# PHR / SPHR Study Guide
## 2015 Version

ISBN 978-1-939536-75-4

Distinctive Human Resources, Inc.
221 N. Horner Blvd.
Sanford, NC 27330

# Table of Contents

# Preparation Manual Introduction

Thank you for choosing these Distinctive HR, Inc. preparation materials. This preparation program, nor any prep system, will guarantee the candidate a 100% chance to pass the certification exam. These tests are difficult and challenging. Memorizing every word of the manual, without fully understanding the meaning of the concepts will not enable the candidate to successfully apply the concepts to the exam scenarios.

We encourage you to read the chapters and work on the practice quizzes in a systematic preparation process. Tackling each chapter until mastery occurs, will greatly facilitate learning, retention, and understanding. We urge you to stick with a chapter or topic until you fully understand it before proceeding on.

We have found that participants who spend approximately 100 or more study hours give themselves the best opportunity to pass the certification test on the first try. However, the amount of hours that you personally need to study will vary based on prior experience and education level.

While this study manual is designed to be used in conjunction with the complete Distinctive HR learning package (audio CD's, online quizzes, online videos, flashcards, etc.), it is sufficient to give the certification candidate a basis for their individual preparations.

This study guide follows the Human Resource Certification Institute's (HRCI) outline for material content to be covered on their certification exam. Various sections of this manual are marked as "SPHR-only." Per HRCI guidelines, PHR candidates need not read or study these sections as this material will not be covered on their exam.

We congratulate you for pursuing professional enrichment. We take our responsibility seriously to aid you in this endeavor.

Best of luck… and let's get certified!

# 10-Week Sample Study Plan

| | | 10-Week Study Plan | Check when finished |
|---|---|---|---|
| **Week 1** | | **Tasks** | |
| | 1 | Watch Class Lecture videos on Test Taking Skills | |
| | 2 | Watch Class Lecture videos on Test Taking Skills (if not already finished) | |
| | 3 | Take the Test Taking Skills quiz | |
| | 4 | Listen to Disc 1 on the Audio CD Set (Test Taking Skills) | |
| | 5 | Determine which exam (or both) to take and sign up with HRCI (www.hrci.org) | |
| | | | |
| **Week 2** | | **Tasks** | |
| | 1 | Read Chapter 1 in Study Guide | |
| | 2 | Watch Troublesome Topics videos (HAZCOM, OSHA Recordkeeping, Lockout/Tagout) | |
| | 3 | Watch Class Lecture videos on Risk Management (90 minutes) | |
| | 4 | Go through flashcards on Risk Management | |
| | 5 | Listen to Disc 2 on the Audio CD Set | |
| | 6 | Take end-of-chapter quiz  **score_____** | |
| | 7 | Take online quizzes for Risk Management (1 & 2) | |
| | | Risk Management 1 score: | |
| | | Risk Management 2 score: | |
| | | | |
| **Week 3** | | **Tasks** | |
| | 1 | Read Chapter 2 | |
| | 2 | Watch TT videos:  Evaluating Training Programs / Kirkpatrick Model; Instructional Design Theory | |
| | 3 | Finish reading Chapter 2 (if not already finished); take end-of-chapter quiz (**score_____**) | |
| | 4 | Watch TT video:  Reliability & Validity; | |
| | 5 | Watch class lecture videos on HRD | |
| | 6 | Go through flashcards on HRD; listen to Audio CD on HRD | |
| | 7 | Take online quizzes for HRD | |
| | | HRD 1 score: | |
| | | HRD 2 score: | |
| | | | |
| **Week 4** | | **Tasks** | |
| | 1 | Read Chapter 3 | |
| | 2 | Watch TT videos:  FLSA - Exempt/Non-Exempt; Central Tendency & Compa-ratio; Job Evaluation | |
| | 3 | Finish reading Chapter 3 and take end-of-chapter quiz (**score_____**) | |
| | 4 | Watch TT videos:  Overtime Calculations; Defined Ben./Defined Contr & Qual. & Unqualified Plans; Begin watching class lecture videos on Comp & Benefits | |
| | 5 | Finish watching class lecture videos on Comp & Benefits | |
| | 6 | Go through flashcards for Comp & Benefits; listen to Audio CD on Comp & Benefits | |
| | 7 | Take online quizzes for Comp & Benefits | |
| | | Comp 1 score: | |
| | | Comp 2 score: | |
| | | | |

| Week 5 | Tasks | |
|---|---|---|
| 1 | Read Chapter 4 (all of chapter) | |
| 2 | Watch TT videos: Motivational Theories; Union Laws; Union Terms | |
| 3 | Take end-of-chapter quiz (**score_____**); Begin watching class lecture videos on Employee & Labor Relations | |
| 4 | Finish watching class lecture videos on Employee & Labor Relations | |
| 5 | Go through flashcards for Employee & Labor Relations; Listen to Audio CD for Employee & Labor Relations; Take online quizzes 1 & 2 | |
| 6 | Play Billionaire Game | |
| 7 | Take online quizzes 3-6 for Employee & Labor Relations | |
| | Employee & Labor Relations 1 score: | |
| | Employee & Labor Relations 2 score: | |
| | | |
| Week 6 | Tasks | |
| 1 | Read Chapter 5 | |
| 2 | Watch TT videos: Job Analysis/Job Desc./Job Spec; EO 11246 & AAP's; | |
| 3 | Finish reading Chapter 5; take end-of-chapter quiz (**score_____**) | |
| 4 | Watch TT video: Adverse Impact & 4/5ths Rule; | |
| 5 | Watch class lecture videos on Workforce Planning & Employment | |
| 6 | Go through flashcards for Workforce Planning & Employment; Listen to Audio CD on Workforce Planning & Employment | |
| 7 | Take online quizzes for Workforce Planning & Employment | |
| | Workforce Planning 1 score: | |
| | Workforce Planning 2 score: | |
| | | |
| Week 7 | Tasks | |
| 1 | Read Chapter 6 | |
| 2 | Watch TT videos: Employment Laws & Number of Employees; Balanced Scorecard; Landmark Supreme Court Cases; | |
| 3 | Finish reading Chapter 6; take end-of-chapter quiz (**score_____**) | |
| 4 | Watch TT videos: Organizational Life Cycle; Business Strategy - Thinking & Planning; Play Billionaire Game | |
| 5 | Watch class lecture videos on Business Management & Strategy | |
| 6 | Go through flashcards for Business Mgmt & Strategy; Listen to Audio CD on Business Management & Strategy | |
| 7 | Take online quizzes for Business Management & Strategy | |
| | Bus Mgmt & Strategy 1 score: | |
| | Bus Mgmt & Strategy 2 score: | |
| | | |
| Week 8 | Tasks | |
| 1 | Review notes | |
| 2 | Go through flashcards for 3 sections; listen to glossary CD's | |
| 3 | Go through flashcards for remaining 3 sections; listen to glossary CD's | |
| 4 | Play Billionaire games | |
| 5 | Take 50-question Sample Test 1 (for the appropriate exam you are taking) | |
| 6 | Review notes; take 75-question Sample Test 2 | |
| | Sample Test 1 score: | |
| | Sample Test 2 score: | |
| | | |
| Week 9 | Tasks | |

| | 1 | Play Billionaire games | |
|---|---|---|---|
| | 2 | Take 100-question Sample Test | |
| | 3 | Review Notes & flashcards; | |
| | 4 | Take 175-question Sample Test | |
| | 5 | Review Notes & flashcards on any "trouble" areas | |
| | 6 | Complete any unfinished study tasks (TT, flashcards, reading, etc.) | |
| | 7 | Take Final Exam (Target score should be 75%+): | |
| | | | |
| **Week 10** | | **Tasks** | |
| | 1 | Take all other online quizzes | |
| | | HRD 3 score: | |
| | | HRD 4 score: | |
| | | Comp 3 score: | |
| | | Comp 4 score: | |
| | | Comp 5 score: | |
| | | Comp 6 score: | |
| | | Comp 7 score: | |
| | | Employee & Labor Relations 3 score: | |
| | | Employee & Labor Relations 4 score: | |
| | | Employee & Labor Relations 5 score: | |
| | | Employee & Labor Relations 6 score: | |
| | | Workforce Planning 3 score: | |
| | | Workforce Planning 4 score: | |
| | | Workforce Planning 5 score: | |
| | | Workforce Planning 6 score: | |
| | | Bus Mgmt & Strategy 3 score: | |
| | | Bus Mgmt & Strategy 4 score: | |
| | | Bus Mgmt & Strategy 5 score: | |
| | | Bus Mgmt & Strategy 6 score: | |
| | | Bus Mgmt & Strategy 7 score: | |
| | | Bus Mgmt & Strategy 8 score: | |
| | | Bus Mgmt & Strategy 9 score: | |
| | 2 | Get a good night's sleep; No studying night before test | |
| | 3 | **PASS HRCI EXAM!!!** | |

# Are you test wise?

Our experience with these national standardized tests has pointed out that many test takers fail the exams, not because they aren't adequately prepared, but because they are not good test takers. Here's a simple test to determine your level of "test wiseness." Read the following carefully and indicate whether each is TRUE or FALSE.

1. Test items should be answered in the order given on the test regardless of how long it takes to arrive at each answer.

2. Even if there is considerable time left after completing a test, it is best not to review any answers, even those of which you were uncertain.

3. If you are uncertain of an answer, it is best to guess, especially when there is no penalty for guessing.

4. When responding to a multiple-choice item, quickly read the stem, then glance over the options until you find one that seems correct.

5. After answering each item, it is a good idea to take the time to check and make sure you have marked the answer you intended to mark.

6. When the test item has two options, which complement or reinforce each other, then neither is correct.

7. In responding to a test item of which you have only partial knowledge, it is better to guess blindly than to spend time trying to figure out the correct option.

8. When you are uncertain of the answer to an item, it is sometimes possible to eliminate options on the basis that they are absurd, or unrelated to the stem.

9. As a general rule, options containing specific determiners (e.g.; always, only, never, all) are probably not correct.

10. Of a four-choice test item, the probability of obtaining the correct answer by blind guessing is 25%.

11. It is a good practice to watch for stem-option resemblances, as such parallelism may give away the correct answer.

12. People who have a high level of test wiseness are able to achieve high scores on tests dealing with areas in which they have little or no knowledge.

13. In some instances, information contained in one item may be helpful in answering another item.

14. You should ignore any grammatical cues in the stem, such as; a, an, was, or were.

# Answer Sheet

1. **False** – You should skip the hard questions and return if time allows.
2. **False** – Always review your answers. You may have made a mistake or you may suddenly recall the correct answer at a later time.
3. **True** – This test is a "no-penalty for guessing" test. Don't leave any questions blank.
4. **False** – Slowly read the stem, then re-read it, until you fully understand the question. Only then, should you look at the answer options.
5. **True** – Double check yourself to ensure you have clicked on the correct answer option.
6. **True** – There can be only one correct answer. Two options that are similar cannot be correct.
7. **False** – Few questions will be fully understood by you. Eliminate the options that you know are incorrect and work on figuring out the best answer option from those remaining.
8. **True** - Eliminate the options that you know are incorrect. That improves the odds of guessing the correct option from the ones remaining.
9. **True** – There are few absolutes in the field of HR. These so-called "hard words" often lead to incorrect answer options. Look for the "soft words" (often, sometimes, may, etc.).
10. **True** – Do the math. Each answer option you can eliminate as incorrect, improves your odds from 25% to 33% then to 50%. What we want is 100%.
11. **True** – This is a national standardized test. It cannot be tricky or it will not be statistically relevant. Occasionally, you can figure out the correct answer based on the clues in the question. Especially useful tip with authors and their theories. Look at the name of the theory and you may figure out the correct answer.
12. **False** – Test wiseness will help your test score but will not allow you to achieve "high scores." Only mastering the body of knowledge will give you high scores. Study hard.
13. **True** – With 175 questions, there may be some questions that cover the same subject. Since each question was authored by a different person, clues may be contained to help answer the other question.
14. **False** - The English must be 100% correct for it to be the correct answer option. No mistakes and no errors on this test. Same for math problems, don't choose it if it's close, choose it if it's exact.

# Chapter 1
# Risk Management
# (PHR 8% - SPHR 7%)

The Human Resources Certification Institute (HRCI) defines the material that will be covered on their certification exam for the Risk Management section which includes: developing, implementing/administering and evaluating programs, procedures and policies in order to provide a safe, secure working environment and to protect the organization from potential liability.

## Liability and Risk Management

Workplace safety was once a fairly routine function that included posters and the emphasis on the number of days without lost work time from accidents. Now, the safety and occupational health function has become a discipline focused on:

- Protecting employee safety and health;
- Controlling and overcoming hazards;
- Controlling and reducing workers' compensation costs;
- Limiting citations and fines resulting from legal violations of the Occupational Safety and Health Act (OSH Act), state safety regulations and laws, and state criminal laws;
- Implementing the provisions of the Drug-Free Workplace Act;
- Taking proactive steps to prevent liability from legislation such as the Americans With Disabilities Act Amendments Act (ADA and ADAAA);
- Reducing the likelihood of an employee lawsuit resulting from expanding product liability litigation and possible criminal liability for disregard of workplace safety;
- Maintaining productivity when injuries and illnesses cause employees to lose workdays and production to experience downtime;
- Hiring, training, and overtime costs for replacements for injured or ill workers;
- Enhancing employee morale;
- Reducing absenteeism and turnover;
- Protecting the company's reputation with the public and community so bottom-line profits and recruiting efforts will not be hurt; and
- Minimizing disruptions that an accident will often cause in the workplace.

Let's address these and other topics to prepare you for this section of the Professional in Human Resources (PHR) or the Senior Professional in Human Resources (SPHR) exam.

# Laws and Regulations

## Occupational Safety and Health Act (OSHA)

The Occupational Safety and Health Act of 1970 (OSH Act) is administered by the Occupational Safety and Health Administration (OSHA). In general, the OSH Act covers all employers and their employees in the 50 states, the District of Columbia, Puerto Rico, and other U.S. territories. Coverage is provided either directly by the federal Occupational Safety and Health Administration or by an OSHA-approved state job safety and health plan. Employees of the U.S. Postal Service also are covered.

The Act defines an employer as any "person engaged in a business affecting commerce who has employees, but does not include the United States or any state or political subdivision of a State." Therefore, the Act applies to employers and employees in such varied fields as manufacturing, construction, long-shoring, agriculture, law and medicine, charity and disaster relief, organized labor, and private education. The Act establishes a separate program for federal government employees and extends coverage to state and local government employees only through the states with OSHA-approved plans.

> **TEST TAKING TIP**
> We've never heard of anyone ever asking a certified professional, "How many times did you take the test before you passed it?" If it takes more than one attempt, there's no shame in it.

The Act does not cover:
- Self-employed persons;
- Farms which employ only immediate members of the farmer's family;
- Working conditions for which other federal agencies, operating under the authority of other federal laws, regulate worker safety. This category includes most working conditions in mining, nuclear energy and nuclear weapons manufacture, and many aspects of the transportation industries; and
- Employees of state and local governments, unless they are in one of the states operating an OSHA-approved state plan.

The Act assigns OSHA two regulatory functions: setting standards and conducting inspections to ensure that employers are providing safe and healthful workplaces. OSHA standards may require that employers adopt certain practices, means, methods, or processes reasonably necessary and appropriate to protect workers on the job. Employers must become familiar with the standards applicable to their establishments and eliminate hazards.

The Act grants employees several important rights. Among them are the right to file a complaint with OSHA about safety and health conditions in their workplaces and, to the extent permitted by law, have their identities kept confidential from employers; contest the amount of time OSHA allows for correcting violations of standards; and participate in OSHA workplace inspections.

Compliance with standards may include implementing engineering controls to limit exposures to physical hazards and toxic substances, implementing administrative controls, as well as ensuring that employees have been provided with, have been effectively trained on, and use personal protective equipment when required for safety and health, where the former controls cannot be feasibly implemented. Employees must comply with all rules and regulations that apply to their own actions and conduct. Even in areas where OSHA has not set forth a standard addressing a specific hazard, employers are responsible for complying with the OSH Act's "general duty" clause.

## General Duty Clause

OSHA enforces thousands of health and safety standards. There are so many rules that often workers and employers get confused or frustrated with the attempt to understand and comply. The Code of Federal Regulations (CFR) contains over 1,000 pages of small print and technical jargon. In addition to all these standards, there is one requirement that covers all hazardous conditions. This is known as the General Duty Clause (GDC).

The general duty clause [Section 5(a)(1)] states that each employer "shall furnish a place of employment which is free from recognized hazards that are causing or are likely to cause death or serious physical harm to his employees."

Therefore, employers are subject to fines and penalties for safety infractions, even when there is no specific standard that has been violated as per OSHA's Code of Federal Regulations.

## OSHA Investigation Procedures

OSHA Inspectors frequently appear with no warning or notice. Before any other steps are taken, first authenticate the credentials of the Inspector. The federal Occupational Safety and Health (OSH) Act allows OSHA to conduct unscheduled visits to worksites and inspect for compliance with safety and health guidelines and standards. As part of these inspections, OSHA may inspect records that employers covered by the act must keep. OSHA may issue citations for alleged violations of OSHA standards, regulations, and guidelines, including recordkeeping violations. Even when a standard does not cover a particular situation, OSHA can cite employers under its general duty clause.

**TEST TAKING TIP**
We find math problems to be the most difficult for most HR professionals to solve. Most of us are good with people and not so great with math.

## OSHA Recordkeeping Requirements

Employers with 10 or fewer employees at all times during the last calendar year do not need to keep OSHA injury and illness records unless OSHA or the Bureau of Labor Statistics (BLS) informs them in writing that records must be kept. However, all employers covered by the OSH Act must report to OSHA any workplace incident that results in a fatality or the hospitalization of three or more employees.

If an employer's business is in an industry that is classified as low hazard, the employer does not need to keep records unless OSHA or the BLS asks them to do so in writing. The partial industry classification exemption applies to individual establishments. If a company has several establishments engaged in different classes of business activities, some of the company's establishments may be required to keep records, while others may be exempt. Industries currently designated as low-hazard include:

- Automobile dealers
- Apparel and accessory stores
- Eating and drinking places
- Most finance, insurance, and real estate industries
- Certain service industries, such as personal and business services, medical and dental offices, and legal, educational, and membership organizations

All other employers are required to use the Form 300 Log of Work-Related Injuries and Illnesses to classify work-related injuries and illnesses and to note the extent and severity of each case. When an incident occurs, the Log is used to record specific details about what happened and how it happened.

If the employer has more than one establishment or site, separate records for each physical location that is expected to remain in operation for one year or longer must be kept.

All occupational injuries and illnesses that require more than basic first aid treatment, or deaths that occurred in the workplace must be recorded on a 300 log. Employers must record work-related injuries and illnesses that result in:
- Death
- Days away from work
- Restricted work activity or job transfer
- Medical treatment beyond first aid
- Loss of consciousness

Employers must record any significant work-related injuries and illnesses that are diagnosed by a physician or other licensed health care professional, such as any work-related case involving cancer, chronic irreversible disease, a fractured or cracked bone or a punctured eardrum.

**TEST TAKING TIPs**
Check out these boxes throughout this manual for tips and advice for passing the certification exam.

Employers must record the following conditions when they are work-related:
- Any needle-stick injury or cut from a sharp object that is contaminated with another person's blood or other potentially infectious material
- Any case requiring an employee to be medically removed under the requirements of an OSHA health standard
- Work-related cases involving hearing loss under certain conditions
- Tuberculosis infection as evidenced by a positive skin test or diagnosis by a physician or other licensed health care professional after exposure to a known case of active tuberculosis

Employers do *not* have to record certain injury and illness incidents such as a visit to a doctor solely for observation and counseling or those requiring first aid treatment only.

All employers must report any workplace incident to OSHA within eight hours after the death of any employee from a work-related incident or the in-patient hospitalization of three or more employees. Employers must orally report the fatality/multiple hospitalization by telephone or in person to the Area OSHA office that is nearest to the site of the incident.

### OSHA's Enforcement Actions

OSHA will impose steep fines for noncompliance with the act's standards, regulations, and guidelines. However, the agency encourages voluntary employer actions to ensure employee safety and health. The agency offers training and consultation, and it considers good-faith efforts to ensure workplace safety in issuing citations. An effective safety and health program is the first place to start.

## Bloodborne Pathogens

Workers in many different occupations are at risk of exposure to bloodborne pathogens, including Hepatitis B, Hepatitis C, and HIV/AIDS. First aid team members, housekeeping personnel in some settings, nurses, and other healthcare providers are examples of workers who may be at risk of exposure.

In 1991, OSHA issued the Bloodborne Pathogens Standard (29 CFR 1910.1030) to protect workers from risk. The standard requires a written exposure control plan, maintenance of medical records for 30 years post termination of every employee, the maintenance of documented training programs and the use of engineering and work practice controls to eliminate or minimize employee exposure to bloodborne pathogens. This includes offering vaccinations to workers with exposure potential, access to clean-up kits and self-protection measures, and other steps deemed necessary by virtue of the particular business enterprise.

Blood is defined as human blood, human blood components, and products made from human blood, and other bodily fluids.

## Hazcom (Hazard Communication Standard)

The "Right to Know Standard" (29 CFR 1910.1200), also known as "Hazcom," requires all employers to develop and communicate, in writing, information on the hazards of products used in the workplace. The primary tool employed to convey the dangers of a particular substance is the Material Safety Data Sheet.

A material safety data sheet (MSDS) is a form containing data regarding the properties of a particular substance. An important component of product stewardship and workplace safety, it is intended to provide workers and emergency personnel with procedures for handling or working with that substance in a safe manner, and includes information such as physical data (melting point, boiling point, flash point, etc.), toxicity, health effects, first aid, reactivity, storage, disposal, protective equipment, and spill handling procedures.

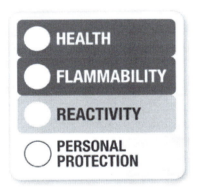

In the U.S., the Occupational Safety and Health Administration requires that MSDS's be made available to employees for any potentially harmful substances handled in the workplace. Also, the employer must maintain a comprehensive list of all the hazardous substances found in the workplace. The MSDS is also required to be made available to local fire departments and local and state emergency planning officials under Section 311 of the Emergency Planning and Community Right to Know Act.

The employer must also train all workers on the safety measures of any hazardous substances they may encounter in the workplace. There is also a duty to properly label substances on the basis of physico-chemical, health and/or environmental risk.

## Drug Free Workplace Act

Passed by Congress in 1988, the **Drug-Free Workplace Act** allowed employers to employ drug tests as a basis for employment. Essentially, the Act requires the employer to maintain a workplace free of illegal or illicit drug use. The Act is limited in that it does not dictate how the employer is to go about complying with its standards other than requiring a written policy on the subject.

Although it is advisable to offer assistance to employees who abuse drugs, employers may terminate employees who violate drug abuse policies without running afoul of laws.

> Both federal and state courts have ruled that current drug addiction is not a disability protected by law, as is the case with alcoholism.

## Reproductive Health Policies

Before 1991, employers adopted fetal protection policies to restrict women of child-bearing age from jobs where exposure to physical, chemical, or biological agents might cause adverse reproductive effects such as miscarriages, stillbirths, spontaneous abortions, or birth defects. Such policies typically applied to all women of child-bearing years — sex-based criteria that applied to a protected group under Title VII of the Civil Rights Act of 1964.

**TEST TAKING TIP**
If you are attending a prep class, sit on the front row. Aggressively ask questions. Don't skip any classes. Read the chapter before you listen to the lecture.

While employers argued for the need to protect women from such hazards, women (locked out of higher paying hazardous jobs as a result of such policies) argued that men were equally at risk. The issue was resolved in 1991, when the U.S. Supreme Court declared sex-specific fetal protection policies unlawful sex discrimination.

This ruling, however, did not clear employers of their duty to provide employees with a safe workplace, including one that protects employees from reproductive hazards. And protecting employees from such hazards is not necessarily easy; in many cases the best answer is removing the employee from the hazard. In some high hazard industries, correcting health hazard exposures is extremely expensive and, in some cases, not even technologically feasible.

Although work-related reproductive problems are difficult to recognize and evaluate, in 1991 the General Accounting Office (GAO) identified 30 chemical, physical, and biological agents generally recognized as human teratogens — causing infertility, impotence, spontaneous abortion, low birth weight, congenital mental retardation, and other genetic diseases.

## Genetic Information Nondiscrimination Act (GINA)

The Genetic Information Nondiscrimination Act of 2008, also referred to as GINA, is a federal law that protects Americans from being treated unfairly because of differences in their DNA that may affect their health. This law prevents discrimination from health insurers and employers.

GINA prohibits discrimination against applicants, employees, and former employees on the basis of genetic information. This includes a prohibition on the use of genetic information in all employment decisions; restrictions on the ability of employers and other covered entities to request or to acquire genetic information, with limited exceptions; and a requirement to maintain the confidentiality of any genetic information acquired, with limited exceptions.

Genetic discrimination occurs if people are treated unfairly because of differences in their DNA that increase their chances of getting a certain disease. For example, a health insurer might refuse to give coverage to a woman who has a DNA difference that raises her odds of getting breast cancer. Employers also could use DNA information to decide whether to hire or fire workers.

## Pregnancy Discrimination

**TEST TAKING TIP**
Failing the certification exam is like failing a driver's license exam; you can retake it as many times as necessary until you pass.

Firing or refusing to hire or promote an employee on the basis of pregnancy, childbirth, or having an abortion was made illegal under Title VII by the Pregnancy Discrimination Act of 1978. Any employment action that is prohibited on the basis of gender also is prohibited on the basis of pregnancy or related conditions.

Temporary disabilities due to childbirth and pregnancy must be treated the same as any other temporary disability. Insurance coverage must be provided for pregnancy-related conditions to the same extent that other medical conditions are covered. Benefit plans that provide for temporary, long-term, or permanent disability must provide the same level of benefits for pregnancy-related conditions. If temporary leave with job and benefit retention is provided for employees with other illnesses or injuries, the same must be granted to women for pregnancy-related disabilities.

### Leaves
Requiring pregnant women to take leaves of absence is prohibited by the law, unless it can be shown that the woman is unable to do her job because of her pregnancy. Likewise, employers cannot require that women remain off the job for a specified period of time following childbirth.

Leave granted for child care purposes and unrelated to a woman's medical condition must be provided on an equal basis for men, according to the EEOC. If an employer provides for a period of paid or unpaid leave after childbirth beyond the period of the mother's medical disability, the same leave opportunity must be granted to fathers.

### Abortions
While employers may not discriminate against a woman on the basis of her having had an abortion, they do not have to provide abortion coverage in employee health insurance plans, except where the woman's life is endangered or where medical complications arise as a result of the abortion. Fringe benefits other than health insurance that are provided to other employees must be provided to women who have abortions — sick leave, for example.

### Unwed mothers
The EEOC maintains that discriminating against unwed mothers violates Title VII. In the unique circumstance where female employees were hired as role models in a girls club's effort to discourage teenage pregnancies, however, a federal appeals court held that marriage before pregnancy was a bona fide occupational qualification.

### Fetal protection policies

Employers may not prohibit fertile women from working in jobs that are potentially hazardous to unborn children unless an equal policy is applied to men. Title VII prohibits discrimination against women because of their ability to become pregnant unless that reproductive potential prevents them from performing the duties of their jobs, the U.S. Supreme Court explained, adding that it is for parents, not employers, to determine what is best for their children.

## Workplace Compensation Laws and Programs

Most employees who are injured on the job have an absolute right to medical care for that injury, and in many cases, monetary payments to compensate for resulting temporary or permanent disabilities. Most employers are required to subscribe to insurance for workers' compensation, and an employer who does not may have financial penalties imposed. It is illegal in most states for an employer to terminate or refuse to hire an employee for having reported a workplace injury or filed a workers' compensation claim.

Workers' compensation provides insurance to cover medical care and compensation for employees who are injured in the course of employment, in exchange for mandatory relinquishment of the employee's right to sue his or her employer for the tort of negligence. The tradeoff between assured, limited coverage and lack of recourse outside the workers compensation system is known as "the compensation bargain". While plans differ between jurisdictions, provision can be made for weekly payments in place of wages (functioning in this case as a form of disability insurance (66 & $2/3^{rd}$ percent of their normal wages), compensation for economic loss (past and future), reimbursement or payment of medical and like expenses, and benefits payable to the dependents of workers killed during employment. General damages for pain and suffering, and punitive damages for employer negligence, are generally not available in worker compensation plans.

Employees may not falsely claim benefits. There have been instances where videos recorded by private investigators show employees engaging in sports or other strenuous physical activities, although the employees allegedly suffered disability or injury. Such evidence may not be admissible at a trial, if it is found that the taping infringed on the employees' reasonable expectation of privacy.

In the vast majority of states, original jurisdiction over workers' compensation disputes has been transferred by statute from the trial courts to special administrative agencies. Within such agencies, disputes are usually handled informally by Administrative Law Judges. Appeals may be taken to an appeals board and from there into the state court system. However, such appeals are difficult and are regarded skeptically by most state appellate courts, because the point of workers' compensation was to reduce litigation. A few states still allow the employee to initiate a lawsuit in a trial court against the employer.

## Employer Liabilities

### Americans with Disabilities Act and its relationship to workers' compensation laws

Even if a state's workers' compensation laws provide the exclusive remedy for a workplace injury, an employee may have additional remedies under the ADA if the injury is a disability as defined by that law. Remedies for violations of the ADA may include hiring, reinstatement, promotion, back pay, reasonable accommodations, or other actions that put the individuals in the position they would have been in had the discrimination not occurred. Attorney's fees, expert witnesses' fees, and court costs also may be awarded.

# Determining Safety Programs

## Worksite Analysis

Worksite analysis involves a variety of worksite examinations, to identify not only existing hazards but also conditions and operations in which changes might occur to create hazards. Unawareness of a hazard that stems from failure to examine the worksite is a sure sign that safety and health policies and/or practices are ineffective. Effective management actively analyzes the work and worksite, to anticipate and prevent harmful occurrences. OSHA regulations require employers to perform these worksite self-inspections and employers are subject to fines and penalties should they fail to comply with this standard.

Personnel who perform comprehensive baseline and updated worksite analysis', analysis of new facilities, processes, procedures, and equipment, and job hazard analyses may require greater expertise than those who conduct routine inspections, since the former are conducting a broader and/or deeper review.

Personnel performing regular inspections should, however, possess a degree of experience and competence adequate to recognize hazards in the areas they review and to identify reasonable means for their correction or control. Such competence should normally be expected of ordinary employees who are capable of safely supervising or performing the operations of the specific workplace. Smaller businesses that need assistance in the development of such competence can receive free assistance from a number of sources, including the OSHA consultative division.

OSHA encourages a personalized approach to the informational and instructional programs at individual worksites, thereby enabling employers to provide the training that is most needed and applicable to local working conditions. Assistance with training programs or the identification of resources for training is available through such organizations as OSHA full-service area offices, state agencies that have their own OSHA-approved occupational safety and health programs, OSHA-funded state on-site consultation programs for employers, local safety councils, the OSHA Office of Training and Education, etc.

## Hazard Prevention and Control

Hazard prevention and control are triggered by a determination that a hazard or potential hazard exists. Where feasible, hazards are prevented by effective design of the job site or job. Where it is not feasible to eliminate them, they are controlled to prevent unsafe or unhealthful exposure. Elimination or control is accomplished in a timely manner, once a hazard or potential hazard is recognized.

A common question that continues to appear on the PHR exam is, "What is the MOST effective way to prevent a hazard?" The answer is, to remove or eliminate the hazardous situation from the work environment. Using guards, applying training, or other safety measures are not as effective as "eliminating" the hazardous situation.

# Implementing Safety Training

## Safety and Health Training

Safety and health training addresses the safety and health responsibilities of all personnel concerned with the site, whether salaried or hourly. It is often most effective when incorporated into other training about performance requirements and job practices. Its complexity depends on the size and complexity of the worksite, and the nature of the hazards and potential hazards at the site.

Various safety laws require "training" as a key element of the compliance actions. Bloodborne pathogens, Hazcom, personal protective equipment (PPE), fall protection, etc. all require the employer to provide "effective training" to employees on those steps necessary to protect themselves from bodily harm.

# Developing Health and Wellness Programs

## Stress Management

Some heart attacks, high blood pressure, peptic ulcers, insomnia, alcoholism, and other medical illnesses can be traced to pressures at work. Occupational stress, a bodily reaction to unpleasant employment stimuli, can also lead to accidents, high absenteeism, and abrupt turnover. Even though some employees appear to thrive on job tension ("I work best under pressure"), many more suffer, unable to use it as a goad to further achievement.

One antidote often recommended for stress is hard regular exercise. It allows workers to "switch gears," to concentrate on physical rather than professional needs, and may provide a "rush" of accomplishment denied at work. The discipline of continuous exercise and the pride taken in becoming fitter, firmer, and trimmer can greatly relieve stress felt in the workplace.

Stress management classes teach employees meditation, self-hypnosis, deep breathing, guided imagery, time management, and assertiveness training.

> **EXAMPLE**
> AT&T Universal Card Services offers a Quiet Room with soft lighting and comfortable seating for its employees. The room is supplied with stress reduction and stress management information. It is open 24 hours a day, seven days a week, to assist with management of stress and for relaxation.

## Smoking Policies

Given increasing medical evidence that smoking is hazardous to smokers as well as nonsmokers (through side-stream or secondhand smoke), smoking in the workplace has become a growing employer concern. This new evidence, combined with the nonsmokers' rights movement, has spurred numerous state and local laws regulating smoking in public places and the workplace. While there is currently no federal legislation covering workplace smoking, pressure is on OSHA to implement a standard protecting employees from workplace smoke.

**TEST TAKING TIP**
Experts tell us there are as many as 1,500-1,800 possible subjects that could be covered on the PHR or SPHR exam. This program chooses to cover the high-probability topics that appear most regularly on the test. Few people are expert in all the fields of HR.

To find a middle ground, many employers use smoking-cessation programs to encourage employees to voluntarily quit smoking. Employees often respond positively to such programs, viewing them as a sincere employer effort to improve employees' health rather than as a mandated lifestyle change.

Employers that develop smoking policies should be aware of numerous liability landmines: Preferential hiring policies could be considered discriminatory, as could complete smoking bans, policies that extend to employees' private life, and terminations of employees who smoke. On the other hand, employers that do not implement and enforce smoking restrictions could be sued for violating nonsmokers' rights. Other legal questions arise such as whether smoking and smoke sensitivity are considered handicaps and whether employers can charge smokers more for their health insurance, which averages higher than that of nonsmokers' costs.

There are four primary areas in which litigation or claims have arisen:
1. the common law (duty to provide a safe workplace, wrongful discharge, negligent hiring),
2. workers' compensation and unemployment compensation,
3. disability discrimination, and
4. constitutional claims.

# General Health and Safety Practices

## Human Factors Engineering (Ergonomics)

Ergonomics is a field of study that evaluates and designs workplaces, work systems, environments, jobs, tasks, equipment, and processes in relation to human capabilities and interactions in order to improve efficiency and reduce fatigue and injury. In its attempt to "fit the job to the person," ergonomics draws on biomechanics, physiology, physics, statistics, and basic engineering.

As a management tool, the effective use of ergonomics can lower medical and workers' compensation costs, reduce accidents and errors, and decrease absenteeism and turnover.

Since OSHA has no official ergonomics standard in place, the agency must use the General Duty Clause to cite employers that have ergonomic problems. This catchall clause requires employers to provide work environments that are "free from recognized hazards that are causing or are likely to cause death or serious physical harm to employees."

If an ergonomic hazard exists, the general duty clause permits OSHA inspectors to issue a citation when the following criteria are met:
- The employer failed to keep the workplace free of a hazard to which employees of that employer were exposed.
- The hazard is recognized or should have been recognized by the employer.
- The hazard is causing or was likely to cause death or other serious bodily harm.
- There is a feasible, useful method to correct the hazard.

# Environmental Protection and ISO 14000

The ISO 14000 environmental management standards exist to help organizations (a) minimize how their operations negatively affect the environment (i.e. cause adverse changes to air, water, or land); (b) comply with applicable laws, regulations, and other environmentally oriented requirements, and (c) continually improve in the above.

The major objective of the ISO 14000 series of norms is "to promote more effective and efficient environmental management in organizations and to provide useful and usable tools - ones that are cost effective, system-based, flexible, and reflect the best organizational practices available for gathering, interpreting and communicating environmentally relevant information".

ISO 14001:2004 does not specify levels of environmental performance. If it specified levels of environmental performance, they would have to be specific to each business activity and this would require a specific EMS standard for each business. That is not the intention.

ISO has many other standards dealing with specific environmental issues. The intention of ISO 14001:2004 is to provide a framework for a holistic, strategic approach to the organization's environmental policy, plans and actions. ISO 14001:2004 gives the generic requirements for an environmental management system. The underlying philosophy is that whatever the organization's activity, the requirements of an effective EMS are the same.

# Incident and Emergency Response Plans

## Crisis Management and Contingency Planning

A crisis can result from any situation with the potential to cause property loss; financial loss; company image problems; or physical harm to an employee; a customer or consumer. Some specific examples include:

- Fire or weather-related problems (floods, earthquakes, tornadoes, snow, ice storms, and hurricanes) resulting in facility damage or loss of operating capability.

- On-site crime resulting in injury to a person or persons (murder, robbery, attack, or rape).

- Equipment or construction malfunction (flooding, broken machinery, or structural building problems).

- Accidents resulting in injury or death of an employee or customer, or environmental damage such as toxic spills or leaks.

- Damage, misuse, or theft of intellectual property such as computer files, trade secrets, or patents.

**TEST TAKING TIP**
Depending on your experience level and which test you're sitting for, to give yourself an excellent shot at passing, you'll need to log about 100 hours of preparation time.

Crisis management is the process by which an organization deals with a major event that threatens to harm the organization, its stakeholders, or the general public. Three elements are common to most definitions of crisis:

1. A threat to the organization,
2. The element of surprise, and
3. A short decision time.

The ability to handle unexpected situations quickly and effectively not only helps to maintain a good reputation with positive community image and customer loyalty but safeguards profitability as well. All the time and money spent in creating a strong, positive reputation will have been wasted if the company is perceived as having jeopardized customers' or employees' best interests.

In contrast to risk management, which involves assessing potential threats and finding the best ways to avoid those threats, crisis management involves dealing with threats after they have occurred.

Risk management is the identification, assessment, and prioritization of risks (defined in ISO 3100 as the effect of uncertainty on objectives, whether positive or negative) followed by coordinated and economical application of resources to minimize, monitor, and control the probability and/or impact of unfortunate events or to maximize the realization of opportunities. ISO 3100 is a family of standards relating to risk management codified by the International Organization for Standardization.

Risks can come from uncertainty in financial markets, project failures, legal liabilities, credit risk, accidents, natural causes and disasters as well as deliberate attacks from an adversary. In ideal risk management, a prioritization process is followed whereby the risks with the greatest loss and the greatest probability of occurring are handled first, and risks with lower probability of occurrence and lower loss are handled in descending order.

## Workplace violence

Workplace violence is any act or threat of physical violence, harassment, intimidation, or other threatening disruptive behavior that occurs at the work site. It ranges from threats and verbal abuse to physical assaults and even homicide. It can affect and involve employees, clients, customers and visitors. Homicide is currently the fourth-leading cause of fatal occupational injuries in the United States.

According to the Bureau of Labor Statistics Census of Fatal Occupational Injuries, about 12% of the fatal workplace injuries that occur each year in the United States are workplace homicides. Homicide is the leading cause of death for women in the workplace. However it manifests itself, workplace violence is a major concern for employers and employees nationwide.

Nearly 2 million American workers report having been victims of workplace violence each year. Unfortunately, many more cases go unreported.

Research has identified factors that may increase the risk of violence for some workers at certain worksites. Such factors include exchanging money with the public and working with volatile, unstable people. Working alone or in isolated areas may also contribute to the potential for violence. Providing services and care, and working where alcohol is served may also impact the likelihood of violence. Additionally, time of day and location of work, such as working late at night or in areas with high crime rates, are also risk factors that should be considered when addressing issues of workplace violence. Among those with higher risk are workers who exchange money with the public, delivery drivers, healthcare professionals, public service workers, customer service agents, law enforcement personnel, and those who work alone or in small groups.

In most workplaces where risk factors can be identified, the risk of assault can be prevented or minimized if employers take appropriate precautions. One of the best protections employers can offer their workers is to establish a zero-tolerance policy toward workplace violence. This policy should cover all workers, patients, clients, visitors, contractors, and anyone else who may come in contact with company personnel.

By assessing their worksites, employers can identify methods for reducing the likelihood of incidents occurring. Typically, a well written and implemented Workplace Violence Prevention Program, combined with engineering controls, administrative controls and training can reduce the incidence of workplace violence. Steps to reduce the potential for workplace violence include:
1. Create a zero-tolerance company policy towards aggressive acts in the workplace.
2. Implement a violence prevention program that includes worker awareness training.
3. Screen applicants vigorously and include a criminal background check.
4. Recognize the warning signs of potentially violent behavior.
5. Be on guard during triggering events such as layoffs, demotions, disciplinary sessions, etc.

6. Provide counseling and therapy for the troubled.
7. Discipline or terminate with respect and dignity.
8. Address ex-employee issues with restraining orders, password changes, revoking security passes, etc.

# Internal Investigations

## Accident Investigations

Many employers have not established comprehensive accident investigation policies. Even among those who have, many never actually follow-through with in-depth investigations. An effective investigation program should fulfill legal requirements, discover the significant factors that contributed to each accident and protect the employer from legal problems.

While physical hazards, dangerous equipment, and unsafe conditions contribute to injuries and illnesses, nearly 90 percent of work injuries are caused by unsafe acts. A principal ingredient of an audit should be to include unsafe acts or dangerous work procedures for inspection, correction, retraining, or even disciplinary action.

If an accident should occur, determine who has responsibility for investigating the incident. Organizations with effective safety programs most often assign that responsibility initially to the immediate supervisor, and management reviews the results of such an investigation. In some cases, safety committee representatives may participate in the investigation or review the results.

An accident reporting questionnaire and procedure is key to assuring reliable results from the investigation. The format of the questionnaire and checklist should elicit the following:
- In-depth description of what happened,
- The employee's statement of what happened,
- The supervisor's statement of what happened (which may be the same as the employee's), and
- A statement of who should take corrective actions and in what time frame, to correct the situation and prevent recurrence.

Following an injury in many organizations, first aid or medical treatment is provided but no formal investigation or reporting procedure has been adopted. Because of this, the correction of safety deficiencies that gave rise to the injury may not take place. Since the employer is in the best position to implement an investigation process, a thorough investigation will likely save the employer money in the long run.

There should be a formal investigation and report to management. Valuable preventive information can come from a thorough investigation of accidents and occupational illnesses. And the investigation should begin as soon as possible after the accident so that eye-witnesses may be questioned while the accident is fresh in their minds, and preliminary safety steps may be begun.

# Communication Strategies

## Safety Promotion

Understand what motivates employees to do a job safely and use this knowledge in safety communication. Here are some proven safety motivators:

- Establish responsibility - Let employees know clearly what they are expected to do to protect themselves, their associates, and property from accidents.
- Integrate safety into the job - The responsibility for doing any job includes the responsibility for doing it safely.
- Tell employees where they stand - Making safety a part of the job also makes it a part of performance evaluations, promotions, and any other form of recognition. Pay attention to whether a job was accomplished free of avoidable errors — the kind leading directly to accidents.
- Be honest - Establish realistic goals and rules and be able to justify them.
- Involve people - When employees help establish procedures and objectives, they will take pride in proving they can do what they promised to do.
- Stress simplicity - It is more important for a safety program to be workable and clearly understood than to be "impressive and eloquently articulated."
- Be consistent - Motivation suffers if policies are followed only when expedient.
- Establish controls - If imposing a safety requirement, establish a means for verifying that the requirement is met.
- Avoid personal fault-finding - It makes little sense to solicit information from those involved in an accident while "keeping score" on who was to blame. If employees suspect they will be put on the hot seat for their errors, they may hold back some facts pertinent to an accident investigation. Reassure employees that the organization is interested in accident causes and cures, not culprits.

> **TEST TAKING TIP**
> Each version of the exam has different questions. Predicting the questions that will be on your version is difficult. That's why you must study all the materials.

# Liability and Risk Management

## Cost considerations of safety

Employers' obligation to protect their employees' safety and health makes good business sense — lost time from job-related accidents and illnesses costs U.S. industry billions of dollars every year. Most companies agree that preventive safety measures pays off and an effective company health and medical program makes good business sense. For example, a program can reduce these company expenses:

- **Workers' compensation costs -** Since these costs are usually based on past injury rate, strict monitoring of claims will likely reveal ways to prevent accidents in the first place and allow the employer to deal with injured workers more cost-effectively when accidents do occur so the employee can get back to work as soon as it is safe to do so.

- **Absenteeism -** Periodic medical examinations and prompt treatment of minor ailments reduce absenteeism for several reasons. Minor illnesses may be prevented from developing into more serious ones. Treatment will relieve employees' discomfort from minor complaints so they will be able to stay on the job. And the company may be able to treat minor work-related ailments on site at less cost than sending the employee to a physician. Some larger organizations have installed an on-site medical clinic to treat workers for personal ailments with the benefits of: workers do not have to leave the worksite for medical care, workers generally stay or return to work quicker, good employee relations, the service more than pays for itself by keeping medical insurance costs down, etc.

- **Turnover** - An efficient medical program can also reduce turnover costs. In these days of tight budgets and soaring medical bills, an employee who believes the company is providing adequate health safeguards is more likely to stay on the job. Employers that implement medical and wellness programs are finding that the return on investment is more than worthwhile in reduced health care costs.

- **Accidents** - The average industrial accident is costly. The compensation payment and medical expenses are only part of the cost. Other indirect costs must also be taken into account: lost time of the injured employee; time of fellow workers; supervisory time; repair to equipment; material spoilage; drop in production; loss of production; and administrative costs.

- **OSHA compliance** - A summary of any OSHA citations and fines will add to the cost of unsafe working conditions. Examples of OSHA compliance costs include: management time expended in OSHA citations such as plant OSHA tours, costs attending OSHA hearings, investigation costs, legal counsel costs, and the like.

## Management commitment and employee involvement

Management commitment and employee involvement are complementary. Management commitment provides the motivating force and the resources for organizing and controlling activities within an organization. In an effective program, management regards worker safety and health as a fundamental value of the organization and applies its commitment to safety and health protection with as much vigor as to other organizational purposes. Employee involvement provides the means through which workers develop and/or express their own commitment to safety and health protection, for themselves, and for their fellow workers.

# Employee Assistance Programs (EAPs)

Many companies sponsor employee assistance programs (EAPs) to provide their workers counseling and referrals for personal problems, including alcohol and substance abuse, divorce, depression, major life events, health care concerns, financial or legal concerns, family or personal relationships, eldercare and aging parents, child care difficulties, etc.

If left unaddressed, personal problems of employees can result in decreased productivity, increased accidents, and higher absenteeism. Employers that sponsored EAPs often report savings on their health care plans.

Employers should consider several variables before choosing an EAP vendor, such as the staff size and type of professionals, coordination with health care coverage, and the kind of program that best fits the needs of their company's workforce. Employers should also make sure their employees understand the benefits of the program.

Confidentiality is maintained in accordance with privacy laws and professional ethical standards. Employers usually do not know who is using their employee assistance programs, unless there are extenuating circumstances and the proper release forms have been signed. In some circumstances, an employee may be advised by management to seek EAP assistance due to job performance or behavioral problems. This practice has been thought to raise concerns for some, who believe that the EAP may place the employer's interests above the health and well-being of the employee. However, when done properly and with a highly qualified vendor, both the employer and the employee benefit. In fact, the goal of these supervisory referrals is to help the employee retain their job and get assistance for any problems or issues that may be impacting their performance.

While there are instances where it is in the employee's best interest to release information to the employer, this may not happen without the employee's prior written consent. The only exception to this rule is covered by Under 42 CFR Part 2, where any instances of suspected child abuse and neglect must be reported to appropriate State or local authorities. Also, when a client commits, or threatens to commit, a crime that would harm someone else or cause substantial property damage, law enforcement personnel must be informed. However, there are regulations (42 CFR Part 2) that require confidentiality of alcohol and drug abuse records, and they provide penalties for unlawful or unauthorized release of information by EAPs.

Every employee will have some type of personal problem during the course of his or her working life. Some will be able to resolve their personal problems without involving their managers. Others, however, may not be able to cope as well, and their problems may begin to affect their work performance and attitude. Having a source of help available to employees can encourage them to voluntarily seek help before their problems become overwhelming.

An employee assistance program not only helps employees cope with their problems, but also helps the company to retain valuable employees.

## Using EAPs

Whether used alone or as an adjunct to drug testing, an EAP can help motivate employees who have personal problems to seek and accept appropriate counseling and treatment. Originally established as resources for alcoholic employees, the scope of EAPs has grown to include other forms of substance abuse, as well as a broad variety of job-related or personal problems.

**TEST TAKING TIP**
Each question is rated for level of difficulty and all the versions of the test (there's about 6) are equally weighted.

An EAP can take many forms — an employee hotline, an information and referral service, or a central diagnostic and referral program. But the first decision of employers that want to initiate an EAP is whether to establish an in-house program or use an outside contractor. Both types of EAPs have advantages:

### Internal EAPs
In-house EAP services range from simple diagnosis and referral to extensive psychological treatment. Larger companies are most likely to provide comprehensive in-house services, while smaller companies frequently contract with community organizations to treat employees with drug abuse and other serious problems. Internal programs can be administered by the company, a union, an employee organization, or a joint committee. Compared to outside contractors, the staff of an in-house EAP can better understand corporate policy, access company services more effectively, respond more quickly to problems, and lend counseling expertise to more areas of the company.

### External EAPs

External EAPs can help a company develop substance abuse policies and procedures, train supervisors to identify problems, provide employee orientation and wellness workshops, report substance abuse activity and usage levels, troubleshoot problems with utilization rates, and follow up on employees who sought treatment. Because an external EAP is viewed as offering greater confidentiality, employees and their families are more likely to use its services.

Smaller companies generally find an external EAP can provide a wider array of services at less cost than an internal EAP.

# Employee Wellness Programs

Interest in wellness programs has increased in response to several factors: Research has shown the **cost-effectiveness of healthier employee lifestyles**; employee health insurance costs have continued to rise faster than inflation, threatening to swallow company profits altogether; and national and international competition is demanding improved productivity and reductions in costs.

> Wellness programs include health education seminars, smoking cessation programs, stress and hypertension management clinics, nutrition and weight-loss programs, exercise programs, on-site physical fitness centers, individual health counseling and risk appraisal and screening, medical exams, and health publications. These programs have also been used to provide safety education or injury prevention courses, such as classes in cardiopulmonary resuscitation (CPR) techniques or first aid.

Some company physical fitness activities don't fall under a particular program. For example, a company may permit use of the cafeteria for an after-hours dieters' group; may install bicycle racks for employees who are pursuing individual physical fitness; or may offer low-cholesterol or low-calorie menus in the company cafeteria.

Employers can also benefit from worksite wellness programs. According to recent research, employers' benefits are:
- Enhanced recruitment and retention of healthy employees
- Reduced healthcare costs
- Decreased rates of illness and injuries
- Reduced employee absenteeism
- Improved employee relations and morale
- Increased productivity

# Workplace Security Risks

## Organization of Security

The dramatic increase in crime, drug abuse, and random violence has increased the importance of workplace security. As a result, HR departments are finding themselves more involved in matters of both internal and external security and crisis management because of their responsibility to provide employees with a safe and healthful environment. An organization that pays attention to this aspect of workplace management breeds fear into would-be perpetrators and gains respect and loyalty from its employees, reduces the possibility of adverse and costly consequences, and enhances its image within the community where it is located.

The primary purpose of workplace security is to protect people and to safeguard both tangible and intangible property. The hallmark of an effective security program is its ability to take proactive, defensive measures rather than reactive or police-action measures.

Firms with 1,000 or more employees often assign security responsibility to a security director. The next position most likely to be responsible for that function is the HR manager or director. Less often, these positions may be named: a management executive such as division or department head or VP; a facilities manager; or administrative staff member, such as an office supervisor.

In nearly one-half of U.S. companies with security programs, responsibility goes to the HR department. HR is often called upon to assist with some security matters by screening job applicants, hiring security specialists or guards, investigating theft and other crimes, and developing crisis management or other security programs.

In a total systems approach to workplace security, an effective program should include (1) physical security measures; (2) procedures or methods to control accessibility, assess vulnerability, and establish accountability; and (3) a program to make employees and management aware of their responsibilities under the security program. However, one of the most fundamental aspects of a security program is the security audit.

**TEST TAKING TIP**
Most people complete the three hour test in about two hours and thirty minutes.

Before setting up a security program or making changes in an existing one, the organization is best served to perform a thorough audit. Typical elements of an audit include:
- Existing risks, hazards, or deficiencies;
- System changes required to accommodate facility or organization revisions;
- Maintenance of security hardware;
- Response time of security personnel to emergency calls or alarms;
- Fire and evacuation drills;
- Alarm system and other hardware tests and examinations for repairs or replacements; and
- Key property and other property inventory.

The components of the security program center on people and procedures. These include:
- Security personnel.
- Internal staff or contracted personnel who are responsible for security tasks.
- Hardware and procedures
  - Hardware such as locks, walls, fences, safes, and alarm systems. Procedures concerning removal of personal and company property from the premises, and procedures concerning visitors on the premises.
- Employee and management cooperation
  - An education and awareness campaign to encourage employees and management to support security measures and abide by them.
- Investigation and other follow-up procedures.
  - A detailed investigation plan for following up on loss or injury to prevent recurrences.

## Proprietary Information

Information and ideas are valuable company assets. They can include everything from trade secrets and computer data to customer and mailing lists, blueprints, and formulas. But companies often fail to realize the importance of protecting their intellectual property. Failure to keep such information confidential can be costly because it can significantly reduce an organization's competitive edge.

To protect the organization's international property, the organization must acquire a copyright, trademark, or patent on its intellectual creations. Under these protections the company has recourse to the court system if they are infringed upon.

- Copyright protects creative works such as photos, graphics, and literary works (computer programs are considered literary works).

- Trademark preserves a name used in association with goods or services such as a company or product name.

- Patent protects a new system, process, or an invention.

# Homeland Security

The United States Department of Homeland Security (DHS) is a Cabinet department of the United States federal government with the primary responsibilities of protecting the territory of the U.S. from terrorist attacks and responding to natural disasters. The DHS works in the civilian sphere to protect the United States within, at, and outside its borders. Its stated goal is to prepare for, prevent, and respond to domestic emergencies, particularly terrorism

The Department of Homeland Security is headed by the Secretary of Homeland Security. The Department contains the components listed below.

- **United States Citizenship and Immigration Services (USCIS)** - Processes citizenship, residency, and asylum requests from foreigners.

- **U.S. Customs and Border Protection** - Law enforcement service that enforces U.S. borders (air, land, sea) including its patrolling and enforcement of immigration, customs, and agriculture laws.

- **U.S. Immigration and Customs Enforcement (ICE)** - Law enforcement service that investigates immigration and customs violations, and enforces deportations and removals.

- **Transportation Security Administration (TSA)** - Responsible for aviation security (domestic and international, most notably conducting passenger screenings at airports), as well as land and water transportation security.

- **U.S. Coast Guard** - Military service responsible for law enforcement, maritime security, national defense, maritime mobility, and protection of natural resources.

- **U.S. Secret Service** - Law enforcement service that provides protective services for important governmental officials and protection of the U.S. currency.

# DHR's Fast 20

DHR's Fast 20's are found at the end of each chapter and are quick review topics to help in preparing for and passing the exam. These topics have all been covered on PHR or SPHR exams in the past. High probability they will appear on future tests. They are written cryptically for quick reading.

1. **EAPs** usually offer assistance/referrals in matters of: mental health, substance addiction, legal needs, financial advice, and family/marital counseling.

2. **NIOSH** is the federal agency responsible for providing research, information, education, and training in the field of occupational safety and health.

3. CVS stands for **Computer Vision Syndrome**.... when using **VDT screens**, eye muscles are most relaxed 24-30 inches from a 15-inch monitor... ergonomics issues.

4. Under **ADA**, a handicapped person is someone who has a disability, has a history of a disability, is treated as if they have a disability, or is associated with someone who has a disability.

5. A variety of health maladies, none serious by themselves, can be lumped together for a **"serious health condition"** under ADA.

6. Intermittent Leave... Employees undergoing continuing treatment for a chronic sickness may be entitled to **FMLA leave** for occasional flare-ups.

7. **Administration Law Judges** (ALJs) conduct the formal legal process of OSHA citations.

8. To **reduce employee theft**: spread responsibility, conduct intensive pre-hire screenings, act decisively on suspicions, implement an anonymous "whistle blower" program, hire a security firm to audit your operating systems, etc.

9. OSHA **"recordables"** (on a 300 log) is any type of treatment "beyond first aide."

10. OSHA form 300A, summary of occupational injuries & illnesses, has to be posted from February 1, until April 30 of each year.

11. The number one **office accident** is "falls". Among others, trip hazards and standing on swivel chairs to reach something high are most common.

12. Top ten **OSHA violations** include: Hazcom, machine guarding, fall protection, abrasive wheels, Lock-Out Tag-Out, eye wash stations, recordkeeping, safety training, and pulley guarding.

13. **OSHA violations** in increasing order of severity are: de-minimus (least severe and sometimes known as "non-serious"), serious, willful, and repeat.

14. OSHA recommends **hearing protection** in areas exceeding 85dB... requires hearing protection over 90 dB.

15. **Fire extinguishers** need three feet of clearance around them... also: mounted at chest height, inspected monthly, a sign above them, and five-year hydrostatic checks... electrical panels also.

16. To compute your **"Incidence Rate"**... total number of recordables, divide by the total hours worked by all employees, and multiply by 200,000.

17. Since **Electromation**, companies need to be careful about the role their **safety committee** plays. Safety committees are limited in discussions to issues that don't include pay, benefits, working hours, or working conditions.

18. **Bloodborne Pathogen Standard** requires training and Hepatitis-B vaccines to be offered to affected employees.

19. **General Duty Clause** requires employers to provide employees with a safe place to work... catch all category when the citation doesn't fit neatly into a defined category.

20. **Department of Homeland Security** combines 22 different government Departments into one… INS is no more, it's now DHS… protects US from terrorism.

# Sample Quiz

1. Which is NOT required under OSHA's Bloodborne Pathogens Standard?
    A. Written exposure control plan
    B. Maintenance of related medical records
    C. Document related training records
    D. Develop plan to isolate and control persons with bloodborne and communicable diseases

2. Work systems, task design, maximizing workplace efficiency, and the design of objects, systems, and environment for human use are BEST described by the term:
    A. QWL
    B. Employee engagement
    C. Workplace simplification
    D. Ergonomics

3. The FIRST step the employer should take when an OSHA Inspector conducts a surprise inspection.
    A. Call the company attorney
    B. Notify all employees to cooperate fully
    C. Ask the Inspector to reschedule the inspection
    D. Check the Inspector's credentials

4. How many employees MUST work for an employer before the employer is required to comply with the Right-to-Know Laws?
    A. 1
    B. 4
    C. 11
    D. 16

5. Which is the LEAST important benefit to the employer who may be considering implementing Wellness initiatives?
    A. Employees feel better about themselves
    B. Lowers employee absenteeism
    C. Reduces health insurance costs
    D. Improves productivity

6. Which is the BEST description of a recordable occurrence on a 300 log?
    A. A vague pain in an employee's back that has developed slowly over time
    B. An employee has a heart-attack while at lunch and off the premises
    C. An illness that was contracted on-the-job and required several visits to the Doctor
    D. An employee is injured in a car wreck while commuting to work

7. Which is NOT required by the Hazard Communication Standard of 1988?
    A. Maintain a list of hazardous materials present in the workplace
    B. Label all containers of chemicals in the workplace
    C. Train all employees on protective measures for handling chemicals
    D. Employers must independently verify the claims of the MSDS prior to requiring employees to handle chemicals

## Answers and Explanations to Practice Quiz:

1. D - While a written exposure control plan, maintenance of medical records for 30 years post termination of every employee, and the maintenance of documented training programs are required by the Bloodborne Pathogen Standard, isolating and controlling persons with communicable diseases is not required and probably illegal under ADA and/or HIPAA.

2. D - The definition of Ergonomics is the design of the equipment, furniture, machinery or tools used in the workplace that promotes safety, efficiency and productivity and reduces discomfort and fatigue. QWL stands for quality of work life and refers to the degree of satisfaction with the working environment. Employee engagement refers to the degree employees are committed and participating in achieving the goals of the organization. Workplace simplification is associated with Lean or Six Sigma process for achieving a more efficient process of production.

3. D - OSHA Inspectors frequently appear with no warning or notice. Before any other steps are taken, first authenticate the credentials of the Inspector. Con artists, Union organizers, and Sales personnel have been known to impersonate inspectors to gain access into workplaces. There is no need to conduct any of the other steps if the alleged Inspector is an imposter.

4. A - Employers need to have only one employee for the Right-To-Know law (HAZCOM) to apply.

5. A - Wellness programs, such as on-site or subsidized fitness centers, health screenings, smoking cessation, weight reduction/management, health awareness and education, target keeping employees healthy, thereby lowering employer's costs associated with absenteeism, lost productivity and increased health insurance claims. Employers are less interested in how employees feel about themselves and more interested in a business related outcome.

6. C - All occupational injuries and illnesses that require more than basic first aid treatment, or deaths that occurred in the workplace must be recorded on a 300 log.
   - A vague pain in an employee's back may be unrelated to the job.
   - The heart attack was during non-working hours in a non-working setting and may be unrelated to the job.
   - Correct answer
   - Commuting time to and from work is not considered to be on-the-job.

7. D - Employers are NOT required to authenticate all the claims of a manufacturer on an MSDS but the Hazard Communication Standard requires employers to:
   - develop and maintain a written hazard communication program
     - including lists of hazardous chemicals present;
   - label containers of chemicals in the workplace, as well as of containers of chemicals being shipped to other workplaces;
   - provide material safety data sheets to employees; and
   - develop and deliver employee training programs regarding hazards of chemicals and protective measures.

# Chapter 2
# Human Resource Development
# (PHR 18% - SPHR 19%)

Developing, implementing and evaluating activities and programs that address employee training and development, performance appraisal, and talent and performance management to ensure that the knowledge, skills, abilities, and performance of the workforce meet current and future organizational and individual needs.

## HRD Introduction

The HRD chapter is basically divided into two main components:
1. **ADDIE model** – The process by which training programs are conceived, developed and delivered.
2. **Performance appraisals** – Different models and techniques for assessing employee's performance.

Sounds simple, right? Unfortunately, not so much. Lots of theories, techniques, models, and more are probable topics to show up on HRCI's exams. Therefore, we've got to be ready by studying the entire process of both training and employee evaluations.

Let's begin by examining the process of how a training program is developed by studying a critical topic for the exam, the ADDIE model. Pay attention to this… this is a class "A" topic on the exam.

## ADDIE

### ADDIE

The ADDIE model is the most common instructional design system traditionally used by professional development designers. The test makers for both the PHR and SPHR exams focus on this theory. It is especially important to learn and understand the various steps affiliated with the creation and delivery of instructional programs as per the ADDIE model.

The acronym "ADDIE" stands for Analyze, Design, Develop, Implement, and Evaluate. It is an Instructional Design model that has withstood the test of time and use. It is simply a "device" to help think through a course's design. Though the model appears linear, it does not have to be followed rigidly or in a sequential approach, especially if course materials are already developed.

The five phases—Analysis, Design, Development, Implementation, and Evaluation—represent a dynamic, flexible guideline for building effective training and performance support tools.

## 1. Analysis Phase

In the analysis phase, also called "needs analysis," instructional problems are clarified, the instructional goals and objectives are established and the learning environment and learner's existing knowledge and skills are identified. This is the pre-planning stage where the program creators think through and gather data to determine the objectives of the course. That way, training interventions are more precisely created based on the "needs" of the programs participants and the organization. Below are some of the questions that are addressed during the analysis phase:

- Who are the audience and their characteristics?
- What do they need to learn?
- What types of learning constraints exist?
- What are the delivery options?
- What are the online andragogical considerations?
- What is the timeline for project completion?

## 2. Design Phase

The design phase deals with learning objectives, assessment instruments, exercises, content, subject matter analysis, lesson planning and media selection. The design phase should be systematic and specific. *Systematic* means a logical, orderly method of identifying, developing and evaluating a set of planned strategies targeted for attaining the project's goals. *Specific* means each element of the instructional design plan needs to be executed with attention to details.

These steps are commonly associated with the design phase:

1. Documentation of the project's instructional, visual and technical design strategy
2. Apply instructional strategies according to the content type
3. Create storyboards
4. Design the user interface and user experience
5. Create prototypes
6. Apply visual design (graphic design)

## 3. Development Phase

The development phase is where the developers build the course structure. They create and assemble the content assets that were created in the design phase. Materials are produced according to design stage decisions. Programmers work to develop and/or integrate technologies. Testers perform debugging procedures.

Common deliverables produced during the development stage include:
- Develop communication packs for program stakeholders.
- Develop session plans, trainer guides, learner guides and trainer and participant resources.
- Develop trainer and on-the-job aids.
- Develop coaching/mentoring guides and resources.
- Develop technology infrastructure and software.
- Develop participant assessments.
- Develop project and program evaluation instruments.
- Conduct pilot program to determine if original requirements are met.
- Review implementation and evaluation costs, effort required and schedule.

## 4. Implementation Phase

During the implementation phase, the actual training program is delivered to the course participants. A procedure for training the facilitators and the learner is developed. The facilitators' training should cover the course curriculum, learning outcomes, method of delivery, and testing procedures.

This is also the phase where the project manager ensures that the books, CD-ROMs, and/or software are in place, and the learning application, webinar technology or website is functional.

## 5. Evaluation Phase

After delivery, the effectiveness of the training product is evaluated. Results of this evaluation form the basis for any program revisions or adaptations. Course feedback is collected to validate content accuracy, completeness, teaching methods, and communication approach. After the program is evaluated, the program will be adjusted for instructional strategies according to the student's reaction to the content, instructor, and peers.

## ADDIE is more than an instructional design tool

In addition to the above, the ADDIE model serves as a template for any procedural process that may be assigned to the HR function. Almost every process begins with the need to study the problem first (or as Carpenters so aptly put it: "measure twice, cut once") and ends with an "evaluation" of the process to see if the projected outcomes were achieved and if any modifications are required.

In summary, the reason the ADDIE model is so universally important is that it has the potential to help the PHR or SPHR candidate prioritize and organize many process-oriented topics that could be asked about on the exam. Often, test makers ask questions about the "FIRST" or "LAST" step in a process. The first will always be the "needs analysis" and the last the "evaluation" phase. Remember this. It's an essential principle on the exam.

# "A" – Needs Analysis

Let's take a deeper look at the first phase in the ADDIE instructional design model—the analysis phase. Great training programs don't come together by accident. They require planning and analysis.

During the "needs analysis" phase, the instructional designer identifies the learning problem, the goals and objectives, the audience's needs, existing knowledge, and any other relevant characteristics to aide in designing a program that targets the "needs" of the individuals and the organization. Analysis also considers the learning environment, any constraints, the delivery options, and the timeline for the project.

## Training Needs Analysis Process

A needs analysis involves collecting information to determine whether a training need exists and, if so, the type of training required in order to satisfy this need. This investigation also should address why the need exists. With this information, trainers can identify the knowledge, skills, or attitudes (KSA's) to include when designing an employee development and training program.

HR professionals can conduct the needs assessment using only training staff, or they can develop a task force or team that includes both trainers and employees. Formally involving employees in the design of training programs offers several advantages:

- The training programs are more likely to address critical needs.

- Employees will feel more ownership of training programs.
- Employees and trainers will share greater accountability for fulfilling training objectives.

## Methods for Assessing Training Needs

No single training program, much less an entire function, can fulfill its purpose without a needs assessment. Needs assessment identifies the performance areas where additional training is needed; it also pinpoints the individuals or groups of employees who could most benefit from the training. Incorporating needs assessment with the design of the training program prevents the duplication of services and maximizes the efficiency of training efforts.

The first step of the process is to determine the best means for assessing needs -- what information to collect, which audience to survey, and what tools to use for collecting and analyzing the data. Training directors can choose from a variety of different methods for conducting the needs analysis. The following sections outline some ways of gathering training information, and discuss the advantages and disadvantages of each approach.

### Checking HR and other records

HR and other types of records can provide clues regarding performance problems and training issues. Advantages of this method are that records provide objective data to identify trouble spots and document performance problems. Disadvantages of this method are that reviewing records can take a long time and may reveal more about past than present situations. Even when the records do reflect current problems, they do not indicate causes or possible solutions.

Some types of records to check include the following:

- **Accident and safety reports.** Excessive accidents or safety problems usually result from inadequate training. If problems tend to cluster in certain departments or certain jobs, employees could benefit from a starter or refresher course in safety training.

- **Attendance records.** High absenteeism and tardiness can occur when employees feel inadequate in their positions and need further training. Or these problems may arise when a department manager needs more training in how to supervise and motivate staff.

- **Grievance filings and turnover rates.** Employee grievances often reflect problems with either the employee or the immediate supervisor. High turnover can result when employees feel that they are not in line for promotion or upgrading. Check trainee turnover. Do new employees leave during their training periods? Do they tend to stay through training, but quit soon after they make the transition to the actual work? If either of these conditions is present, the problem is probably the present training program.

- **Performance evaluations and merit ratings.** Performance evaluations, along with job descriptions, record the skills required for each job and how well current employees are doing. Merit-rating forms also can reveal particular areas where employees slip and might benefit from additional training.

- **Production, sales, and cost records.** Low productivity and wasted time or materials may indicate a need for cost-control or skills training. Declining sales figures can stem from poor customer service or low product quality. Check customer complaints: Do the same problems — either with quality control or with customer service — keep cropping up? If so, perhaps a refresher course is needed for employees in these jobs.

## Conducting individual interviews

Often, when conducting the needs assessment, the Training Manager must interview the potential trainees. Interviews regarding training needs can be done in person or by phone, formally or informally. Advantages of this method are that interviews can reveal feelings, opinions, and unexpected information or suggestions, including potential solutions to problems. Disadvantages of using this technique include the time and labor involved in conducting interviews. In addition, good results depend on an unbiased interviewer who listens well and does not judge, interrupt, or distort responses.

Persons to consider interviewing for information on training needs include the following individuals:

- **Affirmative action officers.** Plans to increase the employment of minorities and women or to improve the promotability of those already employed create training needs for targeted groups. In addition, affirmative action plans could generate a demand for diversity training for co-workers or supervisors.

- **Employment recruiters.** If recruiters are having trouble filling particular jobs because of a scarcity of qualified applicants, on-the-job training of current employees or a remedial course for new hires can remedy the situation. If hiring managers routinely administer pre-employment tests for particular positions, test results could point to common areas of weakness among new hires.

- **Managers.** First-line managers and department heads are directly responsible for performance in their areas. They know what their employees need to learn to improve their present performance and become promotable. Hold regular meetings with research and technical staff directors to keep abreast of changes in their needs.

- **Top executives.** Top executives can provide the information needed to meet changing circumstances. Ask, for example, whether plans call for any expansion or changes in operations that may alter HR needs.

---

**EXAMPLE:**
One company interviewed new hires as part of its effort to identify training needs for its orientation program. These interviews revealed several needs: New employees expressed a desire for privacy as they learned about the company and their jobs, as well as for ongoing access to information, resources, and people. They also wanted to understand the tone, feeling, and spirit of their departments and the company. Finally, new employees liked to know where they fit in the company, what other departments did, who their colleagues were, and where to find the cafeteria, medical department, and the like.

---

## Using focus groups

Focus group meetings resemble face-to-face interviews in many ways. Unlike individual interviews, however, focus groups involve simultaneously questioning a number of individuals about training needs.

The number of focus groups to use depends on the number of different work groups with unique training demands. Focus group sessions are more valuable when participants have similar work processes, work closely with each other, or face common situations, such as working with external customers.

Advantages of this method are that focus groups tap many sources and supply qualitative information often omitted when using other inclusive data collection methods, like written surveys. Focus groups also can build support for training program proposals and develop participants' problem analysis skills for future feedback. Disadvantages include the time needed to conduct focus groups and the possibility that the group leader may sway the direction of the discussion. In addition, good results depend on group members' ability and willingness to attend and participate in meetings.

### Conducting observations

Observations can examine on-the-job performance, simulations of work settings, or written work samples. In a small company, a training director may be able to pinpoint areas where training is needed simply by watching how jobs are done in various departments. Whatever method is used, be sure to talk to employees —they know better than anyone what will help them to improve their job performance.

Advantages of this method are that observations provide a reality check and generate fairly accurate data on performance and work flows with minimal disruption. Disadvantages of conducting observations are that this method is labor-intensive, requires a highly skilled observer, and can be seen as spying.

### Circulating surveys or questionnaires

Surveys and questionnaires generally use a standardized format for gathering information. Common survey methods include polling and other forms of questioning, all of which can be administered by mail, phone, or hand.

Advantages of this technique are that surveys and questionnaires cost little, are easy to administer and tabulate, can reach many people in a short time, ensure confidentiality, and identify the scope of a problem. Disadvantages of using surveys include the time and difficulty of constructing clear and unambiguous questions. In addition, written surveys tend to deter individuals from freely expressing their views, which can sacrifice some of the detail and qualitative information gathered using other methods. Surveys also tend to do a better job of identifying problems than pinpointing causes or possible solutions.

**TEST TAKING TIP**
All the questions on the test will be multiple choice with four answer options.

### Using samples

Sampling is an abbreviated form of surveying. Instead of polling all constituents of the training function, however, sampling surveys a small, selected group of constituents.

Advantages of sampling are that it is less time-consuming than a regular survey and can target the most important users of the training function. Disadvantages of sampling are that inappropriate sample selection can bias the results, and the uniqueness of the sample may make it difficult to compare training survey results from year to year.

### Administering group tests

Testing a group of potential trainees can identify which employees could most benefit from training. It also can highlight weak areas of knowledge or skills that the training program should target. Advantages of using tests are that testing quantifies knowledge and ability levels and provides useful "before" data for later use in evaluating the effectiveness of the training. Disadvantages of tests are that many measure only knowledge, not actual job performance, and designing tests that accurately measure the right knowledge or skill can prove difficult.

## Training Purposes

One of the key goals of any needs analysis is to identify the KSA's that employee's need to develop to cope with today's corporate challenges.

Training, from an employee's perspective, is a career-long, year-round activity that can refresh old skills and teach new talents to further career development. From a management perspective, a systematic training program promotes a variety of aims. It equips the company's workforce to meet business objectives and to satisfy customer needs. Training is also vital to attract, motivate, and retain desired employees.

By helping a company keep pace with internal needs and external changes, training can play a vital role in an organization's agenda.

## Training to Meet External HR Demands

Keeping pace with external forces that affect organizational goals is a challenge facing most HR managers. A forward-looking training program helps a company adapt to the ever-changing external environment. Consider these examples:

- Training programs can give a competitive boost to minorities, women, and people with differing abilities who may never have had a real chance to compete in the labor market.

- Changes in the economy can change workforce composition and turnover rates; training needs and training programs change accordingly.

- New laws and regulations often create new training demands. The Americans With Disabilities Act, the Occupational Health and Safety Act regulations, and the Civil Rights Act of 1991, to name just a few examples, established mandates that often required new employee and management training programs to ensure compliance.

Along with responding to external forces, a good training function helps an HR manager to anticipate needs before they arise. Awareness of technological advances and demographic changes in the labor market should guide the design of an organization's training function.

## Anticipating technological change

A common source of "business needs" involves the practice of keeping employees up to date on the latest technological innovations and cutting edge machinations. Collecting critical information about new technologies and their impact on business practices is a primary consideration for the instructional designer.

Every industry today is affected by the whirlwind pace of technology. Satellite communications, computers, word processors, smart phones, and other technological aids can help any employer become more competitive and productive. New financial theories, marketing strategies, and planning processes also are altering the way companies do business. Employers that do not adapt to these new processes and equipment are left behind, and their profits drop accordingly.

**TEST TAKING TIP**
Almost 50% of the professionals that sit for the exam fail. Many qualified and knowledgeable individuals don't pass the first or even second time. But they stick with it until they succeed.

As a result, training has become more important than ever. To stay competitive, a company may need to introduce new products or processes, or to re-launch existing products into new, sometimes global, marketplaces. The success of these initiatives often depends on training for line and staff in production, sales, and service.

## Attracting a quality workforce

As demographic changes reshape the U.S. workforce, training functions must adapt to develop quality employees from the new marketplace. Some of the labor market projections that a training director should keep in mind include the following:

- Changing profile of entry-level workers. Currently, one out of three entry-level workers is a member of a minority group.

- Mismatch between supply and demand for particular job categories. Certain job categories experience uneven growth, and many companies will continue to face chronic problems finding qualified skilled workers for particular positions. Unskilled workers are plentiful. As a result, training and retraining of displaced workers will take on greater importance.

- Continued participation of women in the workplace. More and more women are entering the workforce to pursue permanent careers. Growing numbers of women work full time, stay in their jobs for at least five years, and seek managerial positions. Nondiscrimination training for supervisors, career development programs for women, and other forms of training must evolve to deal with this trend.

- Growing workforce diversity. Diversity means not only more women and minorities in the workforce, but also new work values and ethics. For employers to attract and retain qualified employees, training programs will need to recognize and plan for this diversity.

Many top executives notice training costs but overlook the impact of training on organizational performance. Often, during periods of economic downturn, one of the first budget items to be reduced is the allocation for training. To gain recognition for its strategic value, the training function must translate a company's strategic goals into clear and achievable training objectives. To do so, the training function must become a strategic planning partner in top company management. To achieve this goal, the training function must focus on aligning all its offerings with operational objectives. No subjective or non-value-added training classes need to be held. Only programs that display an immediate return-on-investment should be scheduled for implementation.

Gaining a foothold in the echelons of top management may involve some homework for training directors. They must learn and understand the company's strategic challenges and basic operational objectives so as to propose training programs that can help solve real and immediate business problems. Training directors can get this business knowledge in a variety of ways:

- Acquire and read company strategic plans, department plans, and other documents that describe the goals of each business unit.

- Read books and industry journals in order to understand the company's position in the marketplace.

- Enroll in outside courses to develop the knowledge and skills necessary to understand the company's business.

- Join and participate in social networking internet sites dedicated to their particular industry or to cutting edge developments in their field.

Once a training director has a feel for the company's business and strategic challenges, the next task is to develop a game plan that highlights ways in which the training function can promote organizational objectives. Asking the following questions can help training directors make the link between company strategy and training activities:

- What is the company's basic business strategy and how does training fit in?
- How is training positioned within the company and the marketplace?
- How can training help move employees in the direction the company wants to go?
- What are the five or six most critical training activities for this year? Which department will oversee these programs?
- What are the training function's five or six most critical assumptions about the company's needs?

**TEST TAKING TIP**
Many candidates fail the test, not because they don't know the material, but because they aren't good test takers. Practice test-taking as much as possible.

A well-run organization knows that employees are its strength. Companies with this philosophy help employees build careers that make them more valuable to the organization. This effort starts by identifying an organization's current and future needs for particular types of employees and skills. Once these needs are identified, the next step is to assess current employees' abilities, performance, and potential. With this information, the company can establish career development plans that ensure employees receive the training needed.

## Needs analysis in summary

In summary, when the Trainer starts their project with a training needs analysis, they collect critical information about business needs, learners' capabilities, and course content. Further, by identifying and analyzing the needs of the organization prior to the implementation of the training, a more structured and efficient program will result.

# "D" – Design Phase

The "Design" phase of the ADDIE model is where the program designer must marry the principles of adult learning and lesson planning with the program objectives or outcomes. The designer is applying "Instructional Systems Design" principles to the professional development experience to ensure the acquisition of knowledge and skill is the most efficient, effective, and appealing.

## Instructional Systems Design

Instructional Design, also called Instructional Systems Design (ISD), is the practice of maximizing the effectiveness, efficiency and appeal of instruction and other learning experiences. The process consists broadly of determining the current state and needs of the learner, defining the end goal of instruction, and creating some "intervention" to assist in the transition. Ideally the process is informed by pedagogically and andragogically (adult learning) tested theories of learning and may take place in student-only, teacher-led or community-based settings. The outcome of this instruction may be directly observable and scientifically measured or completely hidden and assumed. There are many instructional design models but many are based on the ADDIE model.

The chief aim of instructional design is to improve employee performance to increase organizational efficiency and effectiveness. There are basically three main perspectives in modern learning theories:
1. Behaviorism
2. Cognitivism
3. Constructivism

### Behaviorism
Based on behavioral changes. Focuses on a new behavioral pattern being repeated until it becomes automatic. This concept is similar to Operant conditioning theory where participants are rewarded for desirable behavior and punished for undesirable actions.

### Cognitivism
Based on the thought process behind the behavior. Changes in behavior are observed, but only as an indicator to what is going on in the learner's head. Participants are placed in a learning environment where they are encouraged to actively participate and think through the logic of various scenarios until they arrive at their own logical conclusions.

### Constructivism
Constructivism views learning as a process in which the learner actively constructs or builds new ideas or concepts based upon current and past knowledge.

Some other useful models of instructional design include: the Dick and Carey Systems Approach Model, the Smith/Ragan Model, the Morrison/Ross/Kemp Model and the OAR model, as well as, Wiggins theory of backward design. However, these theories have not been covered on either the PHR or SPHR exam as to date and are therefore excluded from further examination in this preparatory manual. Should they appear on the exam, they will most probably be presented as "wrong-answer" options. The other theories covered above are more likely to appear and to be presented as "correct-answer" options.

## Taxonomy of Educational Objectives

Modern instructional theory expanded from the 1956 work of Benjamin Bloom, a University of Chicago professor, and the results of his Taxonomy of Education Objectives — one of the first modern codifications of the learning process.

Benjamin Bloom was an influential academic Educational Psychologist. His main contributions to the area of education involved mastery learning, his model of talent development, and his Taxonomy of Educational Objectives in the cognitive domain. Often called Bloom's Taxonomy, which is a classification of the different objectives and skills that educators set for students (learning objectives). Bloom's Taxonomy divides educational objectives into three "domains:" Affective, Psychomotor, and Cognitive.

### Affective
The affective domain is concerned with the attitudes and feelings that result from the learning process. Skills in the affective domain describe the way people react emotionally and their ability to feel another living thing's pain or joy. Affective objectives typically target the awareness and growth in attitudes, emotion, and feelings.

### Psychomotor
Skills in the psychomotor domain describe the ability to physically manipulate a tool or instrument like a hand or a hammer. Psychomotor objectives usually focus on change and/or development in behavior and/or skills.

### Cognitive

The cognitive domain deals with our ability to process and utilize (as a measure) information in a meaningful way. Skills in the cognitive domain revolve around knowledge, comprehension, and "thinking through" a particular topic. Traditional education tends to emphasize the skills in this domain, particularly the lower-order objectives.

Bloom's taxonomy provides structure in which to categorize instructional objectives and instructional assessment. The foundation of his taxonomy was based on the idea that not all learning objectives and outcomes are equal. For example, memorization of facts, while important, is not the same as the learned ability to analyze or evaluate.

Teaching methods can either be inductive or deductive or some combination of the two.

> The inductive teaching method process goes from the specific to the general and may be based on specific experiments or experiential learning exercises. Deductive teaching methods progress from the general concept to the specific use or application.

Many of the northern European countries employ inductive learning methodologies while most of the world uses deductive approaches. For example, the European School of Management developed a curriculum based on inductive pedagogy.

## Adult Learning Theory

Let's face it, adults learn differently than kids. A primary consideration for the Instructional Designer is to target the design of the professional development program to the learning potential of its audience. In the workplace, to be effective, the designer must describe a set of principles of teaching and learning specifically relating to adults. Thus, instructional designers must understand the fundamental principles of adult learning theory, or andragogy.

Andragogy applies to any form of adult learning and has been used extensively in the design of organizational training programs. Andragogy makes the following assumptions about the design of learning: (1) Adults need to know why they need to learn something (2) Adults need to learn experientially, (3) Adults approach learning as problem-solving, and (4) Adults learn best when the topic is of immediate value.

In practical terms, andragogy means that instruction for adults needs to focus more on the process and less on the content being taught. Strategies such as case studies, role playing, simulations, and self-evaluation are most useful. Instructors adopt a role of facilitator or resource rather than lecturer or grader.

### Learning Curves for Adults

A learning curve is a graphical representation of the changing rate of learning, in the average person, for a given activity. Typically, the increase in retention of information is sharpest after the initial attempts, and then gradually evens out, meaning that less and less new information is retained after each repetition.

Progress in skill learning commonly follows an S-shaped curve, with some measure of skill on the Y axis and number of trials on the X-axis. Progress is slow at first (increasing returns), then a subject may experience a burst of learning that produces a rapid rise on the graph (decreasing returns). The S-shaped learning curve is most obvious when someone learns a highly complex task. The initial part of the curve rises slowly as a person becomes familiar with basic components of a skill. The steep ascending phase occurs when there is enough experience with rudiments or simple components to start "putting it all together." Rapid progress follows until the skill "hits a ceiling" or stabilizes at a high level (plateau).

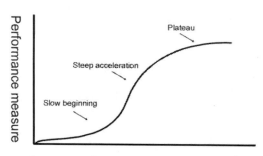

Number of trials or attempts at learning

## Design Consideration and Learning Principles

### Planning and designing a training course

Each training program has unique content and uses different instructional tools, but all training programs share common design issues. They need: course objectives, KSA's to be developed, ensuring the learner learns the content, facilitating actual operational performance, sequencing the learning objectives, and reinforcing the content.

### Purpose of course objectives

A needs analysis should allow a trainer to develop course objectives that target behavioral outcomes. Effective course objectives allow all training constituents —course designers, trainers, management, as well as trainees — to focus on performance expectations.

Course objectives should spell out the following information:

- the knowledge or skills that participants should attain by completing the  course,

- the results that participants should realize on the job, and

- the measurements that trainers will use to evaluate participants' skill retention and production.

---

**EXAMPLE:**

A company with a recently installed computer system needed to set up a group computer training course. The training course goal: Bring employees with varying computer experience up to speed on the new system in a short time without individual training. In setting course objectives, the company first made a list identifying user needs, how each computer would be used, and the software programs employees would need. Next, the company evaluated and prepared for individual learning styles. Training took place in stages, with deadlines for achieving intermediate and final course objectives.

---

## Types of Course Objectives

Specific course objectives vary according to the particular knowledge, skills, and abilities targeted by different training programs. Despite differences in content, however, all training programs should have three basic kinds of objectives:

1. Overall course objectives that state the general purpose of the course.

2. Subordinate or intermediate objectives describing the learning steps that will lead to achievement of the final course objectives.

3. Final course objectives or performance objectives stating what a learner should be able to do after training, under what conditions, and to what standards or performance criteria.

To illustrate, consider a course designed to train workers to use a new computer system. The overall course objective could be stated this way:

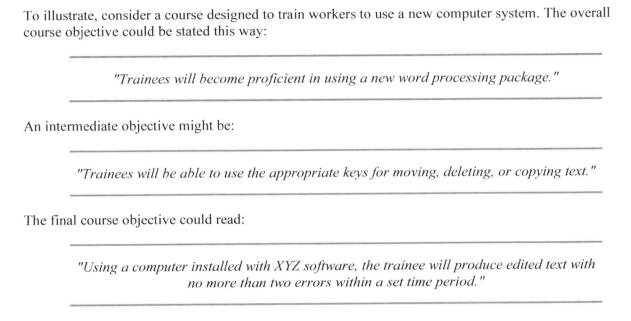

*"Trainees will become proficient in using a new word processing package."*

An intermediate objective might be:

*"Trainees will be able to use the appropriate keys for moving, deleting, or copying text."*

The final course objective could read:

*"Using a computer installed with XYZ software, the trainee will produce edited text with no more than two errors within a set time period."*

## Communicating Course Objectives

The guidelines below can help trainers communicate objectives in specific, measurable terms.

- State objectives in terms of behavioral outcomes. For example, consider the following statement: "Demonstrate effective use of audiovisual equipment, including multi-projector, webinar software, and interactive LCD imaging." Make sure the objectives are realistic and attainable.

- Write objectives as action statements. The word "demonstrate" in the preceding example is the action word that focuses on the activity necessary for success. Show the trainee what method to use for mastering the skill. Role-playing, for example, is one way to enhance mastery of the interpersonal skills involved in an interactive performance appraisal.

- Describe the criteria for evaluating mastery of training objectives. Spell out the conditions under which the trainee must perform, the tools the trainee must work with, the physical environment in which the trainee must perform the task, any assistance the trainee will receive, and criteria for acceptable performance.

- Communicate the direct behavioral results of the training. Three groups should receive information on training outcomes: the organization, the trainee, and the trainer.

Once the Instructional Designer has written the course's learning objectives and confirmed them with the target department head, it's time to begin the instructional design phase. During the design phase, the training specialist plans what the course should look like when it's complete. The designer will create a document that describes the course content but does not contain the course content (that will be developed in the next stage of the ADDIE model, the "Developmental" stage).

In essence, the design phase deals with learning objectives, assessment instruments, exercises, content, subject matter analysis, lesson planning and media selection. Let's begin this analysis of the design phase by looking at different types of training programs the designer has to choose from.

## Types of Training Programs

### Training needed by executives

Executives create a corporate culture through the effective management of organizational values, performance, and systems. As a result, budding executives need training in such areas as:

- long-term planning, strategy, and forecasting;
- corporate goals and the global business environment;
- policy formulation;
- strategic leadership, both in and out of the company; and
- succession planning, including the development of middle management.

Compared with other types of training, executive training involves few individuals and covers highly specialized subjects. As a result, outside courses, seminars, and conferences are often the most practical way for a company to develop top-level managers' skills.

Some types of executive training, however, are better covered through in-house programs. For example, the corporate controller, marketing vice president, or industrial relations director can present overviews of problems facing the organization in the financial, sales, or HR areas. The company's legal counsel likewise can do a better job than an outsider could when explaining how a new law or government regulation affects the organization.

Other types of executive training fit into the category of self-improvement courses. Most executives can benefit from courses in effective speaking and writing; others may want to master speed-reading. In some industries, top managers may need to learn computer science basics, foreign languages, and other skills that could simplify their jobs or give them a competitive edge. If designed as a self-study course, this type of training can accommodate an executive's hectic schedule.

However, the most common way for executive training to be delivered is by use of the informal method of coaching. Executives are often less willing to attend public seminars or formalized development scenarios that include a classroom presentation. They are more willing to listen to a trusted and more experienced individual that they perceive to have the same challenges they face on a day-to-day basis.

Coaching was once viewed by many as a tool to help correct underperformance, today it is becoming much more widely used in supporting top producers. As individuals advance to the executive level, development feedback becomes increasingly important, more infrequent, and more unreliable. Having a coach that will allow the executive to privately discuss daily issues, is considered a highly desirable way of assisting the leader in their own professional development. The idea to engage a coach can originate from either HR and leadership development professionals, or from executives themselves.

### Management training

Even with good supervisory training, most people need additional training when they move into higher management positions. Unlike supervisors, who tend to focus on day-to-day problems, managers must look at long-range goals. Long-time managers may need retraining as well, since some may be using obsolete, instinctive management methods.

Courses in HR, financial management, marketing, labor relations, management theory, information systems, government requirements, and the like can help expand managers' horizons. Large companies with qualified training instructors on staff offer such courses as part of an in-company management training program. Many companies, however, find it is easier and less expensive to use outside training resources.

New managers who are recent graduates and outsiders need special management training. New MBAs and experienced managers hired from outside the firm may have a good grasp of management subjects, but they need briefings on everyday operations and the company's policies and procedures. One training option might have these individuals sit in on pertinent portions of supervisory and pre-supervisory training programs.

Management training should educate managers regarding the strategic framework underlying company goals. It must provide the foundation for managers to keep strategy in mind while carrying out their duties. Management training should address the following areas:

- organizational development and long-term corporate goals;
- company culture, values, and priorities;
- goal-setting and management-by-objectives;
- leadership, employee relations, and team-building;
- communication with employees and other managers;
- legal issues, such as equal employment opportunity and affirmative action programs, Americans With Disabilities Act regulations, and recordkeeping requirements; and
- daily management issues, such as company policies and practices, safety, delegation, productivity, and discipline.

**TEST TAKING TIP**
Many of the "test makers" come from large, white-collar, inner-city and professional organizations. They will generally be more tolerant of undesirable employee behavior than a blue-collar organization.

In planning a management training program, consider the company's need for management training on all levels. Management training should be part of a comprehensive, multi-level program, beginning prior to an individual's promotion and continuing through each step of the career ladder.

## Pre-supervisory training

Pre-supervisory training is preparatory training for employees who want to become supervisors. Some companies accept all employees with supervisory ambitions and offer pre-supervisory training on a voluntary, off-hours basis. Other employers have minimum standards for enrollment in a pre-supervisory course or restrict training to only select high-potential individuals.

An organization benefits from conducting pre-supervisory training because it builds a reserve of qualified supervisory candidates. Although non-management employees generally have their own agendas, it is never too early to start training promising employees for management positions. The programs offer a chance to evaluate each candidate's learning speed, leadership ability, people skills, and other basic attributes before more formal and final promotion decisions take place.

## Career planning

Great leaders recognize the importance of continued improvement and support the concept of a learning organization. Training, from an employee's perspective, is a career-long, year-round, never ending activity that can refresh old skills and teach new talents to further career development. From a management perspective, a systematic training program promotes a variety of aims: It equips the company's workforce to meet business objectives and to satisfy customer needs. Professional development is also vital to attract, motivate, and retain desired employees.

## Team skills

To develop and implement work teams, many employers cross-trains employees so team members know each other's jobs. Normally, the effort begins by explaining cross-training to employees, including an introduction to the team concept. Then team members participate in courses designed to teach essential skills: solving problems, making decisions, resolving conflicts, and giving feedback. At the same time, employees undergo extensive technical training. Team members often serve as peer trainers to make sure each person can do every job on the work team. This enables the employer to be more flexible in reacting to emergency situations such as economic slowdowns, loss of key employees, or implementing a standardized pay system.

## Orientation

Successful orientation programs share certain features that HR managers should keep in mind when designing a program.

- **Stress the value of orientation.** To both new hires and top executives, emphasize orientation's positive payoff — such as lower turnover and higher productivity. Good orientation programs make employees feel valued, help them to fit in, and allow them to begin making a contribution more quickly.

- **Communicate company culture**. New employees need to learn the company's norms, customs, and traditions. Give them an overview of the company's philosophy, operating procedures, work styles, expectations, and definitions of "what's normal." For example, employees need to know if the company has an informal work style that makes it okay to have breakfast at their desks.

- **Use adult learning principles**. Design the orientation program as a learning exercise. Organizations that encourage individual initiative, for example, should consider a self-directed orientation program. Other programs give employees orientation tasks to accomplish within a reasonable deadline. One manufacturing company, for example, allows five days for new hires to complete a checklist of activities, such as finding bulletin boards, locating safety and first aid supplies, and completing new hire forms. Another organization gives its new middle managers and staff people a list of key co-workers to interview and a workbook containing interview questions such as "What do you expect from me when we work together?" and "What are your job and task goals and how do they affect me?"

- **Give specifics.** Like other types of training, orientation programs should have measurable objectives that focus on developing specific knowledge, skills, and attitudes. Poor orientation programs overload employees with more information than they can digest or put to immediate use. Good orientation programs cover not only facts but also practical skills, such as how to use the telephone system.

# Four T's of Training

To develop effective global leaders, organizations often utilize the so-called Four-T's of training. Travel, Teamwork, Training, and Transfer. These measures have proven to be an extremely effective tool for developing global managers.

> **Travel -** exposes managers to various countries, cultures, economies, workforces, political systems, and markets.

**Teamwork** - exposure on an international team teaches managers to operate at an interpersonal level while dealing with business decision-making processes that are embraced by differences in cultural norms and business models.

**Training** - cultural training, language training, and other training programs are beneficial prior to an assignment. However, expatriates report the actual assignment in the field has the most benefit in shaping global leaders.

**Transfer** - more and more organizations are requiring those managers on the fast track to senior corporate leadership positions to have acquired international experience by serving an overseas assignment.

## Diversity and Cross-Cultural Training

In the age of globalization, effective Trainers must learn to reach and teach workers in a manner that allows for individual differences among the class participants and helps foster understanding among workers.

Diversity training is training for the purpose of increasing participants' cultural awareness, knowledge, and skills, which is based on the assumption that the training will benefit an organization by protecting against civil rights violations, increasing the inclusion of different identity groups, and promoting better teamwork. Better teamwork translates into enhanced productivity, improved communications, more innovative problem solving, and a pleasant work environment.

Issues to be considered include the following:

### Communication skills

In different cultures, the same behaviors can have entirely different meanings. For example, the same types of eye contact, body posture and positioning, facial gestures, and personal space considered normal, business-like, and friendly in one culture can be seen as rude, insensitive, or even threatening behaviors in another culture.

International employees need to develop sensitivity to various cultural norms for greeting people, developing rapport, using formal speech, responding with appropriate directness, and so on.

As a result, cross-cultural adjustment training should cover verbal and non-verbal communication skills. Communication skills training should include lessons on how to:

- ask questions or get information without seeming intrusive or rude,
- identify what social protocol to use and when,
- use body language to indicate trustworthiness and attention,
- provide feedback or communicate changes, and
- select methods for focusing on and solving problems.

### Training techniques

Cross-cultural specialists and seasoned multinational expatriates make good trainers since they have learned to read the behavioral nuances that accompany communication in a particular country.

Whenever possible, the trainer should use a "critical incident technique" to reinforce informational presentations. For example, describe social, professional, and personal situations likely to occur in the host country and ask participants to explain how they would handle or resolve the situation, given their understanding of communication in that particular culture.

Role plays, audiovisual materials, interactive presentations, case studies, and discussion groups also are good cultural adjustment training techniques.

### Area studies

These studies explain the host country's geography, history, politics, economy, culture, religion, education, general attitudes, and business and social customs. This type of orientation training is best delivered by a citizen of the foreign country or by a U.S. expatriate who has spent considerable time working and living in the country.

## Instructional Methods and Processes

### Action learning

Action learning is an educational process whereby the participant studies their own actions and experience in order to improve performance. This is done in conjunction with others, in small groups called action learning sets. It is proposed as particularly suitable for adults in the workplace, as it enables each person to reflect on and review the action they have taken and the learning points that resulted. This should then guide future action and improve performance.

The method stands in contrast with the traditional teaching methods that focus on the presentation of knowledge and skills. Action learning focuses on research into action taken and knowledge emerges as a result that should lead to the improvement of skills and performance.

The steps in the Action Learning Model of instruction are:

1. Formulate the hypothesis
2. Design the experiment
3. Conduct the experiment
4. Analyze the results
5. Compare the analysis

### Experiential learning

Experiential learning is simply "learning by doing." The program participants are involved in the tasks or skills sets that they are attempting to acquire and thus, learn by immersion.

To be effective learners, participants must (1) perceive information, (2) reflect on how it will impact some aspect of their life, (3) compare how it fits into their own experiences, and (4) think about how this information offers new ways for them to act. Learning requires more than seeing, hearing, moving, or touching to learn. Workers integrate what they sense and think with what they feel and how they behave. Thus, learning comes from the process of direct interaction.

### Coaching/Mentoring

Coaching or mentoring is a type of field training which is conducted under actual working conditions when classroom or off-site training programs are unnecessary or impractical. A typical type of field training is a buddy or coaching system, which assigns an experienced employee or manager to show a new employee how to perform the job.

Mentoring, a variation of coaching, pairs an employee with a more experienced person — typically a manager — who provides ongoing guidance, often as part of a supervisory or career development program. Mentoring programs establish an on-the-job relationship between an experienced employee, generally a mid-or upper-level manager, and a less experienced individual in the same career track.

Many organizations avoid formal mentoring programs because successful mentoring often involves "chemistry" — something difficult to assign. Instead, some companies use "sponsor" programs that have experienced managers show new managers the ropes without taking formal responsibility for new managers' career development. Mentoring programs generally belong to HR, although not all companies assign oversight to the training function.

**TEST TAKING TIP**
If you subscribe to the phrexamprep.com website, take the online quizzes and play the online games. Get your testing skills razor sharp. Go to phrexamprep.com and have fun.

---

**EXAMPLE:**
Mentoring is one way high-potential employees and less-advantaged female and minority employees learn about company operations and are groomed for more responsibility. Acting as a mentor also can enrich the jobs of plateaued mid-level managers.

---

## Rotation/Cross training
Cross-training and retraining programs prepare employees for various job functions other than the ones they were hired to do. Offering these training programs allows a company more flexibility in its operations. These programs also improve employee morale, since employees feel they play a greater part in the success of the company.

Most companies cross-train or retrain for three reasons:

1. Jobs for certain employees have become obsolete.
2. Technological advances demand employees learn new skills to do current jobs.
3. The organization has created new jobs for which employees need to be trained.

It takes time, effort, and money to train employees in additional job skills. A company should take the following actions before committing to a retraining program:

- Analyze the company's jobs. Not every job needs the back-up protection that cross-trained employees provide.

- Consider how much time might elapse between the training and its use. If an employee is trained in an advanced computer system but might not use this skill for a year, the skill should not be cross-trained, yet. Establish priorities.

- Look at the functions in high-priority jobs and break down each function into steps. These step-by-step descriptions of jobs form the basis for training course content and training manuals. The manuals can also be used to assess employee skill levels before training begins.

## Internships/Apprenticeships
Apprenticeship training is supervised on-the-job training combined with related technical instruction. Another name for this type development system is work-study program. One definition of an "apprentice" is one who:

- learns a skilled trade through structured on-the-job training;
- completes at least 2,000 hours of on-the-job and related training; and
- trains in a recognized occupation and industry.

Common apprenticeship fields include electronics, construction, service, metal working, public administration, and medical and health care. Individual corporations, groups of corporations, or management/union cooperatives can administer apprenticeship programs. For certain trades, joint apprenticeship committees, composed of management and labor representatives, handle administrative duties for local apprenticeships. A joint apprenticeship committee's responsibilities typically include selecting apprentices, setting standards, arranging related instruction, and financing the program.

### Lectures, lecturettes and discussions

Lectures are oral presentations covering particular topics and concepts. Lectures can last an entire class period and are ideal for presenting large amounts of information to groups.

Lecturettes are short lectures lasting less than 15 minutes. They provide participants with the theoretical background needed for learning new skills. Lecturettes can be combined with question-and-answer sessions, discussions, or other instructional methods. Lecturettes are ideally suited for a web-based delivery system such as a webinar when participants are dispersed in a wide geographic area.

Discussions involve more interchange and less structure than other oral instructional methods. Discussions encourage participants and trainers to freely exchange knowledge, ideas, and opinions on a particular subject. Discussions work well when the information presented can be applied in different ways. Discussions also give trainers feedback on how employees are using the knowledge or skills they have learned.

### On-the-job or field training

One of the most common forms of training, field training is conducted under actual working conditions on the job.

Some forms of field training rely less on person-to-person contacts, focusing instead on exposure to developmental experiences. Job enrichment, for example, gradually builds new duties or more challenging responsibilities into an employee's current position, allowing the person to acquire new skills while on the job. Job rotation exposes employees to new challenges by placing them for short-term assignments in different jobs. This technique can be used to prepare a lower-level employee for transfer, or to familiarize candidates for managerial slots with the demands of the departments they will supervise.

On-the-job training can save money, since it requires no special training equipment and makes a new hire at least partly productive right away. For mentoring, coaching, and buddy systems, however, these savings must be weighed against the lost productivity of the skilled person assigned to the trainee. For job enrichment and job rotation, the company must anticipate lowered productivity in whatever position the trainee holds. Quality of training can suffer unless a company trains the right employees and managers to serve as coaches and mentors, and selects the right experiences and skills to include in a job rotation or enrichment program.

## Linking Topics Logically

"Sequencing" organizes the course content into segments that flow logically together. Some job tasks and content topics will complement each other, and are best taught in a specific order. Other topics and tasks may have little or no relation to each other, giving the program designer more flexibility.

> **EXAMPLE:**
> A sales training course might organize tasks chronologically: Greet customer; determine needs; present merchandise and suggest accessories; close and record transaction; thank customer, invite him or her to visit store again, and monitor social networking sites for customer reaction to product use for follow-up or to track customer feedback. Or the trainer might group tasks by topics: customer service; demonstration and description of merchandise; mechanics of recording sales, returns, and other transactions. Another option would use a problem-solving approach, emphasizing problem diagnosis and solutions.

## Assessment Centers

Assessment centers, which first developed during World War II, have become increasingly popular methods of selecting managerial candidates. Many organizations have adopted this approach to managerial or expatriate selection.

The typical assessment center program takes place off-site over a period of one to five days. For in-house programs, facilitators are usually top managers — at least two levels above the candidates — who have undergone assessment training. Independent assessment centers usually have industrial relations psychologists on staff. The assessor-to-candidate ratio can range from one-to-one to one-to-three.

### Pre-evaluation activities

Prior to the session, the assessment center staff gathers information about the managerial position for which candidates are competing. This process might include reviewing previously conducted job analyses; interviewing incumbents about current job demands; and asking top management what aspects of the job are likely to change in the next five to 10 years. In addition, assessors find out what qualities have characterized persons who have succeeded and failed in that position.

### Assessment techniques

Once candidates arrive at the assessment center, they undergo tests and exercises designed to evaluate their managerial potential. Techniques might include the following:

- **Psychological and aptitude tests.** Candidates typically take a variety of tests to determine whether they possess the knowledge needed by managers. In addition, assessment centers often administer personality and other aptitude tests that look for leadership skills; decision-making and long-term planning ability; commitment to quality; motivation and career ambitions; written and oral communication skills; independence; tenacity and determination; organization; and ability to handle stress.

- **In-basket exercises.** Using a sample in-basket, the candidate decides what material requires prompt attention, assigns tasks to subordinates, and/or dictates responses to letters in a simulation exercise. Upon completion of the exercise, an assessor may interview candidates to find out what they learned from the exercise and what reasons they used for their decisions.

- **Group discussions.** In these leaderless activities, candidates either select or are assigned roles in a debate about some issue, such as the type of training needed by college recruits.

- **Individual role plays.** These exercises have candidates act out a specific managerial task, such as interviewing a job candidate or disciplining a subordinate for excessive absenteeism.

- **Business games.** These group activities assign candidates roles to play in handling different situations that a manager might face.

- **In-depth interviews.** Assessors usually conduct in-depth interviews covering candidate's childhood experiences, personal goals, reasons for these goals, expectations for the future, and so forth.

## Final selection

After candidates have completed the evaluation activities, the assessors meet to discuss each individual's performance, sharing their notes and spending at least one hour on each candidate. A standardized rating sheet covering about 20 areas is completed for each individual.

These sheets allow ready comparison of candidates; the highest-rated person typically receives the center's recommendation for the position. Some centers issue final evaluation reports for each candidate, which then can be used by the person's supervisor to plan further training and development activities.

## Advantages and disadvantages of using assessment centers

On the plus side, assessment centers provide one of the most thorough, objective, and well-standardized means of assessing candidates. In addition, research shows good correlations between assessment center ratings and managerial job performance. Another advantage is the common practice of self-nomination that workers can employ thus removing any prejudices or biases the existing management team may have that limits the candidate pool to only those persons deemed worthy. The primary disadvantage of assessment centers is the cost and the time commitment. Outside assessment centers often charge at least $1,000 per candidate.

**TEST TAKING TIP**
Most successful PHR candidates report studying at least one hour per day for ten weeks or more.

## U.S. Copyright Act

Let's conclude our analysis of the Design Phase of the ADDIE model by examining a basic concept that every professional development designer should know and understand, the Copyright Act.

The Copyright Act of 1976 is a United States copyright law and remains the primary basis of copyright law in the U.S. The Act spells out the basic rights of copyright holders, codified the doctrine of "fair use," and for most new copyrights adopted a unitary term based on the date of the author's death rather than the prior scheme of fixed initial and renewal terms.

Fair use, a limitation and exception to the exclusive right granted by copyright law to the author of a creative work, is a doctrine in U.S. Copyright Law that allows limited use of copyrighted material without requiring permission from the rights holders. Examples of fair use include commentary, criticism, news reporting, research, teaching, library archiving and scholarship. It provides for the legal, non-licensed citation or incorporation of copyrighted material in another author's work

Under section 102 of the Act, copyright protection extends to "original works of authorship fixed in any tangible medium of expression, now known or later developed, from which they can be perceived, reproduced, or otherwise communicated, either directly or with the aid of a machine or device."

In conclusion, every professional trainer must guard against the temptation to steal another's work rather than paying them for their effort and ingenuity.

# "D" – Development Phase

If the program designer has done solid work during the "needs analysis" and "design" phases, the development phase should be straight forward and relatively simple. This is the phase of the ADDIE model where the Training Specialist creates the training materials.

Generally, the Designer creates a prototype of the training program and then tries it out on an experimental audience to debug any program deficiencies. However, even though this is a relatively clear-cut step, there are many approaches the Designer may take to accomplish the goals of the program. Let's examine some of these considerations.

## Trainer Selection

Companies that choose to deliver training in-house must decide who should conduct the training sessions. Large employers may have a fully qualified staff of training professionals who can handle most teaching assignments. Normally called "Subject Matter Experts" (SME's), these in-house assets have particular skills pertinent and specific to their operation. Often, in-house experts do not possess the communication skills necessary for training. In these cases, it is often wise to pair the SME with an experienced trainer who will focus on delivering the message while the SME keeps the program from communication misinformation.

As opposed to the larger companies, smaller organizations may have to locate a qualified staff person or outside trainer to handle the assignment. Smaller organizations often do not have the internal resources to conduct high-quality training programs from within and must rely on external sources.

### Using in-house personnel

For many types of training, qualified course instructors can be found within the company. Each executive, for instance, has expertise in a certain area, and most can make time to conduct at least one or two training sessions. Other potential instructors include supervisors and managers; HR personnel, especially those with career counseling and similar experience; and technical and professional employees, particularly ones who have had previous teaching experience.

**TEST TAKING TIP**
There is a calculator on the computer you can use to solve any difficult math problems.

### Hiring outside trainers

Part- and full-time faculty at area colleges and universities are ideal candidates to recruit as trainers. Depending on the nature of the course, other outside professionals to consider as either instructors or guest speakers include consultants, lawyers, psychologists, systems analysts, or efficiency experts. Professional and trade associations, as well as local chambers of commerce, may have the names of experts who would be willing to make presentations; a group that sponsors a speakers' bureau may prove valuable as a training resource.

## Traits of Effective Trainers

When looking for someone to conduct a training program, an organization can turn to professional trainers or enlist an experienced employee, supervisor, or even a retiree. Regardless of instructional experience, a trainer should understand the company and the jobs for which the training program will provide preparation. Beyond knowledge of the company and its jobs, good trainers also display the following qualities:

1. **They do not pretend to have all the answers**. While trainers must understand the subject to communicate it effectively to others, no person can know everything. Trainers gain credibility if they do not set themselves up as exclusive experts. An honest "I don't know" response to a question, a promise to get back with the answer, and a follow-up with the requested information earns employees' respect. Trainers also should encourage participants to offer answers based on the group's knowledge.

2. **They show interest, enthusiasm, and adaptability.**  No matter how relevant the topic, employees lose interest if the trainer acts disinterested. By the same token, even an enthusiastic trainer will lose the audience's attention if the material is too complex, simplistic, or off-base. Whenever it becomes apparent that a lesson plan is not suited for a group's needs, interest, or background, the trainer should switch to another approach.

3. **They get the group involved from the outset.**  Good trainers get to know the employees as individuals and find out what motivates them.

4. **They ask what employees expect to get from the course.**  Trainers should have each employee state his or her expectations for the course and post these responses on a flip chart. This list reminds the trainer of the learning objectives and what the employees want to get out of the course. At the end of the course, a trainer should go back and review the learning objectives, as well as employees' expectations, to make sure all have been met.

## Choosing an Instructional Style

An instructional style defines the manner in which learning will take place. The teaching tools used by one instructional style may differ from those used in other styles; however, instructional styles differ primarily in the underlying beliefs about learning and teaching. In particular, different instructional styles place differing emphases on how active or passive a role trainees and trainers play in the learning process. Four instructional styles are described below.

### Structured approaches
Structured approaches are planned in advance and minimize the trainer's control over trainees' ability to evaluate and draw conclusions from the learning experience. In computer-based training, for example, the computer software drives the learner through the training process. When training is highly structured, the trainer becomes a "consultant" to the training process.

### Nonstructured approaches
Nonstructured approaches give trainers more control over the flow and pace of instruction. These instructional methods generate more participant interaction and feedback since trainees share new behaviors and experiences with others as part of the learning process. For example, group-oriented case studies allow learners to contribute freely to the problem-solving process.

### Participant led programs
Many progressive programs attempt to rely on the skills, knowledge and abilities the participants bring to the program. Instructors attempt to engage the students in discussions that focus on the content of a specific topic. The entire group or individual small groups discuss problem-solving approaches to reach a solution and then apply that knowledge to the next level in the learning process. In this manner, participants feel engaged and learn from each other bringing consistency to their various approaches.

### Lectures
Lectures are passive instructional methods for trainees, since their only role is to listen and take notes. Like a good essay, an effective lecture requires a well-developed beginning, middle, and end, with smooth transitions from one topic to another. Lectures are good vehicles for getting large amounts of information to an audience at one time, but few training programs designed solely around lectures survive. A lecture is most effective when combined with instructional methods such as games, case studies, or demonstrations. While considered a necessary evil, adult learners are less likely to feel engaged in lectures and usually only a small amount of what is taught is retained by participants.

## Choosing Training Facilities

### Classroom conditions

The ideal classroom is square, has high ceilings, carpeting, no windows, located in a quiet area, and is decorated in warm colors. It should have built-in facilities for audiovisual presentations and furniture selected specifically for training. But this ideal exists in relatively few companies. Most organizations instead must look at converting conference rooms or cafeterias into suitable classrooms.

When converting existing space into a training environment, companies should do more than simply pick a room and move in a chalkboard or overhead projector, desks, tables, and so on. The basic requirements for classrooms are simple, but none should be overlooked: adequate lighting, heating, and ventilation.

Typical classroom setups include the following:

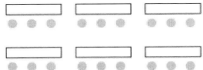

Classroom Style - ideal for note taking, meetings requiring multiple handouts or reference materials, or other tools such as laptop computers. This is the most comfortable set-up for long sessions and allows refreshments to be placed within reach of each attendee.

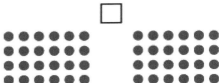

Theatre or Lecture Style - most efficient set-up when the attendees will act as an audience. This set-up is not recommended for food events or if note taking is required.

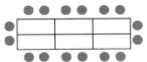

Conference Room Style - often used for Board of Directors meetings, committee meetings, or discussion groups.

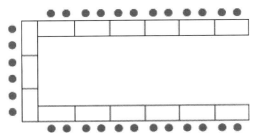

U-Shaped - often used for Board of Directors meetings, committee meetings, or discussion groups where there is a speaker, audio-visual presentation or other focal point.

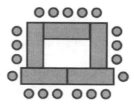

Hollow Square – usually not designed for presentations but for discussions.

**CAUTION:** Employers can be held liable for using off-site training facilities that are not accessible to persons with handicaps or that are otherwise in violation of the Americans with Disabilities Act. As a result, employers should carefully review the facility and training materials for necessary accommodations. A contract with the outside facility spelling out ADA compliance issues and liabilities is a good idea.

## Funding the Training Function

Much research exists that finds increased training budgets are strongly correlated with increased profits and productivity after workforce reductions. However, during periods of economic downturn, the funding for additional professional development tends to be reduced. Training Managers must be pro-active and budgetary conscientious when creating and proposing financial resources be set aside for employee development.

The modern Training Manager must be capable and ready to defend the cost of the training function as a necessary and vital business expense. Being familiar with the operation and the benefits derived from professional development must be explained and presented by utilizing business tools such as ROI, break-even analysis, linear regression charts, etc.

Many federal and state programs offer employers financial assistance and other incentives to encourage them to hire from a larger pool of candidates. Employers can receive benefits by participating in the following federally supported training and hiring programs:

- Apprenticeship programs are designed to give specific skill training to young persons.
- Various veterans' programs promote employment and training of persons who have gaps in their work experience as a result of military service.
- Often, state and federal programs reward employers for employing and training disadvantaged workers that include the hard to employ, disabled workers, seniors, etc.

## Monetary Rewards and Mandatory Overtime Pay

Other consideration for the Trainer, when developing the program, is whether the training will be conducted during business hours or after? Whether the program will be mandatory or voluntary? The morale of the trainees will be affected by these decisions. However, the Fair Labor Standards Act (FLSA) has a direct bearing on these issues.

Time spent in training courses within the regular work day is considered time worked. But if a company decides to hold training sessions before or after regular work hours, trainees should receive overtime pay unless the following conditions apply:

- Training is voluntary — employees do not have to attend to keep their jobs.

- No productive work is involved.
- Training will teach employees a new, different, or additional skill, but is not designed to make them more efficient at their present jobs (although increased efficiency may result incidentally).

# I – Implementation Phase

This is the Trainer's stage. This stage of the professional development process is where the Trainer delivers the message. Usually, the "implementation" phase requires the Trainer to engage in a lot of project management and logistics. Organizing and delivering the course content requires the Trainer to master many forms of instructional methodologies. That is the primary content of this section.

Adults these days not only want to be trained but entertained as well. Holding the workers attention requires the Trainer to have a solid grasp of the concept of training.

Training is a systematic approach to delivering learning to workers. Organizations must keep up with the changing technologies and challenges within their market. One of the critical elements of maintaining pace with the market is the training and development of current workers. This section will detail the typical approaches to the development of a skilled and knowledgeable workforce.

As stated previously, the design and development of learning initiatives follows the ADDIE model. This model advocates a procedural approach that begins with the needs analysis, followed by the design phase, then the development stage, now the implementation phase and finally, the evaluation of the program.

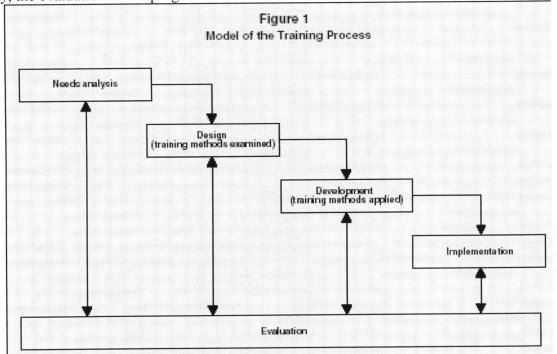

**Figure 1**
**Model of the Training Process**

The merits of different training delivery methods are determined by the unique circumstances of each learning initiative. The desired outcome as well as the workplace environment is key to selecting the appropriate delivery system. The selection of the training system is determined during the development stage.

Learning objectives include: knowledge, skills, and attitudes (KSAs). Knowledge is the ability of the trainee to master the factual information regarding the topic. Skill reflects one's proficiency at specific tasks such as operating a piece of equipment, giving a presentation, or making a business decision. Attitudes are beliefs or opinions about objects and events and the positive or negative feelings associated with them.

The two categories of training delivery are either cognitive or behavioral. Cognitive programs teach conceptual ideas while behavioral programs offer opportunities for workers to practice new skills thus developing newly acquired behaviors. Cognitive programs include: demonstration-performance method, discussion, e-learning, case studies, and lecture. Behavioral programs include: role playing, simulations, business games, in-basket exercises, and behavior modeling.

Let's examine some of the various forms of training delivery systems:

## Lecture

One of the most widely used training systems, the Lecture has both advantages and disadvantages. It is a good method for introducing a topic. Its main advantage is to deliver a large amount of information in a short period of time. However, for this system to be effective, the learners must be adept at both listening and in taking notes on the topic. Depending on the subject, the lecturer, and the context in which the topic is being presented, adults are notorious for not retaining but a fraction of the lecturer's speech.

While modern adult learners have a short attention span and are not good listeners, the lecture is still the optimal delivery system when there is a large audience that all need to hear a consistent message. This delivery system is not as effective when there are a lot of learning points that the lecturer is trying to convey in a short amount of time. Allowing trainees to participate in the process by asking questions and discussing the topic is a more effective way of ensuring that essential learning occurs.

## Discussion

The discussion method is a preferred learning system by trainees as it allows them to actively participate and interact with their fellow trainees. This is not a passive learning system as is the lecture method. This approach requires the participants to work with the ideas and concepts being presented.

The discussion leader walks a fine line between controlling the class and allowing its members to speak. The most common pitfalls in a discussion, lack of organization and clearly defined goals, overly long digressions, pointless arguments, or no real discussion at all. The advantage of the discussion is that it provides an opportunity for the members of the class to work actively with each other in developing a common approach to the training subject.

Another disadvantage, each of the participants must have a common level of understanding and attitudinal opinions of the topic. This delivery system is not as effective for a newly introduced topic where basic learning must occur in a short period of time. In this case, lecture may be a more appropriate way of delivering the subject.

## Demonstration-Performance

This method is also known as "Demonstration and example."

Many adults prefer to learn by doing. In the Demonstration-Performance model, students learn by first watching a skilled worker demonstrate the desired technique, then by repeating the observed demonstration themselves. Truck drivers learn to drive trucks by actually getting behind the wheel; welders learn to weld by practicing welding after watching an experienced welder, etc. Manual jobs are particularly well suited to this form of training delivery. Kinesthetic learners (hands-on) prefer this form of instruction.

This method is very effective in teaching because it is much easier to show a person how to do a job than tell him or give him instruction about a particular job.

## Programmed Instruction (PI)

Programmed instruction is a learning method where the trainee works on their own and at their own pace learning a topic in small increments with a correct response required before the learner may advance to the next unit. This is a fancy way of describing a tutorial.

Training is offered without the intervention of a trainer. Information is provided to the trainee in blocks, either in a book form of through the use of technology such as a computer. This method involves breaking information down into meaningful units and then arranging these in a proper way to form a logical and sequential learning.

## E-learning

E-learning comprises all forms of electronically supported learning and teaching. This is essentially the computer and network-enabled transfer of knowledge. Information is transferred via the internet, intranet, audio or videotape, satellite, or CD.

Some subjects lend themselves to this type of knowledge transfer while others are not well adapted for this type training delivery methodology. For example, programs that require a hands-on approach are not as universally situated for this form of training. However, when trainees are remotely dispersed geographically, this type system is ideal in regards of delivering a standardized message as well as saving on travel time for trainees.

Other names or variations of e-learning include: Computer based training (CBT), Web-based training (WBT), distance learning, etc. Distance learning provides many of the same advantages and disadvantages as the lecture method. Distance learning can be much less expensive than paying for trainees in multiple locations to travel for a lecture, but it may reduce motivation to learn because of the remoteness of the trainer.

There is little difference between CBT and WBT. The primary difference is in how the training program is stored and delivered. A CBT program is stored on a hard-drive while a WBT program is stored in a remote location and is only accessible through the internet.

Advantages of a WBT program is that it may be accessed from any location that has an internet connection. CBT programs are limited in that they may only be operated from a single computer's hard-drive. Thus, WBT programs are easier to update and modify since they are in a central location.

Advantages to e-learning include:
- Flexibility and adaptability of the trainees' time and training site.
- Trainees work at their own pace.
- Enhances organizational standardization.
- Lowers delivery costs by reducing travel and hosting costs.
- Improves learning consistency by offering a standardized format.
- Allows for multi-media presentation formats to be included in the presentation.
- Improves accessibility to training opportunities for remote location trainees.
- Few logistical restraints in regards to booking rooms, schedule accommodations, etc.

Disadvantages to e-learning include:
- No direct contact between trainer and trainee.
- Command of computer or software tools/technologies may be challenging.
- Unmotivated or slow learners may fall behind.
- Cost of computer hardware or software.
- E-learning not always suited for highly specific fields.
- Learners feel isolated.
- Slow or unreliable internet access.
- Hands-on courses are difficult to deliver in this format.

Since there is limited opportunity in e-learning for trainees to benefit from the social discussion aspect of classroom styled approaches, many adult learners prefer a blended approach of both the classroom and e-learning delivery techniques. This so-called "blended approach" is a common learning delivery system utilized by many organizations today.

## Computer Assisted Instruction

Computer Assisted Instruction (CAI) is a form of programmed instruction. CAI provides for accountability as tests are taken on the computer so that the management can monitor each trainee's progress and needs. CAI training program can also be modified easily to reflect technological innovations in the equipment for which the employee is being trained. This training also tends to be more flexible in that trainees can usually use the computer almost any time they want, thus get training when they prefer.

If you have access to Distinctive HR, Inc.'s website and its online tests at phrexamprep.com, then you are using Computer Assisted Instruction to help you prepare for the PHR or SPHR exam.

## Simulations

The use of simulated activities in training is widely becoming recognized as an important tool for enhancing learning in the workplace.

Simulations can be used to provide a representative learning environment for workers. While not rising to the level of on-the-job learning, it comes as close as possible to replicating the real world experience for the trainee. The use of simulations is often cheaper and more practical than employing real life on-the-job training. A flight simulator is far less expensive than maintaining a practice jet.

Vestibule training, equipment simulators, business games, in-basket exercises, case studies, role playing, and behavior modeling, are examples of simulations used in the workplace.

## Vestibule Training

Vestibule training attempts to duplicate on-the-job-situation in a company classroom. It is a classroom training that is often imported with the help of the equipment, machines or operations which are identical to those in use in the place of work. This technique enables the trainees to concentrate on learning new skills rather than on performing the actual job. This type of training is efficient to train semi-skilled personnel, particularly when many employees have to be trained for the same kind of work at the same time. Often used to train: bank tellers, inspectors, machine operators, typists etc. In this, training is generally given in the form of lectures, conferences, case studies, role-play etc.

## Equipment Simulators

Equipment simulator training provides a way for students to gain familiarization and understanding of machine controls, and learn proper operating procedures before training on actual machines or equipment. A variety of training exercises designed to address each of the skills associated with operating actual machines are represented in different work environments such as pilots, machine operators, heavy equipment operators, drivers, etc. This learning delivery method allows workers to practice difficult maneuvers until fully mastered. It improves worker safety, allows for training day or night, breaks bad habits, decreases operator anxiety, reduces wear and tear on actual operational equipment, etc.

Equipment simulators are not only useful in enhancing the learning of trainees, but they have a lot of validity in screening new hires or candidates for promotion. There are few methods more accurate at assessing an applicant's job potential than to actually have them demonstrate a portion of the job they are applying for.

## Business Games

Business games combine fun and learning. Today's adult learner needs to be entertained and challenged while learning for the learning situation to be optimized.

Business games refer to simulation games that are used for teaching business. Business games may be carried out for various business training such as: general management, finance, organizational behavior, human resources and more.

Business games allow trainees to see how their decisions and actions influence not only their immediate issue but also areas that are related to that goal.

Prior to starting the game trainees are given information describing a situation and the rules for playing the game. They are then asked to play the game, usually being asked to make decisions about what to do given certain information. The trainees are then provided feedback about the results of their decisions, and asked to make another decision. This process continues until some predefined state of the organization exists or a specified number of trials have been completed.

Business games involve an element of competition, either against other players or against the game itself. In using them, the trainer must be careful to ensure that the learning points are the focus, rather than the competition.

## In-Basket Exercise

The In-Basket technique simulates the decision making and organizational skills of a trainee. In the typical In-Basket, the test taker is often asked to respond to letters, memos, e-mails, requests, personnel issues, and so forth, in a given amount of time. A time limit may be imposed in order to simulate the time pressure experienced in many jobs. In-Basket exercises are usually designed to assess the candidate's ability to manage multiple tasks, prioritize and delegate work, and analyze information quickly.

When the in-basket is completed, the trainer asks the trainee to explain their actions and decision making process. The trainer then provides feedback, reinforcing appropriate decisions and processes or asking the trainee to develop alternatives.

## Case Study

A Case Study is a form of a business game or simulation where the participants are presented with a fictional situation or case and are asked to work together to arrive at a solution. It is a detailed intensive study of a business issue that stresses factors contributing to its success or failure. Case studies are most often used to simulate strategic decision-making situations, rather than the day-to-day decisions that occur in the in-basket.

Unlike traditional lecture-based teaching where student participation in the classroom is minimal, the case method is an active learning method, which requires participation and involvement from the students. For students who have been exposed only to the traditional teaching methods, this calls for a major change in their approach to learning.

The case study is extremely useful as a training technique for supervisors and is especially valuable as a technique of developing discussion-making skills, and for broadening the prospective of the trainee. The value of the case approach is the trainees' application of known concepts and principles and the discovery of new ones. The solutions are not as important as the appropriateness with which principles are applied and the logic with which solutions are developed.

## Role Play

Role-Play exercises are designed to simulate the interpersonal challenges faced when working with others. In the typical role-play, the candidate is given background information regarding the scenario and asked to play a particular role (e.g., manager, labor relations representative). During the exercise, he or she interacts directly with another role-player.

This actor often plays the role of a subordinate, coworker, or customer and responds to the candidate according to a script. Role-Play exercises are usually designed to assess the candidate's communication and interpersonal skills.

Performance may be observed by a trained evaluator, or may be videotaped and evaluated at a later time. One disadvantage of role play is that if the other trainees are asked to comment on the performance of one of their fellow trainees, they may be reluctant to publicly critique the player's behavior.

This method is especially useful for situations involving employee-employer relationships, such as: hiring, firing, discussing a grievance procedure, coaching, conducting an appraisal interview, etc.

## Behavior Modeling

In Behavior Modeling, the trainee observes a more skillful employee demonstrate the desired behavior, and then attempts to replicate it. The trainee practices the behavior through role plays or other kinds of simulation techniques.

For example, a Team Leader who has never had to discipline an employee before may watch the HR Manager demonstrate the correct leadership behavior through a role play before attempting to replicate these actions. Behavior modeling is used primarily for skill building and almost always in combination with some other technique (such as role playing in our example).

Interpersonal skills, interviewee and interviewer behavior and safety practices are among the many types of skills that have been successfully learned using this method. Behavior modeling differs from role plays and games by providing the trainee with an example of what the desired behavior looks like prior to attempting the behavior.

The desired behaviors may be demonstrated live or through the use of video.

### Simulation summary:

Each of the different simulations has specific learning outcomes for which they are more appropriate:

- Mechanical, machine operation and tool-usage skills are best learned through use of equipment simulators.
- Business decision-making skills, planning, and complex problem solving can be effectively learned through the use of business games.
- The in-basket technique is best suited to the development of strategic knowledge used in making day-to-day decisions.
- Case studies are most appropriate for developing analytic skills, higher-level principles, and complex problem-solving strategies. Because trainees do not actually implement their decision/solution, its focus is more on what to do (strategic knowledge) than on how to get it done (skills).
- Role plays provide a good vehicle for developing interpersonal skills and personal insight, allowing trainees to practice interacting with others and receiving feedback. They are an especially effective technique for creating attitudinal change, allowing trainees to experience their feelings about their behavior and others' reactions to it.

## On The Job Training (OJT)

On-the-job training (OJT) is one of the best and most common training methods because it is planned, organized, and conducted at the employee's worksite. OJT will generally be the primary method used for broadening employee skills and increasing productivity. It is particularly appropriate for developing proficiency skills unique to an employee's job, especially jobs that are relatively easy to learn and require locally-owned equipment and facilities.

OJT is essentially when a more experienced employee with superior technical skill is assigned the task of working with a lesser skilled employee to help them develop or broaden their knowledge of the operation.

There are both advantages and disadvantages to using OJT in the workplace. Let's examine these now.

Advantages:
- Training is targeted to the development of real and pertinent job skills.
  - Trainees become experienced, under controlled settings, with actual operations.
  - Scrap and waste should be minimal during the training period.
- Organizational operations do not have to be halted while training occurs.
- Less costly form of skill development.
  - It does not require the purchase or development of a training program or materials.
  - No outside instructors or contractors.
  - Scheduling of classroom facilities is minimal.
  - No travel time for trainees or instructors.
  - No lodging costs for trainees.
- Excellent for one-on-one or small group training.
- Faster development and delivery of needed programs than traditional classroom methods.
  - Allows for training of new subjects as issues arise.
- Convenient for employees.
- Improves morale of senior employees who serve as trainers.

Disadvantages:
- Training is often inconsistent as different trainers use different approaches.
  - No structured training guide is usually employed.
  - Bad habits and bad attitudes may be transferred from the OJT Trainer to the trainee.
- Some employees prefer the interaction of traditional classroom methods.
- Scrap waste or mistakes may be made with actual company products or customers while the trainee is receiving instruction.
- The trainer is not able to execute their normal job duties while training the trainee.
  - Usually, there is a slight fall-off in operations during the training phase.
- OJT Trainers are often under-qualified to act as an instructor with no background in adult learning.
  - Trainers are often selected because of their familiarity with the training subject, not because they are good communicators or excellent teachers.

Variations of OJT methods include: the job-instruction technique, apprenticeships, coaching, and mentoring.

## Job Instruction Technique (JIT)

Job Instruction Training (JIT) is a proven technique for teaching new skills and safe, healthful work habits faster and more effectively in the workplace while on the job. There are four stages of steps in the JIT system that is often called the four-point method. The steps are: prepare, present, try out and follow up.

1. Prepare: JIT is conducted one-on-one with the trainee and the instructor. The instructor must prepare the trainee by explaining the responsibilities and procedures of the job. The Trainer should also prepare for the instruction phase by documenting the various steps in the operation to aid the trainee in understanding the tasks. The Preparation phase is often overlooked when employing the JIT method.

2. Present: In this phase of instruction, the trainer will tell, show and demonstrate the operation. The trainer explains the operation to the trainee while showing them how it is to be done. Then, the trainer demonstrates how to do the task in the desired manner and why it is done that way.

3. Try Out: The trainee will actually perform the job with the instructor providing coaching. The trainee should explain each step of the operation to the trainer while performing the tasks. The trainee will repeat this process in front of the instructor until mastery occurs.

4. Follow Up: In this stage, the trainer allows the trainee to work independently with frequent check-ins by the instructor. The trainer looks to prevent bad habits from forming. These follow up checks will gradually taper off as the trainee gains mastery.

## Apprenticeships

The Apprenticeship system allows workers to gain new skill sets by understudying a superiorly skilled coworker. These type programs are especially common in the skilled trades. Typical apprenticeship models include a combination of formal classroom training (180 hours+/-) with on-the-job experience (about two years). This type program is an excellent system for introducing entry-level workers into a craft or trade since it provides a structured approach to learning.

The United States does not currently maintain a national apprenticeship program. However, many other countries do. Currently, about 27 states regulate apprenticeship programs within their borders. The U.S. Department of Labor, Bureau of Apprenticeship and Training, maintains a registry of apprenticeship programs and the occupations that are covered throughout the country.

## Coaching

### Business Coaching:
In Business Coaching, the coach works one-on-one with an employee to push them to achieve optimal performance by providing support when needed and teaching or advising when required. The coachee receives guidance, support, accountability and encouragement.

It is unlike other forms of OJT because the coachee is usually a longer-term employee with some performance deficiencies. However, coaching may be employed to assist and motivate a successfully performing employee who benefits from the attention of the coach.

Coaches may be either an outsider or a more senior employee. Often, for lower level employees, the coach is the immediate supervisor. In either case, the goal of coaching is to give an honest effort at improving the coachee's performance. The goal of coaching is not to facilitate the removal of the employee through the disciplinary process but the successful enhancement of their knowledge, skills and attitudes.

The Coach must be trained in the duties and responsibilities of a coach. Not everyone is suited to this task.

## Executive Coaching:

Executive coaching is an experiential and individualized leader development process that builds a leader's capability to achieve short- and long-term organizational goals. It is conducted through one-on-one interactions, driven by data from multiple perspectives, and based on mutual trust and respect. The organization, an executive, and the executive coach work in partnership to achieve maximum impact.

Examples of the uses of executive coaching include:
1. Helping the executive who needs new skills for a new position due to a change in organizational structure.
2. Working with a manager being groomed for promotion.
3. Coaching high performance executives whose personality style impacts negatively on their relationship with peers, staff and clients.
4. Working with executives wishing to develop their career paths and prospects

Coaching is one of the most commonly used approaches for leadership development. Coaching is a professional development tool that has been gaining in popularity for decades. It is especially useful for executives who often feel isolated and vulnerable in today's modern, high-pressured workplace.

## Mentoring:

There is a lot of similarity to coaches and mentors. Both guide and direct the career and performance of a lesser skilled worker. However, where coaching is focused primarily on job performance, the mentor is genuinely invested in the mentee. Successful mentors are looked at as helpmates of the employee who follow their careers throughout. Mentors are more concerned with improving the employee's fit within the organization than improving technical aspects of performance, thus differentiating it from coaching.

There are two basic types of mentoring:
1. The new-hire mentor. In this case, a more experienced person, not necessarily a highly placed executive takes the employee under their wing for purposes of orienting them to the company culture.
2. The high-potential mentorship. Usually, when we think of mentoring, we think of this kind– where specially selected employees are offered the opportunity to develop a relationship with a senior leader. Generally, mentoring is reserved for highly placed employees who demonstrate upward mobility within the organization.

Note: There is overlap between some of the different learning systems that are being presented. Similarities exist between coaching and JIT. Elements of the Journeyman who trains the apprentice also involve coaching and JIT. As stated above, there are only subtle differences between coaching and mentoring. While similar, these difference will be exploited by the test writers and the successful PHR or SPHR candidate must understand them to be successful on the exam.

# Instructional Tools

## Audio training

When a live instructor is impractical, audio CD's and a recorded message can serve as a reasonable substitute. Because CD's are small, easy to use, and inexpensive, recorded programs are useful for training employees who travel frequently. While best suited to language and other verbal instruction, audio recordings can be used to supplement written materials for those with reading disabilities or to vary course content and course presentation. With the aid of a staff member who can write scripts, a trainer can easily produce recorded training courses. As an alternative, trainers can purchase ready-made, professionally developed recordings on a wealth of subjects. Many of these audio-courses are accompanied by workbooks, discussion guides, and other instructional materials. The use of audio programs ensures that all program participants will receive a standardized presentation that presents a consistent message no matter how geographically dispersed the workforce is.

### Video technologies

Video technology has had a lasting effect on business operations. The use of video to communicate business messages has changed the way employees react to workplace communications. Video has been used for highly specialized communications needs and lends itself to several different business related applications, including the ones listed below.

- **Seminars.** Videotapes can be mailed to sites that normally do not get certain programs or loaded onto the internet and tapes of speeches by individuals in different locations can be edited together as part of a single program.
- **On-the-job training.** Taped training sessions can be broadcast over a company's closed-circuit TV system or from a web-based delivery application.
- **International communications.** Video's simulcast capabilities make it an excellent medium for making important announcements to employees worldwide.

### Demonstration models

Scale models and cross-section models can be effective aids when demonstrating job skills and production techniques, especially those used by machine operators or assembly workers who work in a hard-skilled type position. This type application is especially useful for persons who learn from a kinesthetic presentation (hands on) format.

### Charts, posters, diagrams, and maps

Inexpensive and simple to produce, these training aids clearly present complicated concepts, display interrelationships, and reinforce learning. Visual handouts can enhance transfer of training since they can later be posted at the work site as a reference. For example, some fast-food places use charts to remind employees of the steps to follow when preparing an order. These applications are useful for those workers who learn best from a "visual" presentation format.

### Multi-projectors

Multi-projectors use projection technologies, such as LED displays, to project an image onto a screen in a classroom. Typically, the type software most associate with this form of presentation is PowerPoint. To show a class of trainees how to fill out a form, for example, a multi-projector is invaluable. By displaying a picture of the form, the trainer can project the form and fill it out while the class watches.

## Multimedia programs

Because multimedia programs are more interactive than other methods, they can be self-paced to keep trainees' attention for a longer time. These programs often combine such training aids as interactive web-based applications, personal computers, audio recordings, books, and videos. The main disadvantage of multimedia programs is they tend to be expensive.

## E – Evaluation Phase

Arguably, the most important but often the most neglected stage of the ADDIE model is the "Evaluation" phase. A well constructed professional development program requires constant review and revision for continuous improvement. But many employers are either conducting one-off programs where they are not interested in evaluative feedback for improvement or they simply do not go to the trouble to measure the performance of newly trained workers. This is a performance management mistake.

It is understandable that meaningful evaluation of training programs is sometimes costly and difficult, but understanding a program's bottom-line impact is critical to the pursuit of organizational efficacy. The evaluation phase is vital to producing measurable business results, improving morale, making lasting changes in employee behaviors, identifying weak spots, correcting operational errors, etc.

In summary, performance improvement begins and ends with the evaluation phase. It "ends" when the trainer and program designer receives feedback on the programs effect. It "begins" when this information is applied to improving and modifying the program to improve its performance with the next round of training. In effect, forming a closed loop system of never-ending improvements.

Time now to examine some of the common theories on how to conduct a meaningful evaluation of a professional development program.

## Evaluation of Training Effectiveness

The success or failure of a training program ultimately is determined by its impact on employees' ability to achieve organizational objectives. Several factors go into determining whether a training program achieves this final goal. The widely used Kirkpatrick model, developed by Donald L. Kirkpatrick in 1975, includes four key determinants or levels, each of which builds upon the others:

1. **Reactions**, or how participants felt about the training program;
2. **Learning**, or the amount of skills and knowledge acquired in the classroom;
3. **Behavior**, or how well trainees transfer their newly acquired skills and knowledge to the job;
4. **Results**, or how transfer of training affects the organization.

### Level One: Students' Reaction

In this first level or step, students are asked to evaluate the training after completing the program. These are sometimes called smile sheets or happy sheets because in their simplest form they measure how well students liked the training. Tools used to gather the student's reaction include:
- Checklist
- Questionnaire
- Interviews

While the exact number and types of questions to ask will depend on the course objectives, all feedback forms that measure the student's reaction should ask trainees about the following points:
- demographics,
- activities,
- instructional materials,
- trainer qualifications,
- job relevance,
- program characteristics, and
- program objectives.

### Level Two: Learning Results

Did the students actually learn the knowledge, skills, and attitudes the program was supposed to teach? To show achievement, have students complete a pre-test and post-test, making sure that test items or questions are truly written to the learning objectives. By summarizing the scores of all students, trainers can accurately see the impact that the training intervention had. This type of evaluation is not as widely conducted as Level One, but is still very common. Measures used to determine the level of learning include:

- Pre-test; post-test
- Post-test only
- Pre-test; post-test with a control group

Administering a test after training can help tell whether participants have learned relevant skills or knowledge. But unless employees took the same test before training, a good test score could simply reflect prior learning and not any benefit related to the program. An alternative is to compare trained employees' test scores to those of an untrained control group of employees, but few organizations are large enough to conduct this type of assessment. A good test score also does not guarantee transfer of learned skills to the job.

**TEST TAKING TIP**
The exam is a nationalized test. There will be no local- or state-level questions. Only federal or national questions.

The greater the predictive validity of the test used, however, the more likely that transfer of training will take place for high scorers.

### Level Three: Behavior in the Workplace

Students typically score well on post-tests, but the real question is whether or not any of the new knowledge and skills are retained and transferred back on the job. Level Three evaluations attempt to answer whether or not students' *behaviors* actually change as a result of new learning. These evaluations normally include:

- Performance test
- Critical incidents
- Simulation
- Observation

Simulations evaluate a trainee's ability to perform a specific task or a series of tasks, or to apply knowledge to a task. Simulations are best suited for training that involves equipment (such as typing) or discrete operations (such as parts assembly). For managerial training, simulations might involve in-basket or critical-incident exercises. Unlike tests, simulations measure the application of knowledge to a task and more closely predict transfer of training to the job. Like tests, however, a high score on a simulation exercise does not necessarily reflect learning gained through training, unless pretesting or a control group is used.

### Level Four: Business Results

Unfortunately, this is rarely done because of the difficulty of gathering the business data and the complexity of isolating the training intervention as a unique variable. However, even anecdotal data is worth capturing since the overall objective of any training program is to have a positive impact on the business. Typical tools used to capture the "results" on the business of a program include:

- Performance Appraisals
- Progress

The highest level of evaluation is whether the new skills learned in the classroom will "transfer" to better on-the-job performance. Behavioral rating scales, performance appraisals, attitude surveys, and work samples all provide information on whether training has translated into better job performance.

Establishing and maintaining this training assessment demands a long-term investment of time and resources from the training function. It also requires the cooperation and commitment of non-training staff —line managers, sales planners, HR personnel, co-workers, and others who can help track trainees' performance at scheduled intervals. Without this investment of effort, the training function will have difficulty proving its cost value and contribution to the organization.

To evaluate whether trainees use their new skills or knowledge on the job, the training department should consult with line managers to design, develop, and validate performance indicators. If at all possible, the same tools used to measure participants' pre-course performance should be used to assess transfer of training.

## Transfer of training

Another method of evaluating a professional development program's contribution towards enhancing organizational "results" is by looking at the concept of "transfer of training" as mentioned earlier. The definition of transfer of training is the course participants ability to apply the KSA's learned in the classroom to the job.

If the program is designed well, transfer of training to the job should produce measurable improvement in the trained employee's performance, as well as in the supervisor's evaluation of the employee. But the ultimate goal of improving job performance is to contribute to the organization's bottom line. Particularly in tight budgetary times, the training function must show top management how employee development efforts affect overall productivity and profits.

This step often is overlooked in training evaluation, largely because many training managers believe the analysis would prove overwhelming. But much of the data used to evaluate the organizational impact of training already is compiled regularly for department reports and other purposes. All the training function has to do is analyze this data for before-and after-training affects. Sources of information to examine for post-training affects include the following:

- **Productivity reports** - Look at hard production data, such as sales reports, task completion times, error rates, or manufacturing totals. Comparing figures before and after training can help managers and trainers determine whether any training-related performance improvements have taken place that affect the organization's bottom line.
- **HR reports** - Information gathered for HR purposes may show training outcomes that affect organizational goals. Safety reports, for example, may show reductions in workplace accidents or equipment damage after employees received training. Examine other records for reductions in absenteeism, grievance filings, turnover, or customer complaints.
- **Cost analysis** - The training manager should use the costs of trainers' fees, materials, facilities, travel, training time, and the number of trainees to determine the hourly cost of training for each participant.

As the cost of doing business increases and competition intensifies, employers want clear measurement of training's contribution to bottom-line goals. Cost justification for programs and the ability to attract workers into the classroom, are contingent on the Training Manager's ability to sell management on the validity of the training function. To accomplish this goal, the Training Manager must justify the training expense and the cost of tying up employee resources with metrics.

For HR and training managers, this focus on the bottom line has meant undertaking complex evaluations on a frequent basis. It has also led to an emphasis on translating training outcomes into measurements that directly affect an organization's health, such as gross income, percentage of sales, or repeat business.

Items to be considered when determining the cost of training programs include:

- Preparation and administration
- Rental and leasing fees for space and equipment
- Meals or snacks during training sessions
- Lodging, meals, and travel for out-of-town programs
- Trainees' wages
- Instructor's salary
- Full or partial refund of trainees' costs for completing outside programs
- Costs of awards or certificates for trainees
- Profits from selling products or equipment developed or purchased for training
- Revenues from fees charged to trainees

## Basic Formula

There are a number of different methods that may be used in determining the return on investment (ROI) of a training program. A traditional ROI formula involves the following steps:

### Calculate training return
The training evaluation should have produced some payoff measure, such as increased sales, the value of higher productivity, the costs savings of less equipment damage, and so on.

### Determine training investment
This figure reflects the total costs of conducting training. Add together the following expenses:

- **Program expenses.** Include expenses for trainees' and trainers' travel, lodging, and food, as well as trainers' salaries and facility rental.
- **Materials and equipment expenses.** Factor in costs for materials, supplies, and equipment operations.

To figure total training investment, deduct from total expenses any offsetting factors:

- **Program revenues.** Paybacks from training might come from trainees' accumulation of frequent flyer coupons, or from resale or rental of training materials.
- **Equipment revenues.** Resale, rental, or reuse of training equipment for other purposes can offset the cost of purchasing the devices.

Subtract the training investment from the training return. This calculation yields a net (after expenses) training return.

$$\text{Training Return} - \text{Training Investment} = \text{Net Training Return}$$

Calculate ROI by dividing the net training return by the training investment. This final calculation should yield a figure greater than one. If not, the company has actually lost money by training employees.

$$\text{Net Training Return} / \text{Training Investment} = \text{ROI}$$

---

**EXAMPLE**

A classroom training program for sales personnel costs a total of $5,000. From past training evaluations, the company knows that total sales of trained staff run about 20 percent higher than the sales of untrained personnel. For the size of the training class, this improvement in sales should generate about $20,000 more income for the company. The company's return on its training investment is calculated by subtracting the program's costs ($5,000) from the total returns ($20,000), which yields a net training return of $15,000. Dividing the net return ($15,000) by the program's costs ($5,000) shows the company getting a $3 return for every $1 invested in training.

$20,000 - $5,000 = $15,000 = Net Training Return

$15,000 / $5,000 = $3 ROI

---

## Recognizing Training Achievements - Non-monetary Rewards

Recognizing employees for their training achievements will stimulate interest, increase motivation and morale, and enhance the view of training as an important HR function within the organization. An organization can recognize employees for their training efforts in a number of ways. While most employers avoid promising a promotion as a reward, training is sometimes a condition for an employee to be considered for higher positions, particularly in companies that integrate training with formal career development programs. Even when training is not tied to pay or promotions, an employee's training efforts should not go unrecognized during an annual performance appraisal.

# Performance Appraisals

Performance appraisals, and their use, comprise a significant percentage of the material to be covered by the HRD questions on the exam.

The purpose of any good appraisal system is to align the employee's performance with the goals of the organization.

Performance appraisals are a foundational tool for performance management, employee engagement and professional development. The health and well being of the organization lies in the growth and development of the employee. Without a system that assesses each employee's performance in context with the larger organizational goals, inefficiency and wasteful behavior will occur.

## Performance Measurement- The Criterion

An effective performance appraisal system helps an employer meet the following objectives:

### Assess employee potential

An effective performance management system assists employers in making decisions about employee promotions and transfers. It also identifies employees with special abilities and skills.

### Identify training needs

Performance ratings are helpful in evaluating the effectiveness of an established training effort. The employer can design and target its training program to better address the performance problems due to a lack of training. For example, widespread common problems may indicate that a work group needs general or specialized training. Isolated performance problems might identify an individual's need for training in a specific area.

---

## Assist human resource planning

Performance appraisals are valuable in forecasting future personnel needs, calculating anticipated turnover, and formulating hiring projections. They also assist organizations in composing profiles of their work force based on individual, group, and team achievement.

## Assist in compensation planning

Increasing numbers of employers are linking pay to performance. Employers therefore use performance appraisals to validate their compensation practices among their different operating units. A reliable, consistent performance appraisal process enables an employer to predict future payroll costs more accurately.

## Identify and correct poor work performance

Performance appraisals also provide a formal vehicle for discussion between an employee and the employee's supervisor about poor work habits and finding methods of correcting them.

## Validate employment tests

A sound appraisal system exposes weaknesses in the criteria that an employer uses in making hiring, placement, and other personnel decisions. Testing for a particular skill would be inappropriate where that skill is not critical to satisfactory job performance in the position for which an individual is being considered.

**TEST TAKING TIP**
There are between 4-6 versions of each exam given all across the country during each testing period. They have different questions but same level of difficulty.

## Assist in recruitment

Well-defined performance appraisal criteria provide an employer's recruiters with information useful in clarifying the performance expectations for a specific position. With accurate criteria, recruiters are able to describe a position's duties to job applicants and inform them of the employer's performance expectations.

## Defending lawsuits

The performance appraisal process provides employers a means for documenting employees' poor job performance. Employers depend on such documentation to successfully defend themselves against employees' claims of unfair termination or disciplinary action.

## Motivate employees

Performance appraisals help motivate employees to meet the employer's performance standards. A positive appraisal lets an employee know that the employer recognizes the employee's work performance and that the employer will reward the employee for any special efforts.

# Key Performance Indicator (KPI):

A Key Performance Indicator (KPI) helps organizations understand how well they are performing in relation to their strategic goals and objectives. In the broadest sense, a KPI can be defined as providing the most important performance information that enables organizations or their stakeholders to understand whether the organization is on track or not.

Sometimes success is defined in terms of making progress toward strategic goals, but often, success is simply the repeated achievement of some level of operational goal (for example, zero defects, customer satisfaction, safety incidence rate, employee turnover rate, etc.). Accordingly, choosing the right KPIs is reliant upon having a good understanding of what is important to the organization. This often depends on the department measuring the performance; the KPIs useful to a Finance Team will be quite different to the KPIs assigned to the HR department, for example. A very common method for choosing KPIs is to apply a management framework such as the Balanced Scorecard which is discussed elsewhere in this program.

KPIs can also be used in a top-down command-and-control fashion to guide and control people's behaviors and actions. In other words, KPIs can be tied to the reward and recognition system thus ensuring that proper attention will be given to those areas of performance that have the greatest impact on the amount of worker's pay.

## Criterion Problems

One of the most important things a supervisor does as part of the overall task of managing employees' performance is to fairly and legally administer the company's work rules and to confront problems and even discipline employees when necessary. Because any decision that affects an individual's career is open to criticism that the decision was based on some unfair — or illegal — criterion, making expectations clear and documenting shortfalls are very important. Applying the company's work rules consistently and documenting that effort are crucial supervisory functions. The performance appraisal process is an integral tool in achieving this goal.

The following topics offer some examples of employee evaluation criteria.

### Validity
Will the system provide meaningful, relevant, and accurate measurements of performance? Will the system appraise performance rather than potential, personal attractiveness, personal background, or factors outside the employee's control?

### Consistency
Will ratings for the same performance of employees at the same levels of responsibility and experience be essentially the same, regardless of who is doing the rating and who is being rated? Will supervisors appraise employees against the same standards from one appraisal period to the next? How important is it to move toward the goal of obtaining comparable ratings from all supervisors?

### Value as feedback
Will the appraisal system assist employees in improving unsatisfactory performance? Will it present this assistance in a motivating way?

### Rater comprehension
Will supervisors clearly understand what is expected of them as raters? Will they understand the terminology and share with each other and with employee's similar interpretations of qualities rated?

### Rater acceptance
How will the performance appraisal system be perceived by those who have to implement it? Systems that supervisors have helped to develop typically have higher rater acceptance. Systems that are time consuming to administer or that frequently change encounter rater resistance.

### Employee acceptance
Will the system be demonstrably fair? Will it present criticisms constructively? Will it rely on standards that will have been accepted by employees and clearly communicated to them in advance? Can employees be further involved in the appraisal process to promote their acceptance of its results?

## Effectiveness

How effective will the system be in achieving goals set for it? These goals may include:

- recognizing and motivating high achievers;
- bringing the performance of all or most employees up to standard;
- improving overall performance;
- identifying employees who do not contribute sufficiently to the organization;
- showing where and what kind of training may be needed;
- identifying employees who are ready for development and promotion;
- improving communication between supervisors and employees;
- replacing prejudice with unbiased appraisal in salary, promotion, and terminations;
- providing evidence of unbiased decision-making to rebut grievances and lawsuits; and
- providing info needed to assess and measure the effectiveness of employee selection policies, training programs, and other personnel matters.

## Documenting Employee Performance

Many a lawsuit has been lost because the only written records of an employee's performance show that the employee was performing wonderfully. But the need for documentation begins long before any lawsuit is filed. Disciplinary actions and even annual performance reviews are especially hard to undertake if there are no records on an employee's performance.

Spoken compliments or suggestions for improvements may come naturally to leaders and many times is the most appropriate way to work with an individual. But when it comes time to put an assessment of that employee's performance on paper, is there any record of the ratio of compliments to criticism? Or of how many times the leader has pointed out a particular type of shortfall? Creating some written documentation along the way helps ensure that the appraisal of the employee's performance is based on incidents that happened throughout the year and not just on the most recent or memorable events of the year.

Written documentation can also decrease the chances that communications will be misunderstood. It is hard for an employee to claim they were never told that certain behaviors mattered if there is a memo in the file explaining why the behavior is important.

## Types of Appraisals

An organization may want to use more than one type of performance appraisal system. Many companies with effective performance management systems use different measurement systems for different groups of employees. Regardless of which system or systems are chosen, keep in mind that research has shown that systems using objective measurements or measurable criteria are the most effective and the most credible.

Of the many types of performance appraisal models, no one system is right or wrong. HR will need to review, discuss, and evaluate all options when designing a program for the organization. The appraisal system chosen should result from a systematic consideration of several elements, beginning with the objectives that the program is expected to meet. Performance appraisal systems can basically be sorted into several common categories or types. Some models combine factors or techniques from several of the following:

- Rating scales,

- Behaviorally anchored rating scales (BARS),
- Ranking systems,
- Checklists,
- Critical incident reports,
- Narrative or essay evaluations,
- Employee participatory systems (including 360-degree feedback),
- Management by objectives (MBO) systems, and
- Field reviews

## Rating scales and/or Graphic Rating Scales

Rating scales are best suited for a situation in which the supervisor is very familiar with the employee's duties and in which the duties are specific, objective, and easily measured. The supervisor chooses her or his assessment of the employee's performance from a range of numbers on a scale of, say, one to five. The leader then assesses the employee's performance against stated performance areas such as "quality of work," "quantity of work," "attendance," etc. This is a time-saving method of appraisal when a supervisor must appraise many employees at once.

Graphic rating scales, one form of "rating scales," are one of the most common methods of performance appraisal. They require an evaluator to indicate on a scale the degree to which an employee demonstrates a particular trait, behavior, or performance result. Rating forms are composed of a number of scales, each relating to a certain job or performance-related dimension, such as job knowledge, responsibility, or quality of work. It identifies certain subjective character traits, such as 'pleasant personality', 'initiative' or 'creativity' to be used as basic job performance criteria.

Disadvantages to this evaluation method: the traits used for performance evaluation may be unrelated to the job itself. Such traits often tend to be ambiguous and too vague to be used as the basis for employee performance appraisal. Another drawback is that the descriptive terms used in such scales may have different meanings to different raters. Factors such as 'initiative' and 'cooperation' are subject to many interpretations, especially in conjunction with words such as 'outstanding', 'average', or 'poor'.

## Behaviorally anchored rating scales (BARS)

The BARS evaluation system reduces rater bias and error by anchoring the rating with specific behavioral examples based on job analysis information. This type of scale rating is best suited for companies interested in long-range performance of employees in fields that are often changing, such as in research industries. Each job is measured in job-related terms, rather than numbers. It differs from "standard" rating scales in one central respect, in that it focuses on behaviors that are determined to be important for completing a job task or doing the job properly, rather than looking at more general employee characteristics (e.g. personality, vague work habits).

Behaviorally anchored rating scales (BARS) are rating scales whose scale points are defined by statements of effective and ineffective behaviors. BARS utilize critical incidents to focus appraisal on employee behaviors that can be changed. They are said to be behaviorally anchored in that the scales represent a continuum of descriptive statements of behaviors ranging from least to most effective. An evaluator must indicate which behavior on each scale best describes an employee's performance. BARS are constructed by the evaluators who will use them.

The major drawback to this system is that each position must have its own customized listing of behaviors to be measured. This system takes costly resources and time to construct, administer and execute. Despite the difficulties involved in employing a BARS system, it is a very effective appraisal method.

## Paired Comparison Analysis:

The Paired Comparison method involves comparing each employee to every other employee in the rating group, one at a time, to determine the better. A rank order is obtained by counting the number of times each individual is selected as being the better of a pair. Disadvantage of this method: if the number of employees to be ranked is large, the number of comparisons that have to be made may be unmanageable.

## Ranking systems

In this method, the supervisor lists all subordinates in order, from the highest to the lowest in performance. Ranking systems such as this are most appropriate in small companies or small departments. As the number of employees increases, it becomes gradually more difficult to discern differences in their performance. Disadvantages to this method: the size of differences among individuals may not be well defined. For example, there may be little difference between individuals ranked second and third, but a big difference in performance between those ranked third and fourth.

## Forced Distribution:

In Forced Distribution, the supervisor must assign a certain proportion of his/her subordinates to each of several categories on each evaluative factor. A common forced distribution scale is divided into five categories. A fixed percentage of all subordinates in the group fall within each of these categories.

For example, a supervisor with 10 employees must rate one employee as "unsatisfactory," two employees as "below average," four employees as "average," two employees as "above average" and one employee as "outstanding."

The disadvantages to this method are that the actual employee mix of performance does not conform to the fixed percentages. Additionally, supervisors are hesitant to assign employees to the "unsatisfactory" category. Also, as work groups mature and performance increases, it is not uncommon for a larger percentage of workers to perform at the "exceeds" level.

## Checklists

The checklist appraisal is best suited for situations in which supervisors are long-time acquaintances of employees, or are involved to a similar extent in difficult, stressful tasks. The purpose of this type of program is to avoid over-generous, nonspecific appraisals. For each category of performance, the supervisor must choose one phrase describing the employee's performance from a list of three or four phrases. There is usually no allowance for additional commentary.

Employees are evaluated against a large list of descriptive statements concerning effective and ineffective behavior on the job. Evaluators only mark the statements that apply to the worker. Otherwise, the appraiser leaves it blank and moves on to the next descriptive statement. Examples of descriptive statements are, "The employee give support to the Supervisor." "The employee follows instructions properly." Due to the length of the appraisal document, this method is costly and time consuming. Also, it is difficult for the supervisor to evaluate all the elements of the appraisal form.

## Critical incident reports

The Critical Incident method of performance appraisal is where the worker is evaluated on their effectiveness at handling key or critical situations that have arisen during the evaluation period. The manager keeps a written record of the highly favorable and unfavorable actions in an employee's performance. There is little form or format to follow. The evaluator relies on their own judgment as to the examples of critical situations that are to be chosen for review. The disadvantages to this format are that often the negative outcomes are given more weight and attention than positive outcomes. Also, tracking and recording the critical incidents is a difficult and ongoing task for the supervisor.

## Narrative or essay evaluations

This technique is best suited for a situation in which the supervisor is very familiar with the employee's performance and in which the employee's duties are not objective, specific, or easily measurable. In an essay appraisal, the supervisor simply describes in a paragraph his or her impression of the employee's performance. It is helpful if the appraisal is divided into topics such as attitude, creativity, reliability, and so on.

The essay (free-form) appraisal method requires the manager to write a short essay describing each employee's performance during the rating period. The subject of an essay appraisal is often justification of pay, promotion, or termination decisions, but essays can be used for developmental purposes as well. Since essay appraisals are to a large extent unstructured and open-ended, lack of standardization is a major problem. The open-ended, unstructured nature of the essay appraisal makes it highly susceptible to evaluator bias, which may in some cases be discriminatory. By not having to report on all job-related behaviors or results, an evaluator may simply comment on those that reflect favorably or unfavorably on an employee. This does not usually represent a true picture of the employee or the job, and content validity of the method suffers.

## Management by objectives (MBO) systems

The system of management by objectives is widely accepted as a motivating system that appeals to an employee's "ownership" of his or her job. Under an MBO system, the employee and the appraiser collaborate in planning performance goals for the employee to work toward until the next appraisal.

Management by objectives (MBO) involves setting specific measurable goals with each employee and then periodically discussing his/her progress toward these goals. This is considered to be an output-based appraisal approach since the focus is on the job performance outcome.

Disadvantages to the use of this methodology include that MBO is not appropriate for jobs with little or no flexibility. Therefore, the MBO process seems to be most useful with managerial personnel and employees who have a fairly wide range of flexibility and control over their jobs.

## Alternative Performance Evaluation Systems:

All of the above performance evaluation systems are usually executed by the immediate supervisor. However, when supervisors do not have the opportunity to observe each employee's performance, but other work group members do, it is sometimes more effective to allow them to provide performance feedback or to allow the employee themselves to conduct a self examination. Employee participatory systems can incorporate peer reviews, subordinate reviews, and self- appraisals. Examples of multi-rater and alternative evaluation systems include:

1. **Peer Reviews:**

   Peer review is useful when rating professionals in fields requiring highly specialized knowledge. Peer reviews often have a high level of worker acceptance and involvement; they tend to be stable, task-relevant, and accurate. By helping peers to understand each other's work and by airing grievances in a non-threatening manner, peer reviews may also help people to get along better. For the organization, this means higher performance.

   Common performance dimensions on which team members have evaluation expertise include attendance and timeliness, interpersonal skills, group supportiveness, and planning and coordination.

The major disadvantage to this appraisal method is team members resist negatively evaluating colleagues since this can damage relationships. Peer reviews may work best if all parties know that the reviews will not be used for setting pay, promotion possibilities, or disciplinary actions.

2.  **360 Degree Evaluations:**
    Similar to peer reviews, the 360 degree feedback system expands on this idea and includes not just the peers, but superiors, subordinates and even customers. The 360-degree review seeks input from all persons, including customers, who deal regularly with the employee. The 360-degree performance appraisal is a modern approach to evaluate and improve performance.

    This process collects feedback from people all around the person being evaluated and interprets a common theme in it. This outcome is used for professional development and self-improvement of the employee. In many ways, the pros and cons of 360 degree appraisal systems mirror the peer review method.

3.  **Subordinate Reviews:**
    Often, the subordinate is in the best position to provide constructive performance feedback to their superior. Subordinate reviews can provide insight into strengths or weaknesses in management. Pros and cons of this type evaluation system are as follows:
    a.  Subordinates will not be truthful in the performance ratings for fear of repercussions;
    b.  Managers will be over-concerned with pleasing subordinates in order to achieve positive ratings;
    c.  Managerial authority will be questioned;
    d.  Managers' ratings will reflect their popularity among the workers, not their abilities;
    e.  Subordinates are not capable of assessing manager's performance and will, therefore, skew the ratings;
    f.  Subordinates' ratings will be based on the weight of their workload: The harder the work that they are assigned, the more negative ratings will be given to their supervisors;
    g.  Increase in reciprocal leniency- "I'll scratch your back if you will scratch mine" mentality;

4.  **Self Appraisals:**
    When managerial input is not helpful or remote, self- appraisals, combined with one or another appraisal system, can help the employee become more involved in the appraisal process of improved performance or expanded responsibilities. Self appraisal is an important part of the Performance appraisal process where the employee himself gives the feedback or his views and points regarding his performance. Usually this is done with the help of a self appraisal form.

    Often, self appraisals are done poorly when little guidance or preparation training is provided. Employees often write self appraisals that do not accurately reflect their true contribution to the organization because they are unaware of the importance of their role in the organizational effort.

5.  **Field Reviews:**
    One final method of conducting a performance evaluation is where a person outside the concerned department, usually an HR Representative goes into the "field" and assists supervisors in gathering information and rating the appraisee. Field reviews are usually conducted in matters of promoting an executive to the managerial level.

    The advantage of the field review method is that since the rater in an "outsider" the chances of bias are reduced. The rater is usually extensively trained to conduct the appraisal interview.

Disadvantage of the field review method is that the "outsider" may not be aware of the job requirements, work culture and work environment. The outsider has not observed the employee at work and does not know his on-field behavior and performance, except from the report submitted by the employee's supervisor, which may be biased. This method is also time consuming and costly.

## Rating Errors

The pitfalls listed below can be used to help supervisors avoid the most common sources of rating errors in the appraisal process.

- **Bias**. There is a natural tendency for raters to give favorable ratings to someone like themselves. This is sometimes knows as the "similar-to-me bias."

- **Rating personality rather than performance**. Raters may respond quickly and strongly to personality traits, such as charm or aggressiveness, which may bias them when it comes time to assess accomplishments. The appraisal should focus only on actions and accomplishments.

- **Employee's personal background**. Raters may rely on assumptions that employees with more experience are performing better and may fail to test these assumptions rigorously through observation. Ratings that take background into account tend to be inaccurate, unprofitable, and illegal.

- **"Halo/horn effect."** A halo effect occurs when a rater gives an excellent employee top ratings in all areas or gives an unsatisfactory employee low ratings in all areas. The halo or horn effect results when raters let one strong value judgment in one area color their judgment of other behaviors and traits. Poor employees usually have some strengths and high achievers some weaknesses.

- **Lack of clear standards**. Clear, measurable standards are invaluable for producing accurate appraisals. Raters usually benefit from spelling out what behavior would merit each of the ratings before assessing individual employees.

- **Leniency**. Raters may be afraid to hurt employees' feelings or to hurt employees financially. Sometimes a rater may be unwilling to give a low rating to an employee who is likely to bring a grievance or lawsuit, even when the employee's performance is hurting co-workers' morale.

- **Severity**. Some raters have unrealistic expectations about employee performance. Others are simply reluctant to offer praise.

- **Limited use of the rating scale**. Raters may avoid giving very high or very low ratings, since these require greater justification and require the rater to take greater responsibility for the decisions.

- **Inadequate observation**. Raters who are not familiar with all aspects of an employee's performance may feel compelled to fill in a standardized form completely. Raters who do not work closely with subordinates may be unable or unwilling to arrange for a sufficient number of observations. In addition, raters may become set in their opinions and disregard observed behavior that differs from their conclusions.

- **Inappropriate time span (aka "Recency Error)**. Performance appraisals should cover the whole of an employee's behavior and the extent of the employee's progress during the time period from one appraisal date to the next and not just recent issues that may have occurred. Raters who look back to incidents that occurred before the last appraisal are also being unfair to employees.

- **"Contrast effect."** The exceptionally good or bad performance of one or two employees may greatly distort the ratings that the others receive. While contrasting the relative contributions of a group of employees can contribute to the appraisal process and is especially relevant when a fixed amount of rewards must be distributed within a group, morale may fall if the rating of one employee shifts the rating scale for the others.

- **Overemphasis on uncharacteristic performance**. Unusual behavior is more memorable than typical behavior. Raters observing behavior that seems uncharacteristic should make an effort to find out whether it is part of a pattern. Ratings should focus on typical behavior patterns.

## Appraisal Interview

Many raters gloss over the appraisal interview because they are afraid of antagonism or resentment. Instead of criticizing weaknesses or past mistakes, the rater should concentrate on constructive suggestions. The rater should also use the interview as an opportunity to recognize the employee's achievements and future potential.

Raters can take various approaches to the interview, depending upon the situation. The most commonly used interview approaches are (1) the direct approach, where the rater does most of the talking; and (2) the indirect approach, where the rater asks questions, encourages responses from the employee, and spends time listening.

The direct approach is useful for presenting facts and judgments or to orient the employee to a new way of doing a job. This approach is often necessary when an employee is performing poorly and other methods of dealing with the problem have failed.

**TEST TAKING TIP**
HRCI says "not true" but we find many of the longest answers on the exam are the correct answers. Look at the longest and most specific answers that contain value determiner statements when unsure of the options.

The indirect approach is useful because it encourages the employee to think about the reasons for poor performance. Asking questions gives the manager more information about the employee's motives and perceptions. This approach also keeps the employee active in the process. The questions asked will determine the value of the responses raters received. A closed-ended question often elicits a one word "yes" or "no" answer; it asks for specific information. An open-ended question is more general and encourages discussion. Open-ended questions elicit more information.

### Building motivation during the performance appraisal interview
The ideal performance evaluation results in a desire for continued improvement or sustained good performance by the employee. If an employee leaves the evaluation motivated to improve rather than feeling demoralized, the rater can consider the appraisal to be a success.

The following list summarizes techniques an appraiser can use to orchestrate an effective, motivation-building performance interview:

- Point out the employee's achievements and strengths.
- Note progress made towards last year's goals.
- Discuss a limited number of key issues; do not overload the employee.
- Do not spring surprises on the employee; the interview should be a recap of the feedback provided all year.
- Ask questions and listen to the employee's answers.
- Restate employee remarks.

- Pay attention to nonverbal communication.
- Identify and discuss differences that the employee has about the process.
- Try to be empathetic.
- Discuss job performance, not personality.
- Describe behavior and do not interpret motives.
- Avoid discussing personal problems.
- Keep an open mind.
- Translate negatives into areas for improvement.
- Follow through on agreements with the employee.

## Legal Constraints on Performance Appraisal

A hurried, ill-prepared evaluation in the hands of a disgruntled employee can become a weapon against the employer. Employees or former employees have used their evaluations in lawsuits against employers as evidence of intentional discrimination, disparate treatment, and defamation.

Performance appraisals have been the basis of breach of contract suits, and have made possible the tort of wrongful evaluation. Evaluations have sometimes been used to prove that an employee was dismissed without due notice, warning, opportunity to improve, or in violation of an expressed or implied promise.

**TEST TAKING TIP**
The answers are evenly divided between options 1, 2, 3, and 4 on the test. Therefore, 25% of your answers should be option 1, and 25% option 2, etc.

Clearly, a false, incomplete, undocumented, vague, and basically deficient evaluation can be damaging to the employer. While an employer cannot be expected to conduct all evaluations as if a lawsuit were looming, experts suggest that the employer keep the following question in mind: How will this look to a judge or jury? A company that does not take the time to make accurate, complete, and written evaluations might do better with no evaluation at all.

## Goal Setting

In 1955 Peter Drucker advocated Management by Objectives. This involves clearly identifying and communicating the organization's objectives, then specifying objectives for each employee setting out their individual part in achieving these. The SMART acronym has been developed to highlight the characteristics of effective objectives for individual job holders. Objectives should be:

- **S**pecific about the required outcome,
- **M**easurable so that achievement can be determined,
- **A**greed between the manager and the job holder, (sometimes the "A" is for "Achievable,"
- **R**ealistic so that they are stretching but achievable, and
- **T**ime-bound so there is a clear deadline.

## Validity and Reliability

In determining whether performance appraisal systems are discriminatory, federal courts generally apply the same standards used to determine if employee selection devices and tests are discriminatory.

> Under such standards, a performance appraisal system is nondiscriminatory if it is both valid and reliable.

If the system does not satisfy both requirements, the discriminatory impact of the improper factors might cause the system to violate one or more federal or state laws.

### Determining validity

Validity refers to the extent to which an employer's performance appraisal process measures actual job performance. Courts have ruled that employers may establish the validity of their performance appraisal programs using one or more of the following standards:

- **Content validity**. The factors used in a performance appraisal process are content valid if they are both representative of the job and relevant to the job. For example, Content valid factors for appraising a typist's performance may include the typist's typing speed and error rates. However, a typist's performance factor that is based on the typist's ability to lift heavy loads would not be a content valid factor since lifting is not relevant to the job.

- **Predictive validity.** Sometimes called *criterion validity*, is when a performance appraisal process has a positive statistical correlation between an employee's performance appraisal and the employee's performance in later jobs. For example, a requirement that a data entry clerk have neat, legible handwriting probably would not have predictive validity; a severely arthritic employee might have a claim of discrimination based on age or disability if the requirement affected the employee's evaluation (and promotion opportunities).

- **Construct validity.** Performance appraisal factors have construct validity if the employer can demonstrate that the factors are critical to successful job performance. For example, Leadership might be a construct valid factor in a manager's performance appraisal but would not be a valid construct factor in an entry-level employee's appraisal, unless the employer demonstrates that leadership is relevant to successful performance of the entry-level job.

- **Concurrent validity**. The approach whereby people who are successful within a given job, within a given company or industry, are evaluated and generally grouped *Top Third, Middle Third,* and *Bottom Third*. The assessment scores of the people who fit each of these ranges are then compiled and Job Benchmark Standards of the *Top Third* are used to hire, train or manage.

- **Face validity**. This is the simplest form of validity which basically tells us that the personality test or other assessment instrument appears (on the face of it) to measure what it is supposed to measure. Simply put, a test that would be composed of questions concerning the ability to be exact and detailed would have face validity as a measure of the ability to succeed as an accountant. Face validity is not very sophisticated because it is only based on the appearance of the measure. Be careful because the market is flooded with personality testing that has only face validity.

### Determining reliability

In addition to being valid, performance appraisal programs must be reliable. A performance appraisal system is reliable if it provides consistent data about employees regardless of who conducts it. This type of reliability often is referred to as inter-rater reliability.

# DHR's Fast 20

1. "Expectancy Theory" of **motivation** by Vroom... "the trainee must believe his/her effort in the training program will lead to improved skills and thus to a higher salary".

2. "MBT" is techno speak for "**Multimedia Based Training**". Defined as learning that involves computer-based interaction with audio, graphics, video or internet.

3. Most common assessment tool for measuring **classroom effectiveness**... end of class questionnaire... also the worst... measures students reactions... not "learning"!

4. A training course is **evaluated** for effectiveness by measuring: 1) reaction, 2) learning, 3) behavior, & 4) results… per Kirkpatrick.

5. Develop in-house **SMEs (subject matter experts)** to teach recurring topics.

6. **Major steps in training** = 1)assessment, 2) development, 3) implement, & 4) evaluate.

7. **Job rotation** involves moving employees from one job to another to broaden their experience.

8. A **needs assessment** is a systematic, objective determination of training needs.

9. **Computer-based training** is interactive, self-paced, and uses software teaching tools.

10. **In-Basket exercises** require students to role-play realistic job challenges and to problem solve.

11. **Assessment centers** are used exclusively for selecting and identifying managerial candidates.

12. **Vestibule training** programs create realistic simulations and the environment of the actual job-to-be - performed.

13. **Pre-test/post-test** is the commonly accepted way of measuring whether learning occurred.

14. **Adult learners** learn better when an interactive and multi-based presentation style is used rather than straight lecture.

15. Computer assisted training, one form of **Programmed Instruction**, is highly useful because it provides immediate feedback to the student and allows them to work at their own pace.

16. **Critical incident technique** is a method-of-review used to keep a record of uncommonly good or undesirable examples of an employee's work-related behavior.

17. **Behaviorally anchored rating scale (BARS)** is an appraisal method that evaluates good or poor performance based on observable or measurable behaviors.

18. **Training curves** include… S-Shaped curve where the information is learned in a series of increasing and decreasing ability to retain the information… Funnel presentation styles are where the material is presented in a general form first with specific details being taught last… Inverted-Funnel – opposite of Funnel… Plateau – Training is flat and unchanging.

19. **Kinesthetic Learners** learn best by hands-on teaching approach.

20. **Contrast error** occurs when the appraiser compares one employee against another versus the stated performance expectation.

# Sample Quiz

1. Which training method as generally used, does NOT provide for learner involvement, does NOT consider individual differences, and does NOT allow feedback?
    - A. Programmed instruction
    - B. Role playing
    - C. Lecture
    - D. Coaching

2. Job-related knowledge that is obtained in a self-controlled and orderly method, and provides immediate feedback to the learner, is BEST described as:
    - A. Coaching
    - B. Programmed instruction
    - C. Hands-on learning
    - D. Vestibule training

3. According to Kirkpatrick, if you are collecting data by using tests and/or quizzes, or by observation and/or demonstration, you are MOST LIKELY evaluating training effectiveness by which level of criteria?
    - A. Reaction
    - B. Learning
    - C. Behavior
    - D. Results

4. Which statement is BEST concerning HRD?
    - A. Training does not have to align with corporate goals
    - B. Performance improvements cannot happen without training
    - C. It is an informal process
    - D. It is a life-long process

5. The Customer Service manager has asked the Training Manager to help build the core competencies of the CS Reps. The Training Manager should FIRST do:
    - A. Market research
    - B. Review off-the-shelf training packages
    - C. Organize a team of instructional designers
    - D. Develop an evaluation system for the finished product

6. The FIRST step in the Action Learning Model is:
    - A. Design the experiment
    - B. Analyze the results
    - C. Compare the analysis
    - D. Formulate the hypothesis

7. The ultimate objective of any performance review system is to:
    - A. Justify raises
    - B. Form a basis for employee development plans
    - C. Align tactical performance with the organization's strategic direction
    - D. Report on employee performance to determine how the employee measures up

8. An organization is changing their training to entirely internet-based online training. This will result in:
    A. Higher training costs
    B. More employees participating in training
    C. Less satisfaction from students in the delivery methodology
    D. Requiring the company training philosophy to change completely

9. The BEST term for the process of developing a multi skilled workforce by providing employees with training and development opportunities to ensure they have the skills necessary to perform various job functions within an organization.
    A. Cross-training
    B. Performance management
    C. HRD
    D. Continuing education

10. The goal of this type training is to increase awareness and understanding of the differences between workers and also to develop concrete skills among staff that will facilitate enhanced productivity and communications among all employees.
    A. Leadership development
    B. Assessment centers
    C. Diversity
    D. Harassment

## Answers and Explanations to Practice Quiz:

1. C

Lecture is where the instructor speaks with little to no audience participation. Programmed instruction is a broad family of tutorial styled self-paced instructional programs (online tutorials, workbooks, etc.). Role playing is an audience participation activity. Coaching is where a more experienced or skilled individual provides an employee with advice and guidance but with two-way communication.

2. B

See above for further clarification. Hands-on learning (a.k.a. kinesthetic learning) is a model of instructional delivery where the participant learns by doing. Vestibule training is a type of training delivery system where the participant is allowed to learn a job through hands-on methods. Of the answer options, only programmed instruction provides immediate feedback.

3. B

The pre-test and post-test method is the commonly accepted measure for determining whether learning has occurred. The other options use an assortment of methodologies including questionnaires, observation, performance appraisals, etc.

4. D

The other three options are generally considered untrue. HRD is considered a "lifelong" issue as organizations continually need to reinvent themselves and the skills of their workers to keep pace with the modernization of industrialization.

5. A

The first step in any instructional design process is to conduct a "needs analysis." Market research is vital to have when contemplating how to design and deliver a program that targets these CS Reps.

6. D

The steps in the Action Learning Model of instruction are:

6. Formulate the hypothesis
7. Design the experiment
8. Conduct the experiment
9. Analyze the results
10. Compare the analysis

7.  C

The overall strategic goal of any performance review system is to align tactical performance with the goals of the corporation. The other answer options are by-products of the performance review system that are important but not as strategically necessary as aligning tactical execution with strategic goal accomplishment. (Note: you'll see a lot of questions phrased like this one on the test)

8.  B

Online training has proven benefits for reaching employees that are otherwise unreachable (geographically dispersed, telecommuters, etc.). The other options are all wrong. Online training: lowers costs, improves employee satisfaction (especially self-paced programs), and requires little to no change in company training philosophy.

9.  A

The correct answer option is one commonly accepted definition of cross-training. The key to answering this question are the key words of "various job functions within the organization." While a good but not correct answer, HRD is the overall framework for helping employees develop their personal and organizational skills, knowledge, and abilities and less about developing job function skills. Continuing education is better described as courses, programs, or organized learning experiences usually taken after a degree is obtained to enhance personal or professional goals. Performance management is clearly incorrect as it is the process of defining a mission and desired outcomes, setting performance standards, etc. and is not specifically concerned with training & development.

10. C

The key words in the question that provide the clue to the correct answer are, "increase awareness and understanding." Assessment Centers is an incorrect answer as it is a method for assessing potential leaders by utilizing trained assessors using various diagnostic tools. Harassment training, while a good answer, is not the best for the key words above and other key words such as "enhancing productivity and communications." Leadership development is clearly an incorrect option.

# Chapter 3
# Compensation & Benefits
# (PHR 19% - SPHR 13%)

Developing/selecting, implementing/administering and evaluating compensation and benefits programs for all employee groups that support the organization's goals, objectives and values.

## Wage and Hour Laws

### Sherman Antitrust Act

> The Sherman Antitrust Act (Sherman Act, July 2, 1890) was the first United States government action to limit monopolies and is the oldest of all U.S. antitrust laws.

Every contract, combination in the form of trust or otherwise, or conspiracy, in restraint of trade or commerce among the several States, or with foreign nations, is declared to be illegal. In particular, the Act has been interpreted to limit the use of wage surveys between two or more competitors as a form of salary-fixing.

### Davis Bacon Act

> The Davis-Bacon Act of 1931 is a United States federal law which established the requirement for paying prevailing wages on public works projects.

All federal government construction contracts, and most contracts for federally assisted construction over $2,000, must include provisions for paying workers on-site no less than the locally prevailing wages and benefits paid on similar projects.

Representative Bacon initially introduced the bill after a contractor employed African-American workers from Alabama to build a Veteran's Bureau hospital in his New York district. Congress desired to reserve jobs on federal projects for local workers, who nationwide faced epidemic unemployment in 1931. Therefore, Congress enacted the Davis Bacon Act to (1) assure workers a fair wage, (2) provide local contractors a fair opportunity to compete for local government contracts and (3) to preserve its own ability to distribute employment and federal money equitably through public works projects. Opponents of this bill say it's a blatant attempt to appease local union elements.

### Copeland Act

> The Copeland Act (1934) and Anti-Kickback Law (1948) prohibits contractors or subcontractors from in any way inducing an employee to give up any part of the compensation to which he or she is

entitled under his or her contract and requires contractors and subcontractors on certain federally funded construction contracts to submit weekly statements of compliance.

Whoever, by force, intimidation, or threat of procuring dismissal from employment, or by any other manner whatsoever induces any person employed in the construction, prosecution, completion or repair of any public building, public work, or building or work financed in whole or in part by loans or grants from the United States, to give up any part of the compensation to which he is entitled under his contract of employment, shall be fined not more than $5,000 or imprisoned not more than five years, or both.

## Walsh Healy Act

The Walsh-Healey Public Contracts Act of 1936 (PCA) requires contractors engaged in the manufacturing or furnishing of materials, supplies, articles, or equipment to the U.S. government or the District of Columbia to pay employees who produce, assemble, handle, or ship goods under contracts exceeding $10,000, the federal minimum wage for all hours worked and time and one half their regular rate of pay for all hours worked over 40 in a workweek.

The PCA is enforced by the Employment Standards Administration's Wage and Hour Division (WHD) within the U.S. Department of Labor (DOL).

## Fair Labor Standards Act (FLSA)

The Fair Labor Standards Act (FLSA) of 1938, which prescribes standards for the basic minimum wage and overtime pay, affects most private and public employment. It requires employers to pay covered employees who are not otherwise exempt at least the federal minimum wage and overtime pay of one-and-one-half-times the regular rate of pay. For nonagricultural operations, it restricts the hours that children under age 16 can work and forbids the employment of children under age 18 in certain jobs deemed too dangerous. For agricultural operations, it prohibits the employment of children under age 16 during school hours and in certain jobs deemed too dangerous.

The FLSA does not, however, require employers to provide severance pay, sick leave, vacations, or holidays.

The Act is administered by the Employment Standards Administration's Wage and Hour Division within the U.S. Department of Labor.

### Minimum wage
All employers covered by the law must pay employees at least the set minimum wage per hour.

### Overtime pay
Non-exempt employees who work more than 40 hours per week must be paid one-and-one-half times the base wage for any hours over 40.

### Child labor
An employee must be at least 16 years old to work in most non-farm jobs and at least 18 to work in non-farm jobs declared hazardous by the Secretary of Labor. Youths 14 and 15 years old may work outside school hours in various non-manufacturing, non-mining, non-hazardous jobs under the following conditions: No more than:

- 3 hours on a school day or 18 hours in a school week;
- 8 hours on a non-school day or 40 hours in a non-school week.

Also, work may not begin before 7 a.m. or end after 7 p.m., except from June 1 through Labor Day, when evening hours are extended to 9 p.m. Different rules apply in agricultural employment.

## Recordkeeping

Every employer covered by the Fair Labor Standards Act (FLSA) must keep certain records for each covered, nonexempt worker. There is no required form for the records, but the records must include accurate information about the employee and data about the hours worked and the wages earned. The following is a listing of the basic records that an employer must maintain for a period of not less than three years:

- Employee's full name, as used for social security purposes, and on the same record, the employee's identifying symbol or number if such is used in place of name on any time, work, or payroll records;
- Address, including zip code;
- Birth date, if younger than 19;
- Sex and occupation;
- Time and day of week when employee's workweek begins. Hours worked each day and total hours worked each workweek;
- Basis on which employee's wages are paid;
- Regular hourly pay rate;
- Total daily or weekly straight-time earnings;
- Total overtime earnings for the workweek;
- All additions to or deductions from the employee's wages;
- Total wages paid each pay period;
- Date of payment and the pay period covered by the payment.

> **TEST TAKING TIP**
> The certification exam is a national standardized test. Versions of the test are standard across the country and world.

## Exempt status

The FLSA requires that most employees in the United States be paid at least the federal minimum wage for all hours worked and overtime pay at time and one-half the regular rate of pay for all hours worked over 40 hours in a workweek. However, Section 13(a)(1) of the FLSA provides an exemption from both minimum wage and overtime pay. To qualify for exemption, employees generally must meet certain tests regarding their job duties and be paid on a salary basis at not less than $455 per week. Job titles do not determine exempt status. In order for an exemption to apply, an employee's specific job duties and salary must meet all the requirements of the Department's regulations. An employee must meet one of four tests:

1. **Executive Exemption**. To qualify for the **executive** employee exemption, all of the following tests must be met:

   - The employee must be compensated on a salary basis at a rate not less than $455 per week;
   - The employee's primary duty must be managing the enterprise, or managing a customarily recognized department or subdivision of the enterprise;
   - The employee must customarily and regularly direct the work of at least two or more other full-time employees or their equivalent; and
   - The employee must have the authority to hire or fire other employees, or the employee's suggestions and recommendations as to the hiring, firing, advancement, promotion or any other change of status of other employees must be given particular weight.

2. **Administrative Exemption**. To qualify for the **administrative** employee exemption, all of the following tests must be met:

- The employee must be compensated on a salary or fee basis at a rate not less than $455 per week;

- The employee's primary duty must be the performance of office or non-manual work directly related to the management or general business operations of the employer or the employer's customers; and

- The employee's primary duty includes the exercise of discretion and independent judgment with respect to matters of significance.

3. **Professional Exemption**. To qualify for the **learned professional** employee exemption, all of the following tests must be met:

- The employee must be compensated on a salary or fee basis at a rate not less than $455 per week;

- The employee's primary duty must be the performance of work requiring advanced knowledge, defined as work which is predominantly intellectual in character and which includes work requiring the consistent exercise of discretion and judgment;

- The advanced knowledge must be in a field of science or learning; and

- The advanced knowledge must be customarily acquired by a prolonged course of specialized intellectual instruction.

To qualify for the **creative professional** employee exemption, all of the following tests must be met:

- The employee must be compensated on a salary or fee basis at a rate not less than $455 per week;

- The employee's primary duty must be the performance of work requiring invention, imagination, originality or talent in a recognized field of artistic or creative endeavor.

To qualify for the **computer employee professional** exemption, the following tests must be met:

- The employee must be compensated either on a salary or fee basis at a rate not less than $455 per week or, if compensated on an hourly basis, at a rate not less than $27.63 an hour;

- The employee must be employed as a computer systems analyst, computer programmer, software engineer or other similarly skilled worker in the computer field performing the duties described below as their primary job duties:
  a. The application of systems analysis techniques and procedures, including consulting with users, to determine hardware, software or system functional specifications;
  b. The design, development, documentation, analysis, creation, testing or modification of computer systems or programs, including prototypes, based on and related to user or system design specifications;
  c. The design, documentation, testing, creation or modification of computer programs related to machine operating systems; or
  d. A combination of the aforementioned duties, the performance of which requires the same level of skills.

4. **Outside Sales Exemption.** To qualify for the **outside sales** employee exemption, all of the following tests must be met:

- The employee's primary duty must be making sales (as defined in the FLSA), or obtaining orders or contracts for services or for the use of facilities for which a consideration will be paid by the client or customer; and
- The employee must be customarily and regularly engaged away from the employer's place or places of business.

### Highly compensated employees

Highly compensated employees performing office or non-manual work and paid total annual compensation of $100,000 or more (which must include at least $455 per week paid on a salary or fee basis) are exempt from the FLSA if they customarily and regularly perform at least one of the duties of an exempt executive, administrative or professional employee identified in the standard tests for exemption.

### Blue collar workers

The exemptions provided by FLSA Section 13(a)(1) apply only to "white collar" employees who meet the salary and duties tests set forth in the Part 541 regulations. The exemptions do not apply to manual laborers or other "blue collar" workers who perform work involving repetitive operations with their hands, physical skill and energy. FLSA-covered, non-management employees in production, maintenance, construction and similar occupations such as carpenters, electricians, mechanics, plumbers, iron workers, craftsmen, operating engineers, longshoremen, construction workers and laborers are entitled to minimum wage and overtime premium pay under the FLSA, and are not exempt under the Part 541 regulations no matter how highly paid they might be.

### Police, fire fighters, paramedics and other first responders

The exemptions also do not apply to police officers, detectives, deputy sheriffs, state troopers, highway patrol officers, investigators, inspectors, correctional officers, parole or probation officers, park rangers, fire fighters, paramedics, emergency medical technicians, ambulance personnel, rescue workers, hazardous materials workers and similar employees, regardless of rank or pay level, who perform work such as preventing, controlling or extinguishing fires of any type; rescuing fire, crime or accident victims; preventing or detecting crimes; conducting investigations or inspections for violations of law; performing surveillance; pursuing, restraining and apprehending suspects; detaining or supervising suspected and convicted criminals, including those on probation or parole; interviewing witnesses; interrogating and fingerprinting suspects; preparing investigative reports; or other similar work. However, these positions are allowed the use of compensatory leave policies if managed and operated under the auspices of a government entity.

## Equal Pay Act

The Equal Pay Act (EPA) requires equal pay for men and women doing substantially equal work on jobs which require equal skill, effort, and responsibility and are performed under similar working conditions. The EPA is incorporated into the FLSA and applies to all employers subject to that law.

Comparable worth relates jobs that are dissimilar in content and contends that employees who perform jobs that require similar skill, effort, and responsibility under similar working conditions should be compensated equally. However, while many believe the theory of comparable worth to be law, it has not been passed, despite several attempts. Therefore, do not confuse the Equal Pay Act (same pay for same job) with comparable worth (same pay for similar job).

## Lilly Ledbetter Fair Pay Act

The Lilly Ledbetter Fair Pay Act of 2009 amended Title VII of the Civil Rights Act of 1964, the Age Discrimination in Employment Act (ADEA), and the Rehabilitation Act to clarify compensation practices that allow pay discrimination to be determined with the issuance of each new paycheck rather than the old system whereby the complainant had only 180 days to file a complaint from the initial discriminatory wage decision.

Ledbetter had taken her case to the U.S. Supreme Court in Ledbetter v. Goodyear Tire & Rubber Co. where the Supreme Court ruled against her. Congress then took the case and rewrote the law to reset the 180 statute of limitations from the last issuance of a discriminatory paycheck. In her case, it was reset each month when her retirement check was issued. She had been paid less than her male colleagues while employed, unbeknownst to her, resulting in less retirement plan payouts when she eventually retired. She discovered the wage disparity after she had retired. Under the old rules, she was ineligible for restitution since she had not acted to file a claim in a timely manner. Under the new Fair Pay Act guidelines, she was awarded restitution.

## Portal-to-Portal Act

The 1947 Portal-to-Portal Act further defined exactly what time was consider compensable work time. In general, as long as an employee is engaging in activities that benefit the employer, regardless of when they are performed, the employer has an obligation to pay the employee for his or her time. It also specified that travel to and from the work place was a normal incident of employment and should not be considered paid working time.  This Act is an amendment to the FLSA.

> **TEST TAKING TIP**
> 150 of the questions on the exam will count towards your score. Twenty-five of the questions are sample questions that won't be graded. They use them to determine the level of difficulty on future tests.

## McNamara-O'Hara Service Contract Act

The McNamara-O'Hara Service Contract Act (SCA) of 1965 applies to every contract entered into by the United States or the District of Columbia, the principal purpose of which is to furnish services to the United States through the use of service employees. The SCA requires contractors and subcontractors performing services on covered federal or District of Columbia contracts in excess of $2,500 to pay service employees in various classes no less than the monetary wage rates and to furnish fringe benefits found prevailing in the locality, or the rates (including prospective increases) contained in a predecessor contractor's collective bargaining agreement. Safety and health standards also apply to such contracts.

## Wage Garnishment Act

The wage garnishment provisions of the Consumer Credit Protection Act (CCPA) protect employees from discharge by their employers because their wages have been garnished for any one debt, and it limits the amount of an employee's earnings that may be garnished in any one week. CCPA also applies to all employers and individuals who receive earnings for personal services (including wages, salaries, commissions, bonuses and income from a pension or retirement program, but ordinarily not including tips).

### Disposable earnings
Federal restrictions on garnishments are based on an employee's "disposable earnings," a term that differs from gross pay or take-home pay. "Earnings" means compensation paid or payable for personal services,

whether wages, salary, commission, bonus, or otherwise, and includes periodic payments through a pension or retirement program. Tips are generally not earnings. Since employers usually do not collect an employee's tips, employers cannot withhold tips from earnings if a garnishment order is received.

### Deductions

"Disposable earnings" means only that portion of earnings left after deductions required by law. These deductions include federal income tax withholding, federal Social Security taxes, state and city tax withholding, state unemployment insurance taxes, and deductions required under state employees' retirement systems.

Other types of deductions, which are not required by law, do not get taken when calculating an employee's disposable earnings. These non-mandatory deductions include: deductions for savings bond purchases; contributions to religious, charitable, or educational organizations; union dues and union initiation fees; health or life insurance premiums, including retirement programs; board, lodging, or other facilities furnished by the employer; purchase of stock in the employer's corporation; assignment of earnings; repayment of loans or advances made by the employer; or payments for merchandise purchased from the employer.

## Fair Credit Reporting Act

The Fair Credit Reporting Act (FCRA) is an American federal law that regulates the collection, dissemination, and use of consumer credit information. Users of the information for credit, insurance, or employment purposes have the following responsibilities under the FCRA:

- They must notify the consumer when an adverse action is taken on the basis of such reports.
- Users must identify the company that provided the report, so that the accuracy and completeness of the report may be verified or contested by the consumer.

Wage garnishments have certain limitations due to the potential for their negative effect on a person's credit.

## Independent Contractor

If the individual is an independent contractor, the employer generally is relieved of responsibility for withholding and paying employment taxes and for providing the benefits and ensuring the protections of other employment laws.

An employer that incorrectly classifies a worker as an independent contractor can be liable for tax, interest, and penalties. Correct classification of a worker as an employee or independent contractor will protect both the employer and the worker.

Different tests are used under the various laws to determine whether a worker is an employee or independent contractor. The most widely used test is the one employed under the common law. That test focuses on the employer's "right to control" and direct the worker. For example, if your answers to the majority of the following questions are the "employer," the worker should probably be classified as an employee.

- Who sets the hours of work?
- Who sets the pay rate?
- Who pays for the equipment… purchase or rental?

The real determination as to a workers status is answering the question, "is the person in business for themselves?" To answer this question, the following factors must be considered:

- the worker's opportunity for profit or loss depending on his or her managerial skill; and/or
- the degree of the worker's right to control the manner in which the work is performed; and/or
- the worker's investment in equipment or materials or employment of helpers to perform the task; and/or
- the level of special skills required to render the service; and/or
- the degree of permanence of the working relationship; and/or
- the extent to which the service rendered is an integral part of the employer's business.

Other pertinent questions to consider are the following. The more times you answer "no," the more likely they are really your employee.

- Does the worker have other customers?
- Does the worker perform only high-level, skilled tasks and few or no routine tasks requiring little training?
- Does the worker advertise in the yellow pages, newspaper, billboards, etc.?
- Does the worker have an office or permanent business site away from your place of business?

# Benefit Laws

## Social Security Act

Social Security (1935), in the United States, currently refers to the Federal Old-Age, Survivors, and Disability Insurance (*OASDI*) program. Social Security in the United States is a social insurance program funded through dedicated payroll taxes called FICA (Federal Insurance Contributions Act). The Act's major benefits include:

- Retirement
- Disability
- Survivorship
- Death

> **TEST TAKING TIP**
> The test is a computerized exam. It's all point and click.

## Workers' Compensation

Workers' compensation (pre-1949) provides employees with financial protection in the event of a disabling workplace injury or illness and protects employers from potentially costly damage suits. With limited exceptions, employees who are hurt on the job cannot sue their employers for negligence.

## Age Discrimination in Employment Act (ADEA)

The Age Discrimination in Employment Act of 1967, (ADEA) prohibits employment discrimination against persons 40 years of age or older in the United States. The law also sets standards for pensions and benefits provided by employers. The ADEA applies to employers of 20 or more employees.

The ADEA includes a broad ban against age discrimination and also specifically prohibits:

- Discrimination in hiring, promotions, wages, or firing/layoffs.

- Statements or specifications in job notices or advertisements of age preference and limitations.
- Denial of benefits to older employees. An employer may reduce benefits based on age only if the cost of providing the reduced benefits to older workers is the same as the cost of providing full benefits to younger workers.
- Since 1978 it has prohibited mandatory retirement in most sectors, with phased elimination of mandatory retirement for tenured workers, such as college professors.

Mandatory retirement based on age is permitted for only one reason:

- Executives over age 65 in high policy-making positions who are entitled to a pension over a minimum yearly amount.

## Employee Retirement Income Security Act (ERISA)

The Employee Retirement Income Security Act (ERISA) of 1974 requires that employers provide employees with specific information concerning benefit plans. ERISA requires reporting and disclosure of pension and profit sharing plans and welfare plans such as those dealing with group life, group accident, hospitalization, medical and surgical, and dental care insurance. When employers modify their plans, changes must be communicated to employees.

ERISA requires pension plans to provide for vesting of employees' pension rights after a specified minimum number of years and to meet certain funding requirements. It also establishes an entity, the Pension Benefit Guaranty Corporation (PBGC), which will provide some minimal benefits coverage in the event that a plan does not, on termination, have sufficient assets to provide all the benefits employees and retirees have earned.

ERISA covers employee pension plans and, to a lesser extent, employee welfare benefit plans. Pension plans are subject to all of ERISA's requirements. Welfare plans are exempt from most of the requirements dealing with participation, vesting, funding, and plan termination, but are subject to some ERISA-mandated reporting and disclosure rules. Certain plans are totally exempt from ERISA: governmental plans; church plans; workers' compensation, disability, and unemployment insurance plans set up to comply with laws; and foreign plans set up for the benefit of nonresident aliens.

## Form 5500

The Form 5500 is a financial report that must be filed with the Internal Revenue Service, by employers who provide a qualified retirement plan, such as a pension, profit sharing or 401(k) plan, and/or a Section 125 Plan to its employees. This form is also needed when an employer provides group medical, dental, life, or disability, and has 100 or more participants in the plan. The Employee Retirement Income Security Act of 1974 (ERISA) and the Internal Revenue Code (IRC) dictate the format and regulations that apply. All forms and schedules must be filed by the last day of the 7th calendar month after the end of the plan year.

## Pregnancy Discrimination Act

In 1978, the U.S. Congress passed the Pregnancy Discrimination Act (PDA), an amendment to the sex discrimination section of the Civil Rights Act of 1964. Pregnancy discrimination occurs when expectant mothers are fired, not hired, or otherwise discriminated against due to their pregnancy or intention to become pregnant. Common forms of pregnancy discrimination include not being hired due to visible pregnancy or likelihood of becoming pregnant, being fired after informing an employer of one's pregnancy, being fired after maternity leave, and receiving a pay dock due to pregnancy. The PDA requires employers to provide what insurance, leave pay, and additional support that would be bestowed upon any employee with medical leave or disability. This only applies to companies with 15 or more employees (including part-time and temporary workers).

## Consolidated Omnibus Budget Reconciliation Act (COBRA)

The Consolidated Omnibus Budget Reconciliation Act of 1985 (COBRA), is a law that mandates an insurance program giving some employees the ability to continue health insurance coverage after leaving employment. The Act allows employees of a qualifying employer and the employee's immediate family members who had been covered by a health care plan to maintain their coverage if a "qualifying event" causes them to lose coverage.

A qualifying employer is generally an employer with 20 or more full time equivalent employees. Among the "qualifying events" listed in the statute are loss of benefits coverage due to (1) the death of the covered employee, (2) termination or a reduction in hours (which can be the result of resignation, discharge, layoff, strike or lockout, medical leave or simply a slowdown in business operations) that causes the worker to lose eligibility for coverage, (3) divorce, which normally terminates the ex-spouse's eligibility for benefits, (4) employee becomes eligible for Medicare, or (5) a dependent child reaching the age at which he or she is no longer covered. COBRA does not apply, on the other hand, if employees lose their benefits coverage because the employer has terminated the plan altogether.

COBRA does not, unlike other federal statutes such as the FMLA, require the employer to pay for the cost of providing continuation coverage; instead it allows employees and their dependents to maintain coverage at their own expense by paying the full cost of the premium the employer previously paid, plus up to a 2% administrative charge

## Older Workers Benefit Protection Act (OWBPA)

The Older Workers Benefit Protection Act of 1990 (OWBPA) amended the ADEA to specifically prohibit employers from denying benefits to older employees. Congress recognized that the cost of providing certain benefits to older workers is greater than the cost of providing those same benefits to younger workers, and that those greater costs would create a disincentive to hire older workers. Therefore, in limited circumstances, an employer may be permitted to reduce benefits based on age, as long as the cost of providing the reduced benefits to older workers is the same as the cost of providing benefits to younger workers.

In some cases, an employer might offer a severance agreement that includes a waiver of a right to file an age discrimination claim. Such a waiver under ADEA is a legal agreement in which the employee gives up the right to file an age discrimination claim against the employer in exchange for something of value like early retirement benefits or a severance package.

Congress was concerned that an existing employee might be duped or coerced into signing this agreement, and passed the OWBPA with certain restrictions that an employer must meet to make this agreement binding. Severance agreements must be in writing and worded so as to clearly inform the employee of their ADEA rights. Employers are required to give individual employees 21 days to consider signing a waiver and release agreement under the OWBPA. And, once signed, the employee has seven additional days to retract the signed agreement.

# Family and Medical Leave Act (FMLA)

The Family and Medical Leave Act of 1993 (February 5, 1993) is a United States labor law allowing an employee to take unpaid leave due to a serious health condition that makes the employee unable to perform his job or to care for a sick family member or to care for a new son or daughter (including by birth, adoption or foster care).

The FMLA requires employers with at least 50 employees to provide up to 12 workweeks of unpaid leave for certain events during a 12-month period.

These are the events covered:

- the birth, adoption, or placement in foster care of a child; or
- a "serious health condition" involving the employee (when unable to perform one or more essential job functions) or an immediate family member (spouse, child, or parent).

Employees who have worked for an employer for 12 months are entitled to request the leave. Employees may take the leave in one block of up to 12 weeks or in separate blocks of time.

The leave provisions apply to employees or members of their family who have a "serious health condition." The definition of a "family member" is sometimes confusing. Let us attempt to explain the various relationships in today's modern world. Step-relationships are covered while in-laws are not. Thus, the FMLA guidelines define a parent as a biological, foster, adoptive or step parent, or any person who served in loco parentis (served as a parent) to an employee. It does not include a parent-in-law. The same holds true for children (biological, foster, adoptive, etc.). The definition of a spouse is defined by the local state of residence.

In addition, service members are given additional protection under FMLA that provides:
1.  Up to 12 weeks of leave for certain qualifying issues arising out of a covered military member's active duty status, or notification of an impending call to active duty status, in support of a military operation. And/or,
2.  Up to 26 weeks of leave in a single 12-month period for the next of kin of a covered service member recovering from a serious injury or illness incurred in the line of duty on active duty.

# Health Insurance Portability and Accountability Act (HIPAA)

The Health Insurance Portability and Accountability Act (HIPAA) of 1996, was passed to impose portability requirements on group health insurance plans. HIPAA limited restrictions that a group health plan could place on benefits for preexisting conditions. However, the subsequent passing of the Patient Protection and Affordable Care Act guidelines superseded these rules and eliminated any restrictions or conditions for preexisting conditions. In effect, employers may no longer impose any limitations on new hires who have a preexisting medical condition.

However, HIPAA is still relevant to the S/PHR candidate in relation to its privacy provisions. The Privacy Rule took effect in 2003. It establishes regulations for the use and disclosure of Protected Health Information (PHI). PHI is any information about health status, provision of health care, or payment for health care that can be linked to an individual. This is interpreted rather broadly and includes any part of a patient's medical record or payment history. These rules established rather stiff penalties for organizations that don't take reasonable precautions to protect the confidentiality of a person's PHI. The U.S. Department of Health and Human Services (HHS) and the Office of Civil Rights (OCR) are the enforcers of these rules.

## Sarbanes-Oxley Act

Section 306(b) of the Sarbanes- Oxley Act (2002) requires that rank-and-file participants in "individual account plans" be notified in advance when they will be subject to a "blackout period." Whether voluntarily (because they're optimistic about the company's prospects) or involuntarily (because they're subjected to pressure to prove their loyalty by investing their pension accounts heavily in employer stock), many employees put a high percentage of their individual pension accounts in employer stock. The notice provisions are intended to cope with the situation in which rank-and-file workers lose retirement security because they are "frozen" and not allowed to sell shares of their employer company's stock during a "blackout period." The notice must, in plain English, explain the effects of the blackout on participants' rights.  The general rule is that notice has to be given at least 30 days, but not more than 60 days before the start of the blackout period. Exceptions are allowed if for some reason, it's impossible to satisfy this requirement.

## Patient Protection & Affordable Care Act

The Patient Protection and Affordable Care Act (ACA) was passed into law in 2010. Its purpose is to ensure that all Americans have access to quality, affordable health care. The logic is that shared responsibility for health care, by requiring all Americans to obtain a minimum standard of health care coverage, will reduce everyone's overall costs. There is much controversy over whether this will actually occur but despite the challenges to this law, the PHR and/or SPHR candidate must be prepared to field any questions that may appear on the exam.

As of the time of the writing of this study manual, the following points have been passed into law and have been enacted since 2010 and may appear as exam questions. However, the main body of the ACA is not due to be implemented until 2014/2015 and should not appear on the exam until 2016/2017. Therefore, this section will focus only on those items that the current PHR/SPHR candidate should be familiar with and will not provide a full explanation of the ACA. The aspects of ACA that the PHR/SPHR candidate should be familiar with are:

ACA:
1. Eliminates lifetime annual limits on benefits.
2. Prohibits rescissions (cancellations due to health problems) of health insurance policies.
3. Provides assistance to those who are uninsured due to pre-existing conditions.
4. Requires coverage of preventive services and immunizations.
5. Extends dependant coverage up to age 26.
6. Develops uniform coverage documents so consumers can make apples-to-apples comparisons when shopping for health insurance.
7. Caps insurance company non-medical, administrative expenditures.
8. Ensure consumers have access to an effective appeals process and provides consumers a place to turn for assistance navigating the appeals process and accessing their coverage.
9. Creates a temporary re-insurance program to support coverage for early retirees.
10. Establishes an internet portal to assist Americans in identifying coverage options.
11. Facilitates administrative simplification to lower health system costs.

# Total Compensation: Compensation Strategies

Compensation is the single most important element in the employment relationship. Although opportunity for advancement, good working conditions, appropriate supervision, and other non-financial considerations are crucial to productive relations, all employee groups — from top management to hourly workers — consistently rank compensation as a primary factor in deciding whether to accept or continue employment.

In virtually every organization, compensation is the largest component of total labor costs and far exceeds expenses incurred for recruitment, training, administration, or other HR functions. In a labor-intensive setting, compensation costs may account for more than 60% of gross income. However, compensation is one of the few major expense areas that is internally controlled: While a company has limited control over the costs of materials, equipment, transportation, utilities, and outside professional services, an employer can tie compensation levels directly to productivity and profitability. The key is return on investment — maximum performance for every payroll dollar.

## Matching Compensation to Strategic Goals

Compensation is a tool for sharpening and reshaping the behaviors required to achieve business goals. Any discussion of business objectives should take pay policies into account since most business decisions affect compensation.

Understanding a company's business objectives is the most important knowledge a compensation planner can possess. A compensation program that complies fully with all legal requirements and holds a competitive position in the external market will still fail if it does not support corporate goals. Many well-designed pay programs are inappropriate for some organizations.

**TEST TAKING TIP**
Make sure you click on your correct choice before moving on to the next question on the exam.

Compensation programs can both drive and support business objectives. Compensation plans can:

- communicate business objectives,
- provide incentives for employees to maintain or change their behaviors to support those objectives,
- reinforce the relationship between individual or group goals and broader unit or corporate objectives, and
- reward discretionary effort.

## Compensation and HR Goals

The three primary goals of a compensation program are effective recruitment, retention, and motivation.

### Recruitment

Appropriate starting rates and an attractive pay program can position the company to meet its recruitment needs on a consistent basis. If a company lags in its starting rates, it will face a shortage of suitable candidates as potential employees gravitate toward competitor companies or look for jobs in other industries. Low starting rates also can saddle a company with low-potential employees who drag down productivity, competitiveness, and growth. On the other hand, paying the highest rates can generate a different set of problems. Starting salaries that equal or exceed pay rates for experienced workers can undercut internal equity and destroy morale.

### Retention

A compensation program can be used to adjust turnover rates for various positions to achieve an optimal workforce at the lowest cost. Money can provide the leverage to hold valued employees who might find work at other companies. Turnover carries high costs: recruiting and hiring a new employee, orientation and training, and downtime in the position. Organization growth potential diminishes every time an experienced and promotable employee resigns. Turnover also can threaten a company's competitive position if a seasoned and knowledgeable employee moves to a direct competitor. For some positions, however, relatively high rates of turnover are acceptable and keep compensation costs at starting salary levels.

### Motivation

A compensation program based solely on market rates and length of service fails to motivate. A program based on skills and performance turns every paycheck into a concrete statement of a company's business objectives. Pay for performance is the basic premise of compensation today, but turning the idea into a reality requires sound job evaluation, accurate performance measurements, thorough training of and feedback between supervisors and employees, and ongoing support from top management.

Most experts recommend a difference of at least 10 to 15 percent in the pay between high and low performers. Incentive pay plans should reach as far down in an organization as possible. Virtually every employee group can be brought into a performance pay system of one type or another. Use multiple pay plans when needed.

## Traditional Compensation Plans

Traditional compensation programs, designed for mature companies with stable markets and fixed product lines, emphasize cost control, standardization, and high levels of internal equity. They usually have centralized decision-making and administration.

Traditional compensation plans largely consist of base pay — grounded in extensive job evaluation — plus a fixed package of benefits. An employee's compensation level depends primarily on length of service and fulfillment of standard requirements for a position. To the extent that traditional compensation plans include incentive or performance pay, the objectives are usually limited to reducing production costs.

## Alternative Compensation Systems

Alternative reward systems, commonly designed for companies with changing markets, product lines, or growth rates, relate compensation costs to revenues. Compared with traditional compensation systems, alternative systems tend to be less standardized and less centralized. They rely less on job evaluation and more on performance appraisal. They de-emphasize base pay and rely more on incentives for unit, group, or individual performance as defined by growth, market share, or productivity. They often include flexible benefit programs.

Successful alternative reward systems, and the performance pay plans they adopt, are self-financing. They are based on:

- sound projections about the financial returns that will result from improved performance,
- accurate methods of measuring the improvements, and

- effective methods of tying improvements to payouts.

Alternative reward systems are appropriate only if performance objectives are clear and performance criteria are fully identified. Companies that have not developed clear performance objectives and criteria should steer away from alternative pay plans and stick with traditional compensation systems.

## Reward Strategies

A primary objective of a compensation program is to motivate the employee behaviors needed to achieve business goals. Motivation begins with a pay program that employees perceive as fair and equitable. A good compensation program clearly links efforts to outcomes and behaviors to rewards. Some reward theories are discussed below.

### Equity Theory (Adams)

Equity theory is based on an individual subjective determination about his or her perception of pay comparisons. There are three types of equity:

- **Internal** - An employee compares his or her pay to others within the organization.
- **External** - An employee compares his or her pay to a similar job outside the organization.
- **Individual** - An employee compares his or her pay to an individual doing the same job within the same organization.

### Expectancy Theory (Vroom)

Expectancy theory holds that employees' expectations determine effort and performance. Expectancy theory indicates that compensation policies and practices can influence the extent to which employees believe that performance will be rewarded. A performance appraisal system ensures that employees receive the feedback they need to perform well; a well-designed pay system ensures that their performance is rewarded appropriately. Over time, effective performance appraisals and rewards can influence employees' expectations and behaviors.

### Maslow's Needs Hierarchy

Maslow identified five levels of needs, which are best seen as a hierarchy with the most basic need emerging first and the most sophisticated need last. People move up the hierarchy one level at a time. Gratified needs lose their strength and the next level of needs is activated. As basic or lower-level needs are satisfied, higher-level needs become operative. A satisfied need is not a motivator. The most powerful employee need is the one that has not been satisfied. Maslow's hierarchy of needs is often depicted as a pyramid consisting of five levels: the four lower levels are grouped together as deficiency needs associated with physiological needs, while the top level is termed growth needs associated with psychological needs. Level 1 = physiological needs, 2 = safety, 3 = social belonging, 4 = self esteem, and 5 = self actualization.

### Reward Theory or Reinforcement Theory

Reward theory is based on the idea that employees will repeat behaviors that are rewarded and will avoid behaviors that are not rewarded. According to reward theory, paying for time worked fails to motivate high performance because it automatically rewards average or standard levels of performance. Reward theory supports the idea that pay that is contingent on high performance can directly influence behavior.

### Goal-setting Theory (Management by Objectives)

According to goal-setting theory, only those rewards that employees value can motivate behaviors. The key is to set mutual goals for an organization and its employees — goals that will reward both the company and its workers. Goal- setting theory holds that pay can motivate employees if:

- employees participate in setting the goals for which they will be rewarded and accept these goals as their own,
- the goals are specific and set at a sufficiently challenging level, and
- specific monetary rewards are designated for each goal achieved.

### *Intrinsic v. extrinsic rewards*

Total compensation consists of intrinsic and extrinsic rewards. Intrinsic rewards are the psychological and intellectual rewards inherent in the job itself, such as the opportunity to perform meaningful work or gain a sense of accomplishment. They depend on the nature of the work and the values of the individual who performs the work. Extrinsic rewards derive from sources external to the job itself. They include non-financial rewards, such as prestige and positive feedback, and financial rewards, such as wages and benefits. Herzberg's Hygiene theory classifies motivation as either "hygiene" factors (extrinsic), those basic entitlements that employees expect (pay, benefits, working conditions, etc.), VS. "motivators" (intrinsic), those factors that truly change people's behavior (praise, recognition, challenging work, etc.).

> **TEST TAKING TIP**
> Read, then re-read the question before answering.

# Designing the Compensation System

A pay structure guides an employer's decisions about what jobs receive what rates of pay. Most employers use a pay structure consisting of "pay grades" and "pay ranges." Under such pay structures, jobs of similar value are grouped within the same grade. Employees within a particular grade are paid a rate between the minimum and maximum rate, or pay range, specified for their grade.

Pay structures should be designed to support the company's overall business strategies and to provide management with an internal control mechanism for achieving compensation objectives. One of the fundamental questions an employer must address in designing a pay structure is how the company wants its pay rates to compare to pay rates in the marketplace.

Constructing a pay structure involves four basic steps:

1. determining the relative worth of benchmark jobs within the company and collecting data on market rates for those jobs;
2. analyzing how actual pay rates compare to market rates;
3. deciding where target pay rates should be relative to the market rates; and
4. establishing appropriate pay grades and pay ranges.

A pay structure consists of a series of "pay grades" and "pay ranges." Jobs with similar worth are grouped within the same grade. Employees are paid a rate within the minimum and maximum rate, i.e., the pay range, specified for their grade.

The process of creating a pay structure usually begins after the employer has established the relative worth of jobs using job evaluation techniques. A first step in establishing a pay structure is to take the job-worth hierarchy established through job evaluation and compare it to market surveys of pay rates for similar jobs. An employer then decides how the company's actual pay rates should be positioned relative to the market rates. Next, the employer establishes appropriate pay grades and pay ranges.

# Internal Equity Issues

## Job analysis (aka Task Analysis)
The reduction of a job into duties, tasks, and elements for the purpose of establishing a job description, job specifications (required Knowledge, Skills, and Abilities), or a personnel procedure (recruitment, selection, performance appraisal, training, compensation). The process includes the detailed collection of information about the job that normally includes: content, requirements, and context.

The DOL describes the job analysis as (1) what the worker does, (2) how he or she does it, (3) why he or she does it, and (4) the skill involved in doing it.

## Job description
A job description describes the job as it is being performed. In a sense, a job description is a snapshot of the job as of the time it was analyzed. Ideally they are written so that any reader, whether familiar or not with the job, can "see" what the worker does, how, and why.

## Job specification
An analysis of the kind of person it takes to do the job. It is a comprehensive list of the personal qualifications necessary to do the job. Typically this would include:

- degree of education
- desirable amount of previous experience in similar work
- specific skills required
- health considerations
- personality

## Wage compression
Compression refers to situations where pay differences between employees in different jobs are so small that internal pay inequities occur. Compression can occur in situations between supervisors who are exempt from overtime pay and subordinates with large amounts of overtime pay, between newly hired employees and current experienced employees, and among employees in successive job grades.

> **TEST TAKING TIP**
> It takes approximately two years for a question to work its way past all the layers of review before it shows up on the exam. Therefore, you don't have to worry about studying any developments in our field less than two years old.

Compression inequities can be avoided by: establishing meaningful and explainable differences in grade assignments between jobs, moving employees from the minimum to the midpoint of their pay grade in an appropriate time frame, or paying a temporary compression bonus (typically in place of overtime pay).

## Permissible wage differentials
The Civil Rights Act permits wage differentials between sexes if authorized by the EPA. The EPA allows wage differentials if they are based on:

- a seniority system
- a merit system
- a system that measures earnings by quantity or quality of production; or
- any other factor other than sex.

This provision protects employers from charges that wage scales or other terms of employment discriminate against groups that have less skill and experience – often because of past discrimination.

Employers may pay different wages to and provide different terms and conditions of employment for employees who work at different locations. Even if most employees at one plant are of once race, color, religion, sex, or national origin while employees at a second plant belong to another category, wage differentials among locations are allowed, provided the differentials are justified on reasonable business grounds, such as differences in prevailing area wage rates. The wage differentials cannot, however, be a pretext for prohibited discrimination.

## External Equity Issues

External equity is the value differential between the organization's reward system relative to employees in other firms. Usually, the "value differential" is defined by employee perception of local market pay practices.

### Benchmark jobs

Not all jobs are appropriate to use for gathering survey data. Jobs that normally are used in surveys are called benchmark jobs. A "benchmark job" is a job with duties that can be clearly identified, defined, and compared to other jobs in the marketplace. Typically, benchmark jobs are held by many employees, and, over time, have relatively stable work content. Using benchmark jobs assures the highest degree of job comparability between a company's jobs and those that appear in surveys.

> **TEST TAKING TIP**
> There are 25 questions that aren't scored on the exam. You won't know which ones they are. They aren't identified. But, we think they are the really hard ones on which you will want to pull out your hair.

When selecting benchmark jobs to gather market data, a company should include a representative job from as many of the company's job families or function groups as possible. When selected properly, a group of benchmark jobs will accurately reflect the salary practices of a company's competitors.

### Lead vs. lag positioning

A pay structure should support a company's overall business strategies as well as provide its management with a mechanism to achieve compensation objectives. One of the first questions a company must address in designing a pay structure is: How does the company want its pay to compare to rates of pay in the marketplace?

#### Lead policy

In a lead policy, a company projects where the market will be at the end of the structure plan year and matches those rates at the start of the plan year. In so doing, a company leads its competition throughout the plan year.

#### Lag policy

In a lag policy, a company establishes a structure that matches the market rates at the beginning of the plan year. Thus, the structure will be competitive with the market at the start of the year, and as the competition moves ahead throughout the year, the structure will lag behind the market.

*Lead/lag policy*

In a lead/lag policy, a company projects where the market rates will be at the middle of the plan year and matches those rates at the start of the plan year. Thus, the structure will lead the competition for the first part of the year and lag behind the market for the second part of the year.

If it is important for a company to have pay rates that are always at least equal to the marketplace, for example in a very competitive market, then a lead policy is appropriate. For financial or other reasons, a company may choose a lag policy and trail the marketplace rates. A compromise position many companies take is the lead/lag policy, which keeps a structure ahead of the market for six months and never trails the market by more than six months.

# Targeting Pay Rates to the Market

## Compa-Ratio and Measures of Central Tendency

Analyzing pay in relation to both internal and external equity is vital in determining the competitiveness of the organization. Statistical metrics are frequently employed to judge the health of the pay system. Measures of central tendency are used to find the typical or average of a list of numbers.

There are three common ways to find a measure of central tendency. They are the mean, the median, and the mode.

The **mean** is the most familiar to many people. It is often called the average, but its technical name is the mean. It is found by adding all scores and dividing the sum by the number of cases.

*Example: Mean = 38, 38, 40, 42, 47 = (205/5) = 41*

The **median** is the middle-most score when all scores have been arranged in order of size. The median is the point that bisects the distribution, half the cases falling above it and half below it.

*Example: Median = 38, 38, 40, 42, 47 = 40*

The **mode** is the most frequent score.

*Example: Mode = 38, 38, 40, 42, 47 = 38*

The **range** is the difference between the least and greatest values in a set of numbers.

*Example: Range = 38, 38, 40, 42, 47 = (38-47) = 9*

A **compa-ratio** provides an employer with a benchmark to determine how close actual pay rates compare to the company defined midpoint of a pay range. A compa-ratio is the average of employee actual pay divided by the range midpoint.

An employee's Compa-Ratio, or Compensation Ratio, represents how well they are paid compared against an industry standard. Compa-Ratios are position specific. Each position has a salary range that includes a minimum, a midpoint, and a maximum. These three values normally represent industry averages for the position. The Compa-Ratio is calculated by dividing the base salary by the midpoint industry average.

A Compa-Ratio of 1.00 or 100% means the employee is paid exactly what the industry average pays and are at the midpoint for the salary range, while a ratio of 0.75 means they are paid 25% below the industry average. Employees might think they want a high ratio, meaning they are paid more than the market average, but this is the exact opposite of what they should want. Why? Because this ratio, to a large extent, determines whether they are allowed to get any raise at all and if so, how much.

- 80-87% - new, inexperienced, or unsatisfactorily performing incumbents.
- 88-95% - those gaining experience but not yet fully competent in the job.
- 96-103% - fully competent performers performing the job as defined.
- 104-111% - those consistently performing the job at a lever higher than what the job definition requires.
- 112-120% - those universally recognized as outstanding performers, both inside and outside the organization.

If an incumbent's performance appraisal suggests a higher compa-ratio should be applicable, a series of above average salary increases can be used to gradually raise the individual's compa-ratio.

$$\text{Compa-Ratio} = \frac{\text{Actual Salary}}{\text{Mid-Point of Pay Range}}$$

| Title | Actual Salary | Grade Mid | Compa-Ratio |
|---|---|---|---|
| Managing Director | $73,400 | $75,000 | .98 |
| Engineering Manager | $99,000 | $90,000 | 1.1 |
| Marketing Manager | $103,100 | $90,000 | 1.15 |
| Draftsman Manager | $62,550 | $69,500 | .9 |
| Senior Estimator | $44,200 | $52,000 | .85 |
| Estimator | $35,000 | $35,000 | 1.0 |

## Geographic Diversity

A company may have operations in widely separated geographic locations. In order to accommodate different marketplace rates in the separate locations, it may be easier to have separate structures for each location. If there are many locations, some can be grouped together to reduce the number of structures.

# Establishing Pay Grades and Ranges

## Multiple Pay Structures

Another question to answer in establishing pay structures is: How many structures should a company have? For ease of administration, if one structure will encompass all the jobs in a company, then one structure is preferable. It is possible and sometimes preferable to have more than one structure. There are several reasons for establishing multiple structures:

## Range of Pay Rates

The range of pay rates in a company may be so great that one structure may not comfortably accommodate both the highest and lowest rate. For example, in a very large company, the Chief Executive Officer's pay rate may be many times greater than the lowest pay rate, and it may be difficult to design one structure that will efficiently meet the requirements of both ends of the scale. In that case, separate structures should be established. A common example of multiple structures is one structure for nonexempt jobs and another for exempt jobs. Basic design issues can be addressed easily in this type of split.

## Setting Grades

Once a pay line has been established, the next step is to define a series of pay grades. Pay grades group together jobs of similar internal value that will be considered similar for pay purposes. The pay grades provide a convenient way to relate internal and external values. The following items must be considered when developing pay grades:

- the internal relationship of jobs and job groups,
- the number of structures that will be used,
- the number of jobs to be included,
- the system of determining internal values, and
- the external values and differentiations.

**TEST TAKING TIP**
You can miss about 45 questions on the test and still pass (not counting the 25 questions that aren't scored).

## Grouping Jobs

The key to establishing job grades is in the grouping of jobs. This is done by considering both the internal relationships of each job and the type of job evaluation system used. For example, if the internal relationships are established by ranking jobs, then the pay grade groupings are established by identifying natural breaks between jobs. Natural breaks are defined by distinctions such as:

- Reporting relationships — e.g., manager/supervisor, or supervisor/subordinate; and
- Job families — e.g., senior accountant/accountant/junior accountant, or senior clerk/clerk.

# Job Evaluations

Job evaluation is the process of systematically determining a relative value of jobs in an organization in order to set grades and group jobs. In all cases the idea is to evaluate the job, not the person doing it.

Most job evaluation systems divide job factors into the following four broad categories:

## Skill

Skill encompasses job factors such as: education; training; time required to learn; knowledge of equipment, machinery/tools, materials, and processes; initiative and creativity; resourcefulness; manual dexterity; interpersonal skills; and analytical ability.

## Effort

Effort covers both physical and mental exertion and includes job factors such as: mental effort, concentration, and fatigue; eye fatigue and visual application; physical effort, demand, and fatigue; monotony; and deadline and high work volume pressure.

## Responsibility

This category includes job factors relating to responsibility for: other workers or their work product; property, equipment, assets, cash, records, or material; decision making and judgment; independent action; quality, accuracy, and spoilage; coordination of work; and safety.

## Working conditions

Working conditions include job factors such as: temperature; noise; isolation; and health or safety hazards.

Employers may select as many as five to seven factors in each category to adequately describe a job's worth. Appropriate factor selection is a key step in the design phase of a valid job evaluation plan.

To ensure the selection of meaningful job factors employers should:

- focus on the factors that contribute to differences in job worth and select only those factors that truly indicate differences in rates of pay;

- select factors that are independent and unique, so as to avoid redundancy;

- keep factors simple and concrete, so they may be clearly defined; and

- ensure that each factor selected can be realistically and reliably measured.

## Ranking Method

Job ranking involves ordering jobs from highest to lowest based on some definition of value or contribution to the organization. This is the simplest method, least expensive and easiest to understand. A disadvantage to this method is that it does not measure differences between jobs.

## Classification/Grading Method

This method is used by the federal government. Each job is categorized into groups called classes if they contain similar jobs, or grades if they contain jobs that are similar in difficulty but are otherwise different. The Classification method is easy to administer and moderately inexpensive. A disadvantage to this method is that it is difficult to write the class or grade descriptions and considerable judgment is required in applying them.

## Factor Comparison Method

The traditional factor comparison plan that is presented in many salary administration textbooks is seldom used by employers. Employers more often use a modern adaptation of factor comparison that is conducted using a computer and specialized statistical software. This method compares jobs on several factors to obtain a numerical value for each job and to arrive at a job structure. Thus it may be classified as a quantitative method.

Contemporary factor comparison plans consider job worth by analyzing the jobs on a factor by factor basis. Factor comparison involves judging which jobs contain more of certain compensable factors. Jobs are compared with each other (as in the ranking method), but on one factor at a time. The judgments permit construction of a comparison scale of key jobs against which other jobs may be compared.

The compensable factors used are usually:

- mental requirements
- physical requirements
- skill requirements
- responsibility
- working conditions

The evaluation of new or revised jobs also is accomplished through slotting.

**TEST TAKING TIP**
Watch the Distinctive HR videos online at phrexamprep.com to help master the common but difficult topics that may be on your exam. Each video is followed by sample questions to help you prepare.

## Point Method

The point-factor method, or point plan, involves rating each job on several compensable factors and adding the scores on each factor to obtain a point total for a job. A carefully worded rating scale is constructed for each compensable factor. This rating scale includes a definition of the factor, several divisions called degrees (also carefully defined), and a point score for each degree.

Probably the major advantage of the point method is the stability of the rating scales. Once the scales are developed, they may be used for a considerable period. Only major changes in the organization demand a change in scales.

The point-factor system is the most commonly used job content evaluation system. The system assesses the job factors that may be required of the employee holding the job (skill, effort, and responsibility) and reviews the working conditions to which the person is exposed.

The point factor job evaluation process begins by selecting and defining a group of compensable job factors. Job evaluators then apply the following methodology:

- Determine the appropriate number of points for the plan. Although an arbitrary number can be chosen, the decision should take into consideration the number of factors used. Total plan points commonly range between 400 to 1,000 points.
- Assign a range of points, e.g., 10 to 80 points, to each factor based on the factor's relative value to other factors and to total points.
- Divide each factor into degrees to represent varying levels of the characteristic under review. The number of degrees depends on how many discrete differences can be identified logically and practically for the factor. Too few degrees may make it difficult to differentiate between key components of job value, whereas too many degrees become administratively burdensome.
- Define each degree and provide work examples in that definition whenever possible.

- Assign point values to each degree. Use the range of points allotted to the factor as a whole. Typically the lowest point value should be at least 10 percent of the total points assigned to the factor.

- Analyze the specific duties performed by each job by examining the first factor and determining the extent it is present in the job. Compare the results of this analysis to the degree definitions. Select the degree definition that most closely matches your evaluation and assign the job the appropriate number of points for the factor. Repeat this process for each factor.

- Sum up the points for the job and array the total points assigned to each job to establish the relative order of job worth.

- Compare the hierarchy against market values, using between 20 to 25 percent of your benchmark jobs as a test for external equity.

- Make adjustments and develop a final structure.

### Pros and cons

Point factor plans permit full focus on internal job worth by removing market considerations from the initial evaluation process. However, the plans do contain intrinsic deficiencies:

- The plans are costly and time consuming to develop, obtain, and install.

- The plans do not eliminate evaluator bias.

- Many proprietary or generic plans are incompatible with the values of contemporary business. Point factor plans initially were designed to fit multilayered, bureaucratic organizations. Thus, the plans may be of little use to organizations that have relatively flat job hierarchies.

## Guide Chart-Profile Method (Hay Method)

The Guide Chart-Profile Method is the most popular point factor plan. It is the best-known variation of factor comparison. It is described by the Hay Group (a team of management consultants) as a form of factor comparison for the following reasons:

- it uses universal factors

- bases job values on 15 percent intervals

- makes job-to-job comparisons

Once the factors have been identified and described, they are weighted since not all factors are of equal importance to organizations. Next, a factor scale is constructed containing statements of the degree to which the factor is present in a given job. The degree ratings are then recorded and weighted accordingly. This allows for an accumulation of points for each job. Higher ratings equate into a greater number of job evaluation points.

The universal factors in the Hay plan are
- Know-how (skill)
    - procedures and techniques
    - breadth of management skills
    - person-to-person skills
- Problem solving
    - thinking environment
    - thinking challenge

- Accountability
  - freedom to act
  - impact on results
  - magnitude
- Working conditions
  - Hazards
  - Environment
  - Physical demands

## Point Spreads

If a formal job evaluation method, such as a point-factor plan, is used, the internal point values can be used in determining pay grades. The pay grades may be identified by using absolute point spreads or percent-based point spreads. An absolute point spread uses equal or increasing point values to establish pay grades. For example, all grades may be 50 points wide, or the lower grades may be 50 points wide, the middle grades 75 points wide, and the upper grades 100 points wide.

If a percent-based point spread is used, equal or increasing percents are applied to the internal point values. For example, the lower grades may have a 20 percent point spread, the middle grades 25 percent, and the upper grades 30 percent.

## Pay Line as a Continuum

Another method of identifying pay grades is to use the pay line as a continuum. In this method, each internal value point has its own pay value. There is no magical number of grades to use in a structure. The number used will depend on the company's needs and the best fit of the jobs in the structure.

## Setting Ranges

There are three major considerations in establishing pay ranges:

- midpoint progressions,
- range spread, and
- range overlap.

For each of these considerations, there is no right or wrong position, no standard formula. Decisions are based on the structure of the company, the nature of its workforce, the marketplace in which it operates, and its business strategy.

## Midpoint Progressions

Once the number of grades has been selected, the next step is to determine the midpoint progressions between grades. Midpoint progressions represent the percent increase from the midpoint of one grade to the midpoint of the next higher grade. The progression can be a constant percent throughout the structure, or it can increase from grade to grade (that is, the progression increases as the salary grade level increases).

A small difference between midpoints will create a large number of pay grades. Conversely, a large difference between midpoints will create a small number of pay grades. The idea is to create enough pay grades so that there is a sufficient, but not too great, difference between grades. The guidelines to use in determining midpoint differentials include supervisor/subordinate relationships, promotional progressions, and relative pay levels.

As a rule, the midpoint differentials will be smaller for the lower pay grades and will increase for the higher pay grades. This is in part because employees tend to move more quickly through the lower grades than the higher grades, and partly because the dollar values are less in the lower grades. Therefore, more grades are required in the lower end of the pay structure to differentiate between jobs. A typical midpoint progression for the lower grades is 8 percent to 12 percent, with the higher grades using a 14 percent to 18 percent progression.

## Range Spread

The next step is to determine the range spread of the pay grade, which, in combination with the midpoint, is used in deriving the minimums and maximums for the grades. The standard method of expressing the spread of a salary grade is to measure the percent by which the maximum exceeds the minimum.

---

For example, the formulas used to determine the minimums and maximums for a pay grade with a $20,000 midpoint and a 50 percent range spread are:

$$\text{Minimum} = \text{Midpoint} / [1 + (\%\text{Spread} / 2)] \text{ Or}$$
$$= 20,000 / [1 + (.50 / 2)]$$
$$= 20,000 / 1.25$$
$$= 16,000$$

$$\text{Maximum} = \text{Minimum} \times (1 + \%\text{Spread})$$
$$= 16,000 \times (1 + .50)$$
$$= 16,000 \times 1.50$$
$$= 24,000$$

---

As with midpoint progressions, range spread can be a constant percent throughout the structure, or it can increase as the grades increase. Generally, narrow ranges, those with a smaller percent spread, are used for the lower pay grades, and the spread is increased as the pay grade levels increase. For example, jobs in production or maintenance might be in pay grades with a 20 percent to 30 percent spread, clerical jobs in pay grades with a 30 percent to 40 percent spread, exempt professional jobs in pay grades with a 40 percent to 50 percent spread, and managerial jobs in pay grades with a 50 percent to 70 percent spread.

The job content of the jobs in the pay grade affect range spread. There are two key factors:

1. The minimum should represent the minimum salary to be paid for a new employee with minimum qualifications for a job, and the midpoint should represent the company's target rate for a fully qualified employee who is performing satisfactorily. Therefore, in lower level positions where a job can be learned quickly, it is important to keep the midpoint relatively close to the minimum.

2. The greater the opportunity for performance variations in a job, the greater the need to reward that performance. In jobs that allow for a wide range of performance levels, it is necessary to have a wide dollar range to reward performance.

## Range Overlap

Along with range spread, range overlap must be determined. Range overlap represents the amount of overlap between adjacent salary grades. No standard overlap exists, although a rule of thumb is approximately a three-grade overlap before one salary grade's maximum value equals another salary grade's minimum value. For example, if the maximum of pay grade 1 is $20,000, then the minimum of pay grade 5 would be approximately $20,000.

## Broadbanding

Broadbanding involves clustering many different job functions into one broad band as an alternative to more traditional salary grade structures. As a result, an employer may pare away as many as two-thirds of its salary grades into these broader bands. Many companies have considered using a broadbanded structure, although relatively few have implemented it. Those that have, however, are generally satisfied with the results.

**TEST TAKING TIP**
You can skip around on the test. You don't have to start at number one and go to 175. If you get bored, skip around. But, answer them all.

## Unions

It is common for companies to establish a separate structure for union-negotiated pay rates than for the non-union segments of the organization.

## Paying Out of Range

When a pay structure is established, situations inevitably occur where some employees' salaries do not fit into the assigned pay grade. In these situations, the salaries may be either above the maximum or below the minimum. There is no best way to handle these issues. The company must establish a policy regarding paying out of the range, fitting this into the overall pay strategy. The following are two out-of-range situations:

## Red Circle Rates

Red circle rates refer to pay rates that are above the maximum of the pay range. Depending on the company's policy, a pay rate over maximum may be brought into line either immediately or over a period of time. Some options for handling these situations are:

- to reduce the employee's pay to the salary range maximum immediately, in order to slow down the amount and frequency of the employee's increases until pay is within the range; or
- to freeze the employee's pay until the pay range surpasses the salary.

## Green Circle Rates

Green circle rates refer to pay rates that are below the minimum of the salary range. Depending on the company's policy, the pay rate differential may be reduced or eliminated immediately or over a period of time. Some options for handling these situations are:

- to increase the employee's pay immediately to the salary range minimum; or
- to give the employee increases on a more frequent basis until pay equals the range minimum.

# Wages

A wage is a compensation which workers receive in exchange for their labor. In the United States, wages for most workers are set by market forces, or else by collective bargaining, where a labor union negotiates on the workers' behalf. The Fair Labor Standards Act requires a minimum wage at the federal level although states and cities can and sometimes do set their own higher minimum. For certain federal or state government contracts, employers must pay the so-called prevailing wage as determined according to the Davis-Bacon Act or its state equivalent. Activists have also undertaken to promote the idea of a living wage rate which would be higher than current minimum wage laws require.

Wages include all payments made to or on behalf of an employee as remuneration for employment. However, certain payments excluded in computing an employee's regular rate of pay must be taken into consideration in comparing wages of men and women under the EPA. These payments include vacation and holiday pay and premium payments for work on Saturdays, Sundays, holidays, regular days of rest, or other days or hours in excess of or outside regular days or hours of work.

Other payments considered wages for equal pay purposes are: commissions, bonuses, or other payments measured by production, efficiency, attendance, or other job-related factors or agreed to be paid under the employment contract; standby and on-call pay; and extra payments for hazardous, disagreeable, or inconvenient working conditions. But the wages for equal pay comparisons do not include bona fide gifts or discretionary bonuses. Wages also include the reasonable cost to an employer of furnishing board, lodging, and other facilities if employees customarily receive these forms of noncash compensation.

Wage rates include all rates, whether figured on time, piece, job, incentive, or other basis. The term covers both straight-time and overtime rates and all rates at which a draw, advance, or guarantee is paid against a commission settlement.

Generally, there are two types of pay rate structures: fixed rates and step rates. With a fixed rate structure, a company uses one rate of pay for each job. When pay rates change, every employee in that job receives the same pay increase. Fixed rates typically are used for routine jobs where performance does not vary greatly.

For positions in which performance may vary, employers usually use a step rate system where salary ranges are divided into various steps. These steps indicate length of service, performance, or both. Step programs with an automatic progression reward length of service with pay increases. Step rate systems with performance factors reward high level performance. A combination step rate pay system rewards performance with varied increases for employees at periodic intervals.

## Fixed Rates

In a fixed rate pay structure, each job has a single rate of pay, although some employers combine a hiring or starting rate with the fixed rate. In this combined pay structure, a company uses one rate for new employees and another rate for all other employees in that job. The rates are reviewed and increased periodically to keep up with market changes. When the rates change, everyone in the job receives the same increase at the same time. Fixed rates normally are used for routine jobs that do not allow for varying performance levels by employees, such as production jobs where the assembly line sets work pace.

## Step Rates

A step rate pay structure uses salary ranges divided into several steps or pay rates. The various steps are calculated at a constant dollar difference, such as $500, or at a percentage difference, such as 4 percent to 7 percent. The range maximum normally is set at or above the competitive market rate for the job. Once the salary range has been established, an individual's increases are based on length of service only, or on a combination of length of service and performance.

## Performance-Based Pay

A performance-based pay program is a reward system that pays employees based on individual, business unit, or corporate performance, or on a combination of them. Such a program should be based on the company's business strategy and complement its operational processes, management style, and financial objectives. A performance-based pay program informs the employee at the beginning of the performance period what is expected, how much is expected, and what the dollar payout will be for different levels of performance.

## Merit pay

Merit pay is a permanent increase in base salary paid for an individual's outstanding performance. It's the method most widely used for managing performance of individual employees. Other individual incentive plans include skill-based pay, key contributor programs, spot awards, commissions, and piece-rate plans. Generally, each department receives its share of the merit pay pool; managers then decide what amount of pay adjustment, if any, should go to each employee. The key issues to consider when determining individual pay increases include:

- the employee's current performance level,
- the employee's tenure on the current job,
- the employee's common review date or anniversary date,
- the date of the last pay adjustment,
- the reason for the last adjustment, and
- the location in the pay grade, e.g., at midpoint, between 25th and 50th percentile, etc.

When accounting for length of service, managers should be careful not to confuse merit pay with seniority or length of service plans. For example, if 90 to 100 percent of employees receive similar merit increases, the pay increase program is likely a seniority plan and not a merit system.

## Skill-and Competency-Based Pay

Skill-and competency-based pay are nontraditional forms of compensation. They link an employee's pay to the number of skills the employee can perform or the number of competencies he or she has acquired, regardless of the position or length of service.

The "technical skills ladder" approach is one in which employees in the skilled trades and in research and development progress through salary ranges by acquiring new skills and knowledge, usually on the job.

Another approach bases salary levels on the number of different jobs a person, usually a production worker in a manufacturing firm, is able to do over the normally assigned work.

## Advantages

When skill-or competency-based pay programs fit a company's needs and culture, they can offer many advantages, including:

- improved ability to move employees around to meet changing work requirements;
- more available employees who have an understanding of the overall workings of the company and who are more likely to be effective problem solvers; and
- a reinforced company commitment to provide continued employment to its valued employees, although not necessarily in the same job.

## Disadvantages

Some disadvantages of skill-or competency-based pay programs include:

- higher than typical base pay rates for more employees over time as they acquire additional knowledge and skills;
- constant need to balance the trade-offs of meeting production requirements and learning new skills or acquiring new competencies;
- increased complexity of identifying the skills and knowledge the company needs; and
- increased costs and lost work time due to training on new equipment and new procedures to keep employees up to date with technological, business, and company changes.

# Key Contributor Programs

Key contributor plans reward individuals or teams whose skills, abilities, performance, or contributions have enhanced an organization's products, services, or processes and thereby improved its market position, productivity, or profitability. These individuals are recognized as key contributors and receive cash or stock based on their achievement.

This arrangement may base incentive pay on an individual employee's work, with his or her range of minimum/maximum performance expectations linked to a minimum/maximum custom-targeted award. Compensation programs for salespersons usually follow this model.

Another example of a key contributor program is an arrangement in which a company makes cash or stock grants to an employee with the actual grant payouts contingent on the individual's continued employment.

# Spot Awards

Sometimes referred to as "lightning bolt" awards, these performance-based pay programs are discretionary in nature, and payments usually are made after the fact. Small awards often are called "spot" awards because they can be given on the spot, require few approvals (the supervisor's and possibly one other manager's), and are not expensive.

Awards are task or project oriented, with little or no up-front agreement between the employee and manager about the level of performance that might produce an award. Spot awards recognize special efforts in the context of day-to-day job performance.

Spot awards typically are made immediately after the employee completes the event, task, or project. For example, an employee may be given an award after:

- successfully completing a project within an aggressive deadline;
- successfully negotiating with a challenging customer or client; or
- successfully appearing as a stand-in for a co-worker during a crucial presentation.

## Recognition and Achievement Awards

Award programs range from cash awards for employee recognition to incentive awards. Rewards and recognition cover everything from a service badge to a lump sum increase. In designing rewards, management must consider its business objectives and culture to determine what's right for the organization. Generally recognition implies non-monetary rewards, while reward implies a bonus; but both are designed to facilitate improvement.

These programs focus on people and asset effectiveness, team recognition, and individual recognition. Recognition ranges from a certificate to recognition lunches. Site safety, attendance recognition, and supervisor appreciation programs can round out other recognition programs.

## Differential Pay

Differentials are adjustments to base pay made to address factors that create pay inequities. A "differential" is pay an employer provides to employees for working less desirable shifts or for performing particularly unpleasant or arduous work. Differentials generally must be included in an employee's regular rate and may not be credited against any overtime due the employee (i.e.: the employer must include differential pay in calculating overtime).

**TEST TAKING TIP**
Each question on the exam will have been reviewed by about 12 layers of experts before it may be used on a real PHR test. Thus, each question is perfectly worded. No mistakes in wording.

### Geographic differentials

Geographic concerns come into play when a company decides the number of pay structures it will use. If separate structures have not been created to recognize geographic differences, these differences can be handled through pay adjustments. If, for example, a company has offices in locations where market rates of pay are significantly higher than the location for which the pay structure has been priced, these differences can be addressed by pay adjustments called geographic differentials. The focus should be on market rates rather than on cost of living, because a company's need to pay competitively is tied more closely to market rates. The pay adjustments can be made in the form of base pay adjustments, temporary allowances, or supplemental payments.

### Shift differentials

Internal equity concerns may arise in companies implementing work shifts other than regular day shifts (i.e., 9 a.m. to 5 p.m., Monday through Friday). Shift differentials are salary allowances added to the pay of employees working shifts with irregular hours. Employees are granted additional pay to compensate for working a hardship shift. Pay adjustments generally are expressed as a percentage of base pay or in cents per hour, such as a 10 percent night shift differential, or a 35-cent-per-hour shift differential.

### On-call time

On-call employees required to remain on or so close to the employer's premises that they cannot use this time effectively for their own purposes are consider to be working while on call. Employees free to leave the employer's premises but required to leave word of where they may be reached are not considered to be working while on call. Employees who have to wear paging devices, limit their movements, and respond quickly if called may be entitled to compensation for time spent on call.

## Incentive Pay

The incentive pay component is based on the achievement of preset objectives and can be considered recognition for results above and beyond the scope of basic job objectives.

To be successful, an incentive program must motivate the employee as well as link rewards to specific results. The program must be regularly communicated to employees so that they are aware of how to maximize their total compensation.

## Individual Incentives

### Commissions

Commissions are compensation for the sale of products or services, usually calculated as a percentage of the sale. In commission-oriented sales, the higher the sales results, the higher the pay. The payout amount reflects the individual's true performance.

### Piece rate systems

In incentive piecework, which is used where work output is measurable in units of pieces, the piece rate is the rate of pay stated as dollars paid to an employee per piece produced or worked on.

## Bonuses

A bonus is a lump-sum payment for performance in excess of a predetermined standard. Bonuses differ from commissions in that they typically are discrete payments that are paid for achievement of specific, nonrecurring goals. Whereas some salespeople may be paid only commission, salespeople are never paid solely on the basis of bonuses. Bonus payments are always paired with another method of compensation —e.g., commission, salary, salary plus commission, etc.

Typically, bonuses are expressed as either a fixed dollar amount or a percentage of base pay. Sometimes, the bonus may be determined under a formula, such as under a cash profit-sharing arrangement. The performance target set for bonus payments may be quantitative, e.g., sales volume, profit, or cost reduction. Or it may be qualitative, e.g., service visits or other non-sales duties.

## Group Incentives

Group incentive rewards are bonuses awarded to small groups or work teams according to their performance. Many employers tie their group incentives to an organization's strategic goals and objectives or to productivity measures.

Group incentive plans, not widely used a decade ago, are becoming more common.

> Group incentives encompass gainsharing, team incentives, cash profit sharing plans, and combination plans.

In most companies it may be appropriate to adopt a combination of plans. A large company, for example, might want to establish performance measures for project teams or work groups, in which case a company might have a gainsharing plan supplemented by either a team incentive or cash profit sharing.

For this discussion, a group-oriented incentive plan is one in which a variable number of dollars are awarded to employees based on their unit's performance results. Individual contributions to the group are not considered. A key factor in establishing a group-oriented incentive plan is ensuring the selected group operates relatively autonomously, so that the performance of the group can be measured.

## Gainsharing

Gainsharing is a group-oriented incentive pay plan that links pay directly to specific operational and productivity improvements in the company's performance. Employers use gainsharing when quantitative levels of production are measures of success. Gains are shared with the entire unit's employees monthly, quarterly, semiannually, or annually, according to a formula based on the value or gains of production over labor and other costs.

Most employers use a formula to monitor some performance variable as productivity, to measure gains over a targeted baseline, and to share the resulting benefits with employees. The plan permits employees to reap the rewards of their efforts and encourages working as a team, cooperating, and working harder and smarter.

> **TEST TAKING TIP**
> The test will not be sectioned by area. All the questions from each of the six functional areas are blended together for a continuous 175 question exam.

> The most well-known traditional gainsharing plans are the Scanlon plan, the Rucker plan, and Improshare (improved productivity through sharing).

These plans differ in the formula used to compute productivity savings and in the implementation method used. The Scanlon and Rucker plans measure the payroll of the company against total dollar sales and compare it with the average of the past several years. The Improshare plan measures output against total hours worked. All three plans are flexible regarding the makeup of the group involved in the plan. Direct and indirect production workers as well as management may be included.

## Profit sharing

Profit sharing plans provide for employee participation in the profits of an organization. Plans usually include predetermined and defined formulas for allocating profit shares among participants and for distributing funds generated. Funds may be distributed in cash or deferred to act as a qualified retirement plan. Many plans use a combination of cash and deferred compensation.

True profit sharing plans, with tight links between profitability and payouts, are part of the drive to wed compensation and performance. Although profit sharing plans rarely generate direct evidence of dramatic productivity improvements, studies indicate that strong profit sharing plans boost productivity if they are part of a broader corporate commitment to competition and to employee involvement. Simultaneously, they are viable pension plans with potentially substantial benefits for long-term employees at successful firms.

Profit sharing plans may be cash-only plans, with benefits paid directly to participants in cash usually at the end of the plan year. Or profit sharing plans may be deferred plans that hold the contributions in individual accounts until retirement or another event stipulated in the plan, such as termination, disability, or death. Or they may be a combination of cash and deferred profit sharing plans.

Cash profit sharing is a group-driven, performance-based pay program similar to gainsharing in that a portion of the company's financial gain is shared with all employees. If the company meets or exceeds its profit objectives, a portion is distributed to all employees on a pro-rata basis. Payments are calculated by a predetermined formula and made at least annually, but some cash profit sharing plans pay out semiannually or quarterly, depending on the business situation.

For this program to succeed, employees must be able to discern a relationship between their personal performance and the company's, as expressed in profits. To forge this link, a company may establish individual and group-oriented incentive plans where performance results will contribute directly to the company's profit.

A cash profit sharing plan can be established at the business unit or department level if profit/loss accountability is involved. This provides a much clearer line of sight for employees in linking their own performance with the company's success or failure.

## Rewarding Goal Achievement

Unlike traditional gainsharing programs, goalsharing systems can tie employee rewards to achieving nonfinancial outcomes. For example, a goalsharing program may focus on four or five specific problems in a particular unit and reward employees for taking steps to solve those problems. Under this system, employees can get a payout even if the unit itself is losing money.

### Setting unit goals

Using this reward system, a goalsharing plan is set up for each "unit" — a group of employees with common goals. Each unit should be as large as possible and may encompass an entire plant. In most cases, however, a unit is a smaller group of employees, such as a central customer service branch or the security branch at a certain plant.

> **TEST TAKING TIP**
> There are no "tricky" questions on the exam. Some are very hard but not tricky. You must make sure you fully understand the question before choosing an answer option.

Once a unit has been defined, a joint management-employee committee identifies areas where the unit could improve. For instance, in a manufacturing plant, the areas could include overall quality, customer service, job cost, or timeliness. Measurable targets for improvements are then set, with specific employee rewards tied to achieving these goals.

# Factors Affecting Wages

## Inflation

Inflation directly affects wages. Employee buying power is reduced as inflation rises and wages stay the same. When inflation rates are extremely high, wage freezes can be imposed by the president to help control or slow down inflation.

## Interest Rates

Interest rates directly affect the ability of corporations to expand. If interest rates are high, companies are reluctant to expand business. If they are low, it is cost effective for businesses to take out loans for expansion projects. Business growth is usually followed by increased hiring or increased productivity, leading to increased wages.

## Industry Competition

Strong industry competition does not allow industries to pay higher wages. Productivity, on the other hand, can increase profits and therefore increase wages.

## Foreign Competition

Foreign competition has taken many forms in today's global markets. U.S. companies employ several cost cutting options to keep them competitive in a global environment. We realize them through such things as plant relocations from northern to southern states, employing local managers and workers instead of using expatriates at overseas locations, and moving entire companies to foreign shores.

## Economic Growth

Economic growth tells us how much better off the average person is, for example, last year compared to this year. Has the employee's compensation allowed him or her to enjoy the same buying power as the year before? Has inflation increased more than wages?

## Labor Market Trends/Demographics

The labor market is directly affected by supply and demand of human labor. In times of full employment, wages and salaries are pushed upward in order to attract and retain qualified employees. When unemployment is high, employers can pick and choose from the oversupply of labor without having a "wage war" due to competitive pressures.

Demographics also play a part in the supply and demand of labor. The U.S. Department of Labor expects the size of our future labor force to shrink dramatically. At the same time, the workforce composition is changing. More Hispanics, women and minorities are entering the workforce. Educational skills will also change as the composition of the workforce changes.

## Wage Surveys

Location of actual pay in the market of all pay rates is most commonly determined by gathering and analyzing survey data on market rates of pay. Analyzing the data allows a company to understand what competitors are paying for similar jobs, thus, translating business strategy into a compensation plan.

Wage surveys are surveys of the compensation paid to employees by employers in a selected geographic area, industry, or occupation. They are the principal tool used in making compensation decisions. Surveys provide managers with information on market rates for different positions.

A multitude of surveys have been published, including those from the government, industry trade associations, professional societies, and consulting firms. A company should select surveys that contain data describing competitors' pay rates. In this context, "competitors" means labor market competitors: the organizations from which a company may hire employees or to which a company may lose employees. This includes both geographic and job-content competitors.

The geographic labor market for a position is defined as the geographic area from which a company will recruit. For example, a company might recruit nationwide for a CEO, but for a secretary, the recruiting radius may be a 45-minute commute. Therefore, in determining the market rate for a CEO, it is appropriate to use a survey that includes national data, whereas the market rate for a secretary would come from a local area survey.

The same labor market rule applies to industries. Some positions are unique to one industry or a small number of industries. Reliable market data for those positions can be found only in surveys that specialize in those industries.

## Bureau of Labor Statistics Services and Publications

The Bureau of Labor Statistics (BLS) of the U.S. Department of Labor is the principal data-gathering agency of the federal government in the field of labor economics. It is the most extensive source of wage and salary data in the United States. BLS wage and salary surveys are based on large, carefully constructed samples and conducted according to strict methodological standards. Nonwage compensation is covered in a comprehensive survey of employee benefit plans. The BLS also tracks compensation trends through employment cost indexes and wage and benefit changes in major collective bargaining agreements.

BLS reports generally are free or available at a relatively small charge. Although some of the survey data reported suffers from the lag between the reference period and the date of publication, the large sample sizes, level of detail, careful data collection procedures, and low cost make BLS surveys one of the best sources of data for compensation managers in a number of industries. In addition, you can call BLS technical experts for explanations of survey data and consultation on methodologies and results.

### Custom surveys

When survey data is unavailable, unreliable, or insufficient, a company may choose to conduct its own survey. Before undertaking such a project, however, it should consider the time and cost of conducting a survey. If a company uses enough benchmark jobs, the pay rate for other jobs can be based on internal relationships with those benchmark jobs.

# Administering the Pay System

## Setting Communication Objectives

Employers want their compensation and benefits to support their strategic business or organizational goals. However, the effectiveness of compensation and benefits programs often depends on how well they are communicated to employees.

Designing an effective pay and benefits communication program begins with establishing program objectives. Some of the primary objectives of employer communications programs include:

- educating employees about how compensation and benefits programs work and about plan procedures employees must follow;
- helping employees appreciate the total value of their pay and benefit plans;
- complying with legal requirements, such as the Employee Retirement Income Security Act's disclosure requirements;
- streamlining the benefit enrollment process and reducing the time benefits administrators must spend answering employee questions; and
- providing participants the information they need to plan for retirement.

## Effective Communications

In many workplaces, employees are inundated with formal and informal communications about work-related and non-work-related matters. With such competition, it is difficult for employers to capture an employee's attention and focus it on something as complex as compensation and benefits. To effectively compete for employees' attention, communications about pay and benefits programs must be carefully conceived. Breaking through the information clutter requires that an employer's messages be:

- easy to understand,
- as brief as possible,
- tailored to specific segments of the workforce, and
- creative enough to capture the attention of busy workers.

## Need for Effective Communications

Pay satisfaction hinges on employees' perceptions of how their pay compares to that of other workers. In most companies, employees discuss pay among themselves — few work-related topics generate greater employee interest. If the information employees exchange and the impressions they form are accurate, a compensation plan's objectives are well-served. However, studies show that employees frequently overestimate the pay rates of other employees. When these misperceptions occur, even the most lucrative compensation package will not ensure pay satisfaction, high morale, and good productivity.

## Establishing Administrative Controls

Proper compensation administration requires constantly monitoring, evaluating, and adjusting the pay program. The compensation administration process encompasses a sequence of activities, from job analysis to implementation of the pay program. Common activities in which compensation specialists must engage include the following:

- Evaluate compensation policy to ensure that it reflects changes in the firm's business strategy and financial status.
- Conduct job analysis to determine and define the content of different positions.
- Update job descriptions and their "compensable factors," and review job evaluations to determine the relative worth of a firm's jobs and to produce a hierarchy of classifications.
- Track changes in relevant labor markets through salary surveys to ensure that the pay rates and structures are adjusted so the program maintains its competitive position.
- Develop an appropriate pay structure so that it groups jobs into pay grades; establish pay ranges setting a minimum and maximum pay rate for each group of jobs; and provide recommendations on revising pay rates.
- Monitor costs to ensure compliance with budgets and review actual procedures and decisions to ensure that they conform to the policy.
- Implement the program by communicating it to employees and managers; design and develop compensation systems, procedures, and forms.
- Develop and review the efficacy of performance appraisals and make certain that employee appraisals are conducted at least annually.
- Monitor compliance with federal and state laws and regulations pertaining to compensation.

### Centralized or decentralized systems

A number of administration issues hinge on the extent to which pay plan decisions and responsibilities are centralized, with standardized job evaluation, pay rates, and pay programs applied to the entire organization. In centralized systems, corporate staff or the HR department control compensation administration. Small companies, or large companies with a single location and line of business, often adopt a centralized approach, while large multi-business companies and companies with subsidiaries often decentralize decision-making and the administrative process.

Centralization can maximize internal equity, administrative efficiency, defensibility, and cost control, and is probably appropriate for single-business companies organized along traditional lines. A number of compensation experts argue, however, that decentralization offers greater flexibility and effectiveness for many companies, and a growing number of companies are now shifting to a more decentralized approach. Companies organized around distinct business units are moving decision-making responsibilities — including those related to compensation — out of corporate headquarters and into line operations.

## Budgeting – SPHR-Only Section

A significant part of compensation administration consists of the annual process of setting salary budgets. The budget process includes determinations for all forms of increases: general increases, cost-of-living adjustment increases, merit raises, promotional increases, special recognition awards, and adjustments in salary structures.

> **TEST TAKING TIP**
> Take at least two hours of practice exams each week during the preparation period. Keep taking different exams. You'll learn from them and sharpen your skills.

Several different budgets may be generated, including budgets for employees who remain in one position throughout the year and budgets that reflect promotions and workforce expansions or reductions. The types of pay increases used, and the timing of the increases — anniversary date, single effective date, or variable date — will affect the process for constructing the budgets.

### Zero-Based budgeting

A technique of planning and decision-making. It reverses the working process of traditional budgeting. In case of ZBB, no reference is made to the previous level of expenditure. Every department function is reviewed comprehensively and all expenditures rather than only increases are approved. ZBB is a technique, by which the budget request has to be justified in complete detail by each division manager starting from the Zero-base. The Zero-base is indifferent to whether the total budget is increasing or decreasing.

With zero-based processing, budget preparers forget about last year, pretend that the program is brand-new, and see if they can provide a detail of expenses for what they would need to fully accomplish the program. This technique will help them to develop a complete picture of what the program actually needs to cost and not just what it has been costing.

### Incremental budgeting

In traditional incremental budgeting, departmental managers need to justify only increases over the previous year budget. This means what has been already spent is automatically sanctioned.

### Budget information

The amount of the salary increase budget may be influenced by many factors, including:

- developments in relevant labor markets,
- competitors' pay practices,
- company policy on market position,
- turnover rates,
- business growth cycles, and
- financial condition of the company and industry.

Much of the information required for the budget process must come from inside sources. The cooperation of the finance department is essential. Information on competitors' pay practices and relevant labor markets is available from a wide range of external sources.

### Salary increase budget surveys

Information on projected salary increase budgets appears in a number of surveys that are released in every fall. These surveys are available from the World at Work (formerly known as American Compensation Association - ACA) and from most of the major consulting companies. The ACA survey provides projected salary increase budget data by region, industry, employee classification, and type of increase.

When using budget-increase salary surveys, select the surveys of companies that most closely match the size, industry, and workforce characteristics of your company. Then adjust the figures according to the market position desired.

**End of SPHR-only section**

## Calculating Overtime

In the United States, the Fair Labor Standards Act of 1938 applies to employees in industries engaged in, or producing goods for, interstate commerce. The FLSA establishes a standard work week of 40 hours for certain kinds of workers, and mandates payment for overtime hours to those workers of one and one-half times the workers' normal rate of pay for any time worked above 40 hours.

The FLSA does not require overtime pay for work on Saturdays, Sundays, holidays, or regular days of rest. The FLSA does not require extra pay for weekend or night work or double time pay.

To calculate overtime pay, the HR professional must first establish the regular hourly rate of pay. To do this, first calculate the hourly rate of pay. Example: An employee paid $8.00 an hour works 44 hours in a workweek. To calculate the appropriate rate, multiply the 44 hours times $8/hour = $352. The employee is still owed the half-time rate for the remaining four hours. Half of $8 = $4. $4 times the four overtime hours = $16. Add the $16 with the straight-time rate for the 44 hours of $352 = $368.

It becomes more complicated when bonuses are calculated into the equation. Non-discretionary bonuses, any kind of quid pro quo type incentive pay, must be added into the calculation for the hourly base rate of pay first before the overtime calculation may be accomplished. Note: when determining if the bonus is non-discretionary, remember this tip: discretionary = gift; non-discretionary = formula (i.e.; gifts from management (Christmas bonus) do not have to calculated into the base rate while formula-driven pay is almost always a non-discretionary incentive and must be calculated into the base rate of pay.

Example: Using the same example from above, an employee is paid $8.00 an hour and works 44 hours in a workweek. The employee also receives an $88 production bonus (non-discretionary incentive). In this calculation the straight-time regular rate of pay must be established first (44 hours X $8.00/hr = $352); now add the $88 bonus ($88 + $352 = $440); now divide by 44 hours to get the hourly rate of pay ($440 / 44 = $10.00/hr). The regular straight-time rate of pay for the 44 hours is $440 in total. Now, establish the half-time overtime rate of pay (half of $10.00 = $5/hr.); by multiplying the half-time overtime rate by the four hours ($5 X 4 hours overtime = $20). To finish the calculation, simply add the $440 (total regular straight-time pay) to the $20 (total overtime pay) to get $440 + 20 = $460.

---

Exception to the above: Hospitals and Nursing care facilities may pay employees overtime after 40 hours in a 7 day workweek or alternatively, use the "8 and 80" system. Under the "8 and 80" system, the nursing care facility may pay employees -- with whom they have a prior agreement -- overtime for any hours worked after more than 8 hours in a day and more than 80 hours in a 14-day period.

---

An employer may discipline an employee if he or she violates the employer's policy of working overtime without the required authorization. However, federal wage and hour laws require that the employee be compensated for any hours he or she is "suffered or permitted to work, whether or not required to do so." "Suffer or permit" means work the employer knew or should have known about the work.

## Compensatory Time Off

Compensatory time; or comp time refers to a type of work schedule arrangement that allows workers to take time off instead of, or in addition to, receiving overtime pay. A worker may receive overtime pay plus equal time off for each hour worked on certain agreed days. In the United States, such arrangements are currently illegal for private sector workers under overtime laws, but the practice is legal in the public sector.

For example, under current overtime laws in the U.S., non-exempt workers must receive one and one half times their normal hourly wage for every hour worked beyond 40 hours in a work week. So, if a worker clocks 48 hours in one week, then he would receive pay equivalent to 52 hours of work (40 hours + 8 hours at 1.5 times the normal hourly wage). Comp time would permit the worker in this example to forego the 12 hours of overtime pay and instead take 12 paid hours off at some future date.

# Executive Compensation – (SPHR-Only Section)

## Pay Programs for Selected Employees

Effective executive compensation must meet the needs of both the organization and the individual executive. Executive compensation must be tied directly to the organization's strategy and objectives, so executive rewards will promote achievement of the organization's goals. To accommodate changing tax laws, executive pay incorporates more deferred compensation.

Employers frequently include nonqualified deferred compensation plans as part of their executive compensation programs as a way to overcome the restrictions the federal tax code places on qualified plans. Nonqualified plans are not subject to the federal tax code's qualified plan rules that place a cap on annual plan benefits and employer contributions and prohibit employers from directing benefits to executives in a preferential manner. Moreover, nonqualified plans that are unfunded usually are exempt from participation, reporting, disclosure, and other requirements under the Employee Retirement Income Security Act (ERISA).

Nonqualified deferred compensation arrangements are either "funded" or "unfunded." As a general rule, executives are not taxed currently on a deferred compensation arrangement in which the employer makes an unsecured, unfunded promise to pay an amount in the future until the deferred amount is actually paid out. Under a funded arrangement, employer contributions and earnings on these contributions are included in the executive's gross income to the extent that the executive is substantially vested when the contribution or premium payment is made. An executive is substantially vested if employer contributions are not subject to a substantial risk of forfeiture.

Nonqualified arrangements encompass a wide range of plans, including nonqualified retirement plans – excess-benefit plans and supplemental executive retirement plans (SERP's) – nonqualified stock options, top-hat plans, and section 457 plans for state and local governments and tax-exempt organizations. Beyond these basic types of plans, employers have the choice of a variety of ways to fund and structure the plans, including the use of "rabbi trusts," "secular trusts," and revocable trusts.

## Rabbi Trust

"Rabbi Trust" is a nonqualified deferred compensation arrangement under which an employer places funds in a trust that remains under the employer's control. Although the trust remains under the employer's control, it is irrevocable and inaccessible to present or future management. However, to avoid current taxation to the executive, the IRS requires that the trust's assets remain subject to the claims of the employer's creditors in the event of the employer's insolvency or bankruptcy.

Rabbi trusts acquired their name because the IRS's first favorable ruling on these arrangements involved a trust established by a congregation for its rabbi.

Rabbi Trusts are treated as "grantor trusts" under the federal tax code, since trust assets may be used to satisfy the grantor's (i.e., the employer's) legal obligations. Accordingly, the employer is considered the owner of the trust, and as such must include any income or losses attributable to the trust in its tax consequences.

**TEST TAKING TIP**
The more years of practical experience you have making decisions and exercising discretion and judgment, the better chance you'll have on these tests. The less experience you have, the more you'll need to study.

The executive is not taxed on the deferred amount until it is distributed, and the employer will be entitled to a corresponding deduction in the tax year of distribution. However, if more than one executive participates in the trust, no deduction will be allowed unless separate accounts (not separate trusts) are maintained for each executive. Furthermore, any assets remaining in the trust revert to the employer after distribution of the deferred amounts to the executives.

## Split-Dollar Life Insurance

A split-dollar insurance arrangement is another non-qualified way for an employer and employee to share the costs and proceeds of a cash value (whole life or universal life) life insurance policy. However, to avoid current taxation to the executive, the IRS requires that the plan's assets remain subject to the claims of the employer's creditors in the event of the employer's insolvency or bankruptcy.

Under a split-dollar arrangement, the employee and employer agree to share one or more of the following incidents of ownership of a life insurance policy:

- premiums,
- death proceeds,

- policy cash values, or
- dividends on the policy.

These proceeds are tax-free. But the employee must pay tax on the value of the insurance protection plus cash dividends received, reduced by any amount the employee pays. Under a traditional arrangement, the employer pays the premiums and owns the cash surrender value of the policy, with the employee's beneficiary receiving the death benefit less the cash surrender value if the employee dies while the policy is in force.

## Top Hat Plans (SERP)

Another type of nonqualified deferred compensation plan is the supplemental executive retirement plan (SERP). These nonqualified deferred compensation plans are also commonly referred to as top-hat plans because they are used to provide deferred compensation for a select group of top management or highly compensated employees. SERPs provide benefits above and beyond those covered in other retirement plans such as IRA, 401(k) or NQDC plans. There are many different kinds of SERPs available to companies wishing to ensure their key employees are able to maintain their current standards of living in retirement.

A top-hat plan may be either un-funded or funded by the employer. From the employee's standpoint, an un-funded plan means that the employee assumes the risk that the employer may refuse to pay benefits owed under the plan due to a merger, acquisition, insolvency, or other reason. An employee pays tax on the employer's un-funded top-hat plan contributions when the benefits are actually distributed or made available to the employee. If the plan is funded, however, an employer's contributions are includible in an employee's income in the year that the contributions are made.

Similarly, an employer may generally not deduct contributions to a top-hat plan until the benefits are actually distributed or made available to the employee, which varies depending on whether the plan is funded or un-funded. With a funded plan, the employer is also subject to ERISA's participation, vesting, funding, fiduciary responsibility, and plan termination insurance rules.

**End of SPHR-only section**

# Benefits

Benefit planning is the most challenging field in HR today. A well-designed benefit plan can be an effective tool for shaping and motivating the workforce to achieve business goals, with excellent returns on every dollar spent. Benefits represent a significant part of total compensation to employees and total labor costs to the firm.

For most organizations, benefits account for 25 percent to 40 percent of payroll. They include legally required payments, such as Social Security and unemployment compensation, which form the foundation for every plan, plus a huge array of programs that touch virtually every aspect of an employee's life and color the employment relationship.

As a result of the changing economy, and the increasing need for cost containment, businesses must design and strategically plan their benefits programs. An effective employee benefit program should be designed to meet certain objectives for the employer while helping to meet employees' needs and desires. Employers' objectives must accommodate certain economic realities while attracting and keeping competent personnel—all to remain competitive.

## HR Objectives

Benefits can be used to achieve a wide range of business and HR objectives. For example, benefits can be used to:

- recruit targeted groups of employees with particular backgrounds, interests, responsibilities, and aspirations;

- retain valuable employees with plans that heavily reward certain groups or encourage long tenure;

- demonstrate a genuine commitment to workforce diversity;

- beat out the competition without significant additional payroll costs by offering noncash incentives or relatively inexpensive but innovative arrangements;

- increase employee involvement and boost productivity through profit sharing and other performance-related deferred compensation plans; and

- align employee and shareholder interests through Employee Stock Option Plans or stock- based reward programs.

## Administrative Systems

In designing or administering any employee benefit program, it is critical to know whether the program is an employee benefit plan subject to regulation under the Employee Retirement Income Security Act (ERISA). ERISA provides uniform standards for employee benefit plans, particularly pension plans. For employers, ERISA may be both a burden and a blessing. If a benefit program is an employee benefit plan within the meaning of ERISA, it is subject to ERISA, but it is free from state regulation and various common-law suits.

Employee benefit plans are plans that provide either a pension benefit or a non-pension benefit – that is, a welfare benefit. To determine whether a benefit program is subject to ERISA, it is necessary to determine whether it provides a benefit governed by ERISA and whether it is designed to be a plan. In addition, some particular plans are excepted from ERISA coverage entirely.

## Funding/Investment Responsibilities

Certain types of retirement plans – specifically, defined benefit plans and money purchase plans – are subject to minimum funding standards set forth in the Internal Revenue Code. Profit sharing plans and 401(k) plans are not subject to minimum funding.

ERISA requires that employers contribute enough funds to their defined benefit pension plans to cover the amount of benefits that employee-members have accrued during that year, based on an actuarial determination taking into account benefits payable, mortality, earnings on the fund, and turnover. The IRS can grant waivers of all or part of this minimum funding requirement if complying with the requirement would cause substantial financial hardship. Employers also are required to pay for federal plan insurance to guarantee a certain level of benefits to beneficiaries if the employer cannot meet its funding obligations.

Employers with defined benefit plans bear all the risk associated with investment of plan assets. Large gains may allow the employer to reduce future contributions; smaller gains or losses may force larger contributions for adequate funding. Erroneous assumptions about turnover and mortality can increase plan costs. In defined contribution plans, employees bear the investment risk, and the employer's cost is highly predictable.

The Pension Benefit Guaranty Corporation (PBGC) administers ERISA's termination insurance provisions and protects against a loss of retirement benefits when a defined benefit pension plan terminates with inadequate or no funding. The PBGC insurance program guarantees the payment of vested normal retirement benefits up to an indexed monthly amount when the plan terminates.

## Coordination of Benefits

Many employees and their families are covered by more than one health care plan. In cases of duplicate coverage, plan administrators use coordination of benefits (COB) procedures to determine which plan is the primary payer – i.e., the plan that must pay first – and which is the secondary payer – i.e., the plan that pays the remaining expenses up to the total amount of allowable expenses incurred.

Under COB, one plan is designated the "primary payer" and must pay the full benefits required under the terms of the plan. The other plan is designated the "secondary payer" and pays the balance of the participant's allowable expenses, so that the participant is not reimbursed in excess of 100 percent of his or her actual medical expenses.

## Designing Benefit Plans

Employee benefits (also called fringe benefits, perquisites, or perks) are various non-wage compensations provided to employees in addition to their normal wages or salaries. Where an employee exchanges (cash) wages for some other form of benefit, this is generally referred to as a 'salary sacrifice' arrangement. In most countries, most kinds of employee benefits are taxable to at least some degree.

Fringe benefits can also include but are not limited to: (employer-provided or employer-paid) housing, group insurance (health, dental, life etc.), income protection, retirement benefits, daycare, tuition reimbursement, sick leave, vacation (paid and non-paid), social security, profit sharing, funding of education, and other specialized benefits.

The purpose of the benefits is to increase the economic security of employees.

Employee benefits in the United States might include relocation assistance; medical, prescription, vision and dental plans; health and dependent care flexible spending accounts; retirement benefit plans (pension, 401(k), 403(b)); group-term life and long term care insurance plans; legal assistance plans; adoption assistance; child care benefits; and possibly other miscellaneous employee discounts (*e.g.*, movies and theme park tickets, discounted shopping, hotels and resorts, and so on).

Some fringe benefits (for example, accident and health plans, and group-term life insurance coverage up to $50,000) may be excluded from the employee's gross income and, therefore, are not subject to federal income tax in the United States. Some function as tax shelters (for example, flexible spending accounts, 401(k)'s, 403(b)'s). Fringe benefits are also thought of as the costs of keeping employees other than salary. These benefit rates are typically calculated using fixed percentages that vary depending on the employee's classification and often change from year to year.

Normally, employer provided benefits are tax-deductible to the employer and non-taxable to the employee. The exception to the general rule includes certain executive benefits (e.g. golden handshake and golden parachute plans).

American corporations may also offer cafeteria plans to their employees. These plans would offer a menu and level of benefits for employees to choose from. In most instances, these plans are funded by both the employees and by the employer(s). The portion paid by the employees is deducted from their gross pay before federal and state taxes are applied. Some benefits would still be subject to the FICA tax, such as 401(k) and 403(b) contributions; however, health premiums, some life premiums, and contributions to flexible spending accounts are exempt from FICA.

## Retirement Plans

### ESOPs
An employee stock ownership plan is a defined contribution plan that is either a qualified stock bonus plan or a combination qualified stock bonus and qualified money purchase plan designed to invest primarily in securities of the company sponsoring the plan. An ESOP must provide individual accounts for each participant and must base benefits solely on amounts contributed to each account, including attributable income expenses, gains and losses, and allocated forfeitures from other participants' accounts.

### IRAs
Individual retirement accounts (IRAs) are tax- deferred savings programs that allow employees to set aside money for retirement. Earnings are not subject to income tax until distribution. Anyone under age 70 1/2 who has earned income is eligible to establish an IRA. An IRA may not be used as collateral for a loan, and funds may not be borrowed from an IRA.

Employers may establish IRAs for employees or contribute to employees' IRAs. The contributions may be made as additional compensation or as payroll deductions. All amounts contributed by the employer are taxable income.

### SEPs
A simplified employee pension (SEP) is a pension plan that uses an IRA to which both the employer and the employee may contribute. The account is governed by most of the IRA rules on distributions and withdrawals. The employer's contributions are tax deductible for the employer up to the lesser of 15 percent of the employee's compensation.

SEPs can be used by unincorporated businesses, partnerships, corporations, and nonprofit organizations. Once the employer deposits its contribution into the account, it bears no further responsibility for the amount contributed or the income earned.

**TEST TAKING TIP**
Focus, focus, focus!!! No distractions.

### Money purchase plans
Under money purchase plans, the employer makes a fixed contribution for each employee, usually as a percentage of compensation and commonly in the range of 4 to 7 percent. Many of these plans allow voluntary after-tax employee contributions. Money purchase plans are limited to total contributions of 25 percent of earned income, up to a maximum amount in a given year, for all defined contribution plans combined.

Money purchase plan funds are deposited in a trust and used to provide annuities after retirement; some plans offer lump-sum distributions. Money purchase plans are subject to ERISA minimum funding requirements, but as long as an employer makes the contribution required by the plan's formula, the funding requirements are satisfied.

### SIMPLE plans
SIMPLE plans can be adopted by an employer with 100 or fewer employees if it does not maintain another employer-sponsored retirement plan in the same year. Employees who received at least $5,000 in

compensation from the employer during any two earlier years, and who are reasonably expected to receive at least that amount during the current year, must be eligible to participate in the SIMPLE plan.

A SIMPLE plan can be either an IRA for each employee or part of a 401(k) plan. The employer can:

- match employee elective contributions dollar-for-dollar up to 3 percent of compensation (however, flexibility is provided by permitting matching contributions of as little as 1 percent in no more than two of the five years) or
- choose for any year to make a non-elective contribution of 2 percent of compensation for each eligible employee.

Employee contributions are deductible, and not taxable until withdrawn. Employer contributions generally are deductible. Contributions must be credited to employees' accounts within 30 days after the end of the month to which the contributions relate.

Employees must be allowed to end their participation in the plan at any time, and tax-free rollovers can be made from one SIMPLE account to another. Early withdrawals are generally subject to the same 10 percent tax applicable to IRAs, but unlike IRAs, withdrawals during the first two years of a SIMPLE plan are subject to a 25 percent tax.

## Legal Requirements

The Employee Retirement Income Security Act (ERISA) requires that employers provide employees with specific information concerning benefit plans. ERISA requires reporting and disclosure of pension and profit sharing plans and welfare plans such as those dealing with group life, group accident, hospitalization, medical and surgical, and dental care insurance. When employers modify their plans, changes must be communicated to employees. Also, the Consolidated Omnibus Budget Reconciliation Act (COBRA) requires complex communication and notification procedures.

## Vesting

Vesting is the process by which the employee earns a non-forfeitable right to benefits funded by employer contributions. All qualified plans must ensure that employees are vested in employer contributions according to vesting schedules that meet regulatory requirements. Employees are always 100% vested in their own contributions.

An employer may choose between two types of vesting schedules: cliff vesting or graded vesting.

### Cliff vesting

Like it sounds, a cliff vesting schedule means that for a period of time employees won't be vested at all. Then, like going off a cliff, they become vested all at once. Under a cliff-vesting schedule for employer contributions to a Defined Benefit Plan, such as a Pension plan, employee must complete five years of service to become vested in the employer contributions portions of the assets saved. Cliff vesting for a Defined Contribution plan is three years. After this time the employee takes 100% ownership of all plan contributions.

### Graded vesting

Under a graded-vesting schedule for employer contributions to a Defined Benefit Plan, such as a pension plan, employees are 20% vested in employer contributions after completing three years of vesting service. For each subsequent year, the vesting is increased by 20% until it reaches 100%, which occurs after the employee completes seven years of service. Under a graded-vesting schedule for employer matching contributions to a Defined Contribution Plan, the employee is 20% vested in employer contributions after completing two years of vesting service. For each subsequent year, the vesting is increased by 20% until it reaches 100%, which occurs after six years of service.

| Graded DC Vesting | VS. | Graded DB Vesting |
|---|---|---|
| 2 years = 20% vested | | 3 years = 20% vested |
| 3 years = 40% vested | | 4 years = 40% vested |
| 4 years = 60% vested | | 5 years = 60% vested |
| 5 years = 80% vested | | 6 years = 80% vested |
| 6 years = 100% vested | | 7 years = 100% vested |
| **DC Cliff Vesting = 3 years** | | **DB Cliff Vesting = 5 years** |

## Health Insurance Plans

### Cost management

Benefits represent an increasingly sizeable portion of total employee compensation – the average employer spends about one-third of total payroll dollars on employee benefits. However, because most employers offer benefits, employees often view health care and other benefits such as vacations and holidays as an entitlement rather than earned compensation for a job well done. Benefit communications are a key element in the attempt to move employees away from the entitlement mentality and toward a perspective on benefits as a part of total compensation for performance.

Employer's health care programs incorporate a variety of features to limit plan costs. Traditional cost-control measures include cost sharing with employees, setting minimum service and eligibility requirements, excluding certain medical procedures and conditions, and setting limits on the amount of allowable health care charges. While such cost controls have been surpassed by managed care as employers' primary defense against escalating health care costs, traditional cost-control features still play a part in most health care benefits plans.

Most employer health care plans require employees to pay at least part of the cost of health care services covered under the plan. Some common ways that employer programs share costs with plan participants include deductibles, coinsurance, copayments, and premium contributions. Minimum service and eligibility requirements specify who is eligible to participate in the health care plan. Issues to resolve involve newly hired employees, retirees, dependents, spouses, and adopted children.

Another cost limitation method is to exclude coverage of certain procedures that for one reason or another, the plan deems unnecessary to cover. The most common exclusions include unnecessary services, preexisting conditions, and cosmetic surgery.

These measures can leave employees, especially long-time employees who have enjoyed generous benefit packages in the past, feeling resentful and short-changed. A solid communications program can reduce resentment and enlist employees as active partners in efforts to manage benefit costs while maintaining quality programs.

### Flexible benefit plans

Benefit plans that allow employees to choose their own mix of benefits or levels of coverage – are growing in popularity as employers try to control benefits costs and tailor their benefits packages to a diverse workforce with changing needs. Flexible benefit plans are also known as cafeteria plans, reflecting the availability of a menu of benefits choices. The terms are sometimes used interchangeably, though the scope of flexible benefits is considerably broader. The term "cafeteria plan" generally refers to a benefits program under Section 125 of the Internal Revenue code that offers employees a choice between taxable benefits, including cash, and nontaxable health and welfare benefits such as life and health insurance, vacation pay, retirement plans, and child care. The term "flexible benefits" is a general term used to describe any type of arrangement that offers employees a choice among benefits.

## Utilization review

An increasing number of employers are trying to stem rising workers' compensation medical costs by applying "managed health care" techniques. Managed health care describes a range of programs used by health care providers, insurers, and employers to promote the cost-effective use of health care benefits. Managed care techniques with the greatest promise in helping employers contain workers' compensation costs include utilization review, claims review, and case management.

Utilization review (UR) is the process of evaluating the medical appropriateness of health care services with the purpose of ensuring that patients receive cost efficient, high quality health care. Utilization review is conducted by doctors, nurses, and other medical professionals employed by insurers, claims administrators, and specialized utilization review organizations (UROs).

**TEST TAKING TIP**
Many questions on the exam will ask you, "What is the BEST, LEAST, MOST, FIRST, LAST…? These are often some of the more difficult questions as all the options are somewhat correct but you must choose the best answer.

UR encompasses a variety of different programs. However, the most common types of UR include: pre-certification review, concurrent review, case management, and second surgical opinion programs. Because inpatient hospital care and surgical services tend to be the most expensive health care element, UR focuses on those services.

## Health Savings Accounts (HSA)

This is a tax-advantaged medical savings account available to taxpayers in the United States who are enrolled in a High Deductible Health Plan (HDHP). The funds contributed to the account are not subject to income tax, but can only be used to pay for qualified medical expenses. These accounts are a component of Consumer Driven health care.

According to proponents, HSAs encourage saving for future health care expenses and encourage the adoption of High-Deductible Health Plans, which make consumers more responsible for their own health care choices.

HSA's were developed as an improvement over the Medical Savings Account system, as the excess funds are allowed to roll over from previous fiscal years and remain the property of the owner.

Deposits to an HSA may be made by any policyholder of a qualified High Deductible Health Plan (HDHP), by an employer on behalf of a policyholder, or any other person. If an employer makes deposits to an HDHP on behalf of its employees, non-discrimination rules apply — that is, all employees must be treated equally. However, if contributions are made through a section 125 plan, non-discrimination rules do not apply. Employers may treat full-time and part-time employees differently, and employers may treat individual and family participants differently.

Funds in an HSA can be invested in a manner similar to investments in an Individual Retirement Account (IRA). Investment earnings are sheltered from taxation until the money is withdrawn. While HSAs can be "rolled over" from fund to fund, an HSA cannot be rolled into an IRA or a 401(k), and funds from these types of investment vehicles cannot be rolled into an HSA. Unlike some employer contributions to a 401(k) plan, *all* HSA contributions belong to the participant immediately.

## Income Protection

### Accidental Death and Dismemberment Insurance

Group life insurance policies almost always are written with accompanying policies for accidental death and dismemberment (AD&D). However, an employer can purchase a separate policy for AD&D or for accidental dismemberment alone. Life insurance policies with accidental death provisions generally provide for double indemnity—that is, the face value of the policy is doubled in case of accidental death.

In AD&D plans, a schedule sets forth the amounts payable for various losses. The principal sum is paid for accidental death, loss of both hands, both feet, the entire sight of both eyes, or a combination of these losses. Half the amount of the principal sum is paid for loss of one hand, one foot, or the sight of one eye. Exclusions usually include suicide, physical or mental illnesses that require medical treatment, infections other than those caused by a cut or wound accidentally inflicted, acts of war, and travel in any kind of aircraft in any capacity other than paying passenger. AD&D plans are generally noncontributory and usually cover non-occupational accidents only; workers' compensation insurance covers occupational accidents.

### Disability insurance

Disability insurance (also known as sickness and accident insurance) replaces earnings lost when an employee develops a disability that temporarily or permanently prevents the employee from working. There are several sources of disability benefits, including Social Security, workers' compensation, employer salary continuation programs, and long-term disability payments. Short- term disability benefits generally protect workers from loss of income for illnesses of less than six-months to one year. Long-term disability benefits generally provide income replacement for six months or longer — sometimes for the life of the worker.

### Severance pay

Severance pay allows employers to provide for employees who are discharged. Eligibility requirements in severance pay provisions almost always exclude employees who are discharged for cause. In the case of a sale or other transfer of the employer's business, employees who obtain comparable employment with the successor or the employer are also usually excluded. An employer may want to further include employees who reject a comparable job offer from a successor or the employer. The amount of severance pay negotiated is usually proportional to length of service.

### Pay for time not worked

The FLSA requires employees to be paid for all hours worked. However, employers are required by market pressures to offer some or all employees a paid-time-off plan to attract and retain the best employees. Each category of paid time off from work — vacations, holidays, sick leave, personal days, and bereavement — are basic considerations of cost, employee eligibility, calculation of the number of paid days off and amount of pay, scheduling, whether to allow accumulation, and payment upon termination. Typical examples of pay-for-time-not-worked include:
- Holidays
- Vacations
- Personal leave
- Parental leave
- Sick leave

- Other types of paid leave (bereavement leave, jury duty, military leave, etc.)

In addition to the most familiar types of paid time off, unions typically seek payment for time missed from work due to jury duty or short-term military assignments. Lengthy absences from work are generally covered by separate contract provisions, such as a leave of absence clause.

### Unpaid leave

One of the most important fringe benefits an employer can offer is leave – the right to take paid or unpaid time off from work for injury, childbirth, or illness and then to return to the same or a comparable job. Federal fair employment practice laws that deal with leave issues include the Americans with Disabilities Act, the 1973 Rehabilitation Act, Title VII of the 1964 Civil Rights Act, the Family and Medical leave Act, and Executive Order 11246.

> **TEST TAKING TIP**
> Practice test-taking, then practice some more. Take every practice exam you can get your hands on. There are many free sample PHR and SPHR quizzes on the internet. Go forth and search for them.

### Role of Social Security

Social Security provides disability benefits for workers under age 65 who have disabilities that are expected to last 12 months or more or to result in death. There is a five-month waiting period, and employees must have worked enough time to be eligible for Social Security. Combined Social Security disability and workers' compensation benefits may not exceed 80 percent of "average current earnings" before disability.

# Taxes & Accounting Overview

An employee's compensation is subject to several types of withholding and payroll taxes, including federal (and state and local) income tax, social security tax, Medicare tax, and federal and state unemployment insurance taxes. The employer generally must withhold its employee's income taxes and social security and Medicare taxes, match the employee's portion of the social security tax and Medicare tax, and pay the required unemployment tax on wages earned.

## Taxable Earnings

FICA defines wages as "all remuneration for employment including the cash value of all remuneration paid in any medium other than cash." Wages include salaries, fees, bonuses, and commissions on sales or insurance premiums if paid as compensation for services performed by the employee for his or her employer.

Amounts withheld by the employer because of a statutory obligation or an employee's request are also subject to FICA tax. For example, federal, state, and local income taxes that the employer deducts and withholds from an employee's pay do not reduce wages for Social Security tax purposes.

In addition, the employer must provide the benefits of the wage guarantees of the Fair Labor Standards Act (FLSA), pay the costs for federal and state worker's compensation requirements, and generally ensure the protections of the Age Discrimination in Employment Act (ADEA), Title VII of the Civil Rights Act of 1964 (Title VII), the Americans with Disabilities Act (ADA), the Employee Retirement Income Security Act (ERISA), the Labor-Management Relations Act (LMRA), and the Family and Medical Leave Act (FMLA).

## FASB Regulation

Two Financial Accounting Standards (FAS) issued by the Financial Accounting Standards Board (FASB) require significant changes to the accounting practices followed by most companies for reporting their benefit costs. Employers who report their financial statements using generally accepted accounting principles (GAAP) must comply with these standards on their annual financial statements. Historically, most employers used the pay-as-you-go method, which allowed companies to deduct the costs incurred for retirement benefits when the amount was paid. Under the methods prescribed under the FAS's, an employer's financial statement will show a portion of the cost of an employee's retirement benefit as a current cost to the company.

## Taxation of Benefits

In most cases, neither federal taxes, Federal Insurance Contributions Act (FICA) taxes, nor Federal Unemployment Tax Act (FUTA) taxes are withheld from employer contributions or salary reductions. However, 401(k) cash-or-deferred contributions are subject to FICA withholding.

Benefits also may be taxable if the benefit the employee has elected is ordinarily subject to tax or exceeds an applicable ceiling under rules governing qualified and unqualified benefits. In addition, if the plan fails to meet nondiscrimination rules, the value of benefits may be included in the employee's income. The following discussion examines these rules in greater detail.

### Qualified benefits

In general, a benefit is a qualified benefit (and therefore nontaxable) if it does not defer the receipt of compensation, and is not includible in an employee's gross income by reason of an express provision of the Internal Revenue Code. Examples of qualified benefits include:

- cash,
- vacation days,
- contributions to 401(k) cash-or-deferred arrangement,
- group-term life insurance up to $50,000,
- accident and health benefits,
- group legal services,
- dependent care assistance, and
- other benefits that are not includible in gross income pursuant to an express provision of the Internal Revenue Code.

In addition, group-term life insurance policies on family members worth more than $50,000, if paid for with after-tax employee contributions, are qualified benefits.

### Unqualified benefits

Unqualified benefits may not be included in a (section 125) benefit plan, regardless of whether the benefit is purchased with after-tax employee contributions. Examples of unqualified benefits include:

- scholarships and fellowships,
- meals and lodging,
- vanpooling,
- educational assistance,
- no-additional-cost services,
- qualified employee discounts,
- working-condition fringe benefits, and

- de minimis benefits, as defined under (IRC §132.)

# International Compensation (SPHR Only Section)

## Compensation and Benefits for Foreign Nationals and Expatriates

Employees who are assigned to work in a foreign country usually are offered a different compensation package than domestic employees. The international pay package generally consists of: base pay and employee benefits; allowances to offset extra expenses and higher costs; and, in some cases, premiums or incentives to induce the employees to accept foreign assignments.

Employees relocated to fill foreign staffing needs usually are classified as expatriates or third- country nationals (TCNs).

The primary goals of expatriate compensation programs are to encourage qualified employees to accept foreign assignments and to remove financial obstacles that hinder the employee's ability or willingness to relocate to a foreign post. Other goals employers pursue with their expatriate compensation programs include: promoting equity among expatriates assigned to different countries; maintaining equity between expatriates and home-country staff; and staying in full compliance with the tax, labor, and employment laws in both the home country and the foreign country to which the expatriate is assigned.

### Compensation packages for international employees

Many multinational companies need to bring home-country experience and know-how to their foreign operations. This goal often is achieved by relocating experienced employees from the headquarters country or another country.

Many multinationals maintain one international compensation policy that covers both expatriates and TCNs. Generally, the policies are directed toward the needs of expatriates, but may include provisions to accommodate the special needs of TCNs. With a few exceptions, the needs of expatriates and TCNs are the same. Thus, for simplicity's sake the term "expatriate" will be used in the rest of this section to refer to both expatriates and TCNs.

### Purpose of expatriate compensation programs

Expatriate compensation programs serve two primary purposes:

- encouraging qualified employees to accept foreign assignments; and
- removing financial obstacles that hinder the employee's ability to relocate to a foreign post.

Fulfilling these purposes generally requires that the U.S. employer provide a competitive level of base pay, allowances to offset extra expenses and higher costs, and, in some cases, premiums or incentives to induce the expatriates to accept the foreign assignment and its accompanying challenges and burdens.

Beyond the basic objectives of attracting qualified individuals to overseas posts and covering extra costs, expatriate compensation programs also meet some of the following objectives:

- promoting equity among expatriates assigned to different countries;
- maintaining equity between expatriates and home-country staff;
- providing a compensation package that is competitive with that provided by other firms in the same industry;

- providing expatriates resources they need to ensure the education of their children is not adversely affected by the overseas assignment; and

- staying in full compliance with the tax, labor, and employment laws in both the home country and the country to which the expatriate is assigned.

### Expatriate compensation components

Compensation programs for expatriates usually consist of three primary components:

- **Base pay and employee benefits.** An employer's primary goal with respect to expatriate base pay and employee benefits is to ensure that expatriates are not financially disadvantaged by accepting a foreign assignment. Thus, most employers align an expatriate's base pay with what the employee receives in his or her home country and try to ensure health, pension, and other benefits are at least equal to what the expatriate had prior to the assignment.

- **Allowances and expense reimbursements.** Employers include allowances in expatriate compensation packages to cover extra expenses and higher costs. Typically, allowances are provided for the following categories of expenses: goods and services; housing and utilities; taxes; educational costs; and moving and relocation expenses. Although practices vary from company to company, allowances usually do not increase an expatriate's buying power over what it would have been had he or she remained at home.

- **Premiums and incentives.** Premiums and incentives are designed to induce employees to accept overseas assignments. Incentive pay is compensation above and beyond any allowances necessary so the expatriate is not financially disadvantaged. Incentives are offered   in recognition that overseas assignments impose the burden of cultural adjustments and may require the individual to endure lower living standards or even dangerous conditions.

## International Employees

Salary and fringe benefits paid to expatriates are to ensure that international professionals do not suffer any material loss due to working abroad.  Companies attempt to maintain equitable purchasing power between domestic and overseas employees.   Total cost to an employer of maintaining a manager abroad is estimated to be between three and six times the cost of a manager in a position at home.

Compensation for employees of global organizations operating in an international environment consists of four components: base salary, indirect monetary compensation (benefits), equalization benefits, and incentives.

### Base salary

Two alternatives exist for determining base salary for an expatriate: (1) adhering to the established policies and procedures of the parent company's country, including formal job evaluation; or (2) following the policies and practices of the country in which the expatriate works. Since many international assignments are for short durations, usually 3 to 5 years, it may be wise to keep base salary aligned with salaries in the home country. Doing so makes the transition back to the home country less complicated since major salary changes do not have to be made.

### Indirect monetary compensation (benefits)

The benefits package for expatriates is generally the same as the one provided in the home country. However, an organization must be aware that specific countries require benefits that may not be offered in the home country. For example, in France employers are required by law to provide every employee with 25 days of vacation. Although an American working for an American company in France is not legally entitled to such a vacation, the organization may want to follow this practice to avoid morale problems with expatriates. Other countries have retirement, disability, and termination that are different from the U.S.

### Equalization benefits

These benefits are intended to keep expatriates in the same financial condition they were in before accepting an overseas assignment and to reduce any negative aspects of living in a foreign country. A limited selection of the benefits available includes the following:

- Housing allowance
- Educational allowance for children
- Foreign service premium
- Assignment completion bonus
- Emergency leave
- Home leave
- Language training
- Domestic staff
- Club membership
- Spousal employment
- Cultural training for family

**TEST TAKING TIP**
Since the GPHR exam was created, several questions show up on the SPHR exam that are particular to international HR. Expect 4-6 global questions. Be aware of the larger global concepts like those covered in this guidebook.

This list only scratches the surface of the equalization benefits that can be offered in terms of financial allowances, social adjustment assistance, and transitional support for the expatriate's family.

### Incentives

Expatriates may receive a variety of incentives ranging from cash bonuses of various kinds, to stock options, and performance-related payments. Crafting an effective international compensation plan requires a careful consideration of the various types of compensation as well as the specifics of the assignment and employee involved.

## Balance Sheet Approach

Many multinational companies have an international compensation policy designed to ensure that employees on international assignments receive total compensation, housing, living standards and other benefits which are comparable to that which they would have if living in their home country. The intent is to keep the employee "whole" or "balanced", regardless of assignment location. The procedure of keeping an employee whole is known as the "balance sheet" approach.

By employing the balance sheet, the assignment costs to an employer can vary significantly, depending upon the location of an assignment. For example, an employee who is transferred from Toronto to Tokyo will be subject to increased housing expenses. To keep the employee whole, the employer would have to reimburse the employee for these additional costs. The assignment costs are magnified by income tax reimbursements.

Tax reimbursement policy is designed to ensure that an employee will not suffer combined taxes on income (host country taxes, social security taxes and home country taxes) in excess of that which would have been paid if the employee were living back in the home country. The most common methods utilized to accomplish this objective are either:

- tax protection, or
- tax equalization.

### Tax protection

Tax protection plans are designed to reimburse an employee to the extent that the employee's combined total income and social security taxes exceed the amount that he/she would have paid if he/she remained in the home country. If combined actual taxes are lower because of the foreign assignment, then the employee realizes a benefit from the foreign assignment, since he/she is entitled to keep the tax benefit.

**TEST TAKING TIP**
Most successful candidates use a 10 week preparation period to get ready for this beast of an exam. They work hard every day during this 10 week stretch.

### Tax equalization

Many US employers have tax equalization policies which attempt to adjust your net take home pay so that the amount you receive overseas is the same as that you would receive if you worked in the US. These policies use formulas which take into account the US tax, US state tax if any, and the foreign tax, with adjustments for the foreign tax credit and foreign earned income exclusion, and sometimes adjust for housing reimbursements and differences in the cost of living between the US and the expatriate's country of residence.

Tax equalization plans are designed to provide an employee with neither a tax benefit nor tax detriment from the foreign assignment. If combined actual taxes are higher because of the foreign assignment, the employer would reimburse the employee for the additional costs incurred.

## International Social Security Agreements (Totalization)

International Social Security agreements, often called "Totalization agreements," have two main purposes. First, they eliminate dual Social Security taxation, the situation that occurs when a worker from one country works in another country and is required to pay Social Security taxes to both countries on the same earnings. Second, the agreements help fill gaps in benefit protection for workers who have divided their careers between the United States and another country.

Without some means of coordinating Social Security coverage, people who work outside their country of origin may find themselves covered under the systems of two countries simultaneously for the same work. When this happens, both countries generally require the employer and employee or self-employed person to pay Social Security taxes.

The aim of all U.S. totalization agreements is to eliminate dual Social Security coverage and taxation while maintaining the coverage of as many workers as possible under the system of the country where they are likely to have the greatest attachment, both while working and after retirement.

## Legal Aspects of International HR

### Workers' rights
Many foreign countries require that U.S. employees residing within their borders be included in their social benefit programs. Areas to check for legal compliance include the following:

### Workers compensation
Many foreign countries have workers' compensation or similar laws to cover employees' work-related injuries and illnesses. Employers should ascertain whether U.S. expatriates are covered under local workers' compensation laws and whether the protection under the local law is at least equal to that provided under U.S. workers' compensation laws. If not, the employer may want to arrange for supplemental disability insurance.

### Health benefits
Countries such as the United Kingdom, Sweden, and Israel provide free medical care to foreigners employed within their boundaries. Some multinational employers may not extend additional benefits to expatriates covered under national health programs, while other employers may provide supplementary health coverage to allow expatriates to opt out of the government system to consult with a private doctor. Multinational employers sometimes provide special insurance to expatriates assigned to countries with substandard medical care to cover medical emergencies and serious conditions for which the expatriates cannot receive adequate care unless they return to the United States or travel to a third country.

### Pensions
U.S. expatriate employees who are assigned to work for a foreign subsidiary of their U.S. employer usually are directly covered under the U.S. employer's qualified plans. However, the plan document must permit the inclusion of the nonresident employees of the foreign subsidiary. If coverage under a U.S. qualified plan is not available, employers frequently provide coverage under a nonqualified plan or arrange for coverage under a host-country pension plan.


**End of SPHR-only section**

# DHR's Fast 20

1. Most frequently cited/fined mistake by employers, in relation to compensation violations, is in classifying jobs as "**salaried exempt**". USDOL's "Wage and Hour" inspectors are hourly paid.

2. Do you include **bonuses** in your **overtime** calculations?... depends! If the "gift" is "discretionary"... no, while "non-discretionary" (formula driven) are a "yes".

3. Hourly workers who are <u>required</u> to stay on a job site for security and safety (maintenance technicians, security guards, outside craft workers, etc.) during lunch periods must be compensated. Part of **Portal-to-Portal Act**.

4. FLSA requires break periods of less than 20 minutes to be paid-time-off.

5. DOL allows the employment of apprentices, messengers, and students at **subminimum wages**... employer must prove an inadequate supply of qualified workers.

6. **Long-term compensation** is anything of value received 12(+) months after earning it.

7. Definition of "**compensation**"... anything the employee perceives to be of value.

8. **FLSA** covers 5 major areas: 1) Exempt status, 2) Overtime, 3) Minimum wage, 4) Child labor, 5) Recordkeeping.

9. Employers continue to move away from entitlement based pay systems and towards at-risk programs. Called "**incentive pay**" or "pay-at-risk."

10. Lower paying companies have a higher **percentage of benefits costs** as a percent of payroll.

11. Workers rank **health insurance, 401-K plans, and dental insurance**, in order of importance.

12. **Paid-time-off** (vacation, holidays, leaves, etc.) usually account for 15-20% of total costs of a benefits program.

13. **MSAs** (Medical Savings Accounts) and **HSAs** (Health Savings Accounts) provide tax-free savings and tax-free payments of medical bills. Similar to a "Section 125" but different.

14. **COBRA** requires us to notify "any qualified beneficiary" of his/her rights to continued health insurance for up to 18 months following a qualifying event (such as a termination)... includes spouses & dependents. Can deny coverage to a terminating employee only for "gross misconduct."

15. **Mental Health Parity** law took effect 1998 and bars businesses from providing higher annual lifetime caps for physical illnesses than for mental disorders.

16. For qualified plans, **ERISA** requires: 1). annual financial reports filed w/IRS (form 5500) 2). Summary Plan Descriptions (SPDs) must be filed w/DOL, 3). annual premium reports must be filed with PBGC for DB plans, 4). financial statements must be audited.

17. **Green circle rates** - wages that are lower than the bottom of the pay grade and **Red circle rates** - wages that are higher than the top of the pay grade.

18. **Compa-ratio** compares actual pay to the mid-point of their range. (ex: 1.1 = 10% higher and .8 = 20% lower than mid-point).

19. **HIPAA** privacy of "Personal Health Information"... employers are forbidden to have PHI knowledge.

20. **Portal-to-Portal Act** requires employees to be paid for travel time that "cuts across their regular work hours."

# Practice Quiz

1. For a waiver under OWBPA to be enforceable, the employer must provide the employee with all of the following EXCEPT:
   A. 21 days to consider signing the waiver
   B. All benefits for which the employee is eligible
   C. 7 days in which to revoke the waiver after signing
   D. A clearly worded document that specifically refers to their rights under ADEA

2. Which Act provides employees with legal rights to their pension plan?
   A. ERISA
   B. PBGC
   C. HIPAA
   D. Walsh-Healy

3. An organization that compensates employees so that the employee is not financially burdened and can maintain a similar standard of living when working in a foreign country is using which type of compensation program?
   A. Gainsharing plans
   B. ESOPs
   C. Balance sheet approach
   D. Knowledge-based pay

4. FMLA allows an employee to take leave to care for a son, daughter, parent, or spouse with a serious health condition. Which of the following is NOT included in FMLA's definition of "parent"?
   A. Biological parent but absent most of life
   B. Person who raised child but not biologically related
   C. Step-parent
   D. Parents-in-law

5. Which compensation system would MOST probably be employed for blue-collar workers?
   A. ESOP
   B. Rabbi trust
   C. Piecework
   D. Profit sharing

6. Jane worked 44 hours in the workweek. She earns $10 per hour and received a good-housekeeping bonus of $44. What are her gross wages for the week?
   A. $500.00
   B. $502.50
   C. $506.00
   D. $520.00

7. An employee at XYZ Corporation voluntarily continued to work at the end of their normal shift to wait on a customer that had a lengthy problem to solve. The FLSA would require this employer to take what action for this non-exempt employee found working "off the clock."
   A. Pay the employee for these hours
   B. No action required by this employer
   C. Pay the employee only if the "volunteered" time was approved
   D. Take disciplinary action against the employee for working unapproved time

8. John's pay is too low per a new salary survey. He receives an increase to establish a pay rate that corresponds to the same or a similar job's relative value in the market. This is BEST described as:
   A. Internal equity adjustment
   B. External equity adjustment
   C. Merit raise
   D. Compa-ratio factor

9. Which agency handles complaints filed under the FMLA?
   A. Department of Justice
   B. OFCCP
   C. Wage & Hour
   D. EEOC

10. Which is NOT considered a "qualifying event" under COBRA regulations for a spouse of a covered employee?
   A. Spouse loses independent/separate group health insurance coverage
   B. Reduction in hours worked of the covered employee
   C. Divorce or legal separation from the covered employee
   D. Covered employee becomes eligible for Medicare

## Answers and Explanations to Practice Quiz:

1. B
OWBPA amended the ADEA prohibiting all employers from age discrimination in employee benefits programs by either providing equal benefits for older and younger workers or by spending an equal amount on benefits for both groups. It also requires waivers to include: 21 days in which to sign, 7 days to reconsider, and provide a clearly worded document that refers to their ADEA rights. It does not mention "benefits," even though this is a given.

2. A
ERISA sets requirements for the provision and administration of employee benefit plans including pension, health care, and profit sharing plans. While the Pension Benefit Guarantee Corporation is a federal corporation that insures the benefits of defined benefit pension plans, it is not an "Act". HIPAA is the Health Insurance Portability and Accountability Act. The Walsh-Healey Public Contracts Act (PCA) requires contractors engaged in the manufacturing or furnishing of materials, supplies, articles, or equipment to the U.S. government or the District of Columbia to pay employees who produce, assemble, handle, or ship goods under contracts exceeding $10,000, the federal minimum wage for all hours worked and time and one half their regular rate of pay for all hours worked over 40 in a workweek. It has nothing to do with retirement benefits.

3. C
The Balance Sheet Approach is an accounting term applied where the goal is to protect or equalize an expatriate's purchasing power while on assignment abroad. Its primary objective is to ensure equity among expatriates and their home or base country peers. Gainsharing is a profit sharing plan. ESOPs are an incentive system designed to give employees stock ownership. Knowledge-based pay is a reward system that motivates employees to learn more skills.

4. D
Parents-in-law are not covered by the Family Medical Leave Act, while biological parents, persons who raised the individual, and step parents are named in the law as having coverage.

5. C
ESOPs, Rabbi Trusts, and Profit Sharing are more commonly found in white-collar compensation plans. Piece-rate pay systems are only applied to blue-collar workers as anyone doing piecework, by definition, is ineligible for salaried exempt status.

6. C
Always multiply the total hours worked times the base pay rate (44hours X $10/hr. - $440). Now add the $44 bonus since it's a non-discretionary bonus ($440 + $44 = $484). Divide the $484 by 44 hours worked = $11/hr to find the regular hourly rate of pay. Now calculate the overtime by multiplying the 4 OT hours X ($11/hr X .5 overtime rate = $5.5) = (4ot X $5.5) = $22. Add the 44 hour gross rate ($484) to the overtime ($22) = $506.

7. A
Employers are required to pay employees for "all hours worked." The employer may discipline the employee, at the employer's discretion, for working "off-the-clock" but the FLSA requires them to be paid. Covered under the "suffer or permit" to work doctrine.

8. B

The key words in the question give the clues that this is an external equity adjustment (versus an internal adjustment where an employee's wages are disproportionate to their colleagues). The "merit raise" option is clearly incorrect as it pertains to only to the employee's pay based on their performance and not to external equity issues. The compa-ratio factor is a misleading option but it relates more to the employee's position within the pay range and its relation to the mid-point of the grade.

9. C

Complaints filed under the FMLA are handled by the Wage and Hour Division, Employment Standards Administration, USDOL.

10. A

Qualifying events are certain events that would cause an individual to lose health coverage thus enabling them to apply for insurance continuation. Qualifying events for spouses include: reduction in hours of the employee, divorce from the employee, and employee's eligibility for Medicare. Should the spouse lose their own insurance coverage after COBRA is in effect, they usually may not sign up for group coverage.

# Chapter 4
# Employee and Labor Relations
# (PHR 20% - SPHR 14%)

Developing, implementing/administering, and evaluating the workplace in order to maintain relationships and working conditions that balance employer/employee needs and rights in support of the organization's goals and objectives.

This chapter covers two basic issues, unions and employee relations. Usually, the number of questions on the HRCI exam is much more heavily represented with union topics. To be successful, the candidate for certification must master and understand basic union provisions and practices. It is more important to be familiar with unions than employee relations.

## Union Overview

A labor union is an organization of workers dedicated to protecting their interests and improving wages, hours and working conditions. Many different types of workers belong to unions: mechanics, teachers, factory workers, actors, police officers, airline pilots, janitors, doctors, writers and so forth.

Over the last three hundred years, trade unions have developed into a number of forms, influenced by differing political and economic regimes. The immediate objectives and activities of trade unions vary, but usually include:

- **Collective bargaining:** In countries where trade unions are able to operate openly and are recognized by employers, they may negotiate with employers over wages and working conditions.

- **Industrial action:** Trade unions may organize strikes or resistance to lockouts in furtherance of particular goals.

> **TEST TAKING TIP**
> Count your answers to see if you have an under-represented option. If so, mark that option on all the answers you have no idea how to answer to give yourself a better probability of guessing correctly.

Proponents often credit trade unions with leading the labor movement in the early 20th century, which generally sought to end child labor practices, improve worker safety, increase wages for both union and non-union workers, raise the entire society's standard of living, reduce the hours in a work week, provide public education for children, and bring a host of other benefits to working-class families.

To form a bargaining unit -- a group who will be represented by a union in dealing with their employer -- a group of workers must be voluntarily recognized by their employer, or a majority of workers in a bargaining unit must vote for representation. In general, it is legal for employers to try to persuade employees not to unionize. However, it is illegal for a company to attempt to prevent employees from unionizing by promises of violence, threats or other coercive action. It is also illegal for unions to use lies or threats of violence to intimidate employees into joining a union.

An employer is required by law to bargain in good faith with a union, although an employer is not required to agree to any particular terms. Once an agreement is reached through negotiations, a collective bargaining agreement (CBA) is signed. A CBA is a negotiated agreement between a labor union and an employer that sets terms of employment for members of that union and provisions for wages, hours, conditions, vacation, sick days, benefits, etc. After a CBA is signed, an employer can't change anything detailed in the agreement without the union representative's approval. The CBA lasts for a set period of time, and the union monitors the employer to make sure the employer abides by the contract. If a union believes an employer has breached the CBA, the union can file a grievance, which may be ultimately resolved through a process known as arbitration.

Union members pay dues to cover the union's costs. Most unions have full-time and salaried staff that helps to manage its operations. The staff is paid by union dues. Some unions also create strikes funds that support workers in the event of a strike. Dues vary but many are around $50 per month or one-hours pay per week.

A union works somewhat like a democracy. Unions hold elections to determine officers who will make decisions and represent the members. A locally based group of workers who have a charter from a national or international union is known as a union local. The union local might be made up of workers from the same company or region. They may also be workers from the same business sector, employed by different companies.

Union members have the benefit of negotiating with their employer as a group. This basic right gives them much more power than if they were to negotiate individually.

## Types of Unions

### Craft unions
Craft unionism refers to an approach to union organizing in the United States and elsewhere that seeks to unify workers in a particular industry along the lines of the particular craft or trade that they work in. It contrasts with industrial unionism, in which all workers in the same industry are organized into the same union, regardless of differences in skill.

Craft unionism is perhaps best exemplified by many of the construction unions that formed the backbone of the old American Federation of Labor (which later merged with the industrial unions of the Congress of Industrial Organizations to form the AFL-CIO). Under this approach, each union is organized according to the craft, or specific work function, of its members. For example, in the building trades, all carpenters belong to the carpenters' union, the plasterers join the plasterers' union, and the painters belong to the painters' union. Each craft union has its own administration, its own policies, its own collective bargaining agreements and its own union halls. The primary goal of craft unionism is the betterment of the members of the particular group and the reservation of job opportunities to members of the union.

## Union Security

A union security agreement is a contractual clause, usually part of a collective bargaining agreement, in which an employer and a trade or labor union agree on the extent to which the union may compel employees to join the union, and/or whether the employer will collect dues, fees, and assessments on behalf of the union. Designed to protect the union's interests, examples may include: exemptions from their coverage, the scope of union membership that can be required, the requirements for entering into and revoking dues checkoff authorizations, and the legal mechanism for rescinding the union's authority to maintain a union security agreement.

Prior to the passage of the Taft-Hartley Act by Congress over President Harry S. Truman's veto in 1947, unions and employers covered by the National Labor Relations Act could lawfully agree to a "closed shop," in which employees at unionized workplaces are required to be members of the union as a condition of employment. Under the law in effect before the Taft-Hartley amendments, an employee who ceased being a member of the union for whatever reason, from failure to pay dues to expulsion from the union as an internal disciplinary punishment, would usually be fired, even if the employee did not violate any of the employer's rules since they had lost union status.

With the passage of the Taft-Hartley Act, the concept of "closed shops" became illegal. The Act, however, permits employers and unions to operate under a "union shop" rule, which requires all new employees to join the union after a minimum period after their hire. Under "union shop" rules, employers are obliged to fire any employees who have avoided paying membership dues necessary to maintain membership in the union; however, the union cannot demand that the employer discharge an employee who has been expelled from membership for any other reason.

A similar arrangement to the "union shop" is the "agency shop," under which employees must pay the equivalent of union dues, but does not require them to formally join the union.

Section 14(b) of the Taft-Hartley Act goes further and authorizes individual states (but not local governments, such as cities or counties) to outlaw the union shop and agency shop for employees working in their jurisdictions. Under the "open shop" rule, an employee cannot be compelled to join or pay the equivalent of dues to a union that may exist at the employer, nor can the employee be fired if they join the union. In other words, the employee has the "right to work," whether as a union member or not, whether they contribute financially to the union or not.

The Federal Government operates under "open shop" rules nationwide, although many of its employees are represented by unions. Conversely, professional sports leagues (regardless of where a team is located) operate under "union shop" rules.

More recent case law limits the permissible uses of mandatory union dues over nonmember objections and sets some guidelines with respect to the procedures unions adopt to deal with these limitations.

### Terms

A closed shop employs only people who are already union members. The compulsory hiring hall is the most extreme example of a closed shop — in this case the employer must recruit directly from the union. Closed Shops are illegal in the US.

A union shop employs non-union workers as well, but sets a time limit within which new employees must join the union.

An agency shop requires non-union workers to pay a fee to the union for its services in negotiating their contract. This is sometimes called the Rand formula.

An open shop does not discriminate based on union membership in employing or keeping workers. Where a union is active, the open shop allows workers to be employed who do not contribute to a union or the collective bargaining process. In the United States, state level Right-To-Work laws mandate the open shop in some states.

Right-to-work laws are statutes enforced in more than twenty U.S. States which prohibit trade unions from making membership or payment of dues or "fees" a condition of employment, either before or after hire.

### Checkoff

Many collective bargaining agreements contain provisions that obligate employees to pay union dues and bind the employer to deduct dues from the wages of those employees who expressly authorize it. Called "checkoff," this is the process whereby the employer, not the union, uses payroll deduction to collect union dues and render this money to the union.

# Union Laws and Acts

## Clayton Antitrust Act (1914)

The Clayton Antitrust Act of 1914 was enacted in the United States to remedy deficiencies in antitrust law created under the Sherman Antitrust Act of 1890, the first Federal law outlawing practices harmful to consumers (monopolies and anti-competitive agreements).  Section 6 of the Act exempts labor unions and agricultural organizations. Therefore, boycotts, peaceful strikes, and peaceful picketing are not regulated by this statute. Injunctions could be used to settle labor disputes only when property damage was threatened.

## Federal Arbitration Act (1925)

The Federal Arbitration Act (FAA) allows for the private resolution of disputes through arbitration. The decision of the arbitrator is usually both compulsory and binding. Typically, arbitrated decisions are ineligible for appeal. The Federal Arbitration Act requires that where the parties have agreed to arbitrate, they must do so in lieu of going to court.

## Railway Labor Act (1926)

This is the Act that first allowed employees to "organize" and to form a union. The Railway Labor Act is the oldest of the Labor Relations Acts; its significance is that it began the trend towards "worker's rights". It was limited to Railway Workers only. Later, Airline workers were added to the coverage of this Act. Workers covered by this Act, are not subject to the National Labor Relations Act.

## Norris-LaGuardia Act (1932)

The Norris-LaGuardia Act, also known as the "Anti-Injunction Act," substantially limits the jurisdiction and authority of the courts of the United States to issue restraining orders and injunctions in cases involving labor disputes.  Norris-LaGuardia also outlawed the practice of forcing new-hires to sign "yellow dog contracts."  A yellow-dog contract is an agreement between an employer and an employee in which the employee agrees, as a condition of employment, not to be a member of a labor union whilst employed.

## National Labor Relations Act (1935)

The National Labor Relations Act (NLRA), also called the Wagner Act, is a comprehensive federal law granting employees of covered employers broad rights to form or join unions and to engage in collective activity.

As originally enacted in 1935, the NLRA covers almost all private-sector employers. In practical terms, these guidelines mean that all but the smallest private-sector employers must comply with the NLRA. Workers protected by the NLRA include almost all employees below the supervisory, managerial, and executive levels. This federal labor law covers not only full-time and part-time workers, but also nonunion employees exercising rights protected by the NLRA.

The NLRA defines a labor organization as any group, agency, committee, panel, or plan in which employees participate, and which is established at least partially for the purpose of dealing with the employer concerning grievances, conflicts, wages, hours, or other conditions of work

The following kinds of groups have been held to be labor organizations:

- Union federations;

- Trade councils that deal directly with employers;

- Independent unions;

- Employee committees established by an employer to represent nonunion employees with regard to employment conditions (NLRB v. Cabot Carbon Co.); and

- Employee delegations through which members acted in unison to achieve mutual goals with respect to working conditions.

The NLRA does not, on the other hand, cover governmental employees, with the exception of employees of the United States Postal Service, a quasi-public entity.

## Labor Management Relations Act (1947)

> **TEST TAKING TIP**
> Pre-check your testing location. We know of several instances where candidates were just a couple of minutes late and were denied the chance to sit for the exam. No money back, either.

The Labor-Management Relations Act (LMRA), often referred to as the Taft-Hartley Act, establishes the rights and obligations of employers, employees, and unions with respect to collective bargaining. The law's provisions: (1) outlawed the Closed Shop; (2) instituted an 80-day cooling-off period for strikes threatening national security; (3) prohibited unions from using union monies for national elections; (4) allowed suits for Breach of Contract against unions; and (5) defined Unfair Labor Practices of unions. Employers or unions that violate employees' or each other's LMRA-protected rights commit an "unfair labor practice." Unfair labor practice charges may be filed by an employer, employees, or a union with the National Labor Relations Board - the government agency created by the LMRA to enforce federal labor laws.

## Labor Management Reporting/Disclosure Act (Landrum-Griffith)

The Labor Management Reporting/Disclosure Act (LMRDA) was enacted primarily to ensure basic standards of democracy and fiscal responsibility in labor organizations representing employees in private industry. The LMRDA establishes:
- A "Bill of Rights" for union members to combat wrongdoing and to limit control of union leadership. Provides for 1) equal rights, 2) freedom of speech and assembly, 3) limits: dues, fees, and assessments, and 4) provides union members the right to sue if not represented fairly;
- Requirements for reporting and disclosure of financial information and administrative practices by labor unions;

- Requirements for reporting and disclosure by employers, labor relations consultants, union officers and employees, and surety companies, when they engage in certain activities;
- Rules for establishing and maintaining trusteeships;
- Standards for conducting fair elections of union officers; and
- Safeguards for protecting union funds and assets.

Union officers, agents, and shop stewards are obligated:

- to hold the union's money and property solely for the benefit of the organization and its members;
- to expend the union's money and property in accordance with its constitution, bylaws, and resolutions;
- to refrain from dealing with the union as an adverse party in any matter connected with their duties;
- to refrain from holding or acquiring any pecuniary or personal interest that conflicts with the union's interests; and to account to the union for any profit they receive in whatever capacity in connection with transactions they conduct or direct on the union's behalf

The Office of Labor-Management Standards (OLMS) of the U.S. Department of Labor administers and enforces most provisions of the Labor-Management Reporting and Disclosure Act of 1959 (LMRDA). The LMRDA primarily promotes union democracy and financial integrity in private sector labor unions through standards for union officer elections and union trusteeships and safeguards for union assets. Additionally, the LMRDA promotes labor union and labor-management transparency through reporting and disclosure requirements for labor unions and their officials, employers, labor relations consultants, and surety companies. OLMS also administers provisions of the Civil Service Reform Act of 1978 and the Foreign Service Act of 1980 relating to standards of conduct for Federal employee unions, which are comparable to LMRDA requirements.

## Civil Service Reform Act (1978)

The Civil Service Reform Act of 1978 (CSRA) guarantees certain privileges to Federal employees who exercise their statutory right to become a member of a union representing Federal employees. The provisions also impose certain responsibilities on officers of these unions to ensure union democracy, financial integrity, and transparency. One provision of the CSRA was the creation of the Federal Labor Relations Authority (FLRA). FLRA oversees the rights of federal employees to form collective bargaining units (unions).

### Federal Labor Relations Act (1978)

The Federal Labor Relations Act of 1978 (FLRA) is a federal law which establishes collective bargaining rights for most employees of the federal government in the United States. The FLRA was adopted after President Jimmy Carter pushed for legislation to regularize federal labor relations.

In passing the act, Congress declared that it wished to encourage collective bargaining between federal employees and their employers. Congress declared that collective bargaining is "in the public interest" because, among other things, it "contributes to the effective conduct of public business" and "facilitates and encourages the amicable settlements of disputes between employees and their employers involving conditions of employment."

With only a few exceptions, it is patterned on the National Labor Relations Act. The exceptions are however, substantial. The most dramatic differences are:

- Non-negotiability of wages
- No union or agency shops
- No strikes

# The Election Process

## Election Campaign

The NLRB has developed specific rules and processes for conducting union elections, including the use of election petitions, the type of election agreement that will govern the showing of interest necessary for an election, the determination of the election's time and place, the length of the election, and the role of election observers.

In addition, the NLRB makes the legal determinations needed before an election can be scheduled. These determinations include the appropriate bargaining unit; who is eligible to vote, and whether a contract or former election serves as a bar to an election. The NLRB also determines whether challenged ballots will be counted and whether the results of an election will be certified or whether the employer or union engaged in sufficient unlawful activity during the pre-election campaign to nullify the results.

Once a union has filed a petition with the National Labor Relations Board (NLRB) seeking a representation election, most employers wage an organized attempt to persuade employees to vote against union representation This attempt is referred to as the "employer's campaign" and typically involves speeches, letters, and small group discussions aimed at convincing employees that a union will bring unwelcome changes into the workplace, such as dues, the possibility of strikes and permanent replacement, job insecurity, and a tense atmosphere.

There is no legal requirement for an employer to conduct a campaign. However, if the employer does, it must comply with the National Labor Relations Act (NLRA) or risk having the NLRB overturn a management election victory and order the company to bargain. Because the stakes are high, time is short, and the legal rules murky, most employers turn to employment attorneys or consultants for guidance. While these experts may deal with the NLRB, write campaign letters, and draft speeches, the employer must make the ultimate decisions, sign the letters, and deliver the speeches.

If the union wins the election and is certified by the National Labor Relations Board, it has the authority to engage in collective bargaining on behalf of the members of the bargaining unit.

## Interference, Restraint and Coercion

Both the employer and union are entitled to campaign during the period preceding the election. However, if either makes threats, offers bribes, or otherwise interferes with employees' free choice, the NLRB can set aside the election results.

Many employers have rules that restrict employees' and outsiders' ability to talk to employees, distribute materials to employees, or ask employees for support or donations for a cause. These policies have come to be known as "no-solicitation" and "no-distribution" rules. The purpose of such rules is to minimize non-work discussions and activities, thereby promoting a productive work atmosphere. Another purpose for some employers is to limit union activity.

However, the National Labor Relations Act (NLRA) guarantees employees the right to organize unions and to engage in concerted activities. In order for those rights to be meaningful, employees must have some right to talk to co-workers about matters of mutual concern regarding wages, hours, and working conditions. As a result, the National Labor Relations Board (NLRB) and federal courts will invalidate work rules that totally prevent employees from discussing unions or distributing union literature at work, absent special circumstances.

In order to avoid liability under the National Labor Relations Act (NLRA), employers must consider whether decisions to hire or promote employees discriminate based on union status or interfere with employees' protected labor rights. Applicants, as well as employees, are protected under the NLRA.

The NLRA applies to nonunion employers as well as those that are unionized. Employees who act together to complain about work terms or conditions are protected as if they are in a union (known as "concerted activity," it takes two or more employees to qualify). An employer that fails to recognize this can commit an unfair labor practice, with or without a union.

To avoid problems when hiring, employers must be careful not to ask questions about the applicant's present or former union status or attitude about unions in general. Job applications should be free of questions that might reflect past or present union membership. The same is true when an employer decides to promote an employee. If the promotee is to become a supervisor, union status can come into play only after the promotion takes effect. Supervisors are not covered by the NLRA, and the employee may be asked to choose between supervisory status and union membership only after the promotion is offered.

**TEST TAKING TIP**
Pace yourself on the exam, you need to average 58 questions per hour to finish within the time limit. One question per minute is about right.

## Excelsior Lists

An Excelsior list is a list filed by the employer within seven days after a union election has been directed by the National Labor Relations Board (NLRB), stating the names and addresses of all eligible bargaining unit employees.

The NLRB has traditionally held that a union engaged in an organizing campaign is entitled to an Excelsior list, but only after it has filed an election petition with the NLRB. Since a petition cannot be filed without a showing of support from 30% of the employees, this rule effectively requires that unions obtain substantial support before they become entitled to a list of employee names and addresses.

## Domination and Unlawful Support of Labor Organization

The keystone of the National Labor Relations Act (NLRA) is that employees should have the right freely to choose their collective bargaining representative. Accordingly, when an employer dominates or interferes with the formation or administration of a labor organization, the employer undermines the very structure of the statutory scheme.

In the early and middle years under the NLRA, which was enacted in 1935, employer violations took the often obvious form of employer-created company unions, and overt favoritism of a particular union. However, this prohibition more often is applied to the various forms of employee involvement efforts (see the section on "Electromation" in this chapter) that employers have created in response to economic pressures from without and workforce concerns from within.

## Achieving Representative Status

The National Labor Relations Act (NLRA) protects the right of covered employees to join unions. Unionization of a workplace under the NLRA can occur in three ways:

- Voluntary recognition of a union by the employer based on union authorization cards signed by a simple majority (50% + 1) of employees,
- Election of a union by a simple majority (50% + 1) of employees voting in an election conducted by the National Labor Relations Board (NLRB), or
- Involuntary recognition ordered by the NLRB to remedy the employer's egregious unfair labor practices that may have cost the union the election.

Of these three methods, elections are the most commonplace.

## Petitioning for an NLRB Election

Once 30% of bargaining unit employees has signed authorization cards, a petition for a representation election can be filed with the NLRB. The union seeking representation status may not have filed another petition, to cover these same employees, within 12 months of the date of the petition. Only one election per year, anniversary date to the next anniversary date, may be held in any bargaining group.

# Employers Role in the Campaign

## Maintaining Nonunion Status

### Reasons
Employers have many reasons for remaining union-free.  Among those include:

- Restrictions on firings
- Strikes
- Company disloyalty
- Criticism of management
- Limits on scope of jobs
- Violence against employees/property
- Boycotts
- Limits open communications
- ULP's and frivolous lawsuits
- De-emphasis on merit and emphasis on seniority

During contract negotiations, established unions may declare a strike in order to pressure an employer to agree to a contract. Established unions are most vulnerable to union busting when they undertake job actions such as a strike. Union busting is a practice that is undertaken by an employer or their agents to prevent employees from joining a labor union, or to disempower, subvert, or destroy unions that already exist.

Employers faced with a strike have a number of options. They may try to negotiate a settlement, outwait the strikers, break the strike, or act in some combination of these options.

## Managerial rights

Leaders (supervisors and managers) are considered agents of the company under the National Labor Relations Act. They are not allowed to break the law regarding employee rights or the violation "counts" against the company. Should agents of the employer break the law, the National Labor Relations Board can throw out that victory and order the company to bargain with the union.

This does not mean employers should be silent about union issues during the campaign period. Employers wishing to remain union-free must communicate to employees why a union is not in their best interests. Leaders are often reluctant to get involved as they are concerned about misspeaking and creating an unfair labor practice charge against the employer.

Supervisors and managers may do the following without violating the NLRA:

- Talk with employees in groups or one-on-one in the workplace, as long as the discussion does not take place in a private management office or other location that could cause an employee to feel threatened;
- Answer claims the union is making;
- Tell employees the supervisor thinks a union is not a good idea, why the supervisor does not like unions or union policies, how unions have hurt particular industries or firms;
- Relate any negative experiences the supervisor may have had with unions.

In addition to obvious acts of discrimination, such as firing union supporters or treating them less favorably, supervisors may not engage in conduct that coerces employees with regard to union activities. A handy acronym for prohibited activity is **"T.I.P.S."** which stands for Threats, Interrogation, Promise, and Surveillance:

## Threats

Any statement that would be interpreted as a threat of retaliation for union activity is unlawful. Examples include:

- "If a union comes in here, you will all be fired."
- "Where do you think you're going to find another job?"
- "Don't expect any favors from me if a union gets in here."
- "Don't count on those guys [referring to known union supporters] being around here much longer."
- "We know who's involved in this union thing"
- "You didn't hear it from me, but the company is absolutely determined that the union isn't getting in here and anybody who supports the union is really going to be sorry."

## Interrogation

Asking employees about their support of the union or their union activities is unlawful interrogation. Examples include:

- "How are you going to vote?"
- "Did you sign a union card?"
- "Who is for the union? Which way is Sally leaning?"
- "So what do you guys want with a union?"
- "What did you do last night?" [when there was a union meeting that evening].

### Promises

Just as an employer may not threaten to retaliate for union support, it cannot promise benefits for not supporting the union. Examples include:

- "Some of you probably turned to the union because you're upset about not having Thanksgiving off. The boss tells me they will take care of this after the election."
- "Once we get this election behind us, if the employees vote the right way, this company will make everything right."
- "You want a raise this year? Better not vote for the union."

### Surveillance

Management may not do anything that indicates employees' union activities are being spied upon. For example, a supervisor could not lawfully park outside of union headquarters to see which employees entered.

## Other Restrictions Imposed by the NLRB

Employers cannot grant or withhold benefits because of the organizing campaign. If someone was due a raise before the campaign started, they get it. If someone wasn't due a raise before the campaign started, and they get it, it would look like that raise was given in order to bribe workers to vote against the union. This same standard applies to any benefit increases or decreases.

Soliciting grievances is unlawful, even if the employer takes no steps to act on them, since asking about work problems suggests an implicit promise that the company will remedy the problem.

The employer may not talk about union issues on company time to groups of employees within 24 hours of the election. The NLRB considers last minute speeches on company time to be coercive. The employer may speak to employees one-on-one but not in groups of two or more.

The employer may not modify or use alterations of official NLRB documents. This includes photocopies of official NLRB documents as well as anything that is created in such a way that an employee might think it's an official NLRB document. For example, the employer may not take a sample ballot and mark an "X" in the "no" box unless that sample ballot is clearly a mock up.

## Sample NLRB Election Campaign Schedule

| | |
|---|---|
| **Week 6:** | **Kick-Off Campaign** |
| Tuesday, March 17 | Operating VP's group speech (appreciation, concern, nothing union can do that we can't) |
| Thursday, March 19 | Post notices regarding election post flyers: "Your Vote Is Secret" |
| Friday, March 20 | Mail letters home from Operating VP: Only XYZ can develop this operation and protect your job. |
| **Week 5:** | **Importance of Direct Communications** |
| Wednesday, March 25 | Chief Operating Officer's speech: We can communicate without the shield of a union middleman. |
| Friday, March 27 | Payroll stuffer: "It's Still All Yours Now" |
| **Week 4:** | **More on Communications** |
| Wednesday, April 1 | Chief Operating Officer's letters home: Now that we have opened communications with this meeting, please do not erect a shield of union/lawyers between us. Flyer with letter. |
| **Week 3:** | **Information** |
| Tuesday, April 7 | Video: "Is a Union a Good Idea for You?" (Intro and follow-up by operating head). Distribute "Do You Understand All The Facts?" Ask employees to complete questionnaire, for their use only [DO NOT COLLECT UNDER ANY CIRCUMSTANCES], before video. Distribute "Here Are The Real Facts" and the "Benefits" handout Poster. |
| Friday, April 10 | Payroll stuffer: "Don't Open Your Wallet to Local XXX in Exchange for Sweet Talk and Empty Promises." |
| **Week 2** | **Negatives of Unions** |
| Wednesday, April 5 | Speech by operating head - antiunion; dues, strikes, violence. |
| Thursday, April 16 | One -on –ones |
| Friday, April 17 | One -on –ones |
| **Final Week** | **Pro –Company** |
| Monday, April 20 | Operating VP's bargaining speech handout; "Union Only Gets The Right To Ask" - Show other union contracts with insurance contributions - Final letters home: build up for 24-hour speech. Three full days before the election employer must post the NLRB's official "Notice of Election." Check now to make sure notice has been received and has not been misplaced. Call NLRB if you need the notice and send a messenger. The notice must be displayed in a place employees will see it, and it must be protected from marking or other damage. If there's not a locking bulletin board large enough for the Notice, arrange to get some clear plastic to put over it. |
| Tuesday, April 21 | One -on –ones |
| Wednesday, April 22 | Handouts: to be decided. Poster: to be decided. One -on –ones. |
| Thursday, April 23 | 24-hour speech 7:30 - 8:45 AM<br>One-on-ones until polls open |
| Friday April 24 | ELECTION: 9:00-Noon - Cafeteria |

## Sample Letter to Employees

As you know by now, you will have a chance to vote next Tuesday to determine whether or not this company will become unionized. I am sending you this last communication so that you will be fully informed when you cast your vote.

Let me first acknowledge that we have not been a perfect employer. We have made mistakes in the past. We have, however, listened to you and sought to make changes in company policy when our mistakes were brought to our attention. This has been possible because the lines of communication between employees and the company have always been open.

Unfortunately, if the union is voted in, this close communication between the company and employees will cease. The union will demand, and will have the right by federal law, to get involved in personnel matters, regardless of how small. Many of the informal means by which we have been able to resolve differences will be prohibited due to the intervention of this outside third party.

> **TEST TAKING TIP**
> Make sure you have a pictured identification card (driver's license) with you on exam day. Also, have your registration papers with you or they won't let you test.

While we have made mistakes, we have also accomplished a great deal together. Our accomplishments include a wage and benefit package comparable to any in this geographic area and in our industry. The following improvements in our wage and benefit package over the last five years are examples of what we have been able to accomplish together:

- Steady wage increases;
- Contributions for health insurance have held steady for last two years;
- Visual plan added;
- Flexible scheduling introduced last year, expanded earlier this year;
- 401(k) plan now includes contributions from the company;
- Tuition reimbursement policy expanded;
- Shift differential added and increased;
- Safety committee established; and
- Improved plant facilities and working; conditions, including installation of lights in parking lot, additional, vending machines, and new carpeting in break areas.

If you have any questions about the election, or anything we have talked to you about during these last few weeks, please talk to your supervisor or any other management official. The decision is yours. Please VOTE NO on April, 22.

Sincerely,
HR Manager

## Frequently Asked Questions (FAQ's) about Unions

Q. What do union dues pay for?
A. According to records that the union is required to file with the federal government, in the past, the union has spent money on the following matters:

- The international union;
- The "general" fund;
- Rent;
- Salaries and fringe benefits for union staff;
- Furniture;
- Public relations;
- Administrative matters;
- Lawyers and accountants;
- Salaries, fringe benefits, and expense accounts for organizers;
- Travel expenses for union personnel to attend meetings and conventions; and
- Miscellaneous organizing expenses.

[Note: Under the Labor-Management Reporting and Disclosure Act of 1959, unions must file annual financial reports with the U.S. Department of Labor's Office of Labor-Management Standards Enforcement in Washington, D.C. These reports, which an employer may obtain by contacting the DOL, include salaries and other payments to union officials. Total dues received and a schedule of disbursements showing how the union spent its income is also included in the report.]

Q. If it wins, can the union get all the things the union has been promising?
A. Employers are not required to give in to any unreasonable demand that management believes is not in the company's best interests. Under federal law, both the employer and union are required to bargain in good faith. That legal obligation does not require either side to agree to any particular proposal or to make any particular concession.

Q. Won't wages go up if the union wins?
A. There is no clear answer whether wages or benefits will increase if the union wins the election. The employer must agree to raise wages and benefits after the collective bargaining process is concluded. Should the union win, they have the right to ask for an increase in wages and benefits. The company can always say no. The union then has the option to accept management's decision or to withhold their services (strike). Workers on strike do not receive any salary or payments from the company. Additionally, they may be replaced by other workers if the basis for the strike was for economic reasons.

Q. Should workers join the union since the union says everyone else is?
A. A typical union ploy is to tell employees that almost everyone has signed an authorization card and only a few more signatures are needed to make it 100 percent. In reality, the union may have only the authorization cards it needed (30% of workers) to file a petition with the National Labor Relations Board and is trying to pressure workers to sign a card or join so they'll feel obligated to vote for the union. It's entirely up to the employee whether they join the union or sign a card. Workers have the right to sign or not to sign an authorization card. And whether they sign a card or not, whether they join the union or not, they have the right under federal law not to vote for the union. The law requires a secret-ballot election. Workers may vote however they wish.

Q. Why should workers bother to vote if they do not want the union to represent them?
A. Each vote is crucial. The election is determined by a majority of those who actually vote, not by a majority of the employees. If only union supporters vote, the union will win, no matter how many employees don't want the union.

Q. What do workers have to do to vote against the union?

A. The National Labor Relations Board will conduct the election on-site at the company. On the day of the election, when workers arrive at the voting area, a neutral official from the National Labor Relations Board will check them in and give them a ballot. Employees will take the ballot into the voting booth the official provides so they can mark the ballot in private. The ballot usually has two squares at the bottom, with writing outside the boxes indicating what each box means. To vote against the union, they will put an "X" in the square marked "NO." To vote for the union, an "X" goes in the square marked "YES." Workers will not make any other mark on the ballot, and will not be allowed to sign their name to protect the confidentiality of the process.

Q. What's the downside of paying union dues in order to get job security?

A. Any promise the union has made about job security is worthless. The company, not the union, provides jobs and pays wages and benefits. What have unions been able to do about the massive loss of members' jobs in other industries during periods of economic downturn? Nothing. The union cannot provide job security if the economy is in recession and customers are not purchasing the company's goods and services. It is common for employers to challenge workers to ask the union to sign a guarantee containing the sometimes empty promises the organizers may have been making during the campaign. Neither side is allowed to misrepresent the facts during an organization campaign.

> **TEST TAKING TIP**
> If two or more of the answer options are the same, they're all wrong.

Q. If the union wins, and a worker has voted against it, will they be at risk of losing their job?

A. No. The union will not know how each person voted. This is a secret-ballot election conducted by the federal government. Under federal law, workers have the right to vote for or against the union. This means that a union cannot legally try to have anyone fired in retaliation for that person's vote against the union.

Q. If the union wins, and workers realize they liked things better without the union, can they just get rid of the union?

A. It's not easy to arrange for the procedure that results in getting rid of a union (decertification), even if everybody agrees they don't want the union. Under federal law, if the union wins, it will represent workers for at least one year. After that, there are only certain precise times (anniversary date of the election) in which members of the rank-and-file can even attempt to get the National Labor Relations Board to schedule an election to vote the union out.

# Unfair Labor Practices (ULPs)

### Procedures for processing charges of unfair labor practices

The National Labor Relations Act (NLRA) establishes an array of rights, obligations, and prohibitions to support the national labor policy favoring collective bargaining. Should the employer violate any of the act's provisions, it is called an "unfair labor practice" (ULP). Any organization or individual who believes the employer has committed an unfair labor practice may file a charge with the National Labor Relations Board (NLRB). Examples of persons who may file charges are individual employees, attorneys, unions, and employers. Taft Hartley extended the use of ULP's to unions who engage in unlawful practices.

The NLRB arm that deals with unfair labor practice charge processing will be one of 12 regional offices. The particular individual who investigates the charge is called the NLRB or board "agent." A board agent may be a field examiner or an NLRB attorney, depending on the circumstances. Whether an employer is the charged party or a charging party, the employer's representative - often someone from human resources - normally will deal directly with the board agent.

An unfair labor practice charge must be filed and served on the person against whom the charge is made no more than six months (180 days) after the alleged unfair labor practice was committed. Computation of the six-month limitation period begins the day after the commission of the alleged unfair labor practice.

In the course of the NLRB investigation, the board agent will interview, and possibly re-interview, representatives of the parties involved. The board agent will also interview other persons, including rank-and-file employees and union members, believed to have knowledge of the charges. If the charging party's evidence indicates that a case can be made for finding a violation, the board agent will interview the agents of both sides and reduce their statements to writing.

> Example: If the union established its majority status by authorization cards (as opposed to an NLRB election), the NLRB must go to great lengths in refusal to bargain cases to authenticate the authorization cards. The agent would contact individual card signers and subpoena, if necessary, the employer's payroll lists to verify the union's majority status.

If the NLRB's investigation does not reveal a violation, or if the evidence is insufficient to substantiate an unfair labor practice, the regional director will recommend that the charging party withdraw the charge. Likewise, a charging party on its own initiative may request withdrawal of a charge. If the charging party refuses to withdraw an unfair labor practice charge after the regional director has recommended withdrawal, the regional director will dismiss the charge.

If the NLRB's investigation supports the ULP, the regional director will issue a formal complaint based on the charge. The complaint formally notifies the charged party of the claims that are to be judged at the hearing. In framing the complaint, the NLRB is not narrowly confined to the specific matter alleged in the underlying charge. Rather, it may include additional matters related to the events complained of in the charge. This could even include events occurring after the charge was filed.

**TEST TAKING TIP**
Look for the odd answer option that isn't similar to the other three. Frequently it's the right option.

A person against whom an unfair labor practice complaint is issued may file an answer to the original or amended complaint within 14 days from the service of the complaint. The answer is very important in further framing the issues to be litigated. If the respondent does not specifically deny, explain, or state that it lacks knowledge about any specific allegation in the complaint, the NLRB will consider the allegation to be admitted. In addition to addressing the allegations of the complaint, the respondent must include a statement of its defenses in its answer.

The NLRB encourages compromise and settlement of unfair labor practice cases. The Administrative Law Judge (ALJ) assigned to hear the case will provide every opportunity for the parties to reach a mutually satisfactory resolution of the issues. Under normal circumstances, neither the ALJ nor the NLRB may direct a settlement.

The NLRB recognizes two kinds of settlements: formal and informal. Respondents will tend to prefer an informal settlement, and the NLRB will tend to prefer a formal settlement, especially when the General Counsel already has issued a complaint or if there is a history of unfair labor practices suggesting a likelihood of recurrence. Nevertheless, the NLRB's practice is not to sacrifice a remedy for the sake of procuring a formal instead of an informal settlement agreement.

## Employee discrimination to discourage union membership

Basing any adverse personnel decision, including discharge, on union activity violates the National Labor Relations Act (NLRA). Additionally, threats to demote, transfer, or discharge an employee because of union affiliation or protected concerted activity are unlawful.

Both union and nonunion employers may face unfair labor practice charges before the National Labor Relations Board (NLRB) when an employee or union claims that a discharge decision was based on union status or interfered with employees' protected labor rights. If the NLRB finds an employee was discharged because of protected concerted activity or union activity, the employer will probably be required to reinstate the employee and provide back pay from the date of the discharge.

**TEST TAKING TIP**
Studying hard won't guarantee that you'll know all the right answers but it will help you rule out answers that you know are wrong.

## Double-breasted operations

An employer may not divert work from a unionized portion of its facility to a non-unionized part of its facility in order to avoid bargaining with a union. Moving work in a "double-breasted" operation is unlawful discrimination. An employer may not relocate to avoid a union. For example, an employer violated the law when it closed a facility and opened another but refused to transfer unit employees where the company president had stated in a meeting that he did not want a union at the new facility.

## Retaliation

The NLRA prohibits retaliation against and differential treatment of workers who engage (or refuses to engage) in labor activities. It also grants the same protection to employees who file charges with the NLRB or otherwise participate in NLRB proceedings.

Most charges of discriminatory treatment involve an employee who claims some adverse employment action (termination, demotion, transfer, etc.) occurred shortly after management observed the employee taking part in union activity. Whether a cause-effect relationship exists between these two events is a factual question for the NLRB to decide. If the employer can prove legitimate business-related reasons for its action, the NLRB will likely reject the employee's claims of retaliatory discrimination. But if the NLRB is convinced management acted because the employee engaged in protected activity, the board will order the company to restore the employee to his or her previous position and may institute other remedies as well.

While charges of retaliation for involvement with the NLRB are less common, the board takes these charges seriously. The NLRB zealously protects its own powers. Any adverse action taken because an employee visits an NLRB office, telephones the board, or submits a statement to the NLRB will be found to be discrimination.

## Remedies

The NLRB has wide latitude in providing remedies for wronged parties. This includes but is not limited to: reinstatement, reimbursement, attorney fees, back pay, cease and desist orders, mandatory enforcement of contractual obligations, monetary awards, order to compulsory bargain (return to the table), etc. In effect, the NLRB has far-reaching powers. It enjoys almost total control. The court system is reluctant and in some cases powerless to overturn a NLRB decision.

## Union restraint or coercion

Unions, like employers, may not restrain or coerce employees in the exercise of the rights guaranteed them by the NLRA. If coercion is a foreseeable consequence of the union's conduct, a union my commit an unfair labor practice regardless of whether the union intended to restrain or coerce employees, and regardless of whether the union succeeded in its planned purpose.

In addition to regulating the parties' rights, obligations, and restrictions in connection with union security arrangements, the NLRA also prohibits union restraint and coercion with respect to employees' right to self-organization. Such unlawful coercion might include violence or threats of violence, economic coercion, excessive or discriminatory initiation fees, or coercive union discipline. If employees use violence or coercion during a strike, they lose their protection under the NLRA. An employer has the right to terminate them or refuse reinstatement. This applies in the case of unfair labor practice strikers as well as economic strikers.

Union violence against employees is an unfair labor practice if the union's conduct is aimed at the employees' exercise of rights protected by the NLRA.

## Inducing unlawful discrimination by employer

It is unlawful for a union to threaten to strike in order to force an employer to commit an unlawful act. For example, a union violated the NLRA by threatening to strike to force an employer to include a discriminatory hiring hall clause in a bargaining agreement.

**TEST TAKING TIP**
After you choose an answer option, read the entire question and answer option again in one continuous stream to see if it flows properly for you and sounds logical. If so, move on to the next question.

The Labor Management Relations Act (Taft Hartley) lists actions that, if committed by a labor organization, constitute unfair labor practices. This includes: causing or attempting to cause an employer to discriminate against an employee concerning a term or condition of employment to encourage or discourage union membership.

## Excessive or discriminatory membership fees

Unions have the right to charge membership initiation fees, but they may not charge excessive or discriminatory fees. In determining whether a fee is excessive or discriminatory, the NLRB considers, among other things, the fee practices and customs of other labor organizations in the industry and the wages paid to the affected employees.

For example, a $250 initiation fee was excessive where a similar local charged only $75. A $500 fee was excessive where the relevant starting salary was about $90 a week.

Fees in amounts calculated to discourage new, part-time, temporary, or casual employees from joining the union also are unlawfully discriminatory. A union may charge different initiation fees for different classes of persons, but the classifications must be reasonable. Different fees were unlawfully discriminatory where: a union charged higher initiation fees for long-term employees than for new employees, because that distinction infringed on employees' right to refrain from joining a union.

## Duty to successor employers or unions: buyouts, mergers, or bankruptcy

A successor employer's refusal to retain the employees of its predecessor is an unfair labor practice if the successor is motivated by antiunion considerations. A successor employer is under no duty to hire its predecessor's employees if it is motivated by genuine business reasons. For example, a successor lawfully refused to hire its predecessor's employees when the hiring decision was based on poor performance and inefficiency.

Successor employers are guilty of unfair labor practices if they are required to bargain with a union and discharge employees because of their union activity. The test of whether an employer has to bargain with the union is whether the employer made it "perfectly clear" that it would hire its predecessor's employees. An employer may lose its right to set terms of hiring if it misleads employees into thinking it will hire all employees, but really has no intention of it. For example if a successor's refusal to rehire its predecessor's employees is really a plan to defeat the union's status as bargaining representative, the successor will be violating the National Labor Relations Act.

---

**EXAMPLE**

A successor employer blacklisted bargaining unit employees by failing to inform employees that it was hiring. The employer sought applications through newspaper ads that concealed its identity. Of 21 employees hired for the new employer's workforce, none were from the former bargaining unit. As a result, the NLRB determined the predecessor's employees specifically were not hired because of their union status.

---

# The Bargaining Process (SPHR-only section)

## Duty of Fair Representation

When a union is certified by the NLRB, it becomes the exclusive representative of all bargaining unit employees, taking on a corresponding duty to represent all bargaining unit employees fairly. This duty applies in contract negotiations as well as in enforcing a contract through the grievance procedure. A union breaches its so-called "duty of fair representation" when its conduct toward a unit member is arbitrary, discriminatory, or in bad faith.

In particular, with respect to grievance processing, a union must represent all members of the bargaining unit fairly, without hostility or discrimination, and without regard to whether the grievant is a union member. The union's duty of fair representation is owed to bargaining unit employees, not to the employer.

## Collective Bargaining

### Bargaining issues and concepts

Collective bargaining is the process whereby workers organize collectively and bargain with employers regarding the workplace. In various national labor and employment law contexts, collective bargaining takes on a more specific legal meaning. In a broad sense, however, it is the coming together of workers to negotiate the terms and conditions of their employment.

A Collective bargaining agreement is a labor contract between an employer and one or more unions. Collective bargaining consists of the process of negotiation between representatives of a union and employers in respect to the employment of employees, such as wages, hours of work, working conditions and grievance-procedures, and about the rights and responsibilities of trade unions. The parties often refer to the result of the negotiation as a Collective Bargaining Agreement (CBA).

The Labor Management Relations Act (LMRA) requires an employer to bargain collectively with the union designated as the bargaining representative for a unit of the employer's workers. Mandatory subjects of bargaining include rates or pay, wages, hours of employment, or other conditions of employment. Courts have ruled that pension, retirement, and health and welfare plans constitute other conditions of employment and are subject to mandatory bargaining. "Permissive bargaining subjects" are issues that may be raised in negotiations, but which neither party is required to discuss. "Illegal" subjects of bargaining are subjects that conflict with federal or state law and cannot be negotiated or included in an agreement.

The National Labor Relations Act (NLRA) requires an employer to recognize and bargain collectively with the union designated as the bargaining representative for a unit of the employer's workers. A unionized employer must:

- Meet with the union and negotiate in good faith over the terms of an initial contract,

- Sign and comply with a labor agreement whose terms the employer has agreed to,

- Notify the union before the labor agreement terminates if the employer seeks changes and negotiate over the terms of successive renewal contracts,

- Notify the union and bargain over operational changes that affect mandatory subjects of bargaining,

- Deal with the union on contractual grievances and issues that arise concerning the administration of the labor agreement, and

- Disclose information the union requests that is relevant to the negotiation or to the administration of the collective bargaining agreement.

## Negotiation process

In typical collective bargaining sessions, the management and union negotiating teams sit at a conference table facing each other, with their respective spokespersons at the center. At the first meeting, the spokespersons introduce themselves and each member of their bargaining team. Each spokesperson might also offer a preamble couched in terms of the importance of the collective bargaining process and commitment to reaching agreement but which actually serves to introduce arguments in support of the party's bargaining position.

After this introductory phase is over, the party requesting negotiation generally presents its proposals. A union often mails its initial proposals to management with its letter demanding bargaining. The union then may insist that management respond to its proposals at the first meeting. A more effective strategy for management is usually to state that it is not going to respond until the union presents its proposals verbally. As the union reads each of its proposals, management's team can get vital information about which proposals the union considers most serious from the demeanor and statements of the union team's spokesperson and members.

After the union has explained its proposals, management responds by presenting proposals of its own, counterproposals to the union's proposals, questions about the union's proposals, or arguments about why it will not accede to the union's proposal. Of course; management may also accept one or more of the union's proposals. The union then modifies, withdraws, or holds firm on its various proposals and responds to management's proposals, questions, and arguments, putting forth its own questions and arguments.

This process, which can be lengthy and cumbersome, continues until the parties reach agreement, the employees decertify the union, the union seeks legal redress through the National Labor Relations Board, or the union, in extremely rare situations, disavows interest in representing the unit. Depending on the formality of the negotiations and the number and complexity of issues involved, several sessions may be required before each side has presented its proposals.

Once the parties begin responding to each other's proposals and counterproposals, there are frequent breaks in order for each team to confer privately. A typical meeting might begin with one side presenting its current position on some or all of the open proposals followed by a break for the other side to confer. The session reconvenes with the other side presenting its position or counterproposal, followed by a break for the side which spoke first to confer.

This process continues until either an impasse occurs or an agreement is reached. Once the agreement is reached, the new CBA is put into writing and presented to the rank-and-file union members for a vote of ratification. Refusing to put an agreement into writing is a ULP. Once the CBA is ratified, it is enacted and will serve as the primary document governing the employment relationship for the period of time set forth in the document.

### Good faith Requirements

Employers and unions are required to bargain in "good faith." This is a compulsory duty to approach negotiations with a sincere resolve to reach a collective bargaining agreement, to be represented by properly authorized representatives who are prepared to discuss and negotiate on any condition of employment, to meet at reasonable times and places as frequently as may be necessary, and to avoid unnecessary delays.

The good-faith requirement does not require either party to acquiesce to the other's proposals or make any concessions. However, an employer may not implement changes to mandatory terms or conditions of employment until it has reached an agreement with the union or has negotiated in good faith to a genuine impasse. The NLRB can compel either party to bargain in "good faith." They can impose fines, penalties, etc. if they deem it necessary.

### Mandatory bargaining issues

Although the parties need not bargain over every conceivable topic, they must bargain in good faith over mandatory subjects of bargaining, which include wages, hours, and other "terms and conditions of employment." Because these mandatory subjects are very broad, courts over the years have attempted to set standards for determining whether a specific bargaining topic is mandatory. Generally, terms and conditions of employment encompass only issues that "settle an aspect of the relationship between the employer and the employees."

Some decisions, such as advertising and product selection, bear such an indirect relationship to and have such a minimal effect on the employment relationship that they are almost certainly "permissive" subjects of bargaining. Other decisions, such as those regarding hiring, layoffs, and plant rules, are so directly relevant to the employment relationship that they are almost certainly "mandatory" subjects of bargaining.

### Mutual gains bargaining (AKA – principled negotiation)

Mutual gains bargaining (MGB) is an approach to collective bargaining intended to reach *win-win* outcomes for the negotiating parties.

Instead of the traditional adversarial (*win-lose*) approach (aka positional bargaining), the mutual gains approach is quite similar to *Principled Negotiation*, where the goal is to reach a sustainable and lasting agreement that both parties, or all parties in a multi-party negotiation, can live with and support.

### Integrative bargaining

Integrative bargaining (also called "interest-based bargaining" or "win-win bargaining") is a negotiation strategy in which parties collaborate to find a "win-win" solution to their dispute. This strategy focuses on developing mutually beneficial agreements based on the interests of the disputants. The potential for integration only exists when there are multiple issues involved in the negotiation. This is because the parties must be able to make trade-offs across issues in order for both sides to be satisfied with the outcome.

Integrative bargaining is important because it usually produces more satisfactory outcomes for the parties involved than does positional bargaining. Positional bargaining is based on fixed, opposing viewpoints (positions) and tends to result in compromise or no agreement at all. Oftentimes, compromises do not efficiently satisfy the true interests of the disputants. Instead, compromises simply split the difference between the two positions, giving each side half of what they want.

There are often many interests behind any one position. If parties focus on identifying those interests, they will increase their ability to develop win-win solutions. The classic example of interest-based bargaining and creating joint value is that of a dispute between two little girls over an orange. Both girls take the position that they want the whole orange. Their mother serves as the moderator of the dispute and based on their positions, cuts the orange in half and gives each girl one half. This outcome represents a compromise. However, if the mother had asked each of the girls why she wanted the orange -- what her interests were -- there could have been a different, win-win outcome. This is because one girl wanted to eat the meat of the orange, but the other just wanted the peel to use in baking some cookies. If their mother had known their interests, they could have both gotten all of what they wanted, rather than just half.

The first step in integrative bargaining is identifying each side's interests. This will take some work by the negotiating parties, as interests are often less tangible than positions and are often not publicly revealed.

### Distributive bargaining

Distributive bargaining, also called "claiming value," "zero-sum," or "win-lose" bargaining, is a competitive negotiation strategy commonly employed in negotiating collective bargaining agreements (CBAs). When adopting this approach to negotiating a CBA, the parties assume that there are not enough resources to go around and there will be winners and losers at the end of the negotiating process.

Distributive bargaining is important because there are some disputes that cannot be solved in any other way. The stakes are high and are zero-sum gain. Such conflicts can be very resistant to resolution. For example, if the manpower budget in an organization must be cut by 30 percent, and union member jobs are at stake, a decision about whether union or non-union jobs are to be eliminated is extremely critical to the union.

Even in cooperative negotiations, distributive bargaining will come into play. Distributive bargaining and integrative bargaining are not mutually exclusive negotiation strategies. Integrative bargaining is a good way to make the pie (joint value) as large as it can possibly be, but ultimately the parties must distribute the value that was created. If they are able to expand the pie enough, distribution is easy. If there is still not enough to give each side what it wants, however, distributive negotiation will be more difficult.

The strategic role of distributive negotiation hinges on what each party defines as its minimally acceptable outcome. The side that can identify its opposition's goals first, has a tactical advantage in the remainder of the negotiations. Each side is trying to negotiate an agreement that provides them with a result which most closely resembles their pre-negotiation goals.

Information is the key to gaining a strategic advantage in a distributive negotiation. Each side must carefully guard its information and position while trying to gain an upper hand over the opposition. To a large extent, each sides bargaining power depends on how clear they are about their goals, alternatives, and minimally acceptable values and how much they know about their opponents'. Once each side has determined the others' position, each will be in a stronger position to determine when to concede, hold firm, take advantage, or walk away.

## Notice requirements

In a unionized employment setting, a union is required to give the employer 60 days' notice of a strike if the union seeks to modify or terminate an existing bargaining agreement. Under the NLRA, employees cannot strike or be locked out until 60 days after this notice is given or the expiration of the contract, whichever is later. This notice requirement does not apply if the employees strike over unfair labor practices.

---

**EXAMPLE**

If notice to strike is given more than 60 days before a valid bargaining agreement expires, employees cannot lawfully strike until the contract actually expires. If the notice is given less than 60 days before the contract expires, then employees have to wait beyond the contract expiration date to strike.

---

The federal Worker Readjustment and Retraining Notification (WARN) Act requires employers to give unions advance notice and follow other specific procedures when conducting plant closings and mass layoffs.

**End SPHR-only section**

# After the Contract is Signed

## Dispute Resolution

The legal and practical aspects of grievance handling are influenced by:
- The intermingling of explicit NLRA provisions,
- Interpretations of the law by the National Labor Relations Board (NLRB) and the courts,
- The governing of the collective bargaining agreement, and
- The parties' past practices.

There are various remedies and processes for settling disputes between the employer and the union, the employer and employees, or employees and the union. Outlined below are some of the common methods of resolution.

National labor policy favors private settlement of labor disputes through such means as contractual grievance and arbitration procedures. When private dispute resolution fails, however, agency and court proceedings support the enforcement of rights established under the National Labor Relations Act (NLRA) and in collective bargaining agreements. A party may seek vindication of rights protected by the NLRA in unfair labor practice proceedings before the National Labor Relations Board (NLRB). If necessary, a party can then seek enforcement or review of the NLRB's order in the federal circuit courts of appeal. Ultimately, a party can appeal to the U.S. Supreme Court for review.

A party may seek enforcement of rights guaranteed by a labor agreement in a federal or state court suit governed by federal law. The Labor-Management Relations Act (LMRA) allows an employer, union, or employee to file a lawsuit seeking enforcement of rights guaranteed by a labor agreement in federal court.

For example, parties are permitted to sue under the LMRA to enforce the arbitration provision of a collective bargaining agreement. An employer can sue a union for breach of a contractual no-strike provision. An employee can file a suit against both an employer and a union claiming the employer breached the employee's rights under a labor agreement and the union failed to adequately represent the employee's interests.

Because national labor policy favors private settlement of labor disputes, a party must usually exhaust contractual remedies before filing suit.

## Grievance processes and procedures

In the labor relations area, "grievance" is used in two different contexts:

> **TEST TAKING TIP**
> Concentrate solely on the test. Don't let yourself get distracted. Focus, focus, focus.

1. The National Labor Relations Act (NLRA) protects the right of unionized and non-unionized employees to present work-related complaints to their employer on behalf of a group of employees and to be free of any employer discipline for so doing. If the workplace is unionized, the employer must involve the union in any grievance meeting with an employee and may not settle a grievance in a manner that conflicts with an existing collective bargaining agreement.

2. Most collective bargaining agreements contain formal grievance procedures that expand the right to present grievances. Contractual grievance procedures typically state, step-by-step, how the parties are to handle grievances. Labor contracts also usually provide the option of initiating a third-party dispute resolution procedure such as mediation or arbitration if the patties are unable to resolve a grievance by its final step.

With grievances under labor agreements, the union must fairly represent all bargaining unit members in grievance-related matters. Employees also have the right to union representation during an investigatory interview that they believe might lead to discipline. Known as Weingarten Rights, a bargaining unit employee being examined in an investigation (an investigatory examination or interview) is entitled to union representation if: the examination is conducted by a representative of the organization, the employee reasonably believes that the examination may result in disciplinary action, and the employees ask for representation. A performance evaluation is not a Weingarten exam.

## Sample Formal Steps grievance procedure

In the event of any dispute concerning the meaning or application of any provision of the Collective Bargaining Agreement (CBA), there shall be no suspension of work, but the controversy shall be treated as a grievance and shall be settled, if possible, by the employees and the Company in the following manner:

Step 1.　The employee or employees concerned, represented by the shop steward, shall endeavor to adjust the matter with their supervisor.

Step 2.　If a satisfactory adjustment is not reached at Step 1, the matter shall be presented to the Plant Superintendent in writing, signed by the employee and union business agent.

Step 3.　If a satisfactory adjustment is not reached at Step 2, the matter shall be taken up by the International Representative of the Union together with the Plant Human Resource Manager. Such meetings are to be held subject to request by either party at any reasonable time.

Step 4.    If a satisfactory adjustment is not reached at Step 3, the matter shall be referred to binding arbitration by an independent arbitrator. The results of the arbitrated decision are not subject to review or revision.

Grievances with respect to transfers, promotions, demotions, discipline, layoffs, or discharges shall be presented to the company in writing within five (5) days from the date of the action. If such notice in writing is not given the Company within five (5) working days of the occurrence, then it shall be deemed waived and abandoned and shall not thereafter form the basis of a grievance between the parties.

# Decertification

In some situations, the employees choose to undo the certification process and therefore decertify the union as their lawful bargaining agent. The reasons for this may include: they feel misled by the undelivered promises during the campaign, they want their own voice back to represent themselves, they feel repressed by the rules of the international union, they feel they may get a better deal as non-union employees, etc.

Employees, rather than the employer, must play the leading role in decertification. A decertification effort will be set aside by the NLRB if instigated by the employer. Nonetheless, the employer may respond to employee's questions about decertification and render what the NLRB terms "ministerial" assistance. If employees file a valid decertification petition with the NLRB, the employer can present managements views on why decertification is in the employee's best interests. However, the employer is mainly prohibited from extensive involvement in a decertification election. Instead, this process must be led and directed by members of the bargaining unit.

The petition for decertification must be signed by at least 30% of the members of the bargaining unit. After a petition is filed, the employer's decertification campaign is governed by the same rules as an initial campaign opposing the union's election. Certain strategies, themes, and campaign media may also be borrowed from the initial campaign.

Employers need to keep the following three matters in mind regarding decertification:

1.  Only an employee, a group of employees, or a representative of the employees can file a petition for a decertification election. The employer can never file a decertification petition, begin the decertification movement, plant the idea of decertification, solicit employee signatures for the petition, or lend more than minimal support and approval to the petition.

2.  Supervisors are agents of the employer under the NLRA. Supervisors must be trained to ensure they do not engage in coercive practices that could result in a successful decertification victory being overturned.

3.  However, the NLRB's rules regarding the times in which a decertification petition may be filed are inflexible and confusing. Often, employee representatives seeking decertification have a difficult time in executing the requirements of the standard.

# Labor Unrest

## Strikes and Secondary Boycotts

Strikes and boycotts are forms of union pressure designed to force employers to take some kind of action that is considered favorable to the union.

Primary activity, involving a direct dispute between employees and their employer, is generally protected by the National Labor Relations Act (NLRA). Secondary activity, in which workers pressure an employer that is not directly involved in a dispute, is generally unlawful.

There are many different kinds of strikes. An important distinction exists between economic strikes and unfair labor practice strikes. If a strike is over purely economic issues, terms and conditions of employment, then it is considered an economic strike. This means an employer has the right to hire permanent replacements for the strikers and does not have to reinstate the strikers after the strike is over, unless vacancies occur. If the strike is over unfair labor practices, however, an employer may not permanently replace employees.

Some strikes are unlawful. For example, a union may not lawfully strike to force an employer to commit an unfair labor practice. Strike violence and other misconduct will also render a strike illegal. Employers have the right to fire striking employees if the strike is illegal. Otherwise, the employer is only allowed to "replace" workers who are striking for economic reasons.

Picketing, handbilling, and boycotts are other labor actions employers may face. There are different kinds of picketing. Picketing for recognition, informational picketing, and "area standards" picketing are some examples. Picketing by non-employee organizers may be banned from private property as long as the organizers have a reasonable alternative means of getting their message across.

A union may lawfully ask consumers to boycott products of an employer (consumer boycott) if the union has a dispute with that company.

Secondary boycotts, however, are unlawful. A union that has a dispute with one employer may not boycott a neutral company in order to pressure the first company. A secondary boycott occurs when a union encourages its members to boycott products or services produced by a neutral firm (called the secondary employer) in order to force that firm to stop doing business with the firm with which the union has a labor dispute (called the primary employer). Secondary boycotts are unlawful under the NLRA.

**TEST TAKING TIP**
Feelings of insecurity are normal while taking the test. Don't let yourself focus on negative thinking. It's counter-productive.

Specifically, the NLRA prohibits unions from engaging in strikes or refusing to handle, sell, or otherwise deal in goods when the union's objective is to force a person to stop doing business with another person. For example, a union that directed its employees to refuse to handle merchandise from printing plants that hired nonunion workers violated the National Labor Relations Act. This action is known as "hot cargo" and is illegal.

# Strike Preparation

## Employer preparation

The most common reason for workers to strike is to exert pressure on the employer during the collective bargaining process. Often, employers anticipate this tactic and engage in pre-strike preparations. The employer must consider whether it will close during a work stoppage, notify vendors, clients, and others who will be affected, build up an excess supply of inventory during the pre-strike period, or if the company intends to continue operations should a strike occur.

The HR department is often tasked with creating a response plan should the strike become a reality. Usually, pre-strike preparations for HR include:

- Prepare a strike memorandum for distribution to all supervisory and managerial employees that detail their specific responsibilities during the strike.

- Educate supervisory and security personnel as to their responsibilities and duties for maintaining the security of the physical plant and the safety of everyone involved. All personnel should be coached to avoid unnecessary provocation. Supervisors should also receive training to acquaint them with the various laws that apply to their conduct during a strike.

- Be prepared for inspections by health departments, fire departments, the Occupational Safety and Health Administration, or other government regulatory agencies.

- Review comprehensive insurance policies and, if necessary, obtain insurance for all risks, including rioting.

- Prepare plans and maps of the facility. This is important for establishing checkpoints or command posts and protecting the entrances and exits of the facility.

- Photograph entrances to the facility before, during, and after the picketing. However, consult with labor counsel regarding procedures to avoid charges of unlawful spying on protected activities.

- Contact the local police and explain the strike situation to them so they can assist if necessary.

- Contact the telephone company to arrange for extra services or to take preventive measures if taps are anticipated.

- Contact all suppliers and other persons who will have to cross the picket line. Establish alternative methods of obtaining supplies, such as neutral drops or direct pickups.

- Locate warehousing facilities away from the plant to store in-transit material. Ensure that the facilities are staffed, and notify vendors of their locations.

- To monitor events on the picket line, arrange for cameras, videotape equipment, and long-distance microphones. Again, consult with labor counsel regarding procedures to avoid charges of unlawful spying on protected activities.

- Establish a communication center and command post. This can be an office with nothing more than a telephone. This post should be able to accommodate those people involved in the decision-making process, offer access to necessary files and secretarial help, and be accessible in case of any emergency.

- Prepare a list of the home and office telephone numbers of all supervisors and managerial employees, emergency numbers for police, fire, ambulance, and attorneys, and numbers of any other individuals whose services may be required. The list should be distributed to key people in the chain of command and should be on file in the communication center.

- Instruct all supervisors and managers on procedures for investigating and gathering evidence.

- If a long strike is expected, consider paying all moneys owed to employees on the first day of the strike. This may shorten the strike by exhausting the employee's financial resources more quickly. If the employees have all moneys owed to them at the inception of the strike, they are likely to need more money sooner than if they receive a paycheck a week or two into the strike.

- Determine what information is to be communicated to clients. Decide whether to notify all clients or to respond to inquiries only. A standard response to all clients should be prepared. All inquiries by clients should be handled by the press officer immediately and in a reassuring fashion. If a mailing is appropriate, it should be carefully drafted so as merely to report the company's position. Be careful not to alarm clients or negotiate with the union in public.

- Post "No Trespassing" signs at points that warrant them.

- Secure the facility. Supervisors should be alert for strangers on the property. Access through all doors and entrances should be controlled. Consider hiring guards to protect any striker replacements coming to and from work and to watch and control the picketers.

- Prepare alternative shift assignments if workers experience difficulty in crossing the picket line. This permits workers to be at the facility prior to the appearance of the morning picketers. If this fails, arrange to transport workers from a convenient central point.

- Arrange for personnel inside the facility to stay there overnight, if the occasion warrants such action. Make arrangements for meals to be available inside the facility.

- Avoid all contact with strikers. Ignoring them indicates that the company is unaffected by their strike. Furthermore, this increases confusion among the striker's ranks because they cannot learn what arrangements have been made to replace them.

- Direct all inquiries to the designated press officer. A formal position regarding press releases and interviews should be determined in advance. Any statement to the press should be through designated spokespersons. Statements should be designed to build confidence in the company's position and to allay fears in the community.

- Ask labor counsel if gathering the following evidence will be useful in legal proceedings:
  - Names of picketers.
  - Time, date, and location of picket lines.
  - All facts concerning any incidents of violence, threats, mass picketing, or blocking of ingress and egress.
  - Number of picketers.
  - Wording on every sign carried by picketers.
  - Demeanor and manner of picketers.
  - Words spoken by picketers.
  - Conversations between picketers and other persons.
  - Description of picketers' cars and license plate numbers, as well as the automobiles and license plate numbers of persons who are turned away from the facility.
  - Complete and accurate description of any property damage.
  - Police response to requests for assistance.

## Injunctions

The federal Norris-LaGuardia Act strictly limits the circumstances under which courts may grant injunctions in cases involving labor disputes. The statute forbids courts to enjoin certain acts, and imposes procedural requirements on the issuance of any injunction in a labor dispute. Moreover, a court may grant an injunction only after hearing the testimony of witnesses in open court, both in support and opposition, with opportunity for cross-examination.

Temporary injunctions in unfair labor practice cases are expressly exempt from the requirements of the Norris-LaGuardia Act. Rather, to limit the potential harm resulting from an unfair labor practice, the NLRA requires the NLRB to seek a temporary injunction against certain unfair labor practices and gives the NLRB discretion to seek a temporary injunction in other cases

The NLRB must seek a temporary injunction to put a stop to certain classes of alleged unfair labor practices before the NLRB General Counsel issues a complaint. Cases subject to this rule are those involving:

- secondary activities,
- a "hot cargo" agreement, or
- organizational or recognitional picketing.

The reason the NLRB must seek an injunction in these situations is that, in each case, a union's allegedly unlawful conduct enmeshes an employer in a labor dispute with a union that does not represent its employees. Accordingly, the NLRA treats these cases as especially serious unfair labor practices and, in turn, gives them top priority for hearings.

Section 206 of the Labor-Management Relations Act (LMRA) allows the President of the United States to intervene in strikes if national health and safety may be endangered by a strike. Section 208 allows the President to temporarily stop the dispute by asking the Attorney General to issue an injunction against the strike.

# Non-Union Employee Relations

## Human Resource Management (HRM):

There are two broad approaches to the management of the HR function. Hard HRM versus Soft HRM. Hard HRM teats employees as a resource of the business just like a machine. Soft HRM treats employees as if they truly are the most important resource in the business and a source of competitive edge.

Most HR departments adopt elements of both approaches. However, to be successful on the PHR or SPHR exam, the certification candidate must understand the differences between these two conflicting theories. Let's examine them now:

Hard HRM:
- Autocratic leadership style.
- Appraisals are focused on performance evaluation.
- Pay only enough to attract and retain a staff.
- Short term focus on staffing levels. Very reactionary.
- Strong link with corporate business planning in regards to their availability and cost.
- Minimal communication from top down.
- Little focus on employee engagement.
- Pyramid management structure.
- Identifies the needs of the business and staffs accordingly (hiring, laying off, etc.).

Soft HRM:
- Democratic or Theory Y leadership style.
- Appraisals are focused on professional development.

- Competitive pay with performance related rewards such as profit sharing, bonuses, etc.
- Strategic focus on long-term staffing levels. Proactive approach.
- Employees are valued for their individuality and their needs are accommodated.
- Two-way communication systems are established and used.
- Employees are engaged and empowered.
- Decentralized and flattened management structure.
- Concentration on the needs of the employees.

The "hard" approach to HR might be expected to result in a more cost-effective workforce where decision-making is quicker and focused on senior managers. However, such an approach pays relatively little attention to the needs of employees and a business adopting a genuinely "hard" approach might expect to suffer from higher absenteeism and staff turnover and less successful recruitment. Also, there is a persuasive argument for an approach which rewards employee performance and motivates staff more effectively. However, the danger of taking too "soft" an approach is that when all the employee benefits are added up, the cost of the workforce leaves a business at a competitive disadvantage.

## Psychological contract

The Psychological Contract is the unwritten relationship between the employee and the employer that binds them together in the pursuit of both organizational and personal success. In its simplest form, the employer expects the employee to perform well in return for being treated and paid well. However, this issue is much deeper and complex.

This relational balance between the employer and employee is somewhat explained by Vroom's "Expectancy Theory." Employees who perform well, expect to be treated and rewarded well. Employees who perform poorly should expect poor relations with their employer. In other words, the more the employee puts into the job, the higher the expectation for favorable treatment by the employer.

Additionally, employee expectations may form the basis of the psychological contract when they feel they have been promised something by a superior. This is especially common when miscommunications during the on-boarding process result in the creation of expectations that fail to materialize. It is important to note that this is not one-sided. Sometimes, the employee fails to deliver on their potential or promise in regards to job performance.

This sense of expectation creates an unwritten and undefined bond between both parties. This bond is a tenuous relation that can be shattered when one or the other breaks the "rules," such as what happens during layoffs, mergers, obsolescence, etc. It is common for laid off workers to feel anger and resentment towards their employer since they have not broken the covenants of the psychological contract and done nothing personally to deserve the loss of their job.

Even employees who were not personally affected by a layoff may suffer negative morale by observing the treatment of their fellow workers. Perceptions that the psychological contract has been violated may result in performance declines, reduced loyalty, lack of commitment, and an increase in employee misbehavior.

## Procedural Justice

Procedural justice is concerned with providing employees a structured system for resolving disputes that is considered to be fair and impartial. People feel affirmed if the procedures that are adopted treat them with respect and dignity, making it easier to accept even outcomes they do not like. The idea of "due process" is critical to the concept of procedural justice.

## Alternative Dispute Resolution (ADR)

Alternative dispute resolution (ADR) is a general term used to describe problem-solving mechanisms other than lawsuits or government agency investigations. Primarily found in non-union environments, ADR is a method for resolving employer and employee grievances. Employers using ADR mechanisms typically have two goals: to prevent lawsuits and to minimize the time and expense of resolving employees' complaints.

The explosion in the quantity and cost of employment litigation has inevitably led to the use of innovative alternative dispute resolution techniques - mediation, conciliation, arbitration, negotiated rulemaking, and other consensual methods of resolving disputes. The Equal Employment Opportunity Commission anticipates that ADR may be faster, less contentious, and more economical than litigation and is developing a policy on the use of alternative means of dispute resolution in some circumstances

ADR - in the form of negotiated grievance and arbitration procedures - has been the norm for decades in unionized companies. The continuing increase in employment litigation has led to calls for the use of ADR in nonunion companies from employers, government agencies, and federal judges. Typical examples of ADR include mediation and arbitration.

### Mediation and conciliation

Mediation is a non-binding dispute resolution technique in which parties discuss their disputes with a trained, impartial outsider who assists them in attempting to reach a mutually acceptable agreement. While mediators may suggest a variety of means through which to settle a dispute, mediators do not have the authority to impose a settlement on the parties.

Internal mediation, in which the mediator is a neutral party from inside the company, is becoming a popular variation. Although it increases the ease and lowers the cost of obtaining a mediator, internal mediation presents management with a more difficult burden in demonstrating the mediator's neutrality and confidentiality, which are crucial in inducing employees' meaningful participation.

Employers can use mediation as the exclusive means of resolving disputes or mediation can coexist with other forms. For example, grievances that remain unresolved after several setups of a grievance procedure can be submitted to mediation. Similarly, mediation may be permitted or required as a prelude to arbitration.

### Arbitration

Nonunion arbitration is a semiformal trial before one or more trained arbitrators who receive testimony and evidence from the parties. The arbitrator can make factual determinations and award relief. Usually, the arbitrator's decision is binding on the parties, although an employee might later file a lawsuit disputing the binding nature of the arbitration proceeding. However, in Circuit City Stores, Inc. V. Adams, the Supreme Court of the United States upheld the employer's right to require employees to submit to binding arbitration as the exclusive remedy to any employment dispute.

A variant of arbitration is non-binding arbitration. This is an agreement between the parties that the opinion of the arbitrator is advisory only. This procedure is more in the nature of fact-finding. It lacks the finality of typical arbitration procedures and therefore may not represent the best investment of time and resources.

*Arbitration as the final step to other ADR procedures*

Arbitration is often combined with a grievance procedure and or mediation, which precede a formal arbitration hearing. Under this arrangement, the matter will proceed to arbitration only if the dispute cannot be resolved through these less formal processes.

*Ombudsman*

A corporate ombudsman is an individual appointed to investigate internal complaints, report findings, and facilitate equitable settlements. According to surveys, appointing an internal ombudsman is the most-often used form of ADR.

The ombudsman's tasks are to listen, decide whether and how to intervene, and provide feedback. Unlike HR and employee relations officials, who represent management, ombudsmen are neutral.

An ombudsman may have exceptional latitude in deciding how to intervene, but no power to impose a binding result. One view is that any intervention should aim toward making the organization's existing structures - such as a grievance procedure - work properly. To that end, a rule of thumb is to intervene at the lowest possible management level.

## Employee Engagement

Human resource professionals have intuitively known for years that an engaged workforce provides many intangible benefits and can be linked to retention. Employee Engagement is the extent to which workforce commitment, both emotional and intellectual, exists relative to accomplishing the work, mission, and vision of the organization. Employee engagement can be seen as a heightened level of ownership where each employee wants to do whatever they can for the benefit of their internal and external customers, and for the success of the organization as a whole. The three commonly accepted components of "employee engagement" are: employee commitment, how well they participate in the work, and their longevity.

It has been routinely found that employee engagement scores account for as much as half of the variance in customer satisfaction scores. This translates into millions of dollars for companies if they can improve their scores. Studies have statistically demonstrated that engaged employees are more productive, more profitable, more customer-focused, safer, and less likely to leave their employer.

Employee relations programs, how employees are treated, serve a large role in creating, developing and maintaining employee engagement.

## Changes in Terms of Employment

Claims of forced resignation (constructive discharge) are when an employer creates a work environment that is so unpleasant it forces the employee to quit his/her job. In cases of constructive discharge, the U.S. legal system will treat the separation in the same manner as an actual involuntary termination (a discharge).

In order to prove an employee was constructively discharged, the employee must show that a change in work conditions was so intolerable that it caused or was intended to cause the employee to quit.

Constructive discharges sometimes occur due to union-related activity. To be unlawful under the NLRA, the change in working conditions has to be imposed because of the employee's union or concerted activities. Situations that could produce constructive discharge include imposing (because of union activities), pay cuts, benefit changes, work hour changes, transfers to less desirable jobs, assignments to less convenient work places, etc.

If the employer has legitimate business reasons for the change in assignment or conditions, and does not have an antiunion motive, the employer can lawfully make the change. For example, an employer's refusal to give an employee a raise at evaluation time during a union campaign did not amount to constructive discharge if the employee's personnel file showed an unfavorable work record.

## Electromation

Electromation is a landmark decision by the National Labor Relations Board that considered the legality of a modem employee participation effort in a nonunion workplace.

In 1988, Electromation Inc., an Indiana manufacturer of electrical components, created five "action committees" to allow employees and management to confer on the issues of absenteeism, smoking, communications, pay progressions, and attendance policies. Management appointed both the employee and company representatives on the committees.

Facing a Teamsters Union organizing campaign, Electromation dissolved the committees, but the Teamsters nevertheless filed a charge alleging that the action committees were labor organizations formed in violation of the National Labor Relations Act. The NLRB agreed, ruling in 1992, that Electromation's "committees were created for, and actually served, the purpose of dealing with the employees over conditions of employment," and "their only purpose was to address employees' disaffection concerning conditions of employment" (Electromation, Inc. v. NLRB, 1992).

In summary, the NLRB said the employer was trying to "dominate the union" and only the employer or the lawful bargaining agent (the union) is allowed to address "conditions of employment" (since "conditions of employment" are reserved as a mandatory bargaining topic). This ruling put many participatory employee initiatives into a tailspin.

### Lessons for employers
Although finding Electromation's committees illegal, the NLRB emphasized that it was not banning quality circles and could foresee certain circumstances in which labor-management teams would not violate the NLRA. However, board members failed to reach any consensus on what those circumstances might be. Nonetheless, the board's objections to particular aspects of Electromation's committees do offer some guidance:

- Employee participation programs should stay away from traditional bargaining issues.
- Be aware that unions or disgruntled workers may target committees that are questionable.
- Do not force employees to form or participate in committees dealing with working conditions.
- Let supervisors know that the decision does not mean that they can no longer talk to employees about a complaint.

# Other Union Issues – (SPHR-only section)

## Employer's Organizations

An employers' organization, employers' association, or employer's federation is an association of employers usually found in countries outside the United States. They are often mistaken for unions but are different. A trade union, which organizes workers, is the opposite of an employer's organization. The confusion stems from the fact that the role and position of an "employer's organization" differs from country to country, dependent on the economic system of a country.

In countries with a pluralist or Anglo-Saxon economic system (such as the United Kingdom and the United States), where there is no institutionalized cooperation between employers' organizations, trade unions and government, an employer's organization is an interest group or advocacy group that through lobbying tries to influence government policy. In these countries, employer's organizations tend to be weak, with many of their functions taken over by industry trade groups, which are basically public relations organization.

In countries with a social market economy, such as Austria, Sweden and the Netherlands, the employer's organizations are part of a system of institutionalized deliberation, together with government and the trade unions. In tri-partite bargaining, these social partners work out agreements on issues like price levels, wage increases, tax rates and pension entitlements. In these countries, collective bargaining is often done on a national level. It is not between one corporation and one union, but national employer's organizations and national trade unions.

## European Works Council

Many other countries employ the use of "works councils."  Often mistook as a union but they are not.  A works council is a "shop-floor" organization representing workers, which functions as local/firm-level complement to national labor negotiations.

One of the most commonly-examined (and arguably most successful) implementations of these institutions is found in Germany. The model is basically as follows: general labor agreements are made at the national level by national unions and national employer associations, and local plants and firms then meet with works councils to adjust these national agreements to local circumstances.

Most European countries require the establishment of a Works Council or a procedure for informing and consulting employees in every Community-scale undertaking following agreement between the central management and a special negotiating body.

**End of SPHR-only section**

# DHR's Fast 20

1. **Arbitration**: A quasi-judicial process in which two parties agree to submit an unresolvable dispute to a third party for a binding settlement.

2. **Boycott**: Union members agree to not patronize the boycotted firm. This type of boycott is legal.

3. **Collective Bargaining**: A process by which the representatives of the employer meet to work out a contract with representatives of the workers (union).

4. **Decertification Election**: Where a secret ballot election is conducted by the NLRB and the bargaining unit employees vote to oust an in-place union. 50% + 1 vote of cast ballots must vote to keep the union. Can only be held once per year on the "representation election" anniversary.

5. **Grievance**: A complaint lodged by the union against the employer that creates dissatisfaction within the union. Normally there are three steps prior to the arbitration stage.

6. **Hot Cargo Agreement**: Where an employer permits its employees to not work with materials that come from a firm that is being struck by a union. This type of agreement is illegal.

7. **Labor Management Relations Act (Taft Hartley)**: Establishes the rights and obligations of employers, employees, and unions with respect to collective bargaining.

8. **Labor Management Reporting/Disclosure Act (Landrum-Griffith)**: Created a "Bill of Rights" for union members to combat wrongdoing and to limit control of union leadership.

9. **Lockout**: Where employees are denied entry to the facility in order to force the union to stop harassing the employer or to accept the conditions as set by management.

10. **Mediation**: A neutral third party helps labor and management reach a voluntary agreement.

11. **National Labor Relations Act (Wagner Act)**: The main federal law governing labor-management relations. It protects an employee's right to engage in protected group activities such as union organizing and protests.

12. **National Labor Relations Board**: The NLRA created the NLRB as the regulatory agency with jurisdiction over private sector labor-management matters.

13. **Norris-LaGuardia Act**: The Norris-LaGuardia Act substantially limits the courts of the United States in issuing restraining orders and injunctions in cases involving labor disputes.

14. **Railway Labor Act**: The act that first allowed employees to "organize".

15. **Representation Election**: A secret ballot election whereby the bargaining unit vote for, or against representation. 50% plus one vote is needed.

16. **Secondary Boycott**: Where a neutral third party company is threatened with a boycott unless they stop doing business with the primary boycotted company. This type of boycott is illegal.

17. **Steward**: An employee designated and trained by the union to serve as the guardian of the collective bargaining agreement and the employees' on-site representative.

18. **Strike**: Where employees withhold their services so that the employer will make greater concessions at the bargaining table.

19. **Unfair Labor Practice**: Employers or unions that violate employees' or each other LMRA-protected rights commit an "unfair labor practice".

20. **Yellow Dog Contract**: Employers had prospective employees sign agreements that they wouldn't join a union as a condition of employment. Made illegal under Norris-LaGuardia.

# Practice Quiz

1. The extent to which employees commit to something or someone in their organization, how hard they work, and how long they stay as a result of that commitment is BEST defined by the term:
   A. Core values
   B. Strategic plan
   C. Employee engagement
   D. Corporate branding

2. To the company, Alternative Dispute Resolution's (ADR's) main goal is to:
   A. Provide justice
   B. Avoid litigation
   C. Determine the root cause of the grievance
   D. Provide an exhaustive investigation into the grievance

3. Open shops are MOST associated with:
   A. The automotive industry
   B. The steel industry
   C. Right-to-work states
   D. Agricultural workers

4. Which is NOT an illegal subject for collective bargaining?
   A. Hot cargo
   B. Closed shop
   C. No-strike clause
   D. Yellow-dog contract

5. Employees that file ULP's against their employer:
   A. May be terminated for insubordination
   B. Usually do so at the behest of the Union
   C. Will be protected against employer-retaliation by the NLRB
   D. Usually get promoted within the Union

6. What percent of employees must vote for the union in order for the status quo to be maintained in a decertification election?
   A. 30%
   B. 50%
   C. 50% + 1 of voting employees
   D. Simple majority if a quorum of the bargaining unit members are present to vote

7. The central thrust of the Federal Arbitration Act (FAA) of 1925 requires adversarial parties, whom have an arbitration agreement in force, to:
   A. Arbitrate first before bringing litigation
   B. Resort to jury trials when arbitration fails
   C. Equally share the costs of an arbitrated grievance
   D. Be bound by the arbitrator's decision and typically, without legal recourse

8. Examples of mandatory bargaining items does NOT include which of the following?
   A. Rest and lunch periods
   B. Promotion process
   C. Conditions of employment for 1$^{st}$-Line Supervisors
   D. Pensions

9. This is the negotiation process by which disputing parties arrive at a solution.
   A. Litigation
   B. Mediation
   C. Arbitration
   D. Brainstorming

10. Which is MOST likely to be considered an Unfair Labor Practice?
    A. Union holds an open meeting the night before the certification election
    B. CEO holds a meeting with employees to encourage acceptance of the proposed bargaining agreement
    C. HR Manager gives a factual account of union misdeeds to employees during a campaign
    D. An annual step-rate pay raise is given to an employee after the pro-union election was held but before the contract is ratified

11. The legal right to terminate employees who refuse to join the Union after employment is BEST known as:
    A. Closed shop
    B. Agency shop
    C. Union shop
    D. Maintenance of membership

## Answers and Explanations to Practice Quiz:

1.  C

The three commonly accepted components of "employee engagement" are: employee commitment, how well they participate in the work, and their longevity. Core values is more concerned with the key principles guiding the organization, strategic planning concerns the path forward process for growing the business, and corporate branding is about the establishment of a corporate identity in the marketplace by creating a reputation.

2.  B

While the other outcomes are certainly favorable, the company's main interest is using ADR is to avoid the time and expense involved in protracted litigation.

3.  C

The definition of an "Open Shop" is a place of employment at which one is not required to join or financially support a labor union as a condition of hiring or continued employment. Open shops are required by law in right-to-work jurisdictions. This is in opposition to a "closed shop" where applicants must be a union member prior to applying for a position or a "union shop" where new hires must join the union after gaining employment.

4.  C

Hot cargo agreements (the refusal of unionized workers to handle goods produced by replacement workers in a struck facility), Closed shop (see above), and "Yellow-Dog Contracts" (pre-employment contract that forbade workers from joining a union) have all been declared illegal by various Acts and the NLRB. A no-strike clause is a permissible bargaining subject that is usually sought by the employer in return for concessions to the workers.

5.  C

The National Labor Relations Board protects employees against retaliation by their employer when filing an Unfair Labor Practice Charge. The other answer options are generally untrue and incorrect.

6.  C

50% + 1 is defined as a simple majority and is the correct answer. "30%" is the number of employees who must sign authorization cards to <u>call</u> for an election. "50%" is not a correct number. "Simple majority plus a quorum" is incorrect as the vote is taken from those that show up to vote (whether a quorum is reached or not) on election-day.

7.  D

The FAA requires adversarial parties to be bound by the arbitrator's decision. Generally, no option for litigating after the Arbitrator has ruled is allowable, thus negating the other answer options. The answer option requiring the adversary's to share the cost of the arbitration is an agreement between the parties (commonly accepted practice) and is not written into law.

8.  C

Mandatory bargaining issues include any items that may fall into the categories of working hours, working condition, pay, and/or benefits. Since management is excluded from participating in a Union, it stands to reason that no bargaining items may be considered that have to do with Supervisors or other members of the leadership team.

9.  B

The only option where the disputing parties work out an agreement is the correct choice, "mediation." In litigation and arbitration, the disputing parties have the issue resolved by an outside third party (judge or arbitrator). Brainstorming is a problem solving process for creating and generating ideas but is generally not recognized as a dispute resolution tool.

10. B

The CEO may not "bypass the union" and address the employees directly. That is the Union's prerogative. The other answer options are all possibly legal activities that should not result in an ULP, normally.

11. C

A closed shop is a where applicants must be union members before applying (it is an illegal practice). An agency shop is a place of employment where workers must pay union dues whether they are a member of a labor union or not. Maintenance of membership is where union membership may not be rescinded until the current contract expires. Union shop, the correct answer, is where new hires either join the union or pay the equivalent of union dues within a set period of time following their hire. If membership is required by the agreement, then those refusing to join may be terminated from employment.

# Chapter 5
# Workforce Planning and Employment
# (PHR 24% - SPHR 17%)

Developing, implementing and evaluating sourcing, recruitment, hiring, orientation, succession planning, retention and organizational exit programs necessary to ensure the workforce's ability to achieve the organization's goals and objectives.

## Legal & Regulatory Factors

### Title VII of the Civil Rights Act

Title VII of the Civil Rights Act of 1964 prohibits discrimination on the basis of race, color, religion, sex, or national origin. The statute, which applies to virtually all employers with 15 or more employees, bars intentional discrimination as well as practices that seem neutral but have a disproportionate impact on one of the protected classes of employees.

> **EXAMPLE**
> Title VII can come into play when employers treat women differently than men out of concern for safety and health. An example is the practice of setting minimum height and weight requirements for particular jobs on the assumption that only workers of that size can perform the jobs safely. When such requirements have a disparate impact on women, as they almost always will, given the fact that the average woman is smaller than the average man, employers leave themselves open to charges of sex bias under Title VII.

Congress amended the Civil Rights Act in 1991 by providing for the right to trial by jury on claims of discrimination and it introduced the possibility of additional emotional distress damages awards.

### Age Discrimination in Employment Act

The Age Discrimination in Employment Act of 1967 (ADEA) prohibits arbitrary age discrimination against employees or applicants age 40 and older. 1986 amendments abolished mandatory retirement of employees of any age. Amendments also require employers to continue making full contributions to employees' retirement plan accounts until they retire.

### Health, Medical, & Rehabilitation Statutes

#### Pregnancy Discrimination Act of 1978
This act amended Title VII of the Civil Rights Act of 1964. It bars employers from discriminating on the basis of pregnancy related medical conditions. Temporary disabilities due to childbirth and pregnancy must be treated the same as any other temporary disability. Insurance coverage must be provided for pregnancy-related conditions to the same extent that other medical conditions are covered. Benefit plans that provide for temporary, long-term, or permanent disability must provide the same level of benefits for

pregnancy-related conditions. If temporary leave with job and benefit retention is provided for employees with other illnesses or injuries, the same must be granted to women for pregnancy-related disabilities.

## The Family and Medical Leave Act

The Family and Medical Leave Act (FMLA) requires employers with at least 50 employees within a 75 mile radius to provide up to 12 workweeks of unpaid leave for certain events during a 12-month period. See chapter three for more information on FMLA.

## Rehabilitation Act of 1973

Under Sections 503 and 504, employers that have federal contracts worth more than $25,000 or that receive government financial assistance cannot discriminate against handicapped individuals and must take affirmative action to provide employment opportunities for them.

Federal contractors with contracts in excess of $10,000 for personal property or non-personal services, including construction contracts, are required to take affirmative action in the employment and advancement of qualified persons with disabilities. Contractors with 50 or more employees and contracts of $50,000 or more are required to have written affirmative action plans for the employment and advancement of qualified individuals with disabilities.

## Americans with Disabilities Act

The Americans With Disabilities Act (ADA) not only prohibits discrimination in employment on the basis of a person's disability, but also requires that goods and services offered to the public be made accessible to everyone and that architectural barriers be removed.

The ADA does not require employers to make a special effort to recruit individuals with disabilities over other qualified applicants. However, employers must make "reasonable accommodation to the physical and mental limitations of an employee or an applicant," unless such an accommodation would cause undue hardship.

> **TEST TAKING TIP**
> The certification exams are offered twice annually. Once in May-June, and again in December-January. You can pick any day in either of these two periods to take your test.

## Americans with Disabilities Act Amendments Act (ADAAA)

Passed into law in 2008, the ADAAA amended the ADA by broadening its coverage. Many court rulings had interpreted and applied the meaning and scope of the ADA in a limited manner. Congress disagreed with the Supreme Court rulings where individuals with physical or mental impairments were not considered as protected under ADA due to fact that their disability could be "mitigated" or abated due to modern medicines and prosthetic devices.

Thus, the ADAAA came into being and reversed the trend so that persons with major life limitations, even if given a meaningful life due to modern medicine, will still receive protection from discrimination due to their disability. Now, individuals with impairments such as amputation, intellectual disabilities, epilepsy, multiple sclerosis, HIV/AIDS, diabetes, muscular dystrophy, and cancer must receive reasonable accommodations for their disabilities.

Specifically, ADAAA addressed the following issues:
1. It overturned several Supreme Court decisions that Congress believed had interpreted the definition of "disability" too narrowly, resulting in a denial of protection for many individuals with impairments such as cancer, diabetes, epilepsy, HIV infection, and bipolar disorder.

2. It states that the definition of a disability should be interpreted in favor of broad coverage of individuals and be more inclusive of persons with impairments.
3. The law prohibits consideration of mitigating measures such as medication, assistive technology, accommodations, or modifications when determining whether an impairment substantially limits a major life activity.
4. The regulations make it easier for individuals to establish coverage under the "regarded as" part of the definition of "disability."

In summary, the ADAAA made it easier for an individual seeking protection under the ADA to establish that he or she has a disability within the meaning of the statute.

## Vietnam-era Veterans Readjustment Act

The Vietnam Era Veterans Readjustment Assistance Act of 1974 [VEVRAA] requires that federal contractors and subcontractors must take affirmative action to hire and promote veterans and disabled veterans (not limited to the Vietnam era) and Vietnam-era veterans (not limited to the disabled). Federal contractors with contracts of $10,000 or more are required to take affirmative action in the hiring and promoting of qualified special disabled veterans and veterans of the Vietnam era. Those with 50 or more employees and contracts of $50,000 or more are required to prepare written affirmative action plans for hiring and promoting such individuals.

## Immigration Reform and Control Act

To ensure that employers do not employ or continue to employ aliens who are not authorized to work in the United States and do not discriminate on the basis of citizenship status or national origin. The federal Immigration Reform and Control Act (IRCA) provides for an employment verification system. The system requires all employers or other persons that hire, recruit, or refer an individual for employment to:

- require the employee to produce documents that establish both the employee's authorization to work in the United States and his or her identity;
- examine those documents to ensure that they appear to be genuine; and
- attest on the Employment Eligibility Verification Form (Form I-9) under penalty of perjury that it has verified that the employee is not an unauthorized alien by examination of the documents establishing employment authorization and identity.

IRCA is enforced by the Department of Homeland Security's (DHS) two primary immigration related agencies the United States Citizen and Immigration Service (USCIS) and Immigration and Custom Enforcement (ICE).

An employer complies with IRCA's document examination requirement when it has examined the employee's documents and they reasonably appear to be genuine on their face. The employer need not require the production of other documents.

### Federal contractors and agencies

The federal government uses its relationship with its vendors to force compliance with many laws and practices. Failure to abide by these requirements could result in fines, penalties, and/or loss of vendor status with the government or its suppliers.

*Executive Order 11246*

Federal contractors and subcontractors with contracts of more than $10,000, as well as those performing under federally assisted construction contracts of more than $10,000, are prohibited from discriminating on the basis of national origin by E.O. 11246.

Contractors and subcontractors with 50 or more employees and federal contracts of $50,000 or more must develop written affirmative action compliance programs for each of their facilities. These requirements include employers taking positive steps towards the recruitment and advancement of minorities and females.

## Employee Polygraph Protection Act

The federal Employee Polygraph Protection Act of 1988 prohibits most private sector employers from requiring or requesting employees or job applicants to take any lie detector tests or from using the results of such a test, even if an outside agency screens employees or applicants. Further, employees and applicants can't be discriminated against based on polygraph test results or for refusing to take the test. Employers must also inform employees and applicants in writing of their rights under this law or face fines up to $10,000 per violation.

## Worker Adjustment and Retraining Notification Act (WARN)

The Worker Adjustment and Retraining Notification Act (WARN) requires covered employers to give 60 days' notice of a plant closing or large-scale layoff. The law's notification requirements are triggered by a plant closing or mass layoff.

> **TEST TAKING TIP**
> Look for the "soft words" like; "usually," "often," or "sometimes" in the answer options. They're frequently a clue to the right choice.

WARN covers businesses that have at least 100 full-time employees and companies that have 100 or more employees whose combined work hours regularly total 4,000 hours a week, excluding overtime. Part-time employees are considered those who work less than 20 hours a week or six months a year.

## North American Free Trade Agreement

The North American Free Trade Agreement, "Temporary Entry for Business Persons," authorizes Canadian and Mexican citizens engaged in business activities at a professional level to be employed in the United States by a specific employer.

To be eligible for a TN-1 (Trade NAFTA Professional for Canadians) or a TN-2 (Trade NAFTA Professional for Mexicans) visa, the individual must be a member of a profession listed in Appendix 1603.D.1 of NAFTA, most of which require that a Bachelor's Degree be held. These professions include accountant, agriculturist, a wide range of scientists and scientific technicians, lawyer, management consultant, nurse, and teacher.

In addition, the individual must have employment with a U.S. employer or proof that a U.S. employer has agreed to pay for the individual's services. Self-employment is not a basis for obtaining a TN visa. If there is a strike or lockout in progress, the individual's employment may not adversely affect the settlement of that labor dispute.

## Common Law Tort Theories

Common law tort theory of litigation involves some type of wrong that was committed against a person in the absence of a contractual obligation. A civil suit is the result.

Plaintiffs have increasingly included state common law tort claims with federal claims to broaden their scope of recovery for perceived wrong doings done unto them by the employer. Examples of types of these claims include: workplace injuries/illnesses (i.e.; 2nd hand smoke), wrongful termination, invasions of privacy (substance abuse testing), negligent hiring, etc.

## Copyright Statutes

### Copyright Owner

Some companies may want to copyright and be the owner of copyrightable material that is prepared by its employees. What is involved here is "work made for hire," for which the copyright law provides two definitions:

The first definition is "a work prepared by an employee within the scope of his or her employment." The individual (company) that hires an author to create an original work is the author of that work. The creator has no rights whatever in the work unless otherwise specified in a written contract. For example, a research laboratory is considered the author of a report written by a scientist on work done for his or her supervisor. Copyright exception: The law denies copyright to works "prepared by an officer or employee of the United States Government as a part of that person's official duties." This means that, by and large, federal government publications are not copyrighted.

A work is also considered "made for hire" if it is specially ordered or commissioned and fits into one of several categories. In this case, both the creator of the work made for hire and the party doing the hiring must sign a written agreement stating that the work will be considered a work for hire.

## Consumer Credit Protection Act: Garnishments

There are both federal and state laws governing wage garnishments. Employers must comply with state garnishment laws if they are more protective of employees than federal law. The major sources of garnishment law are summarized below.

### Consumer Credit Protection Act

Title III of the Consumer Credit Protection Act is the principal federal law governing wage garnishments. The law sets a limit on the amount of employees' weekly disposable earnings that may be garnished. CCPA includes a general limit on garnishment, as well as a limit that is applicable only to child and family support orders. The law protects employees from discharge because of garnishment with respect to any single debt, but does not protect employees from discharge if their earnings have been subject to garnishment for a second or subsequent debts.

### Internal Revenue Code

Limits on the weekly amount that may be withheld from an employee's wages are different for tax levies than they are for other types of garnishments. The Internal Revenue Code exempts from tax levies a weekly portion of wages equal to the employee's standard deduction plus personal exemptions allowed for the taxable year, divided by 52.

## Fair Credit Protection Act

The Fair Credit Reporting Act (FCRA) regulates the use of consumer reports (which it defines as information collected and reported by third party agencies) as it pertains to adverse decisions, notification to the consumer, and destruction and safekeeping of records. If a consumer report is used as a factor in an adverse hiring decision, the consumer must be presented with a "Pre-adverse action disclosure," a copy of the FCRA summary of rights, and a "Notification of adverse action letter." Applicants are entitled to know the source of any information used against them including a credit reporting company.

## Social Security/Retirement Legislation

The Social Security Act (the Act) provides detailed rules for determining what basic benefit amount is due to a person who is eligible for benefits. The amount of an individual's basic benefit is determined according to one of three calculation methods: the average indexed monthly earnings method; the average monthly wage method; and the transitional guaranty alternative method. The actual benefit paid is determined by reducing or increasing the basic benefit to account for various adjustments, such as cost of living increases, required under the Act.

The Social Security system is a major source of retirement income and family income replacement benefits in the event of the death of active and retired employees. It is funded by employee and employer contributions and collected by the IRS through payroll taxes under the Federal Insurance Contributions Act (FICA). Formally known as Old-Age, Survivors' and Disability Insurance (OASDI), Social Security is a federal insurance program that provides monthly payments to eligible workers and their families when a worker retires, dies, or becomes disabled.

Entitlement to these benefits depends on a worker's insured status. This is measured by the amount of time for which a worker has been credited with coverage under the Social Security Act. Today, more than 90 percent of the workforce is covered by Social Security.

> **TEST TAKING TIP**
> The kinds of math problems you may face on the test include calculations for: turnover rates, accident rates, compa-ratio, 4/5ths rule, overtime, etc.

## ERISA

In designing or administering any employee benefit program, it is critical to know whether the program is an employee benefit plan subject to regulation under the Employee Retirement Income Security Act (ERISA). ERISA provides uniform standards for employee benefit plans, particularly pension plans. For employers, ERISA may be both a burden and a blessing. If a benefit program is an employee benefit plan within the meaning of ERISA, it is subject to ERISA, but it is free from state regulation and various common-law suits.

Employee benefit plans are plans that provide either a pension benefit or a non-pension benefit —that is, a welfare benefit. To determine whether a benefit program is subject to ERISA, it is necessary to determine if it provides a benefit governed by ERISA and whether it is designed to be a plan. In addition, some particular plans are excepted from ERISA coverage entirely.

## Consolidated Omnibus Budget Reconciliation Act (COBRA)

The Consolidated Omnibus Budget Reconciliation Act of 1985 requires employers with group health plans to offer continued coverage to employees and their dependents under certain circumstances where coverage would otherwise end. Health plan sponsors must provide each "qualified beneficiary" whose coverage would be lost because of a "qualifying event" with the chance to elect, within a certain period of time, continued coverage under the plan. No evidence of insurability need be provided. COBRA amended Employee Retirement Income Security Act (ERISA) with these provisions and has been amended itself several times.

The continuation of coverage requirements apply to group health plans that provide medical care to employees, former employees, or their families, either directly or through insurance or reimbursement. The requirements apply to both single and multi-employer plans. COBRA also covers plans that provide dental care, vision care, prescription drugs, and similar benefits. Life insurance benefits provided under a group health plan are not covered by COBRA.

A qualifying employer is generally an employer with 20 or more full time equivalent employees (ERISA cites"(more) than 20 employees on a typical business day during the preceding calendar year"). Among the "qualifying events" listed in the statute are loss of benefits coverage due to (1) the death of the covered employee, (2) termination or a reduction in hours (which can be the result of resignation, discharge, layoff, strike or lockout, medical leave or simply a slowdown in business operations) that causes the worker to lose eligibility for coverage, (3) divorce or legal separation, which normally terminates the ex-spouse's eligibility for benefits, or (4) a dependent child reaching the age at which he or she is no longer covered. COBRA imposes different notice requirements on participants and beneficiaries, depending on the particular qualifying event that triggers COBRA rights. COBRA also allows for longer periods of extended coverage in some cases, such as disability (29 months) or divorce (36 months), than others, such as termination of employment or a reduction in hours (18 months).

## Uniformed Services Employment and Reemployment Rights Act

The Uniformed Services Employment and Reemployment Rights Act (USERRA) requires employers to provide health insurance continuation for individuals performing military duty of more than 30 days for up to 24 months. The employer may charge the military reservist up to 102 percent of the full premium during this time. For military service of less than 31 days, health care coverage is provided as if the service member has remained employed. It allows individuals who leave their jobs to undertake military service and other emergency workers deployed to return to their jobs once their service is over. USERRA also prohibits employers from discriminating against past and present members of the uniformed services, as well as individuals in the process of applying to the uniformed services.

> **Note:** USERRA provides health insurance continuation for military members, not COBRA. This could be an important difference on the PHR or SPHR exam.

## Unemployment Compensation Laws and Regulations

Unemployment insurance is an employee benefit administered through a joint federal-state program designed to provide qualifying workers with financial security while they are temporarily unemployed. The program is funded by an unemployment tax that must be paid by employers (employees may share the payments in Alaska, New Jersey, and Pennsylvania) under the Federal Unemployment Tax Act (FUTA) and state unemployment insurance laws. As a result of the federal-state nature of the program, FUTA allows employers to offset a certain amount of their SUI taxes against their federal unemployment tax obligations.

Employers are responsible for withholding, depositing, reporting, and paying employment taxes. As part of these responsibilities, most employers generally withhold, deposit, report, and pay three separate types of federal taxes:

- federal income tax,

- social security tax and Medicare tax under the Federal Insurance Contributions Act (FICA),
- federal unemployment tax, under the Federal Unemployment Tax Act (FUTA).

## Drug Free Workplace Act

The federal government has enacted a number of laws and regulations concerning substance abuse in the workplace. The broadest of these laws, the Drug-Free Workplace Act, applies to private-sector employers who are federal contractors or grant recipients. Although the act does not mandate employee drug testing, it does require covered employers to establish workplace substance abuse prevention programs or face the loss of their contracts and grants.

Other federal regulations do require drug testing but have a more limited scope. Mandatory drug testing regulations apply primarily to federal agencies and certain private-sector employers in the transportation, defense, and nuclear power industries.

> **TEST TAKING TIP**
> Practice test-taking, keep practicing test-taking, then practice test-taking some more. You've got to get those skills sharp for choosing the correct option.

## Uniform Guidelines on Employee Selection Practices (UGESP)

Adopted by EEOC, the Office of Personnel Management, and the Departments of Justice and Labor in 1978, the Uniform Guidelines on Employee Selection Practices (UGESP) (29 CFR §1607) and the 90 questions and answers attached to them provide employers with a means of determining if an employment selection criteria has an adverse impact on a protected group.

If an adverse impact is found, the selection procedure must by modified, eliminated, or validated as having a clear relationship to performance on the job. The guidelines explain how to validate tests and other selection procedures by content, construct, and criterion-related validation methods.

### Coverage
The guidelines apply to employers, employment agencies, labor unions, and federal contractors covered by Title VII and Executive Order 11246. They do not apply to the ADEA, the Rehabilitation Act, or the ADA. Although the guidelines discuss validation methods in terms of employment tests, they apply to all selection criteria, including interviews, work samples, education requirements, physical criteria, and performance evaluations.

### Four-fifths rule
The UGESP have a "rule of thumb" known as the "four-fifths" or "80 percent rule" for determining the adverse impact of a selection practice. A four-step procedure is used to calculate the impact of a practice:

- the rate of selection for each group is determined;
- the group with the highest selection rate is found;
- the impact ratios are calculated by comparing the selection rate for each group with the selection rate for the highest group; and
- it is determined whether the selection rate for any group is substantially less than the selection rate for the highest group.

The rate of selection is the number of persons selected from a particular group, such as blacks, divided by the number of applicants from that group. The impact ratio is determined by dividing the selection rate for a group by the selection rate for the highest group. If the selection rate for a group is less than four-fifths or 80 percent of the selection rate for the highest group, adverse impact is indicated.

### Making the calculation

If there are 80 white applicants and 40 black applicants for a job classification and 48 of the whites are hired but only 12 of the blacks are hired, the selection rate for whites is 48/80 or 60 percent and the selection rate for blacks is 12/40 or 30 percent. Comparing the black selection rate — 30 percent — with the white selection rate — 60 percent — shows the black rate is 30/60, or 50 percent of the selection rate of whites. Because 50 percent is less than 80 percent (or four-fifths), adverse impact is indicated.

| Applicants | Hires | Selection rate | Percent hired |
|:---:|:---:|:---:|:---:|
| 80 White | 48 | 48 / 80 or | 60% |
| 40 Black | 12 | 12 / 40 or | 30% |

The four-fifths rule is merely a numerical basis from which to draw an initial inference of discrimination. Enforcement agencies will require additional information. Unlawful discrimination may be present regardless of the difference in selection rates for a group. On the other hand, selection criteria may be upheld as job related and necessary for the operation of the business even though the selection rates for various groups are very different.

# Job Analysis, Job Description and Job Specification

Job analysis is the systematic study of an organization's jobs. It involves gathering data about a job to determine and define its "compensable factors" by finding out what the employee does, how and why the job is done, and the skills required for the work. Job analysis provides organizations with information from which they can draft job descriptions and conduct job evaluations, the process of determining the relative worth of a job for compensation purposes.

Job documentation is the data-gathering process. Job descriptions are the most common form of job documentation because they summarize key aspects of a job in an organized, narrative manner. Job documentation becomes obsolete quickly due to new technology, new products, new markets, and reorganizations, so it should be kept up to date.

Employers use job descriptions to identify, define, and describe jobs in order to rate them as part of the pay structure and job evaluation process. A set of job descriptions also may result from job analysis, which is a process for collecting and analyzing information about a job to develop and establish appropriate pay structures within job categories of the organization.

A job consists of essential functions (i.e., core duties) performed under certain working conditions. Essential functions are tasks that are sufficiently critical to a position so that successful completion of those tasks or functions justifies the job's existence. Typically, a job may be described in five to ten function statements.

Job specifications organize information gathered through the job analysis and allow a meaningful comparison of jobs for evaluation and pricing. They are written descriptions of the skills involved and the physical demands of a job. Specifications can be prepared easily and quickly if a thorough job analysis was conducted originally. The analyst who studied the job and prepared the description is usually best qualified to prepare the specification.

## Methods of Job Analysis

| Method | Types of Jobs | Advantages | Disadvantages |
|---|---|---|---|
| Observation | Production | Simple, inexpensive | May be insufficient, time-consuming |
| Interview | All | Thorough | Time-consuming, most expensive |
| Questionnaire | All | Least expensive | Requires follow-up |

### Types of job evaluation systems

Job evaluation methodologies sometimes are referred to as either "job content" or "market-based" approaches. Job content evaluation is the traditional approach to job evaluation. It tends to focus on how a job is valued within the organization and may emphasize internal equity as a goal. A market-based approach focuses more exclusively on how jobs are valued by the broader marketplace of employers and does not give as much consideration to internal equity.

### *Job content evaluation*

A job content evaluation system builds a job-worth hierarchy based primarily on job content. Job content evaluation systems are classified as either non-quantitative or quantitative:

- **Non-quantitative systems**. Non-quantitative job evaluation systems appraise the whole job by comparing each job to one another or against very general criteria. The organization's job-worth hierarchy then is created by using some type of ranking or classification system. The three most common types of non-quantitative plans are ranking, slotting, and classification plans.
- **Quantitative systems.** Quantitative job evaluation systems break jobs down into "compensable factors." Evaluators assign numerical values to each job's compensable factors based on specific criteria. Evaluators then apply statistical methods to such values to derive the job-worth structure.

### *Market-based job evaluation*

Market-based job evaluation systems measure a job's worth based on how the job is valued by the broader marketplace of employers as reflected by the prevailing compensation rates for the particular job. Market-based systems are most appropriate for small companies, businesses undergoing rapid growth, and organizations that must compete for a limited pool of technical or professional talent.

Market-based job evaluations represent a departure from traditional job-content systems. The traditional job-evaluation process begins with job analysis and job descriptions, uses job content methodology to develop a job-worth hierarchy, and then uses the job-worth information and market pay data to develop an organizational pay structure. In contrast, market-based methodologies skip or combine some of these steps, since the primary focus is on external worth of jobs.

The basic approach market-based systems use is to gather data on benchmark jobs from published or custom salary surveys. This data is used to develop the job-worth hierarchy and salary structure.

## Types of Data Gathered in a Job Analysis

The two types of data collection methods used during job analysis are quantitative and qualitative. The job analyst gathers data by observing, measuring, studying relevant literature, interviewing incumbents and supervisors, and obtaining questionnaires from incumbents and supervisors. All job analysis methods of data collection require that certain information about jobs be collected, analyzed, and recorded in a systematic way.

### Quantitative methods

Generally, quantitative methods are conducted through closed-ended questionnaires that focus on tasks or responsibilities. These questionnaires are often tabulated by computers. Quantitative methods are usually used for low-level production jobs.

### Qualitative methods

The qualitative job analysis method uses questionnaires and job descriptions that are prepared by job holders, supervisors, or job analysts. This method combines data collection with human judgment to analyze and summarize information. Qualitative methods include observation, interviews, questionnaires that ask open-ended questions, and other techniques such as activity logs.

## Uses of Job Analysis

In addition to providing information for setting compensation policy, job analysis has many other advantages:

**TEST TAKING TIP**
Look for the "hard words" like; always, never, or all in the answer options. They're frequently a clue to the wrong choices.

- Lines of authority and accountability are set down, and employees know what is expected of them.

- Wage surveys are possible when job duties are known.

- Recruiters can match the right employee with the right job, when they have a description of a job's requirements and the specific qualities needed from an employee.

- Performance appraisal is facilitated by specific knowledge of a job's duties.

- Training programs can be set up when the requirements of a job are known.

## Job Descriptions

A job description is a formal document that describes the essential functions of a particular job. The description includes the job title and a list of the factors considered in determining the appropriate compensation of a person holding that position (i.e., the duties, responsibilities, working conditions, education, training, and experience requirements of the job).

Job descriptions generally may be divided into either of two broad categories. Standard descriptions are general descriptions of the major duties of one or more jobs; and specific job descriptions are comprehensive, detailed descriptions of the duties of a particular job.

## Job/Position Specifications

Job specifications organize information gathered through the job analysis and allow a meaningful comparison of jobs for evaluation and pricing. They are written descriptions of the skills involved and the physical demands of a job.

The specification is not supposed to be another detailed description of the job. But each task covered in the job description should have a corresponding statement in the job specification, indicating the skills involved for performance of the task. It is also important to indicate that no skills are needed, if that is the case.

---

**EXAMPLE**

If a clerical procedure involves assembling a report, the job specification should indicate that an employee merely copies, posts or transcribes data submitted to him; he does not have to compute, analyze or arrive at the information independently, using his own judgment and initiative .

---

Typical questions the specification sheet should answer include these points:

- **Education**: What special knowledge, education, or training is needed? Academic? Technical? Knowledge of a specialized field?

- **Experience**: How long in related or similar work in the same or similar organizations?

- **Complexity of duties**: Independent action? Judgment? Initiative? Independent decisions? Creative effort?

- **Supervision received**: Does supervisor outline specific methods to be followed? Prescribe results to be attained? How closely does supervisor check work or personally handle problems? What dollar loss would result from errors? How often does possibility of loss or error occur?

- **Responsibility**: For loss or damage to tools, equipment, product or materials? Responsibility for safety of others?

- **Contacts with others**: To what extent is employee responsible? How frequent are contacts? Does the employee provide information, make sales, exert influence, or make policy? Are the contacts inside and/or outside the organization?

- **Confidential data**: To what extent are integrity and discretion important? Would unwarranted disclosure cost money, hurt internal or external relationships?

- **Mental and visual demand**: What degree of concentration is required? Is there some or constant eye strain?

- **Working conditions**: Are conditions unusually hazardous or uncomfortable? How intensive, or for what percent of the working time? Are there special physical demands?

- **Supervisory responsibility**: What responsibility for policy, costs, methods, production, or personnel does this position have? Part-time or full- time? How many people are supervised directly or indirectly?

In preparing the specification, job analysts are approaching the first stage of the actual job evaluation. They exercise some judgment, based on their understanding of the job.

# Establish Hiring Criteria

## Identifying Selection Criteria

To minimize the risk of legal action and insure EEO compliance, supervisors should: (1) define very clearly what job requirements must be met; (2) focus on only those areas of an applicant's background and capabilities that are job-related; and (3) insure that all applicants for an opening are evaluated against the same skills and abilities and that those requirements are job-related.

> **TEST TAKING TIP**
> Many successful test-takers report they can get the answer options down to two choices on most questions.

### Clarify job requirements

The first step in the hiring process is to clarify what the person will be doing and what qualifications, knowledge, skills, and abilities are necessary to get the job done. This involves describing job functions as well as scheduling requirements. This is very important because every other step in the hiring process — from advertising to testing, interviewing, and final decision making — depends on what the underlying job requirements are.

Clarifying job requirements is not just the "legal" thing to do; it also helps spell out the job-related criteria for the hiring decision and insures the company gets the best candidates for the job. This should be done before any other step is taken in the recruitment process, including posting notices of openings, advertising, and interviewing.

When clarifying the job requirements needed to get the job done, the description should indicate what are "essential" and what are "marginal" job functions. These terms have specific meanings under the Americans with Disabilities Act and other disability discrimination laws. The description must leave open the possibility of accomplishing tasks in several different ways. This is because the ADA and other disability discrimination laws require employers to provide reasonable accommodations to qualified individuals with disabilities, defined as those who can perform the essential functions of a job, with or without accommodation. Accommodation may mean restructuring a job, particularly its "marginal" functions. Before determining if an accommodation is feasible and will not cause "undue hardship" to the company, the company first needs to know what the "essential functions" of the job are and any alternative ways the job can be performed.

### Review resumes against job requirements

Before conducting any interviews, the interviewer should think through the job systematically and review the job requisition and the job itself to identify relevant factors such as: (1) necessary skills and abilities — work experience, education, technical skills, communication skills, analytical skills, and specialized training; (2) behavioral factors — motivation, interests, goals, drive and energy, reliability, and stress tolerance; and (3) corporate culture — team orientation, independence, social effectiveness, and interpersonal style.

The interviewer should decide what these terms mean when applied to the job to be filled. The supervisor should consult with the HR department to develop criteria for screening candidates and to share the supervisor's concerns. Then a list of specific qualifications and qualities that the successful candidate should have can be prepared to compare with the applicant's resume. The interviewer should have read the applicant's resume and any other written application materials carefully before the interview.

# Identify Internal and External Recruitment Methods

## Internal Sourcing

The first source to tap in filling all but the lowest entry-level jobs is the company's existing workforce. Promotion from within is expected in today's workforce, and not opening jobs for internal candidates may create resentment and high turnover. Most employees do not think of their current job as the last step of their career ladder. If a company does not provide a next step, employees will take the skills and knowledge they have built up and work elsewhere. Even when passed-over employees stay with the company, hiring outsiders to fill positions for which inside personnel are qualified or trainable can cause productivity-robbing turmoil — from resentment of or discrimination toward the new employee to despair and stagnation among passed-over employees.

### Advantages of promoting from within

Filling jobs with internal candidates keeps recruiting costs low since advertising the position costs nothing. It improves employee morale by showing that the company offers opportunities for advancement. Evaluating the skills and strengths of current employees is easier than evaluating candidates based on their resumes and interviews. Promotions also reduce the cost to the company of orientation and administrative processing. Relative to outside hires, promoted employees should become productive more quickly since they need less orientation or "settling in" time. Finally, posting jobs internally lets employees know the requirements of jobs higher on the career ladder and what they must do to become promotable.

### Disadvantages of promoting from within

The chief drawback to promoting from within is that it still leaves a job to be filled — the job left by the promoted employee. Training needs increase because both the promoted employee and the replacement employee need training in their new jobs. The lack of new perspectives from outside recruits can cause stagnation or complacency in an organization. From a legal standpoint, promoting from within will do little to promote affirmative action goals since internal hires perpetuate the characteristics of the workforce. A company that is not doing well in hiring minorities and women can magnify the disparity since its only promotable candidates will be white males.

### Methods of promoting from within

Most companies use some combination of job posting, nominations by supervisors, and skills inventories to find the best qualified candidates within the organization. For each job opening, a notice listing the title, salary range, minimum hiring specifications, and closing date for applications is normally posted in appropriate locations; company intranet sites, bulletin boards in an employee break area/lounge and in the Human Resources Department, or distributed by company e-delivery communication systems. Employees are responsible for monitoring job vacancy notices and for filing an in-house application form following company procedures, electronically or written applications with the Human Resource department by the end of the specified posting period.

### 9-Box Grid

The 9-Box grid is a tool used by managers to assess the potential of individuals so as to devote scarce company resources to those few employees identified as promotional material. Sometimes called a performance or potential matrix, this system is used in succession planning to determine and identify future successors.

Candidates are evaluated on current performance and future potential and placed into a matrix or grid that is three columns wide by three rows deep. The rows are labeled as High, Medium and Low. The columns are titled as Below, Meeting and Exceeding.

The rows signify the potential of an individual to be promoted. The columns signify whether the employee is below, meeting or exceeding her current role's expectations.

This system allows the organization to spend its time and resources on those employees demonstrating both high potential and who are exceeding current expectations. These are the employees who usually are identified for inclusion into the organizational succession plan.

## External Sourcing

When looking outside an organization to fill a vacancy, employers have a number of sources from which to choose. Employment agencies, both public and private, are a commonly used external recruitment tool. Internet based job posting websites provide wide exposure. For upper-management positions, executive search firms offer the specialization needed to identify highly placed persons.

Other sources of applicants include schools and universities, unions, data banks, and career fairs. University placement offices and union hiring halls can identify applicants with particular levels of training, skills, and knowledge. Some computerized data banks cater to particular professional fields. For exposure to a wide range of candidates, career fairs are an alternative.

# Establishing Selection Procedures

## Application Process

Federal fair employment practices laws cover all aspects of employment, including the recruiting, application, and hiring processes. The fact that jobs are available should be made known on an equal basis to members of protected classes. Help-wanted advertisements cannot indicate a preference based on prohibited factors such as race, religion, ethnic background, gender, or age. Application forms cannot contain discriminatory questions. Employment tests that have an adverse impact on minorities or other protected groups are prohibited, and employees must be hired on a nondiscriminatory basis.

Various recruiting methods include: word-of-mouth, nepotism, walk-in applications, employment agencies, and help-wanted ads. The application process includes proper application forms, interviewing techniques, and pre-employment inquiries. Testing and how to validate employment tests are necessary, including content, construct, and criterion-related validation. The Uniform Guidelines on Employee Selection Procedures are commonly accepted and special bona fide qualifications such as height and weight requirements are important considerations. There are potential problems with subjective selection practices and employers should document selection practices under the UGESP.

## Interviewing

The face-to-face employment interview is the most commonly used, yet universally criticized, selection tool. Properly conducted interviews can shed a great deal of light on a job candidate's qualifications, personal characteristics, and background.

However, interviewing has many limitations. Pre-judgment and bias are hard to avoid in interview situations. Research shows that ratings of an applicant's interview performance often mirror the interviewer's pre-existing biases and favor candidates similar to the interviewer in personality or appearance — qualities unrelated to most jobs. Experts also argue that interviews, as conducted in most companies, do not produce valid predictions of job success. These limitations can be lessened by using structured interviews and by educating interviewers in effective interviewing techniques.

Typical interviewing techniques include:

- Screening interviews: Candidates are evaluated informally to determine their suitability to continue in the selection process or to receive an invitation for a face-to-face interview. The process typically includes questions to clarify information found on the candidate's application or resume.

- Stress interviews: Candidates are placed under stressful conditions, which include attempts at intimidation, so as to observe how they handle themselves in demanding environments.

- Structured interviews: All candidates are asked the same set of pre-determined questions, with no deviations or follow-up questions. This system reduces personal prejudice and bias in the interviewer by screening each candidate on qualifications rather than on other factors such as personality.

- Behavioral interviews: Candidates are evaluated as to their past performance on the belief that it is the best predictor of future performance. Behavioral-based interview questions generally start with any one of the following phrases:
    o Tell me about a time when you…
    o Describe a circumstance when you were faced with a problem related to…
    o Think about an instance in which you…
    o Tell me how you approached a situation where…

- Tag-team interviews: Candidates are alternately questioned by two or more interviewers in a fast-paced format designed to give multiple team members exposure to the candidate in order to elicit opinions from various team members as to the candidate's suitability.

- Group interviews: Candidates are interviewed by a group or panel in order to expedite the screening process. This method is more efficient than serial interviewing and all interviewers observe the candidate under the same circumstances.

- Situational interviews: Candidates are asked to respond to various scenarios and how they would respond to each situation.

- Informal interviews: Candidates are evaluated in a casual environment in order to relax them and get them talking so as to elicit additional information about their candidacy.

## Use a structured approach

For each of the job requirements listed as most important, the interviewer should decide what he or she could ask to elicit information to determine whether an applicant has that skill or ability. The process should be kept simple, using only one or two questions per job requirement. An applicant's past performance at similar tasks is a good predictor of future performance. Asking questions that reveal a person's behavioral on-the-job history should help the interviewer to predict how the person will handle the job.

The goal of this form of interviewing is to obtain specific examples of a candidate's past job behaviors rather than to identify general traits and other subjective criteria. The interviewer should include questions along the lines of "Give me an example of a time when you had to: (deal with a difficult person at work, resolve a dispute at work, or coordinate a project that involved many different departments)."

Taking notes during an interview is important. However, the interviewer should be careful not to identify the applicant in writing by any attribute that is unlawful under the fair employment practice statutes. Physical descriptions of an applicant would not be appropriate. Rather, notes should indicate pertinent job-related information about past experience and education that would be useful in making a final selection.

### Questions that can and cannot be asked

Many supervisors fear interviewing because they have heard that the law prohibits asking certain questions. It is easier to remember which questions an interviewer can and cannot ask if a supervisor simply remembers that anything that is not related to whether the applicant can do the job should not be asked, because it would be unlawful — and foolish — to base the hiring decision on it.

Sometimes when people ask an unlawful question, they are trying to find out something job-related, but they are just asking the wrong question. For instance, someone who asks a woman about child care arrangements may be worried about whether the person will be away from work unexpectedly or whether she will be able to undertake the traveling the job requires. If those are important traits for the job, the interviewer should ask everyone about them — both men and women — and ask directly about absences or travel requirements.

Unless there is a proven relationship to the job being sought, the following questions should not be asked of job applicants and information regarding them should not be considered when making hiring decisions:

- medical or mental health history;
- national origin and citizenship status;
- height, weight, or physical characteristics;
- membership in professional or civic organizations that would reveal national origin, race, gender, religion, or any of the other protected classes under fair employment practice laws;
- military service history;
- marital status;
- sexual orientation;
- age;
- previous address;
- names of relatives;
- receipt of unemployment insurance, workers' compensation, or disability benefits;
- foreign languages;
- child care, family planning, or number of children;
- religion or religious beliefs;
- past rejection for bonding; and
- salary history.

Questions should be relevant and job related. Questions regarding an applicant's training and education are normally job related. Other topics that may prove relevant and job related include:

- questioning incomplete information on application form;

- gaps in work experience or education;

- geographic preferences and feelings about relocation, if applicable; normal working hours;

- overnight travel, if applicable;

- reasons for leaving previous jobs;

- personal attributes that could contribute to job performance;

- job-related achievements;

- signs of initiative and self-direction;

- indications of work habits;

- specialized knowledge or expertise;

- lack of detail concerning experience; and

- meaning of former job titles.

## Pre-employment Testing

In a 1971 landmark decision, the U.S. Supreme Court ruled that employers cannot use a selection test unless applicants' scores have a demonstrable bearing on job success. This ruling essentially validated the Equal Employment Opportunity Commission's long-held position on employment tests (Griggs v. Duke Power Co., 1971).

Although the Civil Rights Act of 1964 does not prohibit using pre-employment tests, the Court ruled that employers cannot make test scores the determining factor in a selection decision, unless test results have proven success in predicting later job performance. This limitation holds true whether or not the test was "professionally developed" and regardless of test vendors' claims. According to the Court, the Civil Right Act prohibits "not only overt discrimination but also practices that are fair in form but discriminatory in operation. The touchstone is business necessity." If an employment practice disproportionately excludes blacks or other protected groups and the practice has no proven relationship to job performance, the practice is prohibited, the Court said.

**TEST TAKING TIP**
Get a couple of good night's rest before you sit for the exam.

The Civil Rights Act of 1991 made the Griggs standard into law, requiring employers to show that a challenged hiring practice is a "job necessity." Reasons like customer preference, morale, corporate image, and convenience do not meet this standard.

Employee selection often demands that hiring managers act as fortune-tellers, predicting how an individual will do in the future. To reduce subjectivity and assist in predicting later job success, companies often rely on testing.

Job-relatedness determines how useful any test will be in predicting how a new hire will perform. As a result, different types of tests have evolved for different kinds of work. Some employment screening tools look at an applicant's actual job knowledge; others assess overall intelligence or some specialized cognitive or physical ability that the job requires. In other cases, employers may rely on personality tests to pick the person with the best temperament for the position — an outgoing salesperson or an even-tempered police officer. For positions that involve security concerns or the potential for theft, hiring managers may use polygraph screening and other honesty tests.

## Tests that may violate the Americans With Disabilities Act

| Type of Test | ADA Impact |
|---|---|
| Ability and Aptitude Tests | Job samples like typing tests or "in -baskets" are allowed if they test for abilities required in the job (essential elements) and if employers allow candidates to get the work done any way they can (with accommodation). Intelligence, personality, and cognitive aptitude tests, as well as other tests of skills, knowledge, or abilities must actually relate to the job and be consistent with business necessity. |
| Alcohol Tests | Tests to measure blood alcohol levels are considered medical tests under the ADA (see guidelines below for medical tests). Unlike persons currently addicted to illegal drugs, alcoholics are treated as persons with disabilities under the ADA. |
| Drug Tests | Testing for illegal drug use can be given at the pre-offer stage. However, employers cannot discriminate against recovering and former drug addicts. |
| Genetic Screening | Genetic tests will probably be seen as screening out people with a disability or perceived disability. Job relatedness and business necessity requirements will be hard to prove since genetic tests do not tell anything about a person's ability to do the job. Genetic monitoring of employees (not applicants) for workplace exposure to substances that might cause genetic changes can arguably be job-related. |
| HIV (AIDS) Tests | Barred for virtually all jobs. Can only be justified if the job poses a risk of transmitting the AIDS virus or would endanger the health of the applicant or others in a way that could not be eliminated through accommodation. |
| Medical Tests | Physical exams and other medical tests can only be given after a conditional offer of employment. Exams must be job-related and consistent with business necessity, if used as a reason not to hire someone. Employers can use physical exams to disqualify someone who is a direct threat to health or safety, but cannot disqualify someone based on speculation of future injury. |
| Physical Agility Tests | Strength, flexibility, and endurance tests are not considered medical exams under the ADA and can be given even before making a job offer. |
| Polygraph and Integrity Tests | For paper-and-pencil honesty tests, individuals with certain disabilities may need accommodations in order to complete the tests. |

# Background Investigation

## Why conduct background checks?

### *Negligent hiring*

Employers that hire incompetent or disruptive employees face potential administrative costs and embarrassment. In addition, hiring the wrong person exposes employers to a "negligent hiring" damages claim. Under the negligent hiring principle, an employer has a duty to exercise reasonable care when hiring employees, who, if incompetent or impaired, might pose a risk of injury to the public or fellow employees by means of the employment.

Although this area of the law is still evolving, a majority of states now recognize negligent hiring as a basis for legal action.

> **TEST TAKING TIP**
> For practice purposes, you need to be scoring in the 75-80% range when taking sample tests before you're ready to tackle the real exam.

For example, an employer that hired an employee with a history of violent crimes as the resident manager of an apartment complex was liable to a tenant who was violently raped by the employee. Had the employer done a minimal investigation of the employee, it would have learned that his references were not valid, that he had been convicted of a number of violent offenses, was on probation at the time he was hired, and that he had worked only three months out of the last several years, having spent the remaining time in prison.

However, an employer was not liable when it did not check the criminal record of a door man whose job did not involve the use of guns. The nature of the work was such that checking the applicant's criminal record was not necessary in the exercise of ordinary prudence.

The general rule is that an employer will be liable only if information it could have discovered through a reasonable investigation would have shown that the employee was unfit for the job. If an investigation would not have revealed information that would put the employer on notice that it should not hire the employee, the employer will not be liable if the employee later injures someone.

In some instances, state law may actually prohibit investigation into an applicant's background and employers will not be liable for information that might have been obtained in such an investigation.

For example, Wisconsin law prohibits employers from inquiring into applicants' criminal records. An employer subject to Wisconsin law was not liable for negligent hiring of an employee who killed a child while driving the employer's truck under the influence of alcohol. Even if the employer had checked the employee's record, it would have revealed only that the applicant had a criminal record for battery and burglary, which are unrelated to competence as driver, and a license suspension for 'damage judgment' which does not suggest the use of alcohol or reckless conduct.

As these cases illustrate, employers no longer can afford not to verify past jobs or check references. Such lapses can constitute negligence that skilled attorneys will capitalize on in bringing a claim of negligent hiring.

## How far should the investigation go?

Unfortunately for employers, no hard-and-fast rules apply in determining how extensive a background check to conduct. What is reasonable will depend on the type of job involved and the potential exposure or risk of harm an employee in that position could pose. However, these general tips should help employers guard against negligent hiring lawsuits:

- Complete a background check before hiring any applicant.
- Review the applicant's resume for gaps in work history.
- Obtain the applicant's consent to contact former employers.
- Follow up professional references.
- Managers usually are not hesitant to discuss former employees with excellent records.
- Verify the applicant's previous addresses.
- Do not investigate the applicant's past history of workers' comp claims.
- Look into the applicant's criminal record if possible.
- Monitor employee performance even after hiring.
- Document the investigation.

# Perform or Administer Post-offer Employment Activities

## Medical Examination

### ADA impact

The ADA affects both when and how employers use physicals. Under the ADA, employers cannot use physical exams as pre-employment screens. Hiring policies that automatically eliminate from consideration all persons with certain ailments will almost always be illegal under the ADA.

> Physical exams are lawful only for applicants who have received conditional job offers.

For many employers, complying with this restriction comes easily, since they require physicals only for applicants they expect to hire, as a means of keeping down costs.

The greater effect of the ADA is that employers must make hiring decisions without information on applicants' workers' compensation history or history of diseases and mental illness. Before the ADA, employers routinely asked for this information on application forms, in interviews, or of references.

The ADA does not mean that employers must make hiring decisions without any information about applicants' physical capabilities. Physical agility tests — such as strength, endurance, and flexibility tests — are not considered medical tests and employers can administer them before making the hiring decision.

---

**EXAMPLE**
Rather than ruling out all applicants who have epilepsy from jobs operating dangerous machinery, an employer must consider how the ailment has affected the particular individual. Look at factors like the degree of seizure control, the type of seizures (if any), whether the person has an "aura" or warning of seizures, and whether the person reliably takes prescribed anticonvulsant medication. Automatically rejecting any applicant with epilepsy would illegally discriminate against capable persons who are seizure-free or have adequate warning of seizures. Even when operating machinery might pose a danger to the person, employers should consider possible accommodations, such as placing a shield over the machine to protect the employee.

---

When can an employer require physical examinations? Under the ADA, pre-employment physical examinations are prohibited. An employer can offer a job conditioned on a medical exam showing that the person can safely perform the job. Even when a person's medical history turns up a problem, the employer must consider the impact of the particular ailment on that individual.

At the post-offer stage, employers can require physical examinations only if these practices are followed:

- All other prospective employees in the job category are subject to the same examination before beginning work.
- The applicant's medical history is treated confidentially.
- The results of the exam are not used to discriminate against persons with disabilities covered under the ADA.

## What kind of medical exams meet ADA requirements?

The EEOC has made a few things clear about the medical exam process. First, the inquiry should involve an individual assessment of whether the person is currently able to perform the job, with or without accommodation. Medical studies about work restrictions for people with certain disabilities do not fulfill this requirement since medical research does not reflect the unique circumstances of the individual, the job, and possible accommodations.

Second, the doctor performing the exam must fully understand the position's essential job functions. Medical advice should not be based on general assumptions about what a truck driver or dock worker does. Doctors should know what the person will be doing daily, the company's attendance requirements, overtime expectations, and flexibility or inflexibility of scheduling. For instance, tell the doctor if the person must be able to work six days a week during a busy season that lasts 12 weeks, or if a 9-to-5 work schedule is mandatory. If a person's medical treatment conflicts with this work schedule, the physician can advise the employer of the conflict.

Third, the employer cannot make the doctor responsible for the ultimate hiring decision. Selection should take into account the doctor's advice and other objective evidence, such as the person's experience in similar jobs or non-work activities; the opinions of other doctors knowledgeable about the particular disability; and the advice of rehabilitation counselors, occupational or physical therapists, and others with direct knowledge of the disability or the individual involved.

## Under what circumstances can an offer be withdrawn?

The ADA prohibits employers from using physical exams to screen people out if the exam is not directly related to the job for which the person is applying. Technically, the ADA leaves employers free to require post-offer physical exams that are not job-related. But if an employer withdraws a job offer based on a condition discovered during a pre-employment physical, it should be prepared to show these two facts:

- The reason for withdrawing the offer is job-related, consistent with business necessity, or essential to avoid a direct threat to health or safety.
- No reasonable accommodation would allow the person to perform the job, or making the necessary accommodations would cause the employer undue hardship.

---

Employers cannot disqualify an applicant based on speculation about future risk of injury, increased workers' compensation or health insurance costs, or higher absenteeism.

---

To withdraw an offer based on risk of injury, an employer must be able to document a significant, current risk of substantial harm to health or safety of the individual or others. Even then, the employer must consider whether reasonable accommodations can eliminate the risk or reduce it below the "direct threat" level.

Some examples help clarify how the ADA's standards apply to decisions based on post-offer medical exams:

---

**EXAMPLE 1**

After making a conditional offer of employment, an employer sends an applicant to a doctor for a pre-employment physical. Essential job functions include being available to work every day for the next three months. If the doctor finds a disabling impairment that will cause the person to miss work for a portion of those three months in order to receive treatment, the employer can lawfully withdraw the job offer.

---

**EXAMPLE 2**

An abnormal back X-ray alone does not justify withdrawing a job offer because of fear of increased workers' compensation or health insurance costs. But an employer could reject an applicant for a heavy-lifting job if documentation shows that the person has suffered repeated back injuries in similar jobs, the condition has grown worse with further injuries, and no reasonable accommodation would eliminate the risk of re-injury or reduce it to an acceptable level.

---

**EXAMPLE 3**

A person with a history of repetitive motion injuries has had successful surgery with no further problems. Based solely on the person's history, a doctor recommends against hiring the applicant because the risk of future injury is high. The employer would violate the ADA by acting on this recommendation since the doctor did not consider the person's current condition.

---

**EXAMPLE 4**

After a post-offer medical exam, a doctor recommends a landscaping firm not hire a laborer with curvature of the spine because of the future risk of injury. However, the company failed to give the doctor a job description, which would have shown the job involved riding on a mechanical mower. Once again, the employer would violate the ADA by following the doctor's recommendation, since the risk of injury is speculative and the doctor did not know the essential job functions.

---

## Hiring Applicants with Disabilities

Individuals with disabilities are a frequently overlooked source of qualified workers to fill employer's needs. With low-cost reasonable accommodations, these workers are as productive as any other employee and often have lower absentee and turnover rates. There are many easily tapped recruitment sources for applicants with disabilities, many of which pre-screen individuals to match workers with the jobs for which they are best suited.

For many employers, the most significant impact of the ADA on workers' compensation is the prohibition on asking about an applicant's workers' comp history before making a conditional offer of employment. Equal Employment Opportunity Commission guidance on the interaction of the ADA and state workers' compensation laws makes clear that the ADA allows an employer to ask an applicant questions about prior workplace injuries or workers' compensation claims only:

- after it has made a conditional offer of employment, and

- if it asks the same questions of all employees entering the same job category

## Other major points

- The same limitations apply to medical examinations. An employer may, after making a conditional job offer but before employment has begun, require an applicant to submit to a medical examination to obtain information about the existence or nature of any prior disabilities. Regardless of the obviousness of a disability, this can only be done if all new hires in the same job category are also required to take a medical examination.

- An individual may be considered disabled under a workers' compensation law but not under the ADA. One definition of a disability under the ADA is a physical or mental impairment that substantially limits a major life activity. However, impairments resulting from workplace injuries may not be severe enough to substantially limit a major life activity, or they may be only temporary, non-chronic, and have little or no long-term impact. Such workplace injuries would not be disabilities.

- An employee who does not have an impairment that substantially limits a major life activity, or a record of an impairment, may still be protected under the ADA if the employer regards the employee as being impaired. For example, the following individuals may be regarded as having a disability:

    o an employee with a temporary back impairment whom an employer refuses to reinstate because it believes the employee cannot lift more than a few pounds;

    o an employee with a facial disfigurement whom an employer refuses to reinstate because the employer fears negative reactions by co-workers or customers;

    o an employee who is fully recovered from a temporary back impairment but is discharged because the employer believes that the employee, if allowed to resume heavy lifting, would suffer a totally incapacitating back injury.

- At the time the employee suffers a disabling injury or when the employee seeks to return to work after such an injury, an employer may ask disability-related questions or require a medical examination as long as the questions or examinations are job-related and consistent with business necessity.

- This requirement is met when an employer reasonably believes that the injury will impair the employee's ability to perform essential job functions or raises legitimate concerns that the employee might be a direct threat to the health or safety of the employee or other individuals.

**TEST TAKING TIP**
We suggest people completing a prep course or formalized study group take the test within 10 days of completing the program. The longer you wait, the more you forget.

- The assumption that a person with a disability would pose an increased risk of injury and increased workers' compensation costs is not a proper basis for refusing to hire the person, unless the employer shows that the person's employment would pose a direct threat to the health and safety of the individual or others.

- That a person with a disability experienced a prior workplace injury does not, by itself, establish that the person's current employment poses a significant risk of substantial harm that cannot be lowered or eliminated by a reasonable accommodation.

- An employer cannot require that an employee with a disability related to a workplace injury be able to return to "full duty" before the employee is allowed to return to work. The term "full duty" may include marginal as well as essential functions or may mean performing job functions without an accommodation. Therefore, an employer cannot deny employment to an employee with a disability if these marginal functions can be eliminated or re-assigned or the employee can otherwise be accommodated.

- An employer cannot refuse to return an employee with a disability to work:
  - based on the assumption that the employee poses an increased risk of re-injury, and
  - increased workers' compensation costs,
  - without proof that the employee poses a direct threat to the employee's safety or that of co-workers, or
  - because the employee was found to have a permanent or total disability under a workers' compensation law.

- An employer must reasonably accommodate an employee who is disabled by a workplace injury. Provisions in workers' compensation laws that make them the exclusive remedy for workplace injuries do not limit an employee's ability to pursue relief for disability discrimination under the ADA.

- An employer no longer can elect to keep a qualified employee with a disability in a limited assignment or on a disability benefit program rather than permitting the employee to bid for other jobs.

# Evaluating Selection and Employment Processes for Effectiveness

## Evaluating Recruiting Effectiveness

### Recruitment evaluation systems

The best way to identify effective recruitment techniques is to evaluate recruitment methods. HR managers should conduct separate recruitment analyses for each job or category of jobs, since what works for one job may prove ineffective for another job.

For each recruitment effort, the analysis involves several steps. First, list the key job requirements. This listing will be useful if new openings arise for which the organization has never before recruited. If the new job opening has requirements similar to other jobs in the company, past recruitment experience for those jobs will help the recruiter know where to start.

**TEST TAKING TIP**
There is a countdown clock on the computer screen. It starts at four hours and counts down to zero. You'll know exactly how much time is left.

Next, keep records of applicants who were considered for the position and the recruitment sources used to attract these candidates. List how many qualified applicants came from each recruiting source. This information can be obtained in a number of ways:

- Place a question on the application form that asks "How were you referred to our company?"
- Code the return addresses in advertisements in print media to indicate from where the response came. For instance, a return address of "ABC Co., Dept. LT" would indicate a response from an ad in Legal Times, while "Dept. SFE-1209" would mean the San Francisco Examiner's December 9th edition.

- Ask candidates during the interview how they heard about the company or the job. This method, however, limits recordkeeping to only those candidates who reach the interview stage —typically the most qualified applicants.

For each recruiting source, the following information on applicants attracted from that source can help evaluate its overall effectiveness:

- total number of applicants;

- percentage of minorities and women among applicants;

- average years of experience and education;

- percentage of applicants meeting job requirements;

- average scores of applicants on recruitment screening test; and

- offer and acceptance rates.

Other helpful information for tracking the effectiveness of recruiting sources includes:

- the overall and per-applicant costs of using each source; and

- the length of time between placing the ad or contacting the source and hiring the candidate.

A good strategy for pairing job requirements and recruitment sources is to place the recruitment analysis on the back of the job requisition form.

With this information, a recruiter can figure costs per hire by dividing the cost of each recruitment source by the number of hires obtained through that source. In addition, recruiters should examine the quality of candidates obtained from each source. If successful employees tend to come from a certain school or employment agency, for instance, using that source may prove to be more effective than sources which cost less per hire but produce fewer high-quality candidates.

# Developing and Implementing the Organizational Exit Process

## General Issues

### Reasons for termination

Terminations can be classified by the reason for severing the employment relationship. Determining the cause of a termination is essential for HR managers to carry out company and legal policies governing severance pay, workers' compensation, unemployment compensation, continuation of benefits, and pensions. HR managers also need to make sure the reasons for an involuntary termination do not give grounds for a fired employee to claim wrongful discharge.

### Misconduct

Most disciplinary policies allow termination of employees for gross misconduct, such as theft, dishonesty, violence, or insubordination. Other forms of misconduct leading to discharge include disrespect to co-workers or customers, unsafe acts, violation of work rules, or unprofessional behavior.

### Unsatisfactory performance

Dismissal for unsatisfactory performance can follow repeated absence or lateness, failure to meet deadlines or quotas, or inability to do the work.

### Organizational change

Permanent layoffs occur when positions are eliminated or employees' knowledge, skills, abilities, and/or attitudes do not meet job demands after a reorganization or a change in control. Unlike other forms of involuntary termination, most companies provide severance pay for long-service employees who lose their jobs due to reorganization, downsizing, or change in control.

### Resignation

Employees may voluntarily leave to pursue more attractive job opportunities, to spend more time with family, to deal with personal problems, or merely to escape an unappealing job.

### Retirement

Since mandatory retirement is allowed only in rare cases, retirements are really just voluntary resignations. However, retirement differs from other employee-initiated departures since the separating employee is eligible for pension and other retirement benefits that HR must coordinate.

### Death

At times, an employment relationship can end because of an employee's death. A company's termination policy should address this circumstance and establish mechanisms to inform families of any applicable company-sponsored benefits, such as employee life insurance policies.

## State limits on employment-at-will

Under the traditional employment-at-will doctrine, employers can fire employees at any time and for any or no reason at all. But state laws and court rulings have increasingly restricted this traditional relationship. State public policy may bar terminating employees for such reasons as filing claims for workers' compensation benefits or unpaid wages; refusing to take or failing a lie detector test; AIDS, or drug test; taking a family leave; objecting to unsafe conditions; or smoking in the workplace. In addition, state court rulings have restricted at-will employment based on common-law theories of implied contract, implied covenant of good faith and fair dealing, or wrongful discharge in violation of public policy.

### Implied contract theories

Written or oral communications stating that the employer will follow certain discharge procedures or will terminate employees only for good cause can create an employment contract that discharged employees can use to challenge the employer's claim of at-will employment.

In determining whether an implied contract exists, courts typically examine an employer's:

- written personnel rules as expressed in handbooks, policy statements, or letters to employees; and
- oral promises of job security or fair treatment.

Most states, however, will negate a claim of implied contract if the employee signed an acknowledgment that employment is at-will and that the at-will nature of the employment can only be altered by a document addressed to the employee and signed by the company president.

### Just cause standard

Some companies, to boost recruiting or employee loyalty, allow an implied contract to be formed based on handbook or other statements that limit non-downsizing terminations to "just cause." State courts are split on what an employer must prove when defending a lawsuit challenging a "just cause" discharge. A few states hold that the employer must prove that the employee actually committed misconduct. The majority however, like California, hold that the employer need only prove it conducted a reasonable investigation and reasonably believed, at the time of discharge, that the employee had committed the misconduct.

*Implied covenant of good faith*

Some state courts recognize an implied covenant of good faith and fair dealing as limiting an employer's right to arbitrarily discharge employees. This theory encompasses a range of discharges involving bad faith, some of which are also protected under implied contract or public policy theories.

Examples of bad faith discharges include:

- an abrupt dismissal without cause of a long-tenured employee,

- termination of an employee who had given up a good position and relocated to accept the job offer, or

- discharge of an employee to avoid paying pensions or earned commissions. Many courts, however, have found the implied covenant does not afford any discharge protection to at-will employees.

## Layoffs/Reductions-in-Force

Layoffs, reductions in force (RIFs), and downsizing are terms for employment terminations due to economic, rather than performance, factors. Permanent layoffs are painful for both employees and employers. The company loses trained, experienced employees and tests the loyalties and motivation of its remaining employees. Laid-off employees lose their livelihoods and sometimes their identity and self-esteem. Because of these consequences, employers should explore all alternatives before resorting to layoffs.

> **TEST TAKING TIP**
> You've got to give the test-maker the answer they want. Try to understand their question and where they are coming from, then answer it… their way.

When layoffs are unavoidable, the manner in which the terminations are carried out can greatly influence how both laid-off and surviving employees react.

> Several federal laws affect the manner in which a layoff is carried out. The most important of these laws is the Worker Readjustment and Retraining Notification (WARN) Act, which requires employers give advance notice (60 days) and follow other specific procedures when conducting plant closings and mass layoffs (more than 50 employees and at least 33% of the workforce) for employers with 100 or more employees.

Besides the WARN act, several other federal laws may raise compliance issues when employers are conducting layoffs. The Age Discrimination in Employment Act (ADEA), which prohibits age discrimination against employees over age 40, often is used by terminated workers to challenge a company's layoff selection policies. An employer also can encounter problems when laying off older workers if it carries out the layoffs in a manner that violates the benefits requirements of the Employee Retirement Income Security Act.

## Constructive Discharge

Constructive discharge occurs when an employee resigns to avoid involuntary termination. An employer might offer constructive discharge if it lacks solid grounds for dismissal but feels the employee can no longer function effectively, such as when a political battle or highly publicized charge of sexual harassment undermines a manager's authority. Other situations may involve a long-tenured, once valuable employee whose performance has badly deteriorated but whom the organization would like to offer a face-saving alternative to discharge. Unlike employee-initiated resignations, constructive discharges leave an employer open to a wrongful discharge suit. To make sure an employee's resignation is voluntary and not a constructive discharge, company policy should ask employees to submit resignation letters and undergo exit interviews with HR.

When a resignation is a constructive discharge, sometimes an employee resigns because a supervisor has imposed intolerable conditions on the employee's continued employment that have left the employee little choice but to quit. This is referred to in law as a "constructive discharge." Some courts have held that the standard for determining whether an employee has, in fact, been constructively discharged is whether a reasonable person in the employee's place would have felt compelled to resign. Others require a specific intent to force the person to leave. Constructive discharge can have very serious financial consequences if the employee sues. If the supervisor's motive was discriminatory or otherwise illegal, the employer is no less liable for wrongful discharge than it would be if the employee had been fired. In addition, the supervisor and employer may be liable under state law for both punitive and actual damages for intentional infliction of emotional distress.

### Policy tip

Employers should be alert to the possibility that an employee under pressure will resign because of sexual harassment. If the employee leaves, management may never get the chance to investigate fully and remedy the complaint. In addition, the employee may claim the resignation was a "constructive discharge." If the employer can only say "We didn't do anything about the complaint," the court may agree. Constructive discharge in a harassment case is roughly equivalent to an unlawful discharge. Wages and benefits the employee lost become part of the dollar amount the court will award if the employer is held liable.

## Retaliation

Supervisors sometimes fire employees or harass them until they resign in retaliation for the employee's whistleblowing or exercise of legally protected rights. Retaliatory discharges are very costly in legal, financial, and public relations terms; preventing these firings is up to HR.

Various federal and state laws make it illegal for employers, employment agencies, or labor organizations or their employees or members to discriminate against an employee or job applicant because the person opposed an unlawful employment practice. Persons who file a discrimination charge or who assist or participate in an investigation, hearing, or trial regarding a charge are protected from retaliation.

### Public policy theories

Many states recognize an exception to the employment-at-will rule for a discharge that violates the state's public policy. Most courts extend the exception only when the public policy is clearly expressed in the state's constitution or legislation. The major categories of wrongful discharge claims under this exception are terminations for:

- refusing to commit or participate in an illegal act;
- whistleblowing—reporting the employer's illegal conduct to outside parties such as a state agency or the police;
- performing an important public obligation, such as serving jury duty or aiding a criminal investigation; and exercising a statutory right or privilege, such as filing a workers' compensation claim or refusing to work under unsafe conditions.

The Supreme Court holds that Title VII protects former employees from retaliation, including when an employer gives a former employee a negative reference in retaliation for the employee's having filed a claim against it. Although Title VII's retaliation provision does not mention former employees, it is more consistent with the broader context provided by Title VII's other sections and with the retaliation prohibition's primary purpose of maintaining unfettered access to Title VII's remedial mechanisms to find that former employees are protected than to find that they are not.

## Retirement

Since mandatory retirement is allowed only in rare cases, retirements are really just voluntary resignations. However, retirement differs from other employee-initiated departures since the separating employee is eligible for pension and other retirement benefits that HR must coordinate.

Federal law prohibits targeting pension-eligible employees in a layoff to save the company additional money. However, employers can legally encourage workers to retire by offering early retirement incentives.

The Older Workers Benefit Protection Act amended the ADEA to expressly authorize voluntary retirement plans that further the purposes of the ADEA. Specifically authorized are plans that:

- require a minimum age for normal or early retirement benefits;
- provide subsidized early retirement benefits; and
- provide supplements to employees who retire before they are eligible to receive Social Security benefits.

The legislative history of the OWBPA cites several examples of permissible voluntary retirement programs:

- flat dollar incentives (for example, a bonus payment on termination);
- enhancements tied to years of service (for example, $2,000 per year of service); enhancements based on percentage of salary or pension; and
- imputed additions to age and/or service for purposes of calculating pension benefits.

## Employer Defenses against Litigation

### Documenting reasons for discharge

No law requires employers to record dealings with employees, but written documentation is the best defense against challenged terminations. Discharge decisions based on documented performance deficiencies have the following advantages:

### *Accuracy*

Records made right after an event are more likely to be accurate. Memories may fade and grow distorted over time. The Federal Rules of Evidence recognize the reliability of contemporaneous records by providing, for example, that memos or records made when events are fresh in the writer's mind may be admitted as evidence in courts.

### *Preservation*

If the person making the decision to discharge or the employee witnessing the event leading to termination leaves the company, the employer may find itself with no explanation for its discharge decision. Another concern is that key witnesses may be induced to change their stories; if at the time of an incident, the witnesses made a written record of their observations, this contemporaneous record will carry greater weight than the revised version.

*Believability*

Jurors and judges realize that a supervisor accused of wrongdoing will not necessarily admit to the truth. If a case boils down to an employee's word against a supervisor's claims, human instinct tends to give the employee the benefit of the doubt, considering the repercussions of discharge. Written documentation, even if just the supervisor's personal notes, usually have higher credibility than any statements made after the supervisor was accused of wrongful discharge.

*Communication of expectations*

Sharing written performance evaluations with an employee gives notice of the employer's expectations and warning as to where an individual is failing to measure up. In addition, written warnings, memos, and performance improvement plans carry more weight in an employee's mind than oral reprimands and threats. Showing documentation to the employee at the time of termination also can deter an employee from an impulsive decision to file suit.

> **TEST TAKING TIP**
> Because the questions are prepared by different people, some questions on the exam may give you the answer to another question on the test.

*Proof against defamation charges*

If an employer's reasons for discharge impugn the employee's character, documentation is vital. A fired employee can sue for defamation if the employer acted with reckless disregard for the truth in terminating the individual for such offenses as theft or dishonesty, so an employer should have evidence to support its conclusion about the employee's character.

# Affirmative Action Programs

## Affirmative Action Plans

In the early 1970s, affirmative action plans gained recognition as an integral part of equal employment opportunity law. The purpose of affirmative action is to overcome the effects of past or present discrimination and to remedy the underutilization of women, minorities, and individuals with disabilities by giving express preferences to those groups. The Equal Employment Opportunity Commission has developed guidelines that define affirmative action.

Affirmative action plans are appropriate or required when they are:

- mandated by a court order;
- a remedy for past or present discrimination;
- in compliance with an EEO enforcement agency order; or
- a condition of doing business with the federal government.

*Multiple definitions*

"Affirmative action" is a term that sometimes causes confusion because it has several definitions. Taken very broadly, it means any corrective measure undertaken to overcome past practices that may have excluded or limited access of certain individuals because they belong to a disfavored or disadvantaged group.

*Historical context*

The term "affirmative action" dates back to the 1935 Wagner Act, where it was used in a section prohibiting unfair labor practices. It was applied to fair employment practices in a 1955 Eisenhower White House conference on equal job opportunity.

President John F. Kennedy used the term in 1961 in an executive order that required that companies doing business with the federal government take affirmative action to avoid discrimination in hiring. In 1965, a year after passage of the Civil Rights Act of 1964, President Lyndon Johnson issued Executive Order 11246, requiring all federal contractors to take and report on affirmative action to ensure nondiscrimination in hiring and promotion.

Official notions of affirmative action duties were spelled out in more detail under President Richard Nixon. An order was issued in 1969 requiring every federal contractor to:

- analyze its entire workforce;

- determine the reasons for any disparities in representation of women and minorities;

- establish goals and timetables for hiring or promoting members of underrepresented groups; and attempt, in good faith, to meet those goals and timetables.

## Purpose of AA plans
Congress believes that federal employers, including federal contractors, should be models for the private sector and as such should be held to a higher standard of providing employment opportunities for minorities, women, certain veterans, and individuals with disabilities. In order to ensure that opportunities are indeed equal for those protected groups, applicable laws require affirmative action, which establishes goals and timetables for reaching full utilization of minorities, women, covered veterans, and individuals with disabilities.

**TEST TAKING TIP**
Any math answer options must align 100% with your computations or you've computed wrongly. Even one penny off is a good reason to re-figure.

Affirmative action plans set objectives that an employer commits itself to apply every good faith effort to reach. AA plans strive to correct deficiencies and to achieve the full utilization of minorities and women at all levels and in all segments of an employer's workforce.

There are three essential steps an employer must consider when creating an affirmative action plan:
1. a reasonable self-analysis of the composition of the workforce;
2. an analysis of the make-up of the population in the local labor or recruitment area; and
3. if underutilization of minorities or women is found, the establishment of reasonable goals and timetables to correct the situation.

An affirmative action plan must be specifically tailored to remedy the employer's discriminatory practices. The plan must be narrowly crafted to remedy the effects of the past bias, while not impinging on the rights of other workers. It should be a detailed, result-oriented set of procedures developed to promote the full utilization of minorities, women, or other protected group.

## Utilization analysis
An employer must make an honest and reasonable evaluation of the status of women and minorities within the company by breaking down its workforce into job titles and job groups and then calculating the percentage of women and minorities in those groups. Next, the employer must determine the availability of qualified women and minorities in the relevant job market. Gathering and analyzing this data is called a "utilization analysis." It is a required element of any affirmative action plan.

In addition, a good utilization analysis will help an employer in defending a discrimination charge if the employer uses the information to attempt to correct any problems it finds. The analysis also will help employers monitor their AA plans and determine how the plans are working and what remains to be done.

The following regulations can aid an employer's self-analysis:
- OFCCP Regulations (41 CFR §60-2.1) et seq.); and
- EEOC's Uniform Guidelines on Employee Selection Procedures (29 CFR §1607).

### Internal analysis

An employer must look at its current workforce and prepare statistics on males, females, and minorities at each job level within each job group in each major organizational unit. The present composition of the workforce will reflect the impact of past and present employment practices and also will establish a basis for affirmative action goals by identifying where the problems are. Any figures should indicate both actual numbers of employees in each category and percentages.

The OFCCP advises that underutilization of minorities and women is most likely to occur in the following jobs categories:
- officials and managers;
- professionals;
- technicians;
- sales workers (except over-the-counter sales in certain retail establishments);
- and craftsmen.

**TEST TAKING TIP**
Don't over-analyze the test questions. Many test-takers fall into a trap of circular logic. They over-think each question and try and allow for every possible contingency. Just give the test-taker the answer they want.

Special attention in the analysis should therefore be directed to such jobs. Each job title, ranked from the lowest paid to the highest paid, within each department should be listed. For each job title, the total number of employees, the total number of male and female employees, and the total number of male and female employees by minority subgroup should be listed. The wage or salary rate for each also should be listed.

### External analysis

After determining the composition of its current workforce, the employer must determine the reasonable availability of qualified individuals from each protected group within the available labor pool in the geographic area. Data can be gathered from state and federal labor departments, the EEOC, private organizations, and the U.S. Bureau of the Census.

After obtaining the necessary data, the employer should detail the following information:
- the percentage of each minority group in the total population of the relevant geographical area;
- the percentage of each minority group and of females in the workforce;
- the extent of unemployment of minorities and females in the relevant geographical area;
- the availability of minorities and females with the required skills in the geographical area;
- the availability of promotable and transferable females and minorities in the employer's workforce;
- institutions in the community capable of training people in the needed skills; and
- the employer's capability for training minorities and women to qualify for all job classifications.

*Metropolitan Statistical Area*
The usual method for determining the geographical area from which workers can be drawn is to depend on Census Bureau data for the appropriate Metropolitan Statistical Area where the employer is located. An MSA is a county or group of contiguous counties that contain at least one city of 50,000 inhabitants or more or twin cities with a combined population of at least 50,000, except in the New England states. The MSA is not the only standard used and employers are free to develop their own so long as they are reasonable.

## Reasonable basis for Affirmative Action

After a utilization analysis has been conducted and the internal workforce data has been compared to the external available labor pool data, the employer can determine where there is underutilization of women or minority groups. Any protected group that is under-represented in the employer's workforce signifies a potential need for affirmative action. If a significant under-representation exists due to discriminatory practices or because nondiscriminatory practices adversely impacted on a minority group, the under-represented group should be selected for preferential treatment.

AA plans set goals and timetables for reaching full utilization of minorities, women, covered veterans, and individuals with disabilities. They set objectives that an employer commits itself to use good faith efforts to reach. AA plans are merely goals, however. Due to a variety of circumstances, an employer may not be able to achieve the exact goals set out in the plan. It is important for employers to realize this and to set realistic goals and reasonable timetables in the plans they prepare for the OFCCP.

## Adverse impact

Title VII prohibits employer practices, procedures, and policies that adversely impact women and minorities. If it is determined that an employer's existing or contemplated practices result in actual or potential adverse impact, the employer may institute an AA plan.

The adverse impact does not have to be intentional. A policy that is neutral on its face nevertheless may impact adversely on a protected group. Both intentional and unintentional employment discrimination are prohibited by Title VII. If a hiring policy has resulted in an imbalance in the workplace, the employer may decide to adopt a policy of preferential hiring until the workplace more closely matches the qualified labor pool. As with any voluntary AA plan, care should be taken not to adversely affect the rights of non-protected groups. Employers must remember that courts do not favor quotas, preferring instead that employers use aggressive recruitment techniques.

## Reasonable action

An AA plan must be closely related to its remedial purpose and specifically tailored to correct the problems evinced by the employer's self-analysis. It should not be so broad that it disadvantages other workers who are not members of a protected class.

Reasonable action usually includes, but is not limited to, the following steps:

- setting goals and timetables;
- providing opportunities for groups traditionally discriminated against;
- reviewing the selection practices for positions where underutilization was found;
- creating training programs and focusing recruiting efforts;
- providing transportation when the work site is far from areas with a high minority population; and
- providing on-site or other forms of childcare assistance.

Ideally, the plan should remedy an employer's specific problems without unnecessarily restricting the employment opportunities of non-protected employees.

### Goals and timetables

An employer should establish reasonable interim and long-term goals. The goals should be attainable in view of the employer's deficiencies. They should be significant, realistic, and measurable and they must be established to obtain a specific result in every area of employment where underutilization exists.

The goals should factor the percentage of employees in a job group against the percentage of women and minorities available for the positions in that group. Each goal should have a specific timetable that gages the minimum reasonable time needed to reach the goal.

Other considerations in developing an AA plan include; the AA plan should be enforced by top company officials; and all departments should be encouraged to provide input and to participate in the creation and implementation of the AA plan.

There should be a written statement declaring the employer's intent and policy regarding EEO. An AA policy statement may include the following principles:

- a commitment to EEO for all current and future employees;
- an AA commitment designed to remedy the effects of past discrimination; and
- creating goals to change the current makeup of the workforce.

The AA plan should be disseminated within the company, as well as communicated outside the workplace to the general public. A nondiscriminatory recruitment program should be enacted. All subcontractors, vendors, and other affiliates should be notified of the company's commitment to equal employment opportunity.

For federal contractors, an EEO clause is required for publicly disseminated information and contracts, including:

- want ads;
- leases;
- contracts; and
- purchase orders.

### Who is covered?

The Department of Labor's Office of Federal Contract Compliance Programs is charged with enforcing the affirmative action requirements of Executive Order 11246. Federal contractors with a contract for more than $10,000 are required to take affirmative action to hire and promote minorities and women under EO 11246. Contractors with contracts of $50,000 or more and 50 or more employees are

> **TEST TAKING TIP**
> English majors do well on these tests. Their language skills really help them. If English is not your native language, you'll need to really go slow and work to understand the wording of each question.

required to prepare and maintain a written AA plan for minorities and women for each of their establishments. The OFCCP's regulations suggest that in preparing AA plans, federal contractors should consider the results that could reasonably be expected from putting forth every good faith effort to make an overall affirmative action plan work.

### Workforce analysis

Before an AA plan can be developed, the employer must determine whether there is any underutilization of women or minorities in its workforce and if so, where. The utilization analysis done to determine what affirmative action is required is a necessary part of the contents of an AA plan under OFCCP regulations. The analysis is conducted for each major job classification within the workforce. A separate analysis is prepared for women and for each specified minority subgroup — Black or African American, Hispanic or Latino, American Indian or Alaska Native, and Asians or Pacific Islanders.

*Final availability analysis*

After completing the workforce analysis, the contractor will execute a final availability analysis. This final analysis will show the following:

- entry level jobs requiring no special skills, training, or experience — women and minority availability for these jobs should be close if not the same as their workforce participation rates;

- entry level jobs requiring some skills, training, or experience — the availability of women and minorities should be at a minimum equal to the requisite skills figure for either the reasonable recruiting area or immediate recruiting area, whichever is the larger; and

- jobs filled internally — when all positions are filled internally, availability should be at least the same as the percentage of women and minorities in feeder jobs.

## Special Programs to Eliminate Discrimination

The OFCCP enforces affirmative action required of federal contractors under Executive Order 11246. According to the OFCCP's Affirmative Action Guidelines (41 CFR §60-2), the following may be appropriate affirmative actions:

- developing or reaffirming a policy statement of commitment to equal employment opportunity;

- publicizing the EEO policy through special meetings with executive management, supervisory personnel and all other employees;

- publicizing the EEO policy by posting it on bulletin boards, and announcing and discussing it in intra-company publications and annual reports;

- incorporating an EEO clause in purchase orders, leases, etc.;

- making sure that facilities and company-sponsored social and recreational activities are desegregated, actively encouraging all employees to participate;

- including racially mixed groups of males and females in depictions of employees in ads, employee handbooks, etc.;

- discussing the policy in employee orientation and management training;

- recruiting and selecting human resources employees with sensitivity to EEO needs and issues and training HR staff on the need and means to ensure elimination of bias in all personnel actions;

- meeting with union officials to inform them of the EEO policy and requesting their cooperation;

- including nondiscrimination clauses in union agreements;

- advising recruiting sources of the EEO policy and stipulating active recruitment of women and minorities for all positions;

- actively encouraging employees who are members of underrepresented groups to refer applicants;

- expanding help-wanted advertising to minority news media and women's interest media;

- establishing and maintaining liaison with minority and women's organizations, community agencies, community leaders, secondary schools, and colleges;

- encouraging child care, housing, and transportation programs appropriately designed to improve employment opportunities for minorities and women;

- participating in school and community "career day" and "youth motivation" programs and including female and minority employees among representatives;

- participating in job fairs;

- developing or participating in special employment programs such as co-op programs with minority and women's schools; work-study and summer jobs programs for minority youths; work-study programs for faculty members of minority schools; motivation, training, and employment programs for the hardcore unemployed;

- posting all promotional opportunities;

- compiling an inventory of academic, skill, and experience qualifications of current minority and female employees;

- offering special in-house management and skills training programs and supporting relevant outside education programs for employees;

- requiring written justification of non-selection of qualified minority and female employees for promotions;

- establishing formal career counseling programs for employees;

- appointing an executive to direct and manage EEO programs;

- recording and monitoring referrals, placements, transfers, promotions, and discharges to ensure that the EEO policy is carried out;

- analyzing and classifying position descriptions and making them available to all managers involved in recruiting, screening, hiring, and promoting workers;

- analyzing selection procedures and seniority procedures individually and collectively; and

- performing criterion-based validity studies of selection procedures and seniority practices that screen out disproportionate numbers of any protected class.

Other affirmative actions may include:

- establishing a reporting and investigation system for alleged sexual harassment and other violations of EEO rights;

- appointing women and minorities to the board of directors; and

- factoring EEO compliance as an element in the performance evaluations of managers and supervisors.

## Legal Endorsement of EEO: Supreme Court Decisions

Affirmative action to many employers means "hiring by the numbers"—making sure that a specified percentage of the workforce consists of minority or female employees. While set-aside programs and quotas can be a part of affirmative action, there is a much broader definition that includes making the effort to find and recruit qualified minority and female applicants to create a diverse workforce. This type of affirmative action can be highly useful to employers that are having difficulty finding qualified workers.

As for quotas and set asides, these are fraught with danger if not done in compliance with the strict guidelines established by the Supreme Court. Employers that establish voluntary plans can be liable for reverse discrimination charges from members of groups that are not covered by the plan. On the other hand, there are federal and state laws that require set asides to assist minorities and women. Employers that establish required plans generally are protected from reverse bias claims if they follow enforcement agency guidelines, but the government entities that create the requirements may be liable for reverse discrimination unless the plan meets a compelling governmental objective and is narrowly tailored to accomplish that objective.

## Strict scrutiny applied

The use of quotas, or goals and timetables that seem to work like quotas, has led to claims of "reverse discrimination"—discrimination against qualified members of another group who have not been chosen to receive the benefits of the affirmative action.

Part of a program undertaken to remedy past discrimination may sometimes contain a rigid quota (as for a company-sponsored craft training program), but may not create an "absolute bar to the advancement of whites."

Race or sex also may be a "plus" factor in selection to remedy low participation rates of a protected group, but it may not be the basis for a preference in an affirmative action plan based solely on the proportion to the general population, except for entry-level jobs.

## Government imposed plans

All racial classifications imposed by federal, state, or local governmental actions must serve a compelling governmental interest and must be narrowly tailored to meet that interest. Plans must be analyzed by reviewing courts under strict scrutiny.

Rejecting a prior decision that held the federal government to a lesser standard than that applied to state and local governments, the Supreme Court held in Adarand that the Constitution protects individuals, not groups. Therefore, governmental action based on race—a group classification—must be subjected to detailed judicial inquiry to ensure that the personal right to equal protection of the laws has not been infringed.

The government may not treat people differently because of their race except for the most compelling reasons. The use of race-conscious classifications in affirmative action plans can be justified only if:

- there is a "compelling government interest" in using the classification, such as proof that the employer discriminated;
- a reasonable goal for representation of the minority is set;
- no race-neutral means for achieving the goal has been identified; and
- the proposed action is narrowly tailored to accomplish the goal, it is flexible and temporary, and it is not unduly burdensome to members of other groups.

The government must have a compelling or exceedingly persuasive justification whenever it seeks to impose race or gender-based preferences, regardless of which race or gender is burdened or benefited by the preference. When the government prefers individuals on account of their race or gender, it correspondingly disadvantages individuals who happen to belong to another race or to the other gender.

## Comment

The Supreme Court has limited Congress' authority to establish set asides and quotas. All racial classifications imposed by federal, state, or local governmental actions must be justified by a compelling governmental interest and must be narrowly tailored. Such goals generally must be justified by evidence of past discrimination and analyzed by reviewing courts under strict scrutiny.

## Equal Employment Opportunity Programs

Although closely aligned with affirmative action, an equal employment opportunity policy does not necessarily include hiring goals for specific groups. EEO means simply that regardless of an individual's race, color, religion, gender, national origin, citizenship, age, or disability, all employment decisions, including those involving hiring, promotions, and compensation, will be based only on qualifications.

Some aspects of a complete EEO policy are required of, or strongly recommended for all employers that are covered by Title VII of the 1964 Civil Rights Act and other federal laws. These include posting federal notices of employee rights, reasonable accommodation policies for employees' religious beliefs and people with disabilities, and family leave and sexual harassment policies. Other aspects, such as targeting protected groups for recruitment, are more akin to affirmative action programs and are more apt to be included by some employers than by others.

### Policy statement

An EEO policy begins with a policy statement adopted by the employer. The statement should be comprehensive enough to include all aspects of both applicable federal and state laws. If the state in which the employer does business prohibits discrimination on the basis of marital status or sexual orientation, that factor should be included in the EEO policy statement.

While most experts advise employers to have separate policies on sexual harassment, mentioning the fact that harassment will not be tolerated in the general EEO policy statement is a good practice. A strong sexual harassment policy can serve as a defense in the event an employer is sued for the actions of one of its employees.

Only abbreviated versions of the EEO policy statement will be used in job advertisements, but a complete statement of the company's policy should be adopted and reproduced in employee handbooks or other information given to new hires and communicated to the workforce. The following is an example of an EEO policy statement for an employer operating in a state that has no antidiscrimination requirements beyond those of the federal laws.

---

**EXAMPLE**
**Sample EEO Policy Statement**
It is the policy of this company to select, train, and promote employees based on their ability and job performance and to provide equal opportunities in all aspects of employment without regard to race, color, religion, gender, national origin, citizenship, age, or physical or mental disability. It is the company's policy to maintain a work environment free of racial and sexual harassment and intimidation. It is the company's policy to comply with the letter and spirit of all local, state, and federal laws concerning equal employment opportunity.

---

## Fairness Issues

### Equality for non-minorities

The aim of Title VII and the other federal civil rights laws is to assure equality for all groups regardless of race, color, religion, gender, national origin, age, or disability. When an employment decision is made on the basis of one of those factors, discrimination occurs. If the decision favors a white male, minorities and women may have a claim. If the decision favors a minority or a woman, white males may have a reverse discrimination claim.

Regardless of any imbalance that exists in the workforce, preferential treatment for minorities and women is not required by Title VII. It is, however, required by Executive Order 11246 and other laws covering federal employers and federal contractors.

Employment decisions made on the basis of valid affirmative action plans are permissible even though they result in an adverse impact on members of non-protected classes. The key is determining whether a plan is "valid" in the sense that it will meet the tests established by the Supreme Court.

### Tie breakers

The best qualified candidate always should be chosen, regardless of factors such as race. When two equally qualified applicants are being considered for a promotion, however, using gender or race as a "tie breaker" generally is not discriminatory when used to cure racial or gender under-representation in the workforce.

However, a white teacher was a victim of reverse discrimination in violation of Title VII when she was laid off and a black teacher of equal qualifications and seniority was retained, to maintain racial diversity in the faculty, as called for in the school board's affirmative action plan. The school board presented no evidence of past discrimination or segregation in the workforce caused by past discrimination that would justify the use of race as a tie-breaker in this situation (Taxman v. Board of Educ. of Tp. of Piscataway, 1996).

---

**EXAMPLE**

A federal district court was justified in setting temporary hiring requirements for minorities and women at a percentage higher than their representation in the labor pool or applicant pool. The employer had systematically discriminated against these groups, and little progress had been made to rectify the discrimination. The court cautioned that the duration of this hiring quota could be no longer than necessary to correct the effects of past discrimination (United States v. Buffalo, 1980).

---

**Comment:** After review was granted by the U.S. Supreme Court in Taxman, an out-of-court settlement was reached in which several civil rights organizations and private corporations agreed to pay the white teacher's damages in an effort to avoid a ruling from the Supreme Court that these organizations and corporations feared might cut back further on permissible voluntary affirmative action.

### Hiring quotas

Hiring quotas may be imposed by a court when there is a severe imbalance between the number of women and/or minorities employed and the number of potentially qualified women and minorities in the appropriate geographic area. The court can order an employer to hire either a specific number or a percentage of minorities and/or women.

This type of AA plan is valid and reasonable if it ends when the situation has been remedied and if there is no unacceptable disparate impact on the employment opportunities of another group.

### Promotion quotas

A promotion quota may be imposed by a court when an employer has historically discriminated against women and minorities, thereby leaving them in predominantly lower-level positions. The court can impose either a number of promotions or a percentage of promotions that must be afforded to women and/or minorities. These requirements create greater minority participation in managerial and supervisory positions. Promotional quotas may be implemented by a consent decree or by a collective bargaining agreement.

Promotion quotas are permitted when they are created to combat the effects of long term, open, and hostile discrimination against minorities and women. Court-ordered AA plans are appropriate only when the discrimination cannot be eliminated by less intrusive means.

### Numeric preference plans

In certain instances where the discrimination is pervasive, court-ordered numerical preference plans are justified. A plan that mandated a minority promotion for each non-minority promotion because of the systematic and deliberate exclusion of minorities has been upheld as valid.

### Reverse discrimination

Making employment decisions on the basis of race, color, gender, religion, national origin, age, or disability is discriminatory regardless of who benefits from the decisions. Employment practices that benefit minorities and women to the detriment of whites and men are discrimination in reverse.

Title VII of the 1964 Civil Rights Act does not require preferential treatment for members of protected groups, but Executive Order 11246 and some of the other laws covering federal contractors and federal employers do. Valid affirmative action plans are a defense to reverse discrimination claims against the employers who are required to follow them, even though they may not be for the government entity that established them. The Equal Employment Opportunity Commission and the federal courts have established specific guidelines for determining when preferential plans are permitted and what they must contain to be valid.

> **TEST TAKING TIP**
> Focus your study efforts on those sections on the exam that are not your specialty. If you are knowledgeable about compensation, study labor.

---

**EXAMPLE**
The promotion of a female employee over an equally qualified male employee under an AA plan designed to balance traditionally segregated job classifications does not violate Title VII. The promotion was valid because it was made in furtherance of a valid AA plan and the gender of the employee was just one factor considered.

---

# Recruitment Methods and Sources

## Determining Recruitment Needs and Objectives

All too often, organizations succumb to recruiting "by crisis." Someone gives two weeks' notice and a supervisor desperately calls HR asking it to find an immediate replacement. The alternative to crisis recruiting is strategic recruiting — basing recruitment efforts on where the business wants to go and which types of people it will need to get there. Strategic recruitment can eliminate some recruiting emergencies by anticipating staffing needs and establishing sources to find qualified candidates. A staff planning process tries to answer questions like: What are the HR implications of proposed business plans? What can HR do in the short term to prepare for longer-term needs?

Staff planning is a systematic process for ensuring that an organization has the right number of people with the right skills at the right time to fulfill business needs. It takes into account internal and external changes that will affect the organization and integrates HR planning with the company's overall business plan. By studying historical patterns of employment in the organization, the current inventory of human resources, and external market trends, planners can anticipate and better fulfill staffing needs.

## Sources of forecasting information

A forecast of staffing needs begins with a study of current positions and employees' capabilities, past trends in an organization's workforce, and future business plans and market trends. An inventory that catalogs present employees' skills and abilities can help HR planners predict how closely internal candidates match the company's future HR needs. Strategic business plans and labor market projections also help focus recruiting efforts where they are most needed.

## Recruitment/Selection goals

**Goal 1:** Consults with HR to assure that minorities and women are included in applicant pools from which selections are made, and, when necessary, expands the minimum area of consolidation, extends the closing day of the corporate posting system, contacts minority organizations for referrals, and makes special recruitment efforts to integrate the workforce.

**Goal 2:** Analyzes the racial and ethnic composition of the work unit to identify underrepresentation and underutilization.

**Goal 3:** Establishes realistic and attainable hiring goals (sets specific goals with target dates in each of the areas of underrepresentation).

# Test Reliability and Validity

## Test Validation

The most important element of a testing program is adherence to federal and state equal employment opportunity laws and regulations. The federal government's Uniform Guidelines on Employee Selection Procedures have a major effect on any testing program. Under the guidelines, if the overall selection process for a job shows no evidence of adverse impact on any race, sex, or ethnic group, individual components of the process, such as pre-employment tests, do not have to be validated. But if overall selection procedures do have an adverse or disparate impact on a protected group, each procedure must be validated by proving its relevance to job requirements and performance.

In other words, federal enforcement agencies will usually not pursue cases against employers that are successfully hiring and promoting women and minorities. But even though an employer's "bottom line," or proportions of women and minorities in the workforce, looks good, this diversity is not a defense against a rejected candidate's charges that a test discriminates. An employer's defense instead depends on validation of a test's job-relatedness and its ability to discriminate between good and poor job performers.

Test validation is important from a practical as well as a legal perspective. Even if a test does not show adverse impact, validation makes sure that the test is serving its purpose: helping the company select the best candidates for jobs or promotions. If a test does not promote this end result, it is a waste of time and money, regardless of its impact on affirmative action.

## What does test validity mean?

The lingo experts use in describing test validity can be confusing. Here are the basic types of ways to show that a test is "valid" under the federal Uniform Guidelines on Employee Selection Procedures:

### Content validity

Content validity means that the content of the test is representative of the content of the job itself. These tests are usually work samples, such as a typing test for a typist's job. The behaviors demonstrated in the selection procedure are a representative sample of the behavior(s) of the job in question or that the selection procedure provides a representative sample of the work product of the job.

### *Criterion-related validity*

Criterion-related validity involves proving, through statistics, that people who do well on the test perform better on the job than people who do poorly on the test. It is not as simple as content validity, since the statistics involved require large numbers of individuals. It also requires a reliable way of telling who's performing well in a job and a significant range between good performers and poor performers.

### *Construct validity*

Construct validity involves showing that the test is measuring a certain characteristic (or "construct") that is important to successful performance on the job. A test that measures leadership ability, for instance, may be used for managerial positions. To show construct validity, the employer would have to show that the test does indeed measure leadership ability, and that leadership ability makes a person a good manager. These leadership traits are a "construct" or part of the makeup of an individual as related to actual job performance.

## Validity and Reliability: Job Analysis, Descriptions and Specs

Any validity study should be based on a job analysis that determines the tasks or personality characteristics required for successful performance of that job's essential functions.

The resulting products of a content valid test should closely match actual work products. The testing situation also should approximate as closely as possible the actual work situation. If an employer can show by a job analysis or otherwise that higher test scores are associated with better job performance, test results can be used to rank applicants.

A study of construct validity should include a job analysis that shows the work behaviors required for successful performance of the job. The study then must identify the mental or psychological traits that underlie those work behaviors. The relationship between the characteristic the test purports to measure and the work behavior should be supported by evidence from criterion-related studies.

To conduct a criterion-related validity study, a job analysis should be conducted to determine measures of work performance that are relevant to the job in question. A study that does not include a job analysis but merely compares test results with the subjective ratings of supervisors who have only vague standards for judging job performance will be inadequate.

# Internal Workforce Planning

## Accommodating Organizational and Individual Needs

A career development program must be one that both management and employees see as valuable. HR managers setting up a career development program should take the following steps:

1. Communicate the program's purpose and benefits. Since supervisors' support is critical, stress what the program can do for managers. The best way to get managers to buy the program: Create managerial development plans.

2. Define roles and responsibilities. Initiating a career development program often requires a cultural change in terms of supervisor-employee relationships. Stress that HR will support the career development process and that career development is not "another one of those personnel programs."

3.  Identify a champion who is committed to career development and can sell the program to management. Choose a project manager to oversee development of the program.

4.  Start small and provide adequate support. Avoid elaborate career development programs. Stress preparation for particular types of work, not for particular job titles, and emphasize career opportunities rather than actual job openings.

5.  Keep the career development program visible. Gradually phase in the program, publicize results at each stage, and communicate future plans.

6.  Support career development with training opportunities. Offer both knowledge-based and skill-building training, and include programs for managers and non-managers. Make training a voluntary aspect of participation in the career development program.

7.  Get managers and employees involved. Make career development the responsibility of supervisors and employees, not of the HR department. Get managers and employees to decide directions, to teach others, and to create support materials.

8.  Evaluate efforts. Focus on business needs and check the program's effectiveness in meeting these needs.

## Assigning responsibility

### Organizational role

A career development program needs support from the top. All too often, career planning is incorporated into performance appraisals, where managers cover career plans as an afterthought. By making employee development a separate function, a company will communicate its recognition of the organizational benefits of career planning — which can range from improved employee morale and retention to higher productivity and better placement decisions.

> **TEST TAKING TIP**
> Most test centers will not allow you to take anything into the test room (water, pocketbook, wallet, papers, etc.). Most provide a locker to store your belongings.

### Managers' and employees' roles

Both managers and employees have a role in career development. A supervisor should understand the employee's needs and strengths, provide a "reality check" for the employee's career goals, and arrange appropriate training. Employees should get a clear perspective on their motivations and skills, and learn how to evaluate a job in terms of these motivations and skills. An employee shares responsibility for drafting a written career development plan, discussing it with the manager, and carrying it out.

### HR's role

The HR department plays a supportive role in implementing individual career development plans. Training managers to perform career counseling is the most important role of HR in employee development. The HR department also provides resources needed by managers and employees, such as development planning guidelines, job information, and educational opportunities. Finally, HR should make sure the company's policies and practices, such as internal placement and promotion, support employee development.

## Mobility within the Organization

Once a company has a career development program in place, the next step is to develop a career plan for each employee.

## Checklist for creating a career development program

- ❏ **Predict long-term staffing needs**. Staff planning supports employee development in several ways. It supplies information that employees need to select realistic long-term career goals. It guarantees that openings become available as employees are ready to move up. Finally, by linking employee development to business strategy, staff planning gives the company a supply of interested, well-prepared employees who can fill job openings. These planning efforts can promote career development.

- ❏ **Succession planning**. Forecasting executive and managerial vacancies helps employees assess potential promotional opportunities.

- ❏ **Anticipating organizational change**. Organizational change includes expansion, downsizing, changes in product lines, and other restructuring efforts.

- ❏ **Planning for technological change**. Technological advancements can make some jobs obsolete, change the skills required for other jobs, and create new positions and responsibilities.

- ❏ **Forecasting economic changes and market shifts**. Data on market changes indicate whether job openings will exist when training and development are completed.

- ❏ **Analyze the knowledge, skills, and abilities required for each job**. By identifying the skills required for positions, HR managers can group jobs into categories and identify the additional skills and knowledge that employees must acquire to move into higher-paid positions.

- ❏ **Make employees aware of career opportunities**. The following programs can help employees recognize and evaluate career opportunities:

  - o **Job posting**. Posting descriptions of available job openings provides employees with information about actual job opportunities. Posted information should include the reporting relationship, required skills, and preferred experience. This information, particularly experience requirements, lets employees see the typical career path into a posted job.

  - o **Career paths.** Employees should have several routes into a job and several opportunities for advancement. Career paths encourage employees to acquire the skills needed for upward mobility. They also clarify what supervisors and trainers can do to assist employees.

- ❏ **Motivate managers to develop and promote subordinates**. Employee development must have line supervisors' support. To get this support, upper management can offer incentives such as bonuses and rewards to successful supervisors.

- ❏ **Bonuses and rewards**. Create appropriate programs for supervisors who do a good job of developing employees such as cash awards and other types of recognition.

- ❏ **Links between evaluations of supervisors and employee development**. Supervisors' performance ratings, promotions, and pay raises should depend partly on how well they counsel and develop employees.

- ❏ **Provide formal opportunities for employees to plan their careers**. Such opportunities include: career planning workshops or individual career counseling.

- ❏ **Career planning workshops**. Workshops guide employees in setting career goals and in learning how to realize them.

- ❏ **Individual career counseling**. Employees benefit from individual counseling, whether conducted by a career guidance professional or a manager.

- ❏ **Performance appraisals**. Regular performance appraisals provide an opportunity for employees and supervisors to discuss goals and training needs. Have managers and employees collaborate on a career development plan for the upcoming year and assess progress toward achieving career goals in the preceding year.

- ❑ **Help employees get the knowledge and skills needed for advancement**. Efforts can take several forms including, formal training, tuition assistance or special projects.
- ❑ **Formal training**. Training should develop skills for promotion, not just for a current job.
- ❑ **Tuition assistance**. To achieve some career goals, employees may need outside education.
- ❑ **Special projects and responsibilities that let nonsupervisory employees develop and demonstrate supervisory skills**. Activities could include helping train new employees, participating in quality circles or employee-management committees, or serving as liaisons with other work units. These experiences should foster competencies, such as creative thinking, that are not found in the employee's regular work.

A one-on-one counseling session between an employee and the immediate supervisor is one common employee development technique. Career development workshops, in which a facilitator guides a group of employees through self-evaluation and goal identification, is another employee development technique. Whatever technique is used, career counseling involves the following elements:

**TEST TAKING TIP**
Even if you have to blind guess at a question, you still have a 25% chance of getting it right. Eliminating one answer option improves your odds to 33%.

- performing self-assessment,
- exploring career choices,
- formulation of career development plans, and
- follow-up on progress.

A written employee development plan should reflect the following points from the career counseling session:

**Employee's interests**
- What kind of work involves skills the employee enjoys?
- In which areas of the business would the employee like to make a contribution — both currently and in the future?
- Does the plan match individual motivations and skills to job tasks?
- Does the plan go beyond formal work assignments to include various undefined and unassigned job activities?
- Employee's aspirations.
- What careers interest the employee?
- Does the plan cover short-term (one to two years) and long-term (two or more years) aspirations? Does the plan address both enhancements to the current job and future career possibilities?

**Employee's strengths**
What skills, experience, and education does the employee have to support his or her career interests and aspirations?

**Development needs**
What training or job experiences does the employee need in order to meet or exceed current job requirements and to prepare for future job opportunities?

**Action plans**
- What specific actions should the employee and supervisor take during the next year to address the employee's developmental needs and improve job match?

- For each action, does the plan clearly state the objective, the employee's and the supervisor's responsibilities, and a completion date?

## Illegal Use of Drugs and Alcohol

### Alcohol and drug use

The law allows employers to ban alcohol use or intoxication in the workplace, and to ban illegal drug use. Employers are not required to accommodate alcoholism or illegal drug use. Employees who are not using drugs and are participating in or have completed supervised drug rehabilitation programs are protected by the law. However, employers may apply reasonable policies and procedures such as drug testing to ensure that these employees are no longer illegally using drugs.

### Test methods used

Most employers do drug testing through urinalysis, although some rely on blood samples. Rarely used methods include hair sampling and performance tests. Most employers use a laboratory certified by the National Institute of Drug Abuse to perform the drug testing, and many retest test-positive applicants using a more rigorous test (e.g. gas chromatography rather than first-screen immunoassay test). However, some simply repeat the same test using the sample. Others companies take a new sample but repeat the same test, and still others make no attempt to validate the first test.

### Actions toward applicants testing positive

Very few employers offer probationary employment to applicants testing positive for drugs. The majority refuse to hire test-positive applicants. The remaining employers take other actions, such as retesting at a later date.

The most frequent challenges to drug testing programs have stemmed from concerns over issues of accuracy and invasion of privacy. However, employers have successfully defended the practice as a means of screening for problem employees.

> **TEST TAKING TIP**
> Study the key words in the question. Don't look at the answer options until you have fully understood the key words in the question. Read the question four or five times until you get what they're asking for. Then go to the answer options.

### Privacy

HR policy experts generally agree that an employer cannot and should not try to enforce rules regulating what an employee does when not working, as long as the behavior has no bearing on job performance. Yet when an employer rejects applicants based on a pre-employment drug test, the employer in effect is regulating off-the-job behavior. As a result, individuals have challenged drug testing, both in public debate and through the courts, as an invasion of privacy.

Privacy challenges to drug tests generally have not succeeded in the legal system. Although the U.S. Constitution protects citizens against unreasonable governmental searches and seizures, individuals have no general constitutional right to privacy that would apply to private employment. Courts have tended to support an employer's right to require drug tests of both current and prospective employees.

### Accuracy

The accuracy of drug tests, particularly urine tests, also has generated debate. Urine tests sometimes yield false-positive results. Through inaccurately labeling a sample, an innocent person can test as an illegal drug user. Indeed, urine tests tend to produce false-positive tests more often than false-negative results. This error rate poses problems, since employment decisions based on false-positive results obviously cause far more damage to individuals than do false-negative results.

False results can happen because of poor laboratory procedures, such as technician error, careless handling of samples, or deliberate tampering with samples. False positives also can result because certain commonplace prescription or nonprescription medications show up on tests as illegal substances. Eating certain foods or drinking herbal teas sometimes has caused false-positive drug test results. Exposure to marijuana smoke also might cause someone to test positive even if the person has not smoked marijuana.

To reduce errors caused by the laboratory or type of test, experts urge confirming every positive first test with a second one, preferably using a different lab and a different type of test. This practice will reduce, but not eliminate, problems with false positives. To avoid legal problems, many employers do not tell applicants they were rejected because of a positive drug test.

### Applicant rights

Most state drug-testing laws require disclosure of test results to applicants and provide some means by which applicants can challenge or explain a positive test. Some states also require that employers give prior notice of any drug testing requirement and include this requirement in all job advertisements, employment application materials, or job interview discussions. In some areas, employers also must give applicants copies of both company policy and state regulations governing drug testing. Certain states prohibit performing drug tests unless the applicant has received a conditional offer of employment.

## Companies That Do Not Test For Drug and Alcohol Use

Companies that do not conduct drug and alcohol testing can still take action to prevent and treat substance abuse among employees. Since job performance suffers when a worker develops an addiction, supervisor training on the symptoms of substance abuse is key to successful intervention.

Given the safety, security, and legal risks posed by on-site drug or alcohol abuse, companies also need programs to prevent and detect on-the-job substance abuse. Training security personnel, conducting workplace searches, using electronic surveillance, and employing undercover investigators are options available when employers suspect a problem with on-the-job drug or alcohol activity.

Finally, every employer should have procedures for dealing with employees known to have drug or alcohol problems.

### Off-duty conduct

Conduct during non-working hours can in some instances give rise to lawful disciplinary action. For example, a security guard who shot and killed an individual while off duty demonstrated his unfitness to deal with the stresses of his job and his discharge was lawful. Violating an employer's moonlighting rules also can be a nondiscriminatory reason for discharge so long as the rules are applied fairly and equally to all employees.

Many states have laws governing the off-duty use of lawful products. These states severely restrict the employers' ability to govern the lawful activities of their off-duty employees. Example: companies cannot refuse to hire or discipline for smoking or using lawful tobacco products in some states.

# Individual Employment Rights

## Employment-At-Will Doctrine

The employment-at-will doctrine presumes that both employee and employer are free agents who may terminate their relationship at any time for any reason. This arrangement allows employees to resign at any time and prohibits employers from forcing an individual to complete a term of service, even if covered by contract. For employers, this legal doctrine has given them the freedom to terminate excess or unacceptable employees without fear of litigation.

## Exceptions to Employment-At-Will

While employees retain most of their rights under the employment-at-will doctrine, employers' freedom to discharge employees at will has eroded over the past few decades. Although only one state, Montana, has legislation protecting all employees against arbitrary discharge, other legal limitations have been established through federal laws, state statutes, and court rulings. These legal restrictions allow employees to challenge employment-at-will policies under three broad claims: breach of contract, violation of public policy, and discrimination.

**TEST TAKING TIP**
There are usually only a couple of questions concerning public employers (government, municipalities, etc.). Most questions come from the private sector.

### Breach of contract

- Discharging an employee before the expiration of a fixed-term employment contract entitles the fired individual to unpaid compensation for the portion of the term not served under contract.

- Collective bargaining agreements often restrict the employer's right to discharge a covered employee without cause. Under the National Labor Relations Act, union employees also are protected from discharge for concerted activity or exercise of other rights covered under the act.

- If an employer makes a commitment, orally or in a handbook, not to discharge employees without good cause, some state courts view this commitment as creating an implied contract.

- In other states, the courts have held that all employment relationships are governed by an implied covenant of good faith and fair dealing.

### Public policy violation

- Employers cannot fire an employee to prevent the individual from exercising a right, such as entitlement to pension benefits.

- Most states and some federal laws protect employees against discharge for whistleblowing.

- Various state courts make a public policy exception to at-will employment and prohibit firing employees who refuse to perform an illegal act requested by the employer.

### Discrimination

- If the affected employee is female, belongs to a member of an ethnic or religious minority, is older than age 40, or has a disability, an arbitrary discharge could lead to claims of illegal discrimination.

## Common Law Tort Theories

Under the traditional employment-at-will doctrine, employers can fire employees at any time and for any or no reason at all. But state laws and court rulings have increasingly restricted this traditional relationship. State public policy may bar terminating employees for such reasons as filing claims for workers' compensation benefits or unpaid wages; refusing to take or failing a lie detector, AIDS, or drug test; taking a family leave; or objecting to unsafe conditions or smoking in the workplace.

In addition, state court rulings have restricted at-will employment based on common-law theories of implied contract, implied covenant of good faith and fair dealing, or wrongful discharge in violation of public policy. Common law tort litigation has enabled employees to increasingly file for expanded settlements for violating any of these exceptions to the At-Will doctrine.

## Non-Compete Agreements

Many companies require key employees to sign agreements, called covenants not to compete, stating they will not take after-hours jobs with competitors or in any other way compete with the company. Some of these agreements also prohibit terminated employees from going to work for a competitor or setting up a competing business within a limited distance from the company or within a certain time period after termination.

Given the potential for promoting monopolies and thwarting an individual's ability to make a living, most courts, and certain state laws, have strictly limited the scope of these restrictive covenants. Companies should have legal counsel review any employment agreement containing a non-compete clause, but in general, the following guidelines may help:

- Make sure a legitimate business interest justifies the non-compete clause. Trade secrets, confidential information, customer lists, or loss of unique services supplied by the employee generally qualify as legitimate business interests. The mere threat of competition, however, is usually not sufficient to defend the need for a non-compete clause.

- Set reasonable time and geographic limits. As a rule, a non-compete clause should bar former employees from competing only within those jurisdictions where the employer does business, or, for multistate or international companies, within those areas the ex-employee had worked directly. As for time, courts generally view two to three years as sufficient time for an employer to replace whatever assets it lost when the former employee departed. However, courts have allowed longer time limits in non-compete agreements, particularly if the employer needed to protect trade secrets.

- Limit former employees from seeking employment only in specific positions. Any non-compete clause that bars employees from using their only job skills or that covers all positions in a particular field is not likely to hold up in court.

# Workplace Behavior Issues/Practices

## Discipline

By and large, discipline in the workplace today covers two kinds of "failings:"

- **Misconduct.** In the context of "discipline in the workplace," the term "misconduct" usually refers to any violation of the employer's rules. It would also be used where an employee has engaged in criminal activity at the workplace (like stealing from another employee) or disruptive behavior (like starting a fight) even if the employer's policies are silent on the specific kind of wrongdoing.

- **Failure to perform satisfactorily.** The second broad subject that workplace discipline is concerned with is the individual employee's job performance. Failure to perform satisfactorily is never referred to as "misconduct," however. The main reason is that an employee who is failing to perform is not treated as a loss by many employers; rather, with additional training, or a change in assignments, the employee may succeed, after all. If "failure to perform" were defined as a form of "misconduct," the next step would be management's response to a case of proven misconduct — presumably termination or a lesser punishment.

## Violation of basic conditions of employment

### Poor attendance
Employees may be lawfully terminated for chronic absenteeism, tardiness, or misuse of excused absences. Courts will usually uphold dismissals of employees who fail to follow company procedures for obtaining permission for leave or for extending an excused absence.

### Lying on a job application
Since the qualifications listed on someone's job application or resume often establish the reason for hire, lying on a resume or application, especially about essential qualifications for a position, usually establishes a legitimate grounds for discharge. In fact, some courts even have upheld dismissals that occurred for other reasons when the employer discovered after termination that the employee had lied on the employment application.

> **TEST TAKING TIP**
> Ear plugs or sound depression devices (ear muffs) are provided at most testing centers to help block out distracting noises. Use them.

### Insubordination
An employee's failure to follow a supervisor's instructions has customarily justified an employer's meting out discipline up to and including discharge. Termination for insubordination may involve failure to follow a supervisor's instructions, outright refusals to follow an employer's required procedures, or verbal insults made to the supervisor or about the supervisor to other employees.

### Poor interactions with subordinates
The reverse of insubordination occurs when a manager cannot give employees the respect they deserve. Because a company is liable for the acts of its supervisors, courts usually grant management latitude to fire supervisors who treat subordinates poorly. However, exceptions can arise, as the following case illustrates:

> **Example:**
> Despite 14 years of managing employees in an abrasive manner, a supervisor was fired at age 58 because of poor interpersonal skills. A jury, however, ruled that the reference to the manager's poor interpersonal skills was a pretext for age discrimination, and an appeals court upheld this verdict. Since an evaluation prepared shortly before the termination rated the manager poorly on productivity when just the opposite was true of that manager's department, the jury concluded that the negative evaluation of the manager's interpersonal skills likewise was fabricated to justify an age-biased termination.

### Failure to meet new policy standards
Even if a company changes its employment policies during an employee's tenure, the employer is justified in expecting employees to conform to these new standards. In some cases, management may even be allowed to terminate an employee for past behavior that does not meet the new policy.

## Absenteeism and tardiness
Absenteeism and lateness can be extensive, troublesome problems for an employer, and are best countered through direct action. Choosing a policy for control and enforcement, a company should not only track the absentee patterns within its workforce and determine their accompanying costs, but try to

gain an understanding of the reasons for absenteeism and the underlying societal forces that contribute to missed work-time.

Most companies use some disciplinary measures to keep absenteeism in check, but some use incentives and rewards, such as bonuses, to reinforce good attendance.

Whatever methods you install, however, will make a positive difference in attendance. Recent investigations suggest that major reductions in the rates of absenteeism can be the result of nothing more than establishing some policy and following through with it consistently.

To identify the methods that will work best for the company, consider the absenteeism problems in the organization and the nature of employees who are frequent offenders. Reports show that a system of progressive discipline has some impact on workers with high absence rates, for instance, but comparatively little effect on employees with low-to-average rates. The latter group may respond better to reward programs.

Moreover, a growing number of companies are showing interest in preventive measures to cut back absenteeism, and have begun to explore alternative sick leave programs (such as no-fault leave and paid "absence banks") and to focus on such issues as workers' physical and mental health, child care, eldercare, and flexible work schedules, according to the Bureau of Labor Statistics. These issues may affect the absence behavior of workers.

## Sexual Harassment

Sexual harassment is one of the most explosive issues facing employers today. The law requires employers to provide a workplace free of sexual harassment, and may hold them responsible for harassment suffered by any employee. In some instances, employers may be liable for sexual harassment even if they do not know that harassment is occurring in their workplace.

There are two types of sexual harassment, quid pro quo and hostile environment.
1.  Quid pro quo harassment is the most commonly recognized form of sexual harassment. This occurs when job benefits are made contingent on the provision of sexual favors.
2.  Hostile environment occurs when there is discriminatory conduct or behavior in the workplace that is unwelcome and offensive to an employee or group of employees based on their sex.

One of the main differences between "quid pro quo" harassment and "hostile environment" is in who is committing the harassing behavior. In "quid pro quo", it is someone in a supervisory position. In "hostile environment," it is usually a coworker.

The Civil Rights Act of 1991 is a U.S. statute that was passed in response to a series of United States Supreme Court decisions limiting the rights of employees who had sued their employers for discrimination. The Act represented the first effort since the passage of the Civil Rights Act of 1964 to modify some of the basic procedural and substantive rights provided by federal law in employment discrimination cases: it provided for the right to trial by jury on discrimination claims and introduced the possibility of emotional distress damages, while limiting the amount that a jury could award. Rulings on Sexual Harassment claims such as Burlington Industries v. Ellerth and others opened a veritable floodgate of law suits when combined with CRA of 1991.

HR can perform a valuable service for the organization by adopting a policy prohibiting sexual harassment and instituting procedures for investigating and resolving sexual harassment complaints. Effective sexual harassment policies and procedures can help shield employers from legal liability and adverse publicity should harassment occur. In addition, these policies and procedures can conserve resources by quickly resolving situations that may distract employees from their normal duties.

An effective sexual harassment policy should include examples of prohibited conduct. It also should spell out methods for making and investigating complaints, and provide for discipline of employees who engage in harassment. Once established, the policy should be clearly communicated to all employees.

What is "sexual harassment"? Sexual harassment is a form of sex discrimination and includes unwelcome sexual advances, requests for sexual favors, and other verbal or physical conduct of a sexual nature when:

1. submission to that conduct is made either explicitly or implicitly a term or condition of employment;

2. submission to or rejection of such conduct by an individual is used as a component of the basis for employment decisions affecting that individual; or

3. the conduct has the purpose or effect of substantially interfering with an individual's work performance or creating an intimidating, hostile, or offensive working environment.

Examples of sexual harassment include, but are not limited to, the following conduct, when such acts or behavior come within one of the above definitions:

- explicitly or implicitly conditioning any term of employment (e.g., continued employment, wages, evaluation, advancement, assigned duties or shifts) on the provision of sexual favors;

- touching or grabbing a sexual part of an employee's body;

- touching or grabbing any part of an employee's body after that person has indicated, or it is otherwise known, that such physical contact was unwelcome;

- continuing to ask an employee to socialize on-or off-duty when that person has indicated s/he is not interested;

- displaying or transmitting sexually suggestive pictures, objects, cartoons, or posters if it is known or should be known that the behavior is unwelcome;

**TEST TAKING TIP**
You have to learn the difference between the way your current company operates and the way the rest of the world operates. Questions on the exam cover the rest of the world and not your particular company or regional practices.

- continuing to write sexually suggestive notes or letters if it is known or should be known that the person does not welcome such behavior;

- referring to or calling a person a sexualized name if it is known or should be known that the person does not welcome such behavior;

- regularly telling sexual jokes or using sexually vulgar or explicit language in the presence of a person if it is known or should be known that the person does not welcome such behavior;

- retaliation of any kind for having filed or supported a complaint of sexual harassment (e.g., ostracizing the person, pressuring the person to drop or not support the complaint, adversely altering that person's duties or work environment, etc.);

- derogatory or provoking remarks about or relating to an employee's sex or sexual orientation;

- harassing acts or behavior directed against a person on the basis of his or her sex or sexual orientation;
- off-duty conduct which falls within the above definition and affects the work environment.

# Assessment of Employee Attitudes

## Measurement

In today's organizations, the employee attitude survey is both a tool for collecting information and a way to facilitate strategic decision-making. However, surveys take time to design and analyze properly, and they require a commitment from management to consider and respond to the results.

As a diagnostic tool measuring employee attitudes, surveys are extremely valuable in the development of HR programs that promote shared values and a common purpose. Surveying employees enables management to:

- gather data on attitudes to use as a yardstick in measuring change;
- identify the causes and solutions for such problems as an increase in turnover or a downturn in productivity; and
- give meaning to the phrase "employees are our most valuable resource," by showing employees that their opinions count.

How do employees really feel about their companies and management? Surveys are useful instruments for understanding what is important to employees and how they can be motivated. A formal, in-depth attitude survey is a vital tool management can use for demonstrating a commitment to employee concerns. Surveys give workers a chance to air their views while remaining anonymous. In fact, for management to get uncensored feedback, confidentiality should be guaranteed in the survey process.

The popularity of employee attitude surveys has increased over the past six decades to the point that surveys are now a common HR practice. Most early workforce surveys measured job satisfaction or employee morale, emphasizing that a satisfied worker is a more productive worker. In recent years, however, employers have found many other uses for attitude surveys.

Keep in mind that a survey is not an end in itself. A survey is the beginning of a diagnostic process, which in turn is the beginning of a larger development process. Like other diagnostic tools, surveys identify how certain organizational systems are working.

Surveys can be narrowly focused or broad-based. Some employee surveys involve detailed measures on a limited domain, such as the effectiveness of employee benefit programs. Other surveys measure a larger number of dimensions.

Employee attitude surveys backfire unless action results from the feedback given. One method of improving organizational effectiveness through surveys is known as action research. Action research is a development process that uses employee attitude surveys to provide a framework for action planning, implementation, and change management.

An entire survey project cycle consists of three sequential phases:

- **Design phase**. The research process begins by defining objectives, determining priorities, establishing realistic expectations, and custom-developing a questionnaire that covers a limited set of relevant topics. Senior management or employee focus group interviews are used to develop the questionnaire. At the end of this phase, a clear go or no-go decision becomes apparent.
- **Data collection phase**. Once the questionnaire has been developed and the decision made to proceed, data collection begins. During the data collection phase, the questionnaire is administered, data is processed and analyzed, results are interpreted, and the findings are presented to management. A summary report to employees marks the end of this phase.
- **Deployment phase**. The most important part of a successful action research program is using the results to put words into action. Deployment begins with a feedback process that includes refining the results (i.e., looking behind the numbers) and continues through the action planning process.

## Confidentiality and Anonymity of Surveys

The administration of a survey has a big effect on the quality of the results. The communication plan must confirm absolute confidentiality and anonymity, as well as reiterate management's commitment to report the results.

If a consultant is involved in the project, the report to employees is usually written by the consultant. This system allows the consultant to reaffirm that confidentiality and anonymity were maintained throughout the process.

# International Staffing Concerns (SPHR-only section)

## International Assignment Management

The Global HR Manager must be capable of managing expatriates on international assignment. The basic elements they are responsible for include:
- The establishment of international assignment strategy and policies.
  - This includes planning, implementing, administering and evaluating all activities relating to international assignments or global mobility.
  - It also covers such areas as legal (visa and immigration), compensation, benefits, tax, relocation and security implications for all global assignments–cross-border business travel, short-term, long-term, sequential and permanent assignments.

### The IA Process
Despite terrorist attacks, financial considerations, and disease, global organizations still send employees on international assignments for a variety of reasons, including technology transfer, growth of high-potential employees, development of a cadre of international executives, formation of cross-cultural/cross-functional project teams, or protection of assets in another country for the parent company. Considering that assignment costs are estimated to be approximately three-to-four times the assignee's salary on an annual basis and many assignment costs occur at the onset of the posting, it is prudent to mitigate the risk of the assignment ending prematurely with the business objectives left in limbo.

> To work effectively on an international assignment, the assignee must maintain high-level work performance while working locally, across cultures, time, and distance to achieve the assignment's business goals in the context of the organizational objectives.

This requires:

- conducting business immediately at the new location without distraction from relocation stress, culture shock, family issues, and other predictable barriers to success;
- sustaining high-level business performance and developing complex business relationships necessary to meet or exceed the goals; and
- staying the length of the assignment and repatriating or going on to another posting while depositing the informational wealth gained on the assignment with the organization.

Achieving these goals involves the sustained performance of many employees, not just the expatriate. This section will define the roles and responsibilities of the HR professional working together with the host manager, home sponsor, and the assignee and family to ensure meeting or exceeding the goals of the assignment.

### Step 1:  Assessment & Selection

The first step in the organizational process should be to answer the question, "Why bother with an expatriate for this position? Why is an expatriate necessary for this assignment and what are the alternatives (local staff, commute, or other arrangement)?" If the answer is that an expatriate is appropriate to fill the position, then careful assessment of candidates is essential.

The role of HR is to assist management in the selection of candidates who not only have the technical skills but also the potential for success in another country.

An expatriate assignment is so expensive, it exposes the organization to great risk if the assignment fails to meet the objectives. HR and line managers must not be afraid to paint an accurate picture of the terms and conditions of the assignment to manage expectations up front.

HR activities during this phase should be to:

- assist line management in identifying need for an international assignee and to consider alternatives;
- determine the appropriate candidate (with management);
- conduct assessments (candidate and spouse intercultural assessment, candidate self-assessment); and
- perform a projection of total assignment costs and obtain line management signature.

### Step 2:  Management & Assignee Decision

The time to talk about the impact of living in an unfamiliar, sometimes unsafe, sometimes remote, without-the-comforts-of-home place, is before the expatriate leaves. How does the couple/family cope with the challenges of living in their home country? How effective are they now? How interdependent are they? Can each function separately? There will be fewer problems on the assignment if they can anticipate the situation and work with their coach on how to prepare for and how to overcome predictable obstacles.

Both the assignment manager and the assignee need to be aware of all the details of the assignment so both sides may make an intelligent and informed decision.  Once these details are identified, an assignment document is created that describes all the vagaries of the assignment.

HR activities during this stage should be to:

- collect assignment initiation profile data and track in a database;
- coordinate assignment of home sponsor for assignee;
- generate hypothetical tax calculation, assignee compensation balance sheet, and pay split calculations when necessary;
- **draft assignment letter** outlining terms and conditions;
- conduct HR briefing with assignee and spouse in home location (in person whenever possible);
- conduct tax briefing with assignee and spouse;
- obtain visa/work permit and residence permits;
- process certificates of coverage (totalization agreement forms) where applicable;
- coordinate home selection/reconnaissance visit; and
- arrange destination services/settling-in assistance (including education assistance).

### Step 3:  Pre-Departure Preparation

A home selection trip by the employee and spouse before the assignment begins can help determine what household goods to ship and what to place in storage or donate. It also can quell the fear of the unknown by allowing them to become familiar with what will be their surroundings in the host location.

Cross-cultural orientation before the commencement of the assignment can give the expatriate and family a strong start in the host location, thereby maximizing productivity and minimizing settling-in time.

> Cross-cultural training for the employee and family prepares them to understand the common course of culture shock and to understand the background of the host culture.

It heightens their cultural sensitivity and allows them to be able to communicate more effectively to avoid misunderstandings.

HR activities during this phase are to:

- coordinate policy exception process; monitor and revise policy as needed;
- determine household goods to be shipped or stored and coordinate the service provider;
- arrange intercultural training;
- arrange language lessons where necessary;
- process payments, i.e., miscellaneous allowance, loss on sale, expense reimbursement; and
- process documentation for payroll transfer.

Without proper preparation, the expat with a family most likely will be distracted from work because the family members either will be in chaos or depressed. Depression often is seen as anger and sadness that may be directed at the expatriate because the move was made to accommodate his or her job. In the best of situations, the expat and family members will need a familiar resource who knows what they are experiencing, can help them understand the process and normalize it, and use their strengths to deal with the challenges they inevitably will encounter.

*Step 4: On-Assignment*

The assignment phase begins when the expatriate, with or without the family, arrives at the new location and real-time testing of the selection, contracting, and preparation processes begins. This phase is critically important to the success of the assignment. With proper preparation in previous phases, the expat with a family will be able to begin work without being distracted by the stress the spouse and family are experiencing. Without proper selection, contracting, and preparation processes, the expat, whether single or accompanied, will be confronted with all that is new and different from the home culture (or most-recent location's culture).

HR activities in this phase should be to:

- perform HR and tax briefings in the host location;
- coordinate tax preparation services as required;
- provide notice of benefit plan changes and updates;
- coordinate annual home leave payment;
- coordinate rest and relaxation leave or emergency home leave where necessary;
- coordinate the performance appraisal process;
- update assignee compensation balance sheets during salary review;
- compile year-end compensation summaries for payroll;
- process non-periodic payments, e.g., education assistance;
- settle tax equalization balances;
- process visa/work permit renewals;
- respond to assignee inquiries;
- monitor sponsor/mentor program; and
- deliver monthly/quarterly reports (active assignments, cost information, and repatriation planning) and review with line management.

> For the employee, challenges will include how to leverage culture as a business strategy, how to build effective cross-cultural relationships with team members by intentionally building trust, and how to build global leadership competencies while on international assignment.

*Step 5: Completing the Assignment*

Common repatriation situations are less than desirable for all parties involved. Example: The expatriate is not managing his career while away. Perhaps he thinks he is anointed, hand-picked for this great assignment. If so, he sits back and assumes the company will take care of his high-potential self and has expectations of a promotion on return.

HR activities during this phase should include:

- coordinating pre-departure tax consultation;
- coordinating termination of host country home and automobile leases where required;
- coordinating household goods shipment with service provider;
- processing exit documentation;
- arranging to stop assignment salary payments and coordinate re-entry into home country payroll system;
- processing payments, i.e., miscellaneous allowance and expense reimbursements;

- coordinating repatriation debriefing with assignee and family; and
- conducting assignee satisfaction survey.

> Repatriation may be the most demanding phase of the expat assignment.

Partially because the expat and family-and the corporation-think repatriation will be easy. Even if the expat is happy to return home, he or she has the stress of another relocation. Because the company does not acknowledge relocation stress, the expectation is that the expat either will fit back in without losing a moment to adjustment time, or will be thinking straight enough to negotiate the situation.

## Visas

In most cases, citizens of foreign countries will need a visa to enter the United States.

A visa doesn't permit entry to the U.S., however. A visa simply indicates that the application has been reviewed by a U.S. consular officer at an American embassy or consulate, and that the officer has determined the candidate is eligible to enter the country for a specific purpose. Consular affairs are the responsibility of the U.S. Department of State.

A visa allows a person to travel to the United States as far as the port of entry (airport or land border crossing) and ask the immigration officer to allow them to enter the country.

> Only the immigration officer has the authority to permit a person to enter the United States.

H/she decides how long they can stay for any particular visit. Immigration matters are the responsibility of the U.S. Department of Homeland Security (DHS) as the United States Citizenship and Immigration Services (USCIS).

### Visa Types

There are two categories of U.S. visas: immigrant and nonimmigrant.
Immigrant visas are for people who intend to live permanently in the U.S. Nonimmigrant visas are for people with permanent residence outside the U.S. but who wish to be in the U.S. on a temporary basis – for tourism, medical treatment, business, temporary work or study.

### Nonimmigrant Visas

Nonimmigrant visas give you the right to stay in the United States temporarily with limited rights. Some of the more common visas the HR professional will encounter are:

| Visa Type | Description |
|---|---|
| B1 | Temporary entry for business |
| F1 | Academic students |
| H-1B | Professionals and specialty occupations |

| J | Exchange visitor | | |
|---|---|---|---|
| L | Intra-company transfer | | |
| O-1 | Persons with extraordinary abilities in the sciences, arts, education, business, or athletics | | |

## European Union and the Freedom of Movement

The European Union (EU) has legal personality in its own right. It may enter into contracts and defend its legal interests without intervention from any of the member states.

The treaty that underpins the EU is primarily concerned with the economic relationship between states. From the outset, however, there has been a social dimension in the treaty. The basic social right was the freedom of movement of labor.

> Every EU national is entitled to take up and pursue employment in the territory of another member state under the same conditions as the nationals of the host state (EU Treaty Art 1 and Regulation 1612/68).

A host state may only exclude an individual where there is evidence that their personal conduct poses a present threat to public order. They may, however, impose conditions relating to linguistic competence where this is directly relevant to their employment.

## Decent Work Agenda

Decent work is a concept that encapsulates both the quality of employment as well as the imperative of providing high quality jobs globally.

The decent work agenda seeks not just the creation of jobs, but of high quality jobs around the world.

> According to the International Labor Organization (ILO), decent work has four pillars:
>
> 1. full employment;
> 2. a social safety net;
> 3. fundamental workers' rights; and
> 4. mutually beneficial partnerships between business, labor and governmental actions.
>
> The decent work agenda both affirms and broadens the ILO's core labor standards, which include:
>
> - the elimination of discrimination in employment;
> - the eradication of forced labor and child labor;
> - the freedom of association; and
> - the right to bargain collectively.

The ILO is at the helm of the international campaign to provide decent work to people around the world. The World Commission on the Social Dimension of Globalization, established by the ILO, put the spotlight on decent work by identifying it as central to enabling all people to benefit from globalization. Decent work advocates believe that providing quality jobs globally can lift all boats rather than perpetuate a race to the bottom.

## Human Capital

Human capital refers to the stock of productive skills and technical knowledge embodied in labor.

There is a global debate regarding the fair distribution of human capital. This is most pointed with respect to educated individuals, who typically migrate from poorer places to richer places seeking opportunity, making "the rich richer and the poor poorer." When workers migrate, their early care and education generally benefit the country where they move to work. And, when they have health problems or retire, their care and retirement pension will typically be paid in the new country.

> **TEST TAKING TIP**
> Be careful when answering "negative questions" such as, "Which of these precepts is NOT contained in the Fair Labor Standards Act?" Test takers know there is a higher probability of persons missing these so-called negative questions than a typical straight-forward question.

Colonized countries have invoked this distribution with respect to the "brain drain" or "human capital flight" which occurs when the most talented individuals (those with the most individual capital) depart for education or opportunity to the colonizing country (historically, Britain and France and the U.S.A.).

During the late 19th and early 20th centuries, human capital in the United States became considerably more valuable as the need for skilled labor came with newfound technological advancement. New techniques and processes required further education than the norm of primary schooling, which thus led to the creation of more formalized schooling across the nation. This early insight into the need for education allowed for a significant jump in US productivity and economic prosperity, when compared to other world leaders at the time.

The rights and freedom of individuals to travel and opportunity, despite some historical exceptions such as the Soviet bloc and its "Iron Curtain," seem to consistently outweigh the rights of nation-states that nurture and educate them.

> One must also remember that the ability to have mobility with regards to where people want to move and work is a part of their human capital.

Being able to move from one area to the next is an ability and a benefit of having human capital. To restrict people from doing so would be to inherently lower their human capital.

## Offshoring

One of the areas of talent management that many HR functions have utilized is the high-impact strategy of moving hourly and professional-level work overseas, a strategy known as off shoring.

> Off shoring is the continuous process of moving work away from traditional home-country operations to areas around the world where both high quality and low cost workers are available.

The key to off shoring is to put work where the talent is. Although a handful of multinational firms have begun to identify top talent around the world, very few have taken the next step, which is realizing that it is not necessary (and often more expensive) to bring talent to the home country in order to take advantage of it.

There are three basic elements of off shoring:

1. Letting the very best individuals work wherever they choose to live.

2. Move hourly (production and customer service) work to areas with very low labor costs.

3. Move professional work to locations where the supply of talent more closely fits the company's demand.

## Onboarding

Onboarding is getting your newly hired talent up to speed with the policies, processes, culture, expectations, and day-to-day responsibilities of your company. It is making them feel welcome and excited, confirming why they joined your company. Onboarding is a special challenge for international assignees. They are frequently nervous, lost, and confused when arriving at their new work-site. All too frequently, many companies and local managers are pressured with short-term needs and don't want to spend the extra time and attention required for the long-term need of providing quality orientation and onboarding for the new expatriate.

> The goal of a good onboarding program is to build bonds between the employer and employee that are deep, meaningful and strong.

The stronger the emotional bonds, the greater the likelihood of that employee engaging with the company and remaining with the firm for a long time. Proper preparation and advanced training go a long way to creating a successful onboarding experience for the new assignee

In summary, whether you're a huge brand name corporation with thousands of employees, or a small start-up with 2 employees, all businesses have a similar goal: to attract talented employees and to keep them motivated to continuously contribute to the success of your business. Onboarding is one tool the international HRM needs to execute well.

**End SPHR-only section**

# DHR's FAST 20

1. **Executive Order 11246** requires employers with 50+ employees and w/federal contracts of $10K+ to take affirmative action in regards to race and sex… employers with 50 employees must have an annual written AAP.

2. **"BFOQ"** stands for Bona Fide Occupational Qualification. These are the job duties that you can require of an applicant (i.e.; a fireman is required to carry a 45 lb. hose up a ladder) and still be in compliance with **ADA.**

3. **"Disparate Treatment" vs. "Disparate Impact"**. Disparate treatment relates to a purposeful intent. Disparate impact relates to a non-intentional result. Either is a violation.

4. Beware of the **similar-to-me** bias in recruitment. Perpetuates "old-boy" clubs by unknowingly hiring applicants with the same socio-economic, gender, and racial qualities that we possess.

5. Federal law **(PRWORA)** requires **all** employers to report new hires. It's designed to tighten the noose around child support avoiders. **PRWORA** requires new hire reporting including: employee's name, address, and social; also, employer's name, address, and I.D. number.

6. Reference checking is a vital defense against charges of **"negligent hiring."**

7. **Griggs VS. Duke Power** is the landmark case that led to the demise of pre-employment testing.

8. **Constructive discharge** is literally forcing an employee to quit under pressure. Ex: sexual harassment, changing working conditions, poor or declining treatment, etc.

9. **Implied contract** exists when the employer's written/oral communications or past practices establish certain employee expectations. Ex: employees expect only to be terminated for cause.

10. **WARN** act requires employers to give 60 days advance notice of an impending mass layoff or shutdown.

11. **Public policy** exceptions to the at-will rule include: refusing to commit an illegal act, whistleblowing, filing workers comp, or performing a public act (jury duty, aiding a criminal investigation, etc.).

12. ADA effectively rendered **pre-employment physicals** obsolete.

13. Not having enough minority or female representation in a job classification means that the class is **underutilized**.

14. **Employment-at-will** doctrine stipulates both employer and employee can terminate a working relationship at any time and for any reason other than those situations explicitly covered by law.

15. **The 4/5ths rule** states that discrimination is likely to occur if the selection rate for a protected group is less than 4/5ths of the selection rate for a majority group.

16. **Glass ceiling** refers to the lack of women and minorities in top management positions.

17. **Job analysis** is the systematic process of gathering information about a job. **Job description** defines the job in terms of its content and scope. **Job specification** consists of the KASOC's needed to carry out the job tasks and duties. **KASOC's** are critical Knowledge, Abilities, Skills and Other Characteristics necessary to perform job tasks… similar to BFOQ's.

18. **Pregnancy Discrimination Act** prohibits employment practices that discriminate on the basis of pregnancy, childbirth, or related medical conditions such as abortions.

19. **Sexual Harassment** is unwelcome sexual attention that causes the recipient distress and results in an inability on the part of the recipient to effectively perform the job requirements.

20. **Work process mapping** applies a simplified version of flowcharting to describing work processes. Other related terms on the test may include Lean Manufacturing and Six Sigma that refer to eliminating wasted movements and simplified work processes.

# Practice Quiz

1. The Staffing Manager at ABC Corporation is concerned with the number of discrimination lawsuits brought against various first-line supervisors by several job applicants. Which is NOT a strategy the manager should adopt for this situation?
   A. Structured interviews
   B. Training of supervisors
   C. Team interviews
   D. Stress interviews

2. While USERRA provides re-employment protection for military reservists called into active duty for national emergencies, it does NOT provide protection against employers who deny job opportunities upon initial employment to military servicemen and women. This statement is:
   A. Only true for private employers
   B. Only true for government entities
   C. True
   D. False

3. The only legal subject an interviewer may ask of the applicant is:
   A. Have you filed any work comp claims against other employers?
   B. Are you currently using illegal drugs or abusing prescription drugs?
   C. Do you have an arrest record?
   D. How many children do you have?

4. ABC Corporation hired 25 of the 50 white male applicants. ABC had 30 minority and 80 female applicants. What is the minimal number of minority and female candidates ABC should have hired to prevent adverse impact from occurring?
   A. 24; 32
   B. 12; 54
   C. 12; 32
   D. 24; 54

5. A statistically relevant pre-selection test that measures a selection of behavioral characteristics of the applicant is MOST probably high in:
   A. Construct validity
   B. Reliability
   C. Content validity
   D. Criterion validity

6. A vital element of the strategic staffing plan for any organization is:
   A. Tuition assistance
   B. Succession planning
   C. Bonuses and rewards
   D. Behavioral interviewing

7. The principal compliance component of the Americans with Disabilities Act is (the):
   A. Employer may not refuse to hire disabled persons
   B. Employer must have a written affirmative action plan for hiring of the disabled
   C. Disabled persons may sue employers who discriminate against them
   D. Employer must make reasonable accommodations for disabled employees who can perform the essential elements of the job

8. The last step in the job analysis process is to:
    A. Develop job descriptions for each position analyzed
    B. Perform a job evaluation on all analyzed positions
    C. Conduct a quantitative analysis of the job
    D. Retrain any affected workers

9. Which Supreme Court ruling qualified the use of pre-employment selection instruments, created the terms "disparate impact" and "disparate treatment," and advises employers to validate their hiring process?
    A. Griggs v. Duke Power
    B. Sides v. Duke Hospital
    C. Washington v. Davis
    D. University of California v. Bakke

10. Per EO 11246, the term "underutilization" is BEST characterized by the example of:
    A. Certain members of protected groups are inadequately represented within the workforce.
    B. Minorities are purposefully dealt with in a manner different from majorities
    C. Minorities are leaving employment at a disproportionately faster rate than majorities
    D. Protected groups are represented in the workplace at a 15% less ratio than majorities

11. Quid Pro Quo Harassment is BEST exemplified by:
    A. A sexy pinup in an employee's locker
    B. Staring or leering at other workers
    C. Can only be perpetrated by someone in a position of power or authority over another
    D. A male employee who goes out of his way to tell one particular female extremely dirty jokes

12. An employee requests a day off to attend a religious ceremony. The HR Manager is tasked with dealing with this issue. The MOST legal response for this request is to:
    A. Honor the request unconditionally
    B. Make a reasonable accommodation
    C. Remain consistent with prior precedents
    D. Deny any and all similar requests

13. Jason is fed up with ABC, Inc. due to poor quality issues, inconsistent production, and tardy deliveries of its products. As a Sales Rep who knows the local market, he feels he can start his own firm and go into competition with ABC. When Jason was first hired, he agreed to not go into competition for a period of time after terminating his employment. This contractual agreement is BEST termed a(n):
    A. Condition of employment
    B. Civil law
    C. Trade secret agreement
    D. Non-compete agreement

## Answers and Explanations to Practice Quiz:

1. D

Stress interviews put the candidate into an uncomfortable and stressful environment. The Stress interview is sometimes confrontational and unpleasant and is likely to increase the number of complaints by applicants. The other interviews are typical strategies employed by HR Managers to reduce the subjectivity of individual supervisor's actions.

2. D

USERRA does provide protection for job applicants who are military reservists. The statement is entirely untrue for all employers.

3. B

Drug Free Workplace Act allows the employer to take steps up to and including testing of applicants for illegal drug use. It stands to reason the employer is certainly allowed to ask about illegal drug use prior to making an offer. The other options are violations of Americans with Disabilities Act and Uniform Guidelines on Employee Selection Procedures.

4. C

The 80% rule is applied here. Since the company hired the white males 50% of the time (25 hirees / 50 applicants = 50%), apply the 80% standard to the 50% white male hiring rate (80% X 50% = 40%) to arrive at the 40% minimum threshold rate. 40% of the 30 minorities is 12 and 40% of the 80 females is 32. Therefore the answer, 12; 32.

5. A

Construct validity measures traits and characteristics. Thus the correct answer. Reliability measures the degree of repeatability of the test, content validity measures certain vital components of the job itself, and criterion validity measures and predicts future performance.

6. B

While all of the options may prove useful to an organization, should it decide to employ these measures, only by planning for and providing for the future staffing needs of the organization will the entity hope to weather unexpected staffing emergencies. It often takes years of careful grooming to develop effective senior managers and technologists.

7. D

Three of the answer options are untrue under ADA (disabled applicants not able to perform the essential elements with accommodation are not required to be hired, there is no "written affirmative action" requirement under ADA, and only after the EEOC has issued a "right to sue" letter may the disabled person bring suit but this is not a principle component of compliance. Only by making "reasonable accommodations" can the employer comply with ADA.

8.  A

First comes a thorough analysis of the job where the position has its core tasks broken down and defined into discrete units. After this step, then the job description (an "executive summary" of the position) is crafted from the highlights of the job analysis. Job evaluations is a process of creating a relative ranking of jobs to determine internal equity of each position, the job analysis itself conducts a quantitative and qualitative analysis of the job, and retraining (aka: cross-training) may occur at any point in the process as it is basically unrelated to the question.

9.  A

Griggs is the correct answer because Sides concerns "implied job contracts," Washington v. Davis is about anti-discrimination laws and their relationship with BFOQ requirements, and Bakke is about so-called "reverse discrimination."

10.  A

Underutilization is when minorities are disproportionately under-represented in the workplace. Minorities being purposefully dealt with differently than majorities is best known as "disparate treatment." Minorities leaving employment at an excessive rate is probably "disparate impact" or a possible violation of the 80% rule (aka: 4/5ths rule). 15% under-representation is not a violation of the 80% rule (>20% is a violation).

11.  C

"Quid Pro Quo," by definition, means "something for something" or "this for that." Therefore, Quid Pro Quo sexual harassment must be perpetrated by someone in a higher placed position. The other three answer options are examples of "hostile environment," not quid pro quo harassment.

12.  B

Title VII Civil Rights Act of 1964 requires employers to "make reasonable accommodations" for religious observances. The other three answer options could cause compliance and precedent problems with unilateral application in all cases.

13.  D

A non-compete clause or covenant not to compete (CNC), is a term used in contract law under which one party (usually an employee) agrees not to pursue a similar profession or trade in competition against another party (usually the employer). As a contract provision, a CNC is bound by traditional contract requirements including the consideration doctrine. The use of such clauses is premised on the possibility that upon their termination or resignation, an employee might begin working for a competitor or starting a business, and gain competitive advantage by abusing confidential information about their former employer's operations or trade secrets, or sensitive information such as customer/client lists, business practices, upcoming products, and marketing plans.

# Chapter 6
# Business Management & Strategy
# (PHR 11% - SPHR 30%)

Developing, contributing to and supporting the organization's mission, vision, values, strategic goals and objectives; formulating policies; guiding and leading the change process; and evaluating organizational effectiveness as an organizational leader.

## Landmark and Precedent Setting Court Cases

While there are many significant landmark decisions that have had a significant impact on shaping employment law, the following is a list of some of those that are likely to appear on either the PHR or SPHR exams. While memorizing all on this list is daunting, there is usually one or two of these that will appear on your exam. To save yourself some study time, try and learn which cases go with specific categories (i.e.; sexual harassment, discrimination, etc.).

**Griggs v. Duke Power Co.**, (1971), was a court case argued before the United States Supreme Court on December 14, 1970. The Supreme Court ruled against a procedure used by the company when selecting employees for internal transfer and promotion to certain positions, namely requiring a high school education and certain scores on broad aptitude tests. African-American applicants, less likely to hold a high school diploma and averaging lower scores on the aptitude tests, were selected at a much lower rate for these positions compared to white candidates. The Court found that under Title VII of the Civil Rights Act, if such tests disparately impact ethnic minority groups, businesses must demonstrate that such tests are "reasonably related" to the job for which the test is required.

**McDonnell Douglas v. Green**, (1973), the McDonnell Douglas v. Green case established the order and framework that employment discrimination cases must follow. 1. The plaintiff (employee) must first establish a prima facie case of discrimination. 2. The defendant (employer) must produce evidence of a legitimate non-discriminatory reason for its actions. If this occurs then the presumption of discrimination dissipates. 3. The plaintiff must then present facts to show an inference of discrimination. In practice, the third step is the most difficult step for plaintiffs to successfully achieve.

**NLRB v. J. Weingarten, Inc.**, (1975), was a case decided by the Supreme Court of the United States that ruled that employees in unionized workplaces have the right under the National Labor Relations Act to the presence of a union steward during any management inquiry that the employee reasonably believes may result in discipline. While this ruling has been reversed several times, since 2007, workers who are not union members do not have the right to the presence of a representative during management inquiries.

**Albermarle Paper v. Moody** (1975), African American employees charged that the company's seniority system perpetuated the overt segregation that existed in the plant's departmental job assignment system prior to 2 July 1965 (the effective date of Title VII), and they sought injunctive and back pay relief. They won. The Supreme Court clarified the job-relatedness defense, requiring a careful job analysis to identify the specific knowledge, skills, and abilities necessary to perform the job. They also required the employer to use specific criteria on which to evaluate job performance in showing the job relatedness of a test.

**Washington v. Davis**, (1976), was a United States Supreme Court case regarding the application of the Equal Protection Clause. Two African Americans had applied for positions in the Washington, DC police department, and sued after being turned down. They claimed that the department used racially discriminatory hiring procedures, by implementing a test of verbal skills (Test 21), which was failed disproportionately by African Americans. The Court ruled against them, finding that use of the test did not violate the Equal Protection Clause. The important general rule created by Washington v. Davis is that, under the Equal Protection Clause of the Fourteenth Amendment, "[an] official action will not be held unconstitutional solely because it results in a racially disproportionate impact." Instead, a plaintiff must prove discriminatory motive on the state actor's part. The court noted that "disproportionate impact is not irrelevant, but it is not the sole touchstone of an invidious racial discrimination forbidden by the Constitution". The purpose-based standard elucidated in the Court's 1976 opinion has made it much more difficult for plaintiffs to prevail in discrimination suits.

**Regents of the University of California v. Bakke**, (1978) was a landmark decision of the Supreme Court of the United States on affirmative action. It bars quota systems in college admissions, but affirms the constitutionality of affirmative action programs, giving equal access to minorities. Bakke, a white medical school candidate, filed suit when he determined lesser qualified minority candidates were obtaining entrance into medical school because the school had set aside (reserved) 16 of the 100 openings each year. He claimed he was discriminated against because of his race. This was one of the first "reverse discrimination" cases.

**United Steelworkers of America v. Weber**, (1979), was a case regarding affirmative action in which the United States Supreme Court held that the Civil Rights Act of 1964 did not bar employers from favoring women and minorities. The Court's decision reversed lower courts' rulings in favor of Brian Weber whose lawsuit beginning in 1974 challenged his employer's hiring practices.

**Bundy v. Jackson** (1981), the District of Columbia Circuit Court of Appeals characterized hostile environment cases as presenting a "cruel trilemma." In *Bundy* the victim had three options: (1) to endure the harassment, (2) to attempt to oppose it and likely make the situation worse, or (3) to leave the place of employment. A hostile work environment, the court held, represented discrimination under Title VII and constituted grounds for legal action. This ruling determined that someone who is harassed does not have to suffer financially or lose job benefits in order for the harassing to be a violation of Title VII.

**Davis v. United Steel Corp.** (1985), this ruling said that if a supervisor or a manager notices sexual harassment and does nothing about it, a company is legally liable.

**Meritor Savings Bank v. Vinson**, (1986), marked the United States Supreme Court's recognition of certain forms of "hostile environment" sexual harassment as a violation of Civil Rights Act of 1964 Title VII, and established the standards for analyzing whether conduct was unlawful, and when an employer would be liable. Plaintiffs with hostile environment-styled claims must prove that the challenged conduct: 1) was severe and pervasive, 2) created a hostile or abusive working environment, 3) was unwelcome, and 4) was based on the plaintiff's gender.

**Burlington Industries v. Ellerth** (1988), Ellerth quit her job at Burlington Industries because she allegedly suffered sexual harassment by her supervisor. The court found the company liable for damages due to "constructive discharge," even though they had no knowledge of the allegations and Ellerth had suffered no adverse affect due to the alleged harassment.

**City of Richmond v. J.A. Croson Co.**, (1989) was a case in which the United States Supreme Court held that the city council of Richmond's minority set-aside program, giving preference to minority business enterprises (MBE) in the awarding of municipal contracts, was unconstitutional under the Equal

Protection Clause. The court found that the city failed to identify both the need for remedial action and that other non-discriminatory remedies would be insufficient.

**Martin v. Wilks,** (1989), was a U.S. Supreme Court case brought by Robert K. Wilks challenging the validity of race-based hiring practices. In 1974, the Jefferson County, Alabama Personnel Board signed a consent decree that required them to hire and promote African-American firefighters. Wilks, a white fireman, took issue with the agreement, claiming that he and other white firefighters (who were not parties to the original consent decrees signed in 1974) were more qualified than some of the black firefighters receiving promotions. The Supreme Court of the United States upheld the appeal of the white firefighters in a 5-4 decision on the issue of whether the white firefighters have a constitutional right to challenge the previously established decrees.

**Ellison vs. Brady** (IRS) (1991), The California 9th Circuit Court of Appeals determined that behavior alleged to be sex harassment must be analyzed from a "reasonable woman's" point of view, as opposed to the previous standard of a reasonable person's point of view. In this case, Ellison had been called "supersensitive" by a lower court ruling with regard to her reaction to unwelcome love letter from Brady.

**Piscataway Board of Education v. Taxman**, (1996) was a racial discrimination case begun in 1989. The school board of Piscataway Township, New Jersey needed to eliminate a teaching position from the high school Business Education department. Under New Jersey state law, tenured teachers have to be laid off in reverse order of seniority. The newest tenured teachers, Sharon Taxman and Debra Williams, white and African-American respectively, had started working at the school on the same day. In the interest of maintaining racial diversity (Williams was the only black teacher in the department, and 50% of the students were

> **TEST TAKING TIP**
> Some candidates who are unsure of whether to sit for the PHR or the SPHR exam choose both. It's expensive but you can sign up for both in the same test period. They usually sit for the SPHR first and if they pass, they skip the PHR exam.

minorities), the school board voted to lay off Taxman, even though she had a master's degree and Williams only had a bachelor's degree. Taxman complained to the Equal Employment Opportunity Commission, saying that the board had violated Title VII of the Civil Rights Act of 1964. The United States Court of Appeals for the Third Circuit ruled in favor of Taxman. The school board appealed to the United States Supreme Court and a hearing was scheduled, but civil rights groups, fearing that the case could lead to the prohibition of affirmative action, provided money for the board to settle the case out of court, so the case was never heard. Taxman was subsequently rehired.

**Oncale v. Sundowner Offshore Services**, (1998), was a decision of the Supreme Court of the United States on a suit for sex discrimination by a male oil-rig worker, who claimed that he was repeatedly subjected to sexual harassment by his male coworkers with the acquiescence of his employer. The Court held that Title VII's protection against workplace discrimination "because of... sex" applied to harassment in the workplace between members of the same sex.

**Circuit City Stores, Inc. v. Adams**. (2001), is a case where the Supreme Court upheld the employer's right to require mandatory arbitration to settle any legal disputes from the employees, rather than providing them the right to bring a lawsuit against the employer.

**Burlington Northern & Santa Fe (BNSF) Railway Co. v. White**, (2006), was a United States Supreme Court case about sexual harassment and retaliatory discrimination. A job reassignment which is dirtier and more strenuous may constitute retaliatory discrimination under the Civil Rights Act of 1964, as may a month of suspension without pay even when the employee receives back pay.

**Sereboff v. Mid Atlantic Medical Services, Inc.,** (2006), was a case decided by the Supreme Court of the United States involving the ability of an Employee Retirement Income Security Act (ERISA) plan fiduciary to recover medical costs from a beneficiary who has been reimbursed for injuries by a third party. The Court ruled unanimously that ERISA permitted the fiduciary to recover costs from the settlement proceeds a beneficiary received in a personal injury lawsuit.

**Ledbetter v. Goodyear Tire & Rubber Co.,** (2007), is an employment discrimination decision of the Supreme Court of the United States. Justice Alito held for the five-justice majority that employers are protected from lawsuits over race or gender pay discrimination if the claims are based on decisions made by the employer 180 days ago or more. This was a case of statutory rather than constitutional interpretation. The plaintiff in this case, Lilly Ledbetter, characterized her situation as one where "disparate pay is received during the statutory limitations period [i.e. less than 180 days ago], but is the result of intentionally discriminatory pay decisions that occurred outside the limitations period [i.e. more than 180 days ago]." In rejecting Ledbetter's appeal, the Supreme Court said that "she could have, and should have, sued" when the pay decisions were made, instead of waiting beyond the 180-day statutory charging period.

# Application of Laws to Employers

HR Professionals must be aware of whether certain laws and Acts apply to their particular business enterprise. The federal labor laws generally apply to employers above a certain size, defined in terms of the number of employees they have. But how do you count your employees if you have part-time workers, or if your payroll ebbs and flows with the seasons? Generally, you must count all the employees who are on your payroll during a week. This means that you must count each of your part-timers, temporary workers, and leased workers as employees; however, don't count your independent contractors. Do this for each week in the year. If you meet the threshold number of employees under a given law for at least 20 weeks in a year, you are covered by that law for the entire year.

The following chart demonstrates that most laws are applied to employers based on the number of full-time-equivalent employees the employer has.

| Minimum # Employees | Law(s) | Other |
|---|---|---|
| 100 | WARN | |
| 50 | Affirmative Action<br>FMLA | $10,000 or $50,000 |
| 20 | ADEA<br>COBRA | 40 and over |
| 15 | ADA<br>Title VII<br>Civil Rights Act of 1964 and 1991<br>Pregnancy Discrimination Act (PDA) | |
| 1 | All others | |

# Strategic Planning

## Changing HR roles

Over the last few decades, the role of an HR manager has changed from processor of personnel paperwork to strategic, proactive business partner. Today's HR professionals act as conduits between employees and management, monitor compliance with employment laws, and manage an organization's human resources to meet corporate goals and objectives.

> HR's primary mission now is to design and implement legally sound HR policies that will support strategic business goals and fulfill the organization's workforce needs as economic conditions change.

## HR's Role in Strategic Planning

> To serve as a global strategic business partner, an HR manager must fully understand the organization's business, its competitors, and the internal and external factors affecting short- and long-term planning.

This knowledge is essential not only to develop HR plans consistent with the overall business strategy, but also to establish HR as a valuable player in organizational planning. Top executives value input from HR managers who can foster organizational development, predict future legislation and regulations, and recommend corrective actions.

In hiring, training, motivating, and retaining employees, HR managers increasingly must think like senior management.

### Reasons a business focus in HR is becoming more important

#### Accelerated competitive change
Given the rapid pace of change, senior managers cannot afford the time and patience to instruct HR managers of each new development. The effective HR manager, like the effective CEO, follows the industry news and reads the trade journals. In fact, HR executives increasingly are expected to instruct senior management of pending changes and appropriate responses.

#### Increased demand for skilled labor
Equipment, materials, and mechanical-electronic systems are becoming expendable commodities, while information, customer goodwill, and skilled employees are becoming prime, hard-to-replace business assets. The increased value of skilled employees reflects several trends:

- Skilled labor is becoming scarce, and any scarce commodity increases in value.

- Cost-conscious managers are subcontracting out production work and reducing finished-product and materials inventories, so these resources account for a smaller percentage of a company's value.

- More employers are leasing buildings and equipment, which reduces a company's physical assets.

> **TEST TAKING TIP**
> On any question that asks about something "strategic," seek the option that says something about aligning or supporting the overall business plan or company goals.
> **Example:** HR's primary strategic concern in developing a new HRD program is:
> 1. The program supports top management's business plan.

- The value of intangible assets, like patents and technology, is more volatile and has a shorter half-life due to the faster pace of competitive and technological developments.

As a result, the success of an organization and its HR manager may depend on finding people with the right skills, training and motivating employees appropriately, and retaining them successfully.

### Bottom-line orientation

Other departments long have been measured on their contribution to revenue and profits. Today, HR departments also are coming under bottom-line scrutiny.

To demonstrate profitability, HR executives must develop functional objectives, track results in achieving these objectives, and quantifying their dollar impact wherever possible. For example, consider the cost value of the following HR activities:

- recruitment, such as acquiring a product manager who introduced a winning new line;

- employee morale, such as implementing policies to prevent dissatisfaction and costly attrition in the systems department;

- position and compensation control, such as recommending leased instead of permanent employees to cut benefit costs; and

- equal employment activities, such as briefing senior managers about recent antidiscrimination decisions to reduce the company's risk of expensive lawsuits.

**TEST TAKING TIP**
Remember, you are to choose the BEST answer option. Often, the BEST option is a poor option for the situation described on the exam, but it's better than the other three choices.

## Forecasting Models

In any planning process, there is a certain amount of guesswork involved. The prudent planner will hedge their bet on future predictions by employing a scientific approach to forecasting. Commonly accepted models include:

1. Judgmental forecasting: This is where the planner uses their own experience, education and opinion to form the basis for a prediction as to what the future may bring. In other words, it is an educated guess.

2. Delphi technique: This is a systematic forecasting method that involves the use of a panel of experts who are kept separate and isolated from one another while rendering opinions and predictions within their area of expertise. Usually, several rounds of questions and answers are conducted. After each round, a consensus forecast is compiled on the subject being planned.

3. Nominal group technique: A variant of brainstorming, the Nominal Group Technique requires a group of knowledgeable team members to write down their ideas or predictions, on a specific subject, independent of the other team members input. Once the ideas are written down, they are discussed and prioritized one by one by the team. The steps of this process normally follow:
    a. Generation of ideas or predictions
    b. Record the ideas or predictions
    c. Discuss the ideas or predictions
    d. Vote on the ideas or predictions

## HR Research:

### Research design and methodology

One method of improving organizational effectiveness is applying scientific principles of problem solving and research to the resolution of organizational issues. Scientific research is a development process that uses objective criteria and data to provide a framework for action planning, implementation, and change management.

The following outlines the steps to use in conducting an action-oriented investigation, from the initial phase of deciding what to survey, to the final phase of making changes based on the data received. An entire survey project cycle consists of four sequential phases:

### 1. Design phase

The research process begins by defining objectives, determining priorities, establishing realistic expectations, and custom-developing a questionnaire that covers a limited set of relevant topics.

### 2. Data collection phase

Once the investigatory process has been developed and the decision made to proceed, data collection begins. During the data collection phase, data is processed and analyzed, results are interpreted, a hypothesis is formulated, and the findings are presented to management.

### 3. Deployment phase

The most important part of a successful research program is using the results to put words into action. Deployment (or testing the hypothesis) concerns implementing the plan.

### 4. Evaluation phase

The successful use of this model is incomplete unless the process includes evaluating or measuring the results of the plan. It is imperative that follow-up occur, and any flaws discovered are corrected in the hypothesis and, starting over at the Design Phase, if necessary.

## Goal Setting

Part of the process of strategic planning for the HR Professional is to acquire the ability to set realistic goals. The common model adopted by many planners is to make goals and objectives more explicit by following the guidelines associated with the S.M.A.R.T. acronym:

- **S**pecific: one should precisely define objectives or goals rather than tolerating diffuseness or nebulousness
- **M**easurable: one should define a method of measuring the objectives/goals
- **A**chievable: all parties need to agree to the objectives/goals, and to their achievability
- **R**ealistic: one must define realistic objectives/goals, the accomplishment of which must make sense
- **T**imely: completion must occur within an agreed time-scale

## SWOT Analysis (SPHR-only section)

SWOT Analysis is a strategic planning method used to evaluate the **S**trengths, **W**eaknesses, **O**pportunities, and **T**hreats involved in a project or in a business venture. It involves specifying the objective of the business venture or project, and identifying the internal and external factors that are favorable and unfavorable to achieving that objective.

- **S**trengths: attributes of the organization that are helpful in achieving the objective.

- **W**eaknesses: attributes of the organization that are harmful in achieving the objective.
- **O**pportunities: *external* conditions that are helpful in achieving the objective.
- **T**hreats: *external* conditions which could do damage to the business's performance.

SWOT is generally employed at the beginning of the planning process. Identification of SWOT is essential because subsequent steps in the process of planning for achievement of the selected objective may be derived from the SWOT.

SWOT is sometimes considered part of an environmental scan, just as the OT (opportunities and threats) are external to the organization.

**End SPHR-only section**

## Action Plans and Programs

For a career development program to succeed, an organization must have job paths and career tracks that provide growth opportunities for employees. The traditional career development pattern directs employees on a single career path toward managerial positions through promotions. However, this approach can present several problems:

- Managerial positions have become fewer as companies have downsized and streamlined organizational hierarchies, and as the number of traditional industrial enterprises has dropped. At the same time, the demand for technical and research expertise has grown.
- Not all employees who succeed in technical or skill-based positions make good managers. In fact, the same characteristics that account for a technical employee's success in some fields can work against that employee becoming a successful manager.
- Successful employees, even those who might prefer to stay in their area of expertise and avoid management, have no alternative but to pursue supervisory positions if they want to continue career and salary growth.
- A company that relies exclusively on managerial promotions to reward high performers winds up losing the expertise of its best technical employees once they are promoted.

As part of the process, it is the responsibility of the HR head (working with other employees in the unit) to develop action plans to implement business unit strategy. Action plans give a clear idea of the following:

- what resources are needed (e.g., people, technology, time, and finances);
- what the goals, objectives, and desired results are;
- what the priorities should be; and
- what the impact will be on others in the organization.

The business strategy and action plans can be developed at the same time that the unit budgets are being developed and approved. Marrying the planning and the budgeting is important. Many firms fail to see the connection between planning (deciding what to do) and budgeting (allocating the resources to do it). It is not uncommon to have business units work on goals and objectives that are not financially sound undertakings for the company, or to have them focus on completing specific goals and objectives with no allocated resources.

## Balanced Scorecard

In 1992, Robert S. Kaplan and David Norton introduced the balanced scorecard, a concept for measuring a company's activities in terms of its vision and strategies, to give managers a comprehensive view of the performance of a business. Recognizing some of the weaknesses and vagueness of previous management approaches, the balanced scorecard approach provides a clear prescription as to what companies should measure in order to 'balance' the financial perspective.

*"The balanced scorecard retains traditional financial measures. But financial measures tell the story of past events, an adequate story for industrial age companies for which investments in long-term capabilities and customer relationships were not critical for success. These financial measures are inadequate, however, for guiding and evaluating the journey that information age companies must make to create future value through investment in customers, suppliers, employees, processes, technology, and innovation." - Robert S. Kaplan -*

**TEST TAKING TIP**
Choose the touchy feely answer option. Test makers usually seek the option that is most nurturing and supportive of employees.

The key new element is focusing not only on financial outcomes but also on the human issues that drive those outcomes, so that organizations focus on the future and act in their long-term best interest. The scorecard drives implementation of strategy using perspectives which generally include:

**1. Financial Perspective** - measures reflecting financial performance, for example debtor management, cash flow, or return on investment. The financial performance of an organization is fundamental to its success. Even non-profit organizations must make the books balance.

Financial figures suffer from two major drawbacks:
I.     They are historical. While they tell us what has happened to the organization, they may not tell us what is currently happening, or be a good indicator of future performance.
II.    It is common for the current market value of an organization to exceed the market value of its assets.

**2. Customer Perspective** - measures having a direct impact on customers and their satisfaction, for example time taken to process a phone call, time to deliver the products, results of customer surveys, number of complaints or competitive rankings.

**3. Business Process Perspective** - measures reflecting the performance of key business processes, for example the time spent prospecting, number of units that required rework or process cost.

**4. Learning and Growth Perspective** - measures describing the company's learning curve -- for example, number of employee suggestions or total hours spent on staff training.

Kaplan and Norton found that companies are using the scorecard to:
- Clarify and update budgets
- Identify and align strategic initiatives
- Conduct periodic performance reviews to learn about and improve strategy.

## Evolution of the HR Mission

- Increased international competition has shaken U.S. complacency in the world market. The United States no longer dominates markets nor dictates management and business practices.

- Government regulation and legislation have grown, which further restricts U.S. competitiveness and increases the chances of government fines and employee litigation.

- Technological advances make training increasingly important, especially as the pool of skilled workers shrinks. Employers have to train new recruits in the skills that U.S. high school graduates lack, and retrain current employees to handle new skill demands.

- Economic stagnation, downsizing, and reorganizations have emphasized employee involvement, HR development, and career counseling. Companies must involve and develop employees to maximize productivity and achieve total quality management goals without increasing staff. Today's leaner organizations also must find creative ways to reward talented employees despite declining job security and advancements opportunities.

- Changing workforce demographics have created new employee needs and demands that companies must address to attract and retain talent. Diversity in recruitment and employment practices has become essential for employers to maintain critical labor force levels. Besides hiring more women, minorities, and immigrants, highly competitive organizations adopt HR policies that respond to the needs of the new workforce such as flextime, child care, and telecommuting.

# Outsourcing

## Outsourcing the HR Functions

Given the complexity of many employment tax and benefits laws, most small businesses start out by outsourcing certain human resource (HR) functions. For many companies, small and large, using outside vendors to process payroll, track and deposit employment taxes, and handle benefits administration is more efficient and cost-effective than trying to hire and train in-house staff to handle these matters. In fact, increased government regulation and oversight have spurred even the largest companies to turn these HR activities over to outside specialists.

In choosing a vendor to handle certain functions, businesses usually can choose from a wide array of potential providers. The key to success is knowing how to locate a qualified service provider, and how to manage and monitor the quality of services provided. Employers ultimately are responsible for compliance with employment and tax laws, and can be held liable for mistakes made by an outside service provider. Therefore, choosing the right vendor is of paramount importance, as well as monitoring the vendor's activities.

Outside providers can:

- perform technical tasks of legal compliance;

- handle complicated or volatile situations like sexual harassment; and

- take over the time-consuming but essential paperwork duties associated with many HR activities.

Even companies with a dedicated HR staff commonly outsource certain activities. These activities typically require specialized knowledge, such as administration of a 401(k) plan or an employee assistance program, or involve routine, repetitive, administrative functions, such as payroll processing.

## Advantages of outsourcing

While using an outside vendor costs money, it often provides a better quality of service at less cost than hiring someone to perform the activity. In addition, minimizing in-house time devoted to cumbersome HR activities lets a company focus on its primary business mission. Reducing the compliance burden associated with offering benefits also may allow smaller businesses to offer packages they otherwise could not afford. Expanded benefits, in turn, help small businesses to compete for talented workers who would otherwise seek opportunities available only in large companies.

## Disadvantages of outsourcing

Despite these benefits, outsourcing HR activities does have some potential disadvantages. Any use of an outside provider means loss of control and the possibility of a lower quality of service. In the HR area, picking a bad vendor can wreak havoc on employee morale, such as when paychecks are issued late. It also can cost a company millions if employment laws are violated in the process. As a result, some in-house time still must go toward managing and monitoring vendor services.

# Evaluate HR's Contribution

## Evaluation of Human Resource Planning

Before conducting an evaluation, HR managers must first decide what aspects of the HR function to assess. Making this decision prior to conducting the evaluation is essential to ensure that appropriate data are available for conducting the evaluation. HR evaluations can take place at any of the following levels:

### Program level

Program evaluations measure the impact of specific HR activities or services. Examples of this type of evaluation include:

- calculating the cost savings associated with a change in benefit options;
- collecting employee ratings of a training program;
- tracking absenteeism rates before and after instituting a program to reward good attendance;
- comparing the accident rate of employees receiving safety training to that of workers not receiving the training;
- monitoring the staff time saved by developing a personnel record form that can be scanned into the computer system;
- comparing the number of qualified applicants obtained through different recruitment media;
- tallying the costs of a change in salary structure against the associated savings in terms of employee retention, reduced recruitment costs, and so forth.

### Departmental level

This type of HR evaluation focuses on the overall effectiveness of the HR function. Approaches to evaluating HR department effectiveness include:

- surveying HR programs, services, and activities to ensure the HR department is adequately meeting employee needs and legal mandates;
- tracking annual HR department costs, staffing levels, and activities to evaluate HR productivity over time and in comparison to industry norms;
- polling employees and managers regarding their satisfaction with the quantity and quality of HR programs and services; and

- auditing HR processes to determine if better HR staff training or different methods of performing these activities would improve efficiency or quality.

## Organizational level

At the organizational level, HR evaluation involves looking at the overall company norms, goals, or issues that HRM could address. Examples of organizational HR evaluation include:

- tracking the number of consultations with employees and managers to assess HR staff impact on the workforce;

- measuring the impact of instituting flextime on measures of organizational performance, such as productivity, absenteeism, or recruitment goals;

- determining the number of HR plans to facilitate organizational strategic goals and assessing the impact of these HR plans;

- surveying employees to determine areas in which managerial training could improve HR policy implementation; and

- analyzing aspects of organizational culture that facilitate or hinder effective HR management.

> **TEST TAKING TIP**
> SPHR candidates need to spend a lot of time mastering the Distinctive HR flashcards. Flashcards force you to fully understand a subject.

## Evaluating HR Effectiveness

### Types of evaluations

#### Qualitative vs. quantitative evaluations

Qualitative evaluations examine the types of programs and services an HR function is providing, how well it delivers those programs and services, and which HR areas or customers could benefit from new programs or improved processes. Quantitative evaluations calculate averages, ratios, or cost-benefit values for different HR activities. These measures can be tracked over time and compared to internal or external norms.

#### Internal vs. external norms

Evaluations using internal norms track ratings or statistics over time or between different areas. For example, an organization could compare employee ratings of health benefit plans to those given the pension benefit program, or it could track how highly employees rate the benefit plan from year to year. External norms might include statistics on HR department budgets as a percent of operating revenues, average number of HR staff to total employees, and other commonly available survey standards.

### Conducting an HR evaluation

A variety of sources can provide information regarding the effectiveness of the HR function.

#### Interviewing HR customer

Obtain customer feedback using individual interviews, focus group discussions, or written surveys. Whatever technique is used, get different perspectives by including HR staff, line managers, top executives, and employees. Find out whether policy design, communication, or implementation accounts for the level of satisfaction or dissatisfaction expressed. Interviews and surveys work particularly well for collecting qualitative information about the adequacy of HR services and the level of HR customer satisfaction.

An HRIS audit covers all aspects of the system, the people who use it, and the organizational purposes which the HRIS serves. In a sense, auditing an HRIS is similar to conducting a needs analysis. In general, the following areas of HRIS operations should receive a thorough analysis:

### *Documentation*

User's manuals, computer programming specifications, on-line instructions, written forms, and the like usually require updating over time. Changes made to the system through routine maintenance can make the original HRIS documentation outdated, incomplete, or erroneous if supportive documents are not updated as part of routine maintenance.

### *Procedures and policies*

Review procedures for operating and maintaining the HRIS, as well as current and future organizational policies relevant to HRIS operations. Some procedures may benefit from streamlining, as users become more familiar with the system and its capabilities. For example, an organization that originally processed new hires by having managers fill out written forms and HR staffs retype this information into the database, may want to begin using optical scanners or the hiring manager's staff to handle input. On the other hand, some seemingly simple procedures may prove unworkable: A company that made departmental managers responsible for assigning staff to input new employee information may find that fewer errors and delays occur when HRM handles this activity instead.

### *HRIS personnel and other users*

Lines of communication between staff engaged in hands-on HRIS activities and users who request their services deserve close attention. Other issues to consider include the delegation of HRIS activities, the performance of individuals assigned those responsibilities, and the level of HRIS staffing. Training needs also may change with staff turnover and system updates over time.

### *System hardware and software*

Look at the efficiency of HRIS performance capabilities and the effectiveness of maintenance procedures in keeping the database current and operations flowing smoothly. Technological advances also may make it attractive to replace, update, or augment current software and/or hardware. Even when no dramatic technological breakthroughs have occurred, some HRIS components that the organization originally ruled out as too expensive may have become more price-competitive over the years.

### *Organizational directions and business needs*

Future changes in the overall business and its competitive environment may create a demand for new HRIS functions or reduce the need for other HRIS programs. A change to using a third-party administrator for benefits activities, for example, will reduce this aspect of in-house HRIS activity. On the other hand, an organization that decides to move from outsourcing its benefits programs to self-insurance and self-administration will need significant enhancement of its HRIS capabilities.

# Organizational Change

## Organization Life Cycle

The HR Professional must be ready to adapt to change. Change is a constant. As the organization changes, so must the Human Resources department to support operational achievement.

Some changes are predictable. As the company matures, the organization has different needs that can be planned for. To understand these needs, the HR Manager must allow for the classic product life cycle, which has four stages: introduction; growth; maturity and decline.

### *1. Introduction Stage:*

At the Introduction (or development) Stage market size and growth is slight. It is possible that substantial research and development costs have been incurred in getting the product to this stage. In addition, marketing costs may be high in order to test the market, undergo launch promotion and set up distribution channels. It is highly unlikely that companies will make profits on products at the Introduction Stage. Therefore, there is little money to pay employees so they are normally below market rates. Instead, employees are generally given stock options or promises of growth potential. When staffing, business managers prefer to hire experienced personnel since there is no infrastructure to train and develop inexperienced staff.

### 2. Growth Stage:

The Growth Stage is characterized by rapid growth in sales and profits. Profits arise due to an increase in output (economies of scale) and possibly better prices. At this stage, employees are paid at market rates. Some training occurs as the company continues to grow and hire a mix of both experienced and inexperienced workers.

### 3. Maturity Stage:

The Maturity Stage is, perhaps, the most common stage for all markets. This is the stage that competition is most intense as companies fight to maintain their market share. The Maturity Stage is the time when most profit is earned by the market as a whole. Any expenditure on research and development is likely to be restricted to product modification and improvement and perhaps to improve production efficiency and quality. Employees are paid well, normally above market rates. Recruiting is easier since top candidates are attracted by the plethora of pay and benefits. Monies are plentiful and training budgets are large enough to accommodate extensive employee development.

### 4. Decline Stage:

In the Decline Stage, the market is shrinking, reducing the overall amount of profit that can be shared amongst the remaining competitors. Usually, the company looks to take out some production cost, to transfer production to cheaper facilities, sell the product into other, cheaper markets, layoff employees, reduce or eliminate the training budget, hire only replacement workers when necessary. The goal is to re-invent the organization and re-enter the growth stage heading back into maturity again.

### 5. Demise Stage:

If the business doesn't turn around and profit doesn't improve, the organization may decide to end itself or may fall into bankruptcy.

## Change Agent

The HR professional is frequently front-and-center when the organization is undergoing change. The HR professional is usually the position most responsible for communicating and selling the required changes to the workforce.

Downsizing and increased work pressures can create uncertainty and fear among employees. This in turn can rob employees of enthusiasm, cooperation, dedication to detail, innovation, and other qualities essential to a positive, productive corporate culture. The resulting HR challenge is to implement programs and practices that maintain employee morale and commitment despite continuing change.

Successful approaches include implementing quality programs that provide employees with methods and time for analyzing their own results. Forming cooperative project teams to develop and test innovations encourages creativity without increasing staff size. Sound, conservative hiring and termination practices also are essential because workforce stability eliminates uncertainty and provides the continuity needed for a positive corporate culture.

## Change Process Model – Kurt Lewin's Theory

Lewin's Change Theory Model is based around a 3-step process (Unfreeze-Change-Freeze) that provides a high-level approach to change. It gives a manager a framework to implement a change effort, which is always very sensitive and must be made as seamless as possible.

The 3 phases of the Kurt Lewin model provide guidance on how to go about getting people to change: a manager will implement new processes and re-assign tasks, but change will only be effective if the people involved embrace it and help put it into practice.

1.  The first stage is called "unfreezing". It involved overcoming inertia and dismantling the existing "mind set". Defense mechanisms have to be bypassed.
2.  In the second stage the change occurs. This is typically a period of confusion and transition. Workers are aware that the old ways are being challenged but do not have a clear picture as to what are replacing them.
3.  The third and final stage is called "freezing". The new mindset is crystallizing and one's comfort level is returning to previous levels.

## Mergers and Acquisitions (SPHR-only section)

Mergers and acquisitions bring uncertainty and confusion to workers. Whether being acquired or acquiring, workers are concerned for their job, corporate culture, and the amount of change forced on most all positions. The HR professional must accept responsibility for helping workers deal with and accept change.

The phrase mergers and acquisitions refers to the aspect of corporate strategy, corporate finance and management dealing with the buying, selling and combining of different companies that can aid, finance, or help a growing company in a given industry grow rapidly without having to create another business entity.

Merger is a tool used by companies for the purpose of expanding their operations often aiming at an increase of their long term profitability. Acquisitions can also happen through a hostile takeover by purchasing the majority of outstanding shares of a company in the open market against the wishes of the target's board.

---

Usually mergers occur in a consensual (occurring by mutual consent) setting where executives from the target company help those from the purchaser in a due diligence process to ensure that the deal is beneficial to both parties (note: the HR Manager frequently conducts a due diligence on people related items such as: funding of pension plans, employment law compliance liabilities, retention of key personnel, etc.).

---

An acquisition, also known as a takeover, is the buying of one company (the 'target') by another. An acquisition may be friendly or hostile. In the former case, the companies cooperate in negotiations; in the latter case, the takeover target is unwilling to be bought or the target's board has no prior knowledge of the offer. Acquisition usually refers to a purchase of a smaller firm by a larger one. Sometimes, however, a smaller firm will acquire management control of a larger or longer established company and keep its name for the combined entity. This is known as a reverse takeover.

## Types of Acquisition

**Full Acquisition:** The buyer buys the shares, and therefore control, of the target company being purchased. This form of transaction carries with it all of the liabilities accrued by that business over its past and all of the risks that company faces in its commercial environment.

**Asset-Only Acquisition:** The buyer buys the assets of the target company. A buyer often structures the transaction as an asset purchase to "cherry-pick" the assets that it wants and leave out the assets and liabilities that it does not. This can be particularly important where foreseeable liabilities may include future, non-quantified damage awards such as those that could arise from litigation over defective products, employee benefits or terminations, or environmental damage. A disadvantage of this structure is the tax that many jurisdictions, particularly outside the United States, impose on transfers of the individual assets, whereas stock transactions can frequently be structured as like-kind exchanges or other arrangements that are tax-free or tax-neutral, both to the buyer and to the seller's shareholders.

The rise of globalization has exponentially increased the market for cross border M&A. This rapid increase has taken many M&A firms by surprise because the majority of them never had to consider acquiring the capabilities or skills required to effectively handle this kind of transaction. In the past, the market's lack of significance and a more strictly national mindset prevented the vast majority of small and mid-sized companies from considering cross border intermediation as an option which left M&A firms inexperienced in this field.

Due to the complicated nature of cross border M&A, many cross border actions have unsuccessful results. Cross border intermediation has many more levels of complexity to it than regular intermediation seeing as corporate governance, the power of the average employee, company regulations, political factors customer expectations, and countries' culture are all crucial factors that could spoil the transaction.

**End SPHR-only section**

## Organizational Development

Organization development (OD) is a systems approach, based on valid information, to help organizations and teams manage change. It uses behavioral science knowledge and experiential methods to help teams and organizations learn how to become more effective and to develop action plans that improve organization effectiveness.

A basic tenet of organization development is that interventions are based on research about a company, including its goals and environment. Organization development is less concerned with individuals and more concerned with team interactions. Its holistic approach focuses on the welfare of the overall organization. For a company to reinvent itself, it must undergo a process of change. Organization development can help identify, implement, and manage changes in a systematic and effective fashion.

### Grid Model

Grid organization development is a planned intervention approach popular in the 1960s and 1970s. This model sees organization development interventions as progressing through these stages:

| Phase 1 | This stage is an educational process for organization members, starting with top management, to learn about management styles. |
| --- | --- |
| Phase 2 | During this phase, the task focuses on teamwork development, again starting with top management teams. |
| Phase 3 | The teamwork developed for top management is extended at this stage and directed at intergroup, or cross-functional team effectiveness. Goals might include reducing conflict and blockages between R&D, manufacturing, accounting, and marketing, for example. |
| Phase 4 | At this stage, the organization engages in creative strategic planning. |
| Phase 5 | The strategic plans are implemented during this phase. |
| Phase 6 | This final phase involves the systematic measurement and critique of progress toward organization goals, including quality goals and related measurement. |

### Kepner-Tregoe Model

Organization development interventions can include building different kinds of problem-solving and decision-making skills to help quality teams achieve their goals. One option for facilitating development of these skills might be to use processes similar to the Kepner-Tregoe problem-solving and decision-making model:

Problem-solving steps:

- Analyze the situation.
- Identify and specify problem(s).
- Determine priority problems.
- Identify possible causes of problem.
- Determine most likely causes.
- Specify corrective action.

Decision-making steps:

- Establish decision objectives.
- Assign priorities to decision objectives.
- Generate alternative actions.
- Evaluate alternatives against objectives.
- Identify tentative best alternative.
- Explore potential adverse consequences of best alternative.
- Determine and implement actions to prevent possible problems created by possible adverse consequences.

> **TEST TAKING TIP**
> Take breaks during the exam. They'll let you get up and get water or use the facilities. Stretch your legs and back and get the blood flowing. The clock keeps running but you've got the time.

### Force field analysis

All organization development interventions entail some type of change. Kurt Lewin's force field analysis process is a helpful technique to use with a group contemplating change. The force field analysis helps gauge the magnitude of a contemplated change, any risks, and possible actions necessary to implement changes.

Lewin's force field analysis involves identifying the driving forces, or conditions and factors that facilitate the changes, and the restraining forces, or conditions and factors that could prevent or resist the change. These driving and restraining forces are represented by vectors on a chart, with the length of each vector determined by the significance of that factor.

## Types of interventions

Interventions are the tools of organization development. They are planned, structured activities that serve as a means to accomplish organization development goals.

An organization development effort can include multiple interventions, including any of the dozens of proven and documented interventions. Classified by type, organization development inventions fall into three categories: intervention mode, target group focus, and problem/opportunity orientation.

### Intervention mode

This type of intervention might include:

- training or education,
- coaching/facilitating,
- data gathering/feedback,
- confrontation,
- planning,
- problem-solving/decision-making, and
- technical/structural.

## Participative Management

Organizations that aggressively pursue lower costs, higher quality, and improved customer service have borne out the efficacy of participative, high-involvement management. Radical and positive transformations in cost, quality, and service based on participative management principles have been documented across industry, government, and nonprofit sectors.

The following principles are important to keep in mind when embarking on a change effort to increase participative management:

- The top level must commit to the effort. This commitment assures effective role modeling and reinforcement and communicates that the change effort will not go back to "business as usual" when resources are short or the organization experiences a crisis.

- The idea is not to implement participative management for participative management's sake or solely to improve the quality of work life. Participative management, like any other management tool, needs to be focused on attainment of organization goals and improvement of quality, service, and costs.

- Changing management style alone often does not yield the desired results. Implementing participative management usually needs to be accompanied by changes in structure, work and job design, compensation, and other systems. For example, gainsharing programs that provide incremental financial incentives/rewards for measurable improvement in key areas, have produced good results when introduced with participative or high involvement management efforts.

- Attempts to increase participative management mean change, and are subject to all the change management principles covered earlier.

Some people will naturally resist change. Middle managers may resist a switch to participative management because they feel their roles are threatened and that they will lose power. Non-managers, or those who directly get a bigger say and more responsibility, can also resist change. Change is different from what they know, and for some managers, anything different represents a potential threat. Empathy, clear communication, and training for all parties can minimize the potential downside of attempts to increase participative management.

## Top management's role

Tell employees that the company is interested in their ideas, and that these ideas matter. After increasing employees' awareness of the demand for their input, management must begin to increase the amount and quality of communication among the different corporate levels. Involving employees will make them feel that they are an important part of the company team. Employees who feel that their work contributes to the success of the company will likely work more productively and be more amenable to helping cut costs.

# Organizational HR Policy

### Organizational Structures

Design of the HR department reflects overall organizational design. As a result, HR department structures vary from company to company according to several factors: line vs. staff functions, centralization vs. decentralization, span of control, responsibility and authority, and availability of personnel. The following discussion examines these five issues and their impact on HR department design.

### Line vs. staff functions

Organizations with line functions establish separate departments for different products or services. Each line manager has direct responsibility for a single area with little crossover of authority between departments. Examples of line functions include shipping and mailing, production, and marketing and sales. Staff functions supplement the line function and have an advisory, facilitative, or specialized support role. Unlike line managers, staff managers generally are responsible for providing services across all departments within a company. Examples of corporate staff functions include HR, legal, accounting, and the like.

### Centralization vs. decentralization

Centralization is said to be a process where the concentration of decision making is in a few hands. All the important decision and actions at the lower level are subject to the approval of top management. Decentralization refers to the systematic effort to delegate to the lowest level of authority except that which can be controlled and exercised at central points.

Larger organizations typically have multiple locations and handle more than one line of business or service. Most large companies set up line organizations for each location or business. In contrast, staff functions, like HR, can remain centralized at headquarters, be decentralized to each site or business, or be divided between the corporate and unit levels. In practice, while some decentralized functions, such as legal and finance, may continue to report directly to a corporate manager, most decentralized functions like HR report to a local line manager on straight-line basis and to a corporate staff head on a dotted-line basis.

### Span of control

The number of subordinates reporting directly to a supervisor determines that manager's span of control. An appropriate span depends on the nature of the work, the capabilities of the staff, and the organizational culture. The current trend is to eliminate management layers and establish flat organizations, which usually increases a manager's span of control.

---

**EXAMPLE**

Ford of Europe recently removed two of seven management layers, and British Airways reduced the number of levels between CEO and front-line managers from an average of eight or nine to five. Spans of control at some General Electric divisions have increased from the traditional five to eight staffers, to 15 or more.

---

### Responsibility and authority

Responsibility and authority are two key organizational imperatives. Clear lines of responsibility facilitate the flow of information, let subordinates know to whom they report, and establish firm control over operations. Authority goes hand-in-hand with responsibility. Although one management principle says that authority, unlike responsibility, can never be completely delegated, managers must have the requisite authority to accomplish their objectives.

### Available personnel

The optimal organization structure is always affected by the availability of competent personnel. At times, an organization's structure may need modification to adapt to changing personnel availability. For example, staff shortages may make it necessary to merge different functions into one; in other cases, an organization might need to create new positions to retain qualified incumbents or to recruit new employees. For HR departments, the current trends toward downsizing and outsourcing have prompted some departments to abandon functional specialization and hire staff with a generalist orientation suited to handling different activities.

# Leadership

## Leadership Theories

### Blake and Mouton model

Robert Blake and Jane Mouton characterize leadership style as the degree of concern for production a leader expresses relative to concern for people. By plotting low, medium, and high levels of "concern for production" on the horizontal axis and "concern for people" on the vertical axis, they identified a grid of managerial styles. Under this model, managers display one of five basic leadership styles:

| | |
|---|---|
| **Task manager** | This type of manager has high concern for production; low concern for people |
| **Country club manager** | This managerial type is characterized by high concern for people; low concern with production |
| **Middle of the road/compromise manager** | This individual has neither a high concern for people or production, but a medium level of concern for both. The manager's assumption is that a high concern for production and a high concern for people are opposing priorities, so strong behaviors in either dimension are avoided to balance allegiances |
| **Impoverished or laissez-faire manager** | This type of manager's behavior and performance indicate neither concern for production or for people |
| **Team leader** | This individual acts on the belief that high levels of attention both to production and to people are possible |

## Hersey-Blanchard model

The Hersey-Blanchard model, also known as the Situational Leadership model, stresses that the best leadership style is dependent on the situation. They believe that leaders should adapt their style to the level of maturity of the worker and the organization. Situational leadership differentiates itself from other leadership theories in that it emphasizes the need for the leader to change their style rather than being dependent on one dominant style.

The leader must consider three dimensions when determining the optimal leadership style:

- Task behavior involves defining the roles and organizing and directing the tasks required to accomplish a job.

- Relationship behavior concerns how a leader maintains contact and relationships with and among team members.

- Task maturity is the degree that an individual or a team is confident, competent, and experienced in a particular work or task situation.

This theory asserts that in situations where task maturity is low, an effective leadership style is one that provides a fairly high degree of task structure for team members, even telling them what needs to be done and how to accomplish a task. At medium levels of task maturity, much contact with and among team members are appropriate. This interaction allows for adequate coaching and builds teamwork so team members develop capabilities to be more autonomous. At very high levels of task maturity, neither much direction (task behavior) nor contact (relationship behavior) is required because a team and team members function effectively autonomously.

## Likert model

Rensis Likert portrayed a range of possible leadership styles on a continuum with four systems from left to right:

> **TEST TAKING TIP**
> Review your answer choices when you finish the exam but don't change any unless you have a clear and logical reason to do so. Often, your first choice will be the best choice.

- Exploitative-Authoritative (System 1). This leadership style, located on the far left of the spectrum, is autocratic and task-centered.

- Benevolent-Authoritative (System 2). This style of leadership bears similarities to the first but is not as autocratic.

- Consultative (System 3). These leaders are more willing to seek employee input but retain most decision-making responsibility and authority.

- Participative-Group (System 4). Found on the continuum's far right, this leadership style is democratic, participative, and employee- centered.

In his research, Likert consistently found that the most successful organizations exhibit System 4 characteristics and that the least successful show System 1 and System 2 characteristics. The implication of this model and research for organization effectiveness is to develop and sustain System 4, organizations need to encourage highly participative management practices while focusing on goal attainment.

## McGregor's model — Theory X and Theory Y

One of Douglas McGregor's major contributions to management/leadership theory is his Theory X/ Theory Y model. Theory X and Theory Y are meant to represent two opposite sets of assumptions about people and work teams:

- Theory X managers, and by extension Theory X organizations, view people by and large as lazy, not very bright, and irresponsible.

- Theory Y managers and organizations view people as basically bright, responsible, motivated, and wanting control over their work and lives.

While no individual manager or organization may be pure Theory X or Theory Y, McGregor's model can be a helpful tool for teams and managers to assess some of their basic orientations and assumptions about others they work with. For example, organizations and managers operating from a Theory X position will find it very difficult to make the transition to high-involvement work teams.

### Clark Wilson Task Cycle model

Clark Wilson's Managerial Task Cycle is a framework useful for evaluating the effectiveness of managers and, by extension, their teams and organizations. Wilson found that effective management involved six phases of a managerial task cycle. Each of these phases, when done well, will lay the groundwork for successive tasks in the cycle:

- **Making goals clear and important**. Relevant others must understand what is expected and know the priorities.
- **Planning and problem-solving**. Once the goal is clear, plans must be laid and potential problems solved.
- **Facilitating the work of others**. With a goal and plans, managers must provide resources, coaching, training, time, tools, and money.
- **Obtaining and providing feedback**. As work proceeds, managers must observe progress and give feedback to those doing the work.
- **Making control adjustments**. If feedback indicates the task is not on track, performance must be adjusted.
- **Reinforcing good performance**. Upon task completion or expenditure of optimum effort, effective managers recognize and reinforce good performance.

Research has indicated that the quality of relationships, overall climate, and motivation of team members increase when these tasks are performed well. Wilson discusses how both management and leadership are necessary for achieving stated goals. He developed a separate Leadership Cycle as a framework for assessing the leadership effectiveness of individuals and teams in an organization. Changing habits and cultures require a balance of these leadership skills in a logical sequence:

- **Entrepreneurial vision**. Change leaders must be able to see what should be changed and have the fortitude to make it happen.
- **Sensing the environment**. To succeed, a leader must know the stakeholders — i.e., who will help, who will resist, and who will sit on the fence.
- **Gaining commitment**. No one can become a leader unless others are willing to follow. Skills to gain commitment are crucial.
- **Drive**. No leader is worth his or her salt without high expectations and standards, plus the push and perseverance to see that they are met.
- **Reinforcing change**. Anyone who wants to continue in a leadership role must share the credit.

## Effect of Leadership in Organizations

### Building leadership

The quality and extent of leadership is a significant indicator of an organization's effectiveness. Part of an organization development project should involve assessing and developing effective leadership.

Leaders exert power of some kind to influence others. When evaluating the leadership exercised in an organization or team, analyze the source of power exercised to influence team members. Leaders can possess several distinct kinds of power:

- **Position power** reflects the function of someone's designated role in an organization's official structure or hierarchy. A person with high position power would expect orders and suggestions to be carried out by virtue of his/her position in the organization.

- **Expert power** is based on the respect shown and inclination to follow directions or suggestions based on someone's expertise, skill, or knowledge.

- **Coercive power** rests on fear and the belief that not complying or following directives will lead to punishment.

- **Reward power** is a function of people believing that compliance will lead to increased pay, recognition, promotion, or other rewards.

- **Personal power** is based on a liking for or admiration of personal traits or accomplishments, and identification with a leader.

> **TEST TAKING TIP**
> The test question and answer option must read 100% grammatically correct. If the sentence syntax or grammar isn't proper, it's not the correct answer.

### Employee empowerment

Successful organizations are learning that power and influence should not rest solely with managers and those with position power. In fact, empowerment of all employees to exercise leadership in the interest of improving quality and service is generally in the organization's and customers' best interest.

Empowering employees involves expanding the power base in an organization by creating a work environment where employees take initiative and exercise leadership to maximize quality and service. Empowered employees, for example, will shut down a production line on their own when observing a problem that could result in poor quality. Another example is an employee who does whatever seems reasonable to satisfy an important customer.

## Leadership styles

Leadership styles vary. One leadership theory is the "**path-goal view**," which recognizes four kinds of leadership behavior:

- **Directive leadership.** Directive leaders take a structured approach to supervision, giving subordinates specific guidance about what to do, how to do it, and when to complete it.

- **Supportive leadership.** Supportive leaders emphasize their concern for employees' needs and welfare. They demonstrate their friendliness to subordinates and strive to create a pleasant workplace atmosphere.

- **Participative leadership.** Leaders with a participative style adopt an open attitude toward suggestions from subordinates and actively solicit their input when making decisions.

- **Achievement-oriented leadership.** This leadership style emphasizes setting goals and communicating confidence in subordinates' ability to meet high expectations. An achievement-oriented leader encourages employees to improve their performance and challenges them to perform at high levels.

Which leadership style works best for a particular company depends on the nature of the work, the organizational controls, and individual characteristics — such as the maturity, experience, and dedication of the staff and the executive's own traits and abilities. Good executives "read" a work situation before deciding what type of approach to take with employees. For example, an executive who typically uses a consulting approach may adopt an autocratic style because the occasion demands it.

## Leadership training

Executives must be leaders if they are to motivate and direct the rest of the company to maintain the highest possible productivity. A job title alone does not guarantee that an executive is a capable leader. The following traits distinguish good leaders from poor ones:

- Leaders are self-starters who desire to excel. They like to be in charge and make things happen and are willing to work hard to achieve success.

- Leaders have self-confidence and can make sound decisions quickly.

- Leaders are open to change and encourage subordinates to find better ways to do a job.

- Leaders devote their time and energy to supervision and planning; they do not get sidetracked into doing their subordinates' work.

- Leaders bring order into disorganized situations and clarify a group's goals so that they can be more easily attained.

- Leaders have the stamina to withstand the pressures of their positions and the resilience to bounce back from defeat.

- Leaders have a sense of responsibility. They are not afraid to accept obligations and challenges.

- Leaders have integrity. They are honest with themselves and with subordinates.

- Leaders have enthusiasm and communicate this enthusiasm to others. An uninspired leader attracts few followers, but an enthusiastic executive generates renewed energy and commitment from employees.

**TEST TAKING TIP**
Most questions will have two answer options that look really good, one that is OK as an option, and one that is not a good choice. The trick is choosing the best of the two good options, especially for you SPHR candidates.

Good leaders have exceptional human relations skills. Leaders are involved with fellow employees, analyzing their needs and trying to understand their problems. Researchers have found that executives who care about employees and their problems have higher productivity than work-centered executives. An executive with good human relations skills engages in these efforts:

- Makes employees feel involved in reaching company goals.

- Gives credit for work well done and helps employees learn from mistakes.

- Deals fairly and frankly with subordinates, keeping them informed about their performance.

- Shows confidence in employees' ability to get their work done by permitting them a degree of freedom in their jobs.

## Power Distance Rating (SPHR-only section)

Geert Hofstede is an influential Dutch expert on the interactions between cultures and the organization. His theories on Power Distance are applicable in any country or any organization. His theory concerns the degree to which the *less powerful* members of society expect there to be differences in the levels of power. A high score suggests that there is an expectation that some individuals wield larger amounts of power than others. A low score reflects the view that all people should have equal rights.

Latin American and Arab nations are ranked the highest in this category; Scandinavian and Germanic speaking countries the least. Countries with high power distance rating are often characterized by a high rate of political violence.

In High Power Distance cultures: obedience to authority (parent, boss, officials) is expected; language filled with power or hierarchy indicators; managers / teachers tend to be autocratic while subordinates expect direct supervision. In Low Power Distance cultures, emphasis is on challenging decisions, expecting autonomy and independence.

**End SPHR-only section**

# Ethics

Ethics in business is not an expedient concept, something to practice only when convenient. It is more complicated than deciding what is "right" and what is "wrong." A company's ethics reflect its character, its mission, and its goals. When ethical considerations are wanting or inadequate, the enterprise itself is vulnerable. It has opened itself up to the risk of legal liability, along with—in the event misconduct is identified and punished—loss of face, customer loyalty, and market share. Investors may also shun stock in a company which does not meet their standards, or which appears to be in a precarious legal position.

### Personal and professional conduct
When drafting guidelines for employees' behavior, many employers choose to be as general as possible. A phrase asking employees to refrain from conduct that could be "harmful" or "viewed unfavorably" by most people covers many forms of unacceptable behavior without tying management's hands should it need to discipline employees.

### Entertainment, gifts, favors, and gratuities
The area of exchange of goods and services that have intrinsic value is a murky one. Is treating a supplier to a restaurant meal a gift? What about sending a basket of food or a case of wine? Most would view an invitation to dinner as simple hospitality, but look askance at a weekend at a hunting lodge. Other kinds of gifts are equally ambiguous from time to time. A coffee mug will not raise red flags in most places, but a china tea service imported from London surely would.

Some companies, and the U.S. government, settle the problem by assigning an arbitrary limit in monetary value to gifts that may be received. Others expect their employees to exercise some judgment.

### "Inside" information
So-called "inside" information is not available to the general public. For practical reasons, any company may wish its decision making to remain confidential until signed off on, in order not to give the impression of instability while different options are being discussed. But for companies whose stock is traded publicly, the necessity to play decisions close to the vest has market implications. It is against the law to act on, or to provide to others, information about any acquisition or sale contemplated by a company before that information has been released to the general public.

### Conflicts of interest
Such conflicts usually involve compensation of one kind or another. Usually a conflict of interest is one in which an employee's loyalty may be divided between self-interest and the interest of the employer.

### Confidential and proprietary information

Confidential information may be of the "inside" type, which has to do with trading stock or other items of value, or it may be information with no value. For example, for a supervisor or HR professional to gossip about an employee's credit record or medical history would be at least unethical if not illegal.

### Outside employment

This area is one similar to conflict of interest. Employees may not usually work for a competitor, or work in a position that would compromise their work with the chief employer.

### Nepotism

Here again, to do business with family members in a company's name causes a conflict of the employee's interest and the employer's, and is for that reason usually forbidden.

### Political contributions

An employer may not interfere with an employee's exercise of political rights, other than to forbid them on company time. It is of course against the law for an employer to require employees to contribute to a particular candidate or party, although a number have done so in recent years (and been caught).

### Financial reporting

This is for the most part a reiteration of policies forbidding theft or fraud.

### Blanket and acknowledgment statements

It is important to have on file an acknowledgment that each employee received a copy of the ethics policy. In the event of any difficulty down the road, the employee will not be able to protest that the policy was not communicated.

**TEST TAKING TIP**
Count your answers! Check to ensure you've got an even spread of answers when completing the exam. If you're close to the count of 44 on each answer option, then it's time to submit your exam for grading. If you've got too many of one option, go back and re-check those you were unsure of. Don't change them unless you have good reason.

## Whistleblower protections

With the recent spate of revelations at companies such as Enron, WorldCom, Tyco and others, interest in encouraging employees to come forward with allegations of misconduct has expanded even further. In 2002 President Bush signed into law the Sarbanes-Oxley Act of 2002. Drafted in response to disclosures of corporate wrongdoing, the law contains provisions related to accounting oversight, pension administration and Securities and Exchange Commission (SEC) investigations, among other issues. The objective of the law is to restore investor confidence in public companies by establishing greater accountability and stiffer penalties related to shareholder fraud.

Public contractors may not discharge or otherwise discriminate against employees who report a violation of state or federal laws or regulations related to performance of the contract. The Whistleblower Protection Act also protects employees who report misuse of public funds.

Employees must make a written report of the violation and must first submit the report to their employer, unless the employer is the party suspected of violating the law. Employees who believe their employer is engaged in a legal violation may submit a report to any government agency authorized to receive reports from the state ethics commission. If, after the initial report is made, the employer does not make a good faith effort to correct the problem within a reasonable time, the employee may report the incident to "any person, agency, or organization."

## *Sarbanes-Oxley*

Section 806 of the Sarbanes-Oxley Act strengthens the protections accorded to employees who allege wrongdoing at organizations governed by SEC regulations. Under Section 806, no publicly traded company, or "any officer, employee, contractor, subcontractor, or agent of such company," may discharge, demote, suspend, threaten, harass, or in any other manner discriminate against an employee for providing information about activities that he or she reasonably believes constitutes a violation of SEC rules or involves shareholder fraud. The provision covers employees who share this information with any person who has supervisory authority over the employee; any person with the authority to investigate, discover and terminate misconduct; federal regulatory agencies; law enforcement; and/or members or committees of Congress. Employees also are protected if they participate in any proceedings related to SEC rules violations.

Employees who believe they were subject to adverse employment actions due to their role in exposing wrongdoing have 90 days from the date the violation occurred to file a complaint with the U.S. Department of Labor. If there is no resolution of the complaint by the Secretary of Labor, the employee may file suit against his or her employer 180 days after filing the complaint.

Companies found to have discriminated or retaliated against employees under the provisions of Section 806 may be required to reinstate the employee with the same seniority status the employee would have had, but for the discrimination; provide back pay with interest; and compensate the employee for any special damages sustained as a result of the discrimination, including litigation costs, expert witness fees, and reasonable attorney fees.

In addition, the Act prescribes criminal penalties for various violations of its provisions. For example, individuals at companies covered by the Act who alter, destroy, mutilate or conceal a record, document, or other object, or attempt to do so, with the intent to impair the object's integrity or availability for use in an official proceeding can be both fined and imprisoned for up to 20 years. While the criminal penalties are not specific to the whistleblowing section of the law, illegal actions taken in response to employee complaints can put companies at risk for criminal penalties.

## *In the courts*

When charges are brought under whistleblowing statutes, courts are willing to side with the employees, as a recent decision by the U.S. Court of Appeals for the 11th Circuit shows. In the case, the 11th Circuit ruled in favor of Marvin Hobby, a former executive at Georgia Power Company, who alleged he was fired after he raised questions about violations of federal regulations at two of the company's nuclear plants. The Court affirmed a lower court decision that awarded Hobby $4 million, required the company to reinstate him and ordered Georgia Power to send a letter to every employee of the company welcoming Hobby back.

## *Avoiding liability*

Given the proliferation of whistleblowing provisions in new laws, employers must proceed with caution before taking action against employees who have lodged complaints against their companies. By following a few basic guidelines, companies can reduce their potential liability. The first step in reducing exposure is establishing a process for employees to report suspicions of wrongdoing.

## HR's Code of Ethical and Professional Standards in HR Management

The Society of Human Resource Professionals (SHRM) has a code of Professional Standards that may be the source of questions on the test. SHRM's code covers such diverse topics as: Professionalism, Professional development, Ethical leadership, Fairness and justice, Conflicts of interest, and Use of information. Essentially, SHRM's standards do not allow HR Professionals to abuse the power of their position for personal gain or to act unprofessionally.

*Kickbacks*

Employees may think taking kickbacks from vendors does not harm the company and so is not a serious offense. Understandably, employers view the practice otherwise, and so do arbitrators.

## Establishing Ethical Behavior in the Organization

The two basic types of conduct codes are the compliance-based and the integrity-based.

### Compliance-based code

The compliance-based code, as its name suggests, aims to defend an organization from liability by making sure it is complying with all relevant laws and regulations. A code based on compliance is driven by legal considerations, drafted or reviewed by lawyers, and amounts to a defensive posture.

### Code based on integrity

A code based on integrity, on the other hand, is designed to solve any dilemmas employees may face by providing an ethical basis for decision making. If the compliance-based strategy is defensive, the integrity-based conduct code could have the motto: "The best defense is a good offense."

Many organizations think of a code of conduct as a safe conduct pass through the shoals of legal liability. Seeking to operate within the law is a necessary but not sufficient standard. Setting up a compliance system, however, can be the first step in designing a more comprehensive, integral system.

The basic framework for a compliance system, from the federal sentencing guidelines, includes the following elements:

- standards,
- oversight,
- avoiding delegation,
- communication,
- reasonable compliance,
- responsibility, and
- preventing recurrence.

---

**EXAMPLE**
**K-MART POLICY**
No KMART associate shall directly or indirectly accept any personal benefit, including but not limited to any bribe, commission, kickback, payment, loan, gratuity (including travel and entertainment), gift, sample, service, promise of employment (hereinafter collectively referred to as "benefits") from any vendor, supplier, subcontractor or competitor or their agents or representatives.

Meals associated with a business purpose are acceptable if reasonable in cost, appropriate as to time and place, and occasional in nature.

No KMART associate, without exception, may personally benefit from any transaction involving KMART.

---

## The limits of a compliance-based model

A compliance program, based on a careful reading of applicable laws and a plan to ensure the company works within those laws, although necessary, is insufficient. Conduct that is within the law can still be ethically questionable. Selling hazardous products like DDT overseas is legal but may not meet ethical standards. Buying goods made overseas by children, or manufactured in sweatshops or prisons, may not risk a jail sentence but, again, can be seen as conduct that infringes on recognized standards of human rights and decency.

Cases of questionable though legal behaviors have arisen in the U.S., especially in securities, banking, and insurance. Although it is legal for those industries to use a "hard sell," their aggressive pursuit of elderly or uninformed people was deplored by the public and the industries have had to alter their practices in order to maintain or regain the public trust. No law was broken, but something amounting to a "common law" ethic was breached.

Avoiding punishment is not the highest calling for business. "It is not an adequate ethical standard to aspire to get through the day without being indicted," as former chair of the Securities and Exchange Commission Richard Breeden has said.

Lawyers often develop corporate ethics programs, using as a rationale the 1991 Federal Sentencing Guidelines. These kinds of programs emphasize prevention, and are based on deterrence theory — the notion that people will be deterred from committing crimes by fear of paying the penalty. This theory has its limits, however. For one thing, surveillance can have a boomerang effect on people. Some will rebel and act out simply because they resent not being trusted, or because it becomes a challenge to beat "the system." Studies have shown that people weigh a law or regulation against their own beliefs in what is legitimate and moral. Finding such a law lacking in legitimacy or morality, they will not obey it. So merely assigning more surveillance and penalties, and making no other changes, will not necessarily accomplish the goal.

So although discipline is necessary—for some much more so than for others—overemphasizing threats can be both superfluous and counterproductive. Some employees will rebel. Others will resent the implication that they are untrustworthy. The cynical may see the announcement of an ethics policy as liability insurance for management, which may not be far off the mark.

## Components of an integrity-based system

Though there is not just one way to put an integrity based system into effect, many successful efforts in this area have had the following components:

- The guiding values and commitments make sense and are clearly communicated.
- Company leaders are personally committed, credible, and willing to take action on the values they espouse.
- The espoused values are integrated into the normal channels of management decision making and are reflected in the organization's critical activities.
- The company's systems and structures support and reinforce its values.
- Managers throughout the company have the decision-making skills, knowledge, and competencies needed to make ethically sound decisions on a day-to-day basis.

Differences between compliance and integrity systems

| Characteristics | Compliance Strategy | Integrity Strategy |
|---|---|---|
| Ethics | conformity with externally imposed standards | self - governance according to chosen standards |
| Objective | prevent criminal misconduct | enable responsible conduct |
| Leadership | lawyer driven | management driven with aid of lawyers, HR, others |
| Methods | education, reduced discretion, auditing and controls, penalties | education, leadership, accountability, organizational systems and decision processes, auditing and controls, penalties |
| Behavioral assumptions | autonomous beings guided by material self-interest | social beings guided by material self - interest, values, ideals, peers |

| Implementation | Compliance Strategy | Integrity Strategy |
|---|---|---|
| Standards | criminal and regulatory law | company values and aspirations; social obligations, including law |
| Staffing | lawyers | executives and managers with lawyers, others |
| Activities | 1. develop compliance standards<br>2. train and communicate<br>3. handle reports of misconduct<br>4. conduct investigations<br>5. oversee compliance audits<br>6. enforce standards | 1. lead development of company values and standards<br>2. train and communicate<br>3. integrate into company systems<br>4. provide guidance and consultation<br>5. assess values performance<br>6. identify and resolve problems<br>7. oversee compliance activities |
| Education | compliance standards and system | Decision-making and values; compliance standards and system |

# Organizational Budgeting

## HR Budgeting Process

HR heads are responsible for effectively using the assets of the company allotted to them to support the corporate strategy.

The operating budget forms the focus of compensation planning, since this budget sets the organization's operating revenues and expenses, including the totals for HR and compensation. The HR portion of the operating budget covers adjustments in salary structures and all forms of increases, including general increases, cost-of-living adjustment (COLA) increases, merit raises, promotions, benefits, upgrades, bonuses, commissions, special recognition awards, and other incentives. The HR part of the budget usually accounts for all labor costs in gross figures; it indicates the total number of employees in each unit and the money needed to pay them for the upcoming budget year.

## Types of Budgets

- A zero-based budget is one where the total income minus the total expenses equals $0. In other words, it forces the budgeter to assign every dollar of income to an expense (or savings) category." Each year, during the budgeting process, the budgeter must start over at a zero balance and justify every dollar of expense.

> **TEST TAKING TIP**
> Any time you can rule out answer options as being unrelated or incorrect is improving the odds of choosing the right answer.

- A formula-based budget is one where the budgeter applies a formula to determine budget allocation for a business unit. It may be based on units produced, or on number of employees, etc. There could be a base amount of the budget and the rest is determined by the formula applied.
- Incremental budgeting is one where the budget is prepared using a previous period's budget or actual performance as a basis with incremental amounts added for the new budget period.
- A rolling budget is a method in which a budget established at the beginning of an accounting period is continually amended to reflect variances that arise due to changing circumstances.
- A capital budget is a plan for raising large and long-term sums for investment in plant and machinery, over a period greater than the period considered under an operating budget. Techniques such as internal rate of return, net present value, and payback period are employed in creating capital budgets.

## Balance Sheet

In financial accounting, a balance sheet or statement of financial position is a summary of an organization's financial position. Assets, liabilities, and ownership equity are listed as of a specific date. These three measurements are the common accounting standards for qualifying a company's net worth. Of the ways to measure a company's financial worth, the balance sheet is the only statement which applies to a single point in time (i.e.; the balance sheet is a "snapshot" of the company's financial value on a given day).

The difference between the assets and the liabilities is known as equity (or net assets or net worth). The sum of net worth minus liabilities equals assets, thus the term balance because the opposing measurements must balance.

# Environmental Scanning (SPHR-only section)

An Environmental Scan requires identifying the external threats that will affect the short- and long-term goals of the organization. Problems can arise when projecting past trends into even the near future. The forecasting process must certainly look at internal factors that may affect future business plans. However, environmental scanning is the process of including; issues, trends, demographics, or other data that are external to the organization.

## External factors

External factors, such as a competing employer expanding its operations, or an increase in demand for computer programmers, also can cause turnover rates to counter past trends. Social and economic policies and local labor conditions can have a sudden impact on traditional labor patterns. For instance, record-high unemployment or prosperity nationally or locally may alter past turnover rates. Intermediate and long-range plans are even more unpredictable than short-term forecasts. The planning process should include a procedure for adjusting these forecasts based on external changes.

## Internal Scanning

Internal changes, such as shifts in workforce demographics and composition, can alter the accuracy of staffing forecasts. For instance, if a larger percentage of the company's workforce is nearing retirement age, future turnover rates will be higher than in the past. Or a change in retirement policy may affect traditional retirement patterns.

Examples of internal scanning include; skills inventory, staffing projections, business trends, needs assessment, human resource inventory, etc.

## Strategic choice

Decision makers and problem solvers are valued within today's modern organization. The factors that affect the decisions of organizations and the direction and goals of the organization are often external to the company. Often, these external factors are so vital and critical that they shape or demand a certain response from an organization thus limiting the true autonomy of the decision maker. This shaping of decisions by external influences is the basis for the Choice theory of decision making.

The competition that a firm faces, along with the expectations of the market in which it is competing, has a lot to do with any strategy that is taken. For instance, a decision to expand one of ABC Corporation's facilities will be necessitated by an environmental scan that will examine labor availability, legal and regulatory factors, cost of manpower, cost of facilities, etc. The result of this environmental scan of external challenges will determine the suitability of each location as a candidate for facility expansion.

Every situation has its own unique contingent factors that determine the correct strategic choice. Therefore, strategic choice theory asserts that these external influences must be accounted for in order to make the best decisions.

**End SPHR-only section**

# Human Resource Information Systems (HRIS)

Before HR managers can understand human resources information systems uses and intelligently assess the benefits of automating various HR management functions, they must have knowledge of computer systems and relevant technical terminology.

Like all computer systems, the components of an HRIS fall into two broad categories: hardware and software. The individual hardware components and how they fit together is largely determined by the type of computer system or platform used to operate the HRIS: mainframe computer, minicomputer (also known as midrange or midframe computer), microcomputer (commonly called personal computer or PC), or some combination of these three platforms.

The sophistication and efficiency of an HRIS depend not only on the hardware and software used, but also on the extent of the database of personnel information. Together, the platform, hardware, software, and database make up the system's design, or what computer professionals refer to as system architecture.

An HRIS database contains information, or data, regarding an organization's personnel and HR services, as well as the software required to carry out various HR activities. A database is like a filing system: Similar data can be grouped into records, and similar records can then be placed into files.

Files fall into two general categories:

- System files contain the software programs and applications.

- Data files contain information created by users. In an HRIS, this information would include the facts about an organization's employees and HR programs that will be needed in various computer operations. For example, one file might contain a record for each employee showing home address and phone number; other files might contain records for each employee showing position, starting date, and current salary; yet another file might combine these separate records into employee "master files."

Just like any filing system, the quality of the database management system determines how easily information can be located and how efficiently the overall computer system operates. The exact method used to arrange all these records and files depends on the type of database management system software used in the HRIS: hierarchical or relational.

## Conducting an HRIS Cost-Benefit Analysis

An HRIS can bring about both direct and indirect savings for the HR department and the entire organization. Direct dollar savings occur when an HRIS reduces the number of clerical positions or eliminates the need to contract outside agencies or hire temporary help to perform HR activities and analyses.

Other, less easily quantified savings arise from more efficient HR performance and processes. Besides the dollar benefits of higher HR staff productivity, a more efficient HR process can produce savings in every department affected by that process. For example, lower turnover, faster applicant processing, and more rigorous applicant screening can reduce costs of recruitment ads and agencies, relocation reimbursements, training expenses, lost productivity due to vacancies and inexperienced personnel, and so forth.

The savings associated with an HRIS purchase vary depending on the planned uses of the HRIS and on whether the organization is automating the affected HR activities for the first time. In selling top executives on the benefits of an HRIS investment, HR managers should emphasize the ways in which planned uses of the HRIS match organizational goals and objectives. They also should use annual budget reports to quantify current costs and potential dollar savings in areas affected by the proposed HRIS purchase.

## Areas to Examine for Savings

### Payroll

Moving from use of an outside firm to in- house payroll administration and processing eliminates the contract fees paid for payroll processing. In addition, experts estimate that the improved efficiency associated with automating salary and benefit administration can produce savings equal to at least 1 percent of the total payroll.

Automation also may allow a company to offer more complex but cost-effective salary and/or benefit packages. For example, many benefit consultants estimate that implementing flexible benefit and cafeteria plans — difficult to achieve without automation — can cut total payroll by 1 to 3 percent. An HRIS that can perform "what if" analyses of proposed salary or benefit changes can safeguard against the costs of poor decisions, or at least eliminate the need to hire an outside consultant to perform these analyses.

### Investment in employees

Finding, training, and keeping qualified employees is a major strategic goal for most companies, and the associated costs in dollars and staff time can prove considerable. The improvements in applicant tracking and screening, and in turnover analysis resulting from automation, can save from 5 to 10 percent of the total budget costs in these areas. Expenses associated with employee investment that should receive consideration include:

- recruitment costs, both external (i.e., advertising and agency fees) and internal (i.e., reimbursement of out-of-town applicants' travel expenses, costs of recruitment trips made by in-house staff, or dollar-value of staff time spent sorting applications, contacting candidates, conducting interviews);

- relocation expenses, if reimbursed by the company;

- training costs, including both on-the-job and classroom training;

- costs of losing high-performing employees, whose loss can be far more expensive for the company than the loss of low performers; and

- estimated lost productivity, including time required to fill vacancies and to conduct training.

### Government compliance reporting

Government regulations have greatly increased the burden on HR functions over the past few decades. Simply collecting and processing relevant data required for EEO, COBRA, OSHA, and other regulatory reports can lead to staff increases, overtime, or the hiring of temporary help or consultants. The cost of noncompliance, as measured by penalties and fines, also can prove substantial. Automating data collection for these various compliance reports will produce immediate savings.

### Routine clerical and recordkeeping activities

An HRIS can reduce the amount of staff time required to produce salary review notices, mail benefit selection renewal forms, maintain employee files, respond to management or employee inquiries, generate reports, and handle the myriad day-to-day HR activities. All organizations automating an HR activity should realize some improved productivity and efficiency. For some companies, these improvements are significant enough to eliminate some clerical positions or to expand services to employees.

## Enterprise Resource Planning

Enterprise resource planning (ERP) is a business strategy that combines all the various company-wide computer programs into one cohesive system. By linking all the different software and hardware packages together, the organization is better able to facilitate a single cohesive business approach to customer service and operational excellence.

By providing management with immediate access to all daily operational information and financial data, better decision making results from the more immediate analyzing of data, identifying trends, planning for the future and the tracking of goals.

Traditionally, the various company functions such as accounting, inventory, customer service, human resources, etc., did not share their information through a common technological link. Each department acted autonomously and only indirectly shared information with other departments. By bringing together all the functions into one harmonious system that is tied together, the left hand will know what the right hand is doing. This approach replaced a tangle of complex computer applications with a single, integrated system.

In today's global marketplace, reacting swiftly and taking proactive steps to gain competitive advantage requires speed. To gain this competitive advantage, businesses must process information in a seamless and integrated manner. ERP is the backbone of this initiative.

While the HR department holds employee records such as employee compensation, payroll, medical, benefits, staffing compliance, etc., it must integrate these programs with Sales, Finance and Manufacturing. What occurs in these other departments has a down-stream impact on compensation and the other HR records that are based on headcount in these departments.

With ERP, all who need information can easily access all elements in the supply and production chain. This leads to efficiency and responsiveness.

# Management Functions: Planning, Organizing, Leading and Controlling

The four major functions of management are summarized by the P-O-L-C model. This acronym stands for planning, organizing, leading and controlling. The P-O-L-C model has widespread acceptance as a very useful way of classifying the activities managers engage in as they attempt to achieve organizational goals. Managers are expected to engage in creative problem solving and the POLC model provides a framework for decision making and creating a smoothly running organization.

Even more importantly, the underlying principles of this theoretical model appear regularly on the PHR and/or SPHR exam. So let's examine it more in depth.

| Planning | Organizing | Leading | Controlling |
|---|---|---|---|
| 1. Vision & Mission <br> 2. Strategizing <br> 3. Goals & Objectives | 1. Organization Design <br> 2. Culture <br> 3. Social Networks | 1. Leading <br> 2. Decision Making <br> 3. Communications <br> 4. Groups / Teams <br> 5. Motivation | 1. Systems / Processes <br> 2. Strategic Human Resources |

## Planning

The planning function sums up future impact on today's decisions. All other activities are very much dictated by planning. A manager can only organize and staff the company only after setting the goals and drawing up plans to achieve them.

The planning process begins with environmental scanning. This is the act of analyzing the critical external contingencies facing an organization in terms of economic conditions, competitors, and customers.

Planners must establish objectives, which are statements of what needs to be achieved and when. Planners must then identify alternative courses of action for achieving objectives. After evaluating the various alternatives, planners must make decisions about the best courses of action for achieving objectives. They must then formulate necessary steps and ensure effective implementation of plans. Finally, planners must constantly evaluate the success of their plans and take corrective action when necessary.

### Planning involves:

- Vision statement: A nonspecific directional and motivational guidance to the entire organization. This usually comes from the top management. It describes the desired future state of the business.
- Mission statement: The existence or purpose of the organization. This explains the scope of the business and uniquely identifies the business house from similar businesses. The mission reflects organizational culture and ethics.
- Objectives: These refine the mission and address key issues like market standing, innovation, productivity, physical and financial resources, profitability, management and work force performance and efficiency.
- Goals: These are rational estimates of anticipated results. The goals are usually Specific, Measurable, Attainable, Rewarding, and Timely (SMART).
- Organizational culture: Comprises the shared attitudes, experiences, beliefs and values of an organization.

There are a myriad of planning techniques among which "Strategic planning" is very important. It encompasses certain parameters like Strengths, Weaknesses, Opportunities and Threats (SWOT) which help in formulating strategies appropriate for task completion.

## Organizing:

Organizing is the function of management that involves developing an organizational structure and allocating human resources to ensure the accomplishment of objectives. The structure is usually represented by an organization chart, which provides a graphic representation of the chain of command within an organization.

"Organizing" focuses on division, coordination, and control of tasks and the flow of information within the organization. A manager distributes responsibility and authority to each employee as part of this function of management. In an organizational structure a managers' decision reflects the mission, objectives, goals and tactics that are the result of the planning function.

### "Organizing" involves:

- Division of labor: An organizational chart reveals that complex jobs can usually be less expensively completed by a large number of people each performing a small number of specialized tasks.
- Delegation of authority: This is the legitimized power vested with an individual. The ability to influence others, whereas delegation is the distribution of authority.
- Departmentation: This is the grouping of jobs for the purpose of planning, coordination and control. The extent of departmentation is dictated by different nature of jobs.
- Span of control: The number of employees a manager can effectively supervise.
- Coordination: This is essentially liaison between different departments and employees to produce a finished product.

Organizing at the level of a particular job involves how best to design individual jobs to most effectively use human resources. Traditionally, job design is the process of putting together various elements to form a job. This concept is based on the principles of division of labor and specialization, which assumed that the more narrow the job content, the more proficient the individual performing the job could become.

However, experience has shown that it is possible for jobs to become too narrow and specialized. Many jobs are now designed based on such principles as empowerment and job enrichment which is a job redesign technique that allows workers more control over how they perform their own tasks. Also, teamwork is a job redesign objective as it hopes that a cooperative effort by the members of a group or team will be a more efficient method for achieving a common goal.

## Leading:

Leading is the most important function of management. The definition of management is "accomplishing things through others." To do this, leaders must motivate, communicate, educate, lead and discipline workers.

Managers must study and understand their subordinates' personalities, values, attitudes, and emotions. Studies of motivation and motivation theory provide important information about the ways in which workers can be energized to put forth productive effort. Studies of communication provide direction as to how managers can effectively and persuasively communicate. Studies of leadership and leadership style provide information regarding questions, such as, "What makes a manager a good leader?" and "In what situations are certain leadership styles most appropriate and effective?"

### "Leading" involves:

- Motivation: Highly motivated people with steely resolve perform better than unmotivated people. There is also an inherent danger of employees losing focus and becoming demotivated over the course of time. A manager guards against this. Some elements of motivation are rewards, citations and recognition.
- Communication: This involves removing barriers to communication. Giving a better access to the work force to contact management and remove the obstacles to performance improvement.
- Performance appraisal: Every employee should receive performance appraisal as part of continuous improvement process. It is the responsibility of the manager to see that such appraisals do not negatively affect the morale of the employee but are a useful tool to improve professional development.
- Discipline: Allowing disorderly behavior like coming late to work, not following safety regulations, complacency in work ethic could result in great loss to the firm. A manager must deal with situations firmly. A manager should not hesitate to punish the offending employee consistent with the severity of the issue and help maintain order at all times

## Controlling:

Controlling involves ensuring that performance does not deviate from standards. Controlling consists of three steps, which include (1) establishing performance standards, (2) comparing actual performance against standards, and (3) taking corrective action when necessary. Managers at all levels engage in the managerial function of controlling to some degree.

The managerial function of controlling should not be confused with control in the behavioral or manipulative sense. This function does not imply that managers should attempt to control or to manipulate the personalities, values, attitudes, or emotions of their subordinates. Instead, this function of management concerns the manager's role in taking necessary actions to ensure that the work-related activities of subordinates are consistent with and contributing toward the accomplishment of organizational and departmental objectives.

Effective controlling requires the existence of plans, since planning provides the necessary performance standards or objectives. Controlling also requires a clear understanding of where responsibility for deviations from standards lies.

Two traditional control techniques are budget and performance audits. An audit involves an examination and verification of records and supporting documents. A budget audit provides information about where the organization is with respect to what was planned or budgeted for, whereas a performance audit might try to determine whether the figures reported are a reflection of actual performance. Although controlling is often thought of in terms of financial criteria, managers must also control production and operations processes, procedures for delivery of services, compliance with company policies, and many other activities within the organization.

The management functions of planning, organizing, leading, and controlling are widely considered to be the best means of describing the manager's job, as well as the best way to classify accumulated knowledge about the study of management. Although there have been tremendous changes in the environment faced by managers and the tools used by managers to perform their roles, managers still perform these essential functions.

# Roles and Strategies of the HR Function

## HR Roles

### Core HR responsibilities

While the specific structure and organization of an HR department will vary from company to company and from industry to industry, all HR departments share functional, managerial, and strategic purposes. Regardless of the particular organization or marketplace in which an HR department operates, it must carry out the following activities:

- Design and deliver HR programs, practices, and processes that meet and support the needs of the company and its employees.

- Support line supervisors' efforts to achieve business goals through effective management of employees.

- Contribute to organizational development and strategic planning through developing HR practices that enhance overall competitiveness.

**TEST TAKING TIP**
The test is three hours in length and is brutally taxing. Be in shape for this event. You'll feel like you ran a marathon when it's over.

The HR role is a pure service function. All of an organization's employees are considered their customers.

## HR Generalist and HR Specialist Roles

### HR specialists

The competencies required of HR personnel traditionally have reflected the functional or operational divisions of an HR department. The HR job descriptions have become increasingly more specialized as the complexities of this field have deepened. Illustrations of the different types of expertise required for particular HR areas include: compensation and benefits, EEO planning, recruitment, and so forth. The focus of these specialists is much more narrowly defined than for an HR generalist.

Specialized HR departments deliver state-of-the-art competence in each HR practice area, such as staffing, training and development, appraisal, rewards, organization design, and communication. The overall effectiveness of the HR function depends on the individual skills of the staff assigned to each HR activity and how efficiently these individuals deliver services. For example, the training function demonstrates specialist capabilities when it designs training and development programs using the latest training technology.

## HR generalists

In recent years, the trend toward outsourcing complex HR activities such as benefits administration, combined with a new emphasis on strategic HRM, has led to a growing demand for HR generalists. Instead of in-depth expertise in a particular HR area, generalists must have only broad knowledge of different HR activities. However, HR generalists do need special managerial and consulting skills to provide guidance to and locate resources for employees, line supervisors, and top executives. In addition, computer skills have become essential as new software programs allow HR generalists to perform activities that once required the talents of in-house specialists or outside HR contractors.

Generalist HR departments emphasize integration rather than specialization of HR activities. HR effectiveness depends on how well the department as a whole operates and is not merely the sum of individual HR activities. For example, a generalist HR function emphasizes integrating training activities with performance appraisal results and promotion plans, rather than focusing on state-of-the-art training techniques.

> **TEST TAKING TIP**
> There is no substitute for preparation. Study, study, study. 100 hours or more in total.

## Education and experience requirements

In today's organizations, exempt-level HR staffs typically possess at least a bachelor's degree, and advanced degrees have become common. For HR personnel, business administration degrees are the most common majors, with specialization in HR or labor relations. However, the growing emphasis on HR as a strategic business partner has prompted more HR staff to seek Master's in Business Administration (MBA) degrees. It is becoming more commonplace for organizations to require HR accreditation such as the Professional in Human Resources (PHR) or Senior Professional in Human Resources (SPHR) certification from HRCI. For HR executives, prior HR managerial experience is a typical requirement, although a significant number of HR executives also have managerial experience in non-HR departments.

## Organizational Context

The skills needed by HR staff vary depending on the overall structure and orientation of the HR department and its role within an organization. A company with a centralized HR department structured according to functional activities, for example, will have greater demand for HR specialists than a company that has a decentralized HR department or that outsources many HR activities.

The industry in which a company operates and the organization's overall philosophy of employee relations also influence HR competency requirements. A unionized company, for example, will need HR personnel with labor relations and negotiating skills, while an entrepreneurial firm with a flat organizational structure will have greater demand for HR staff skilled in recruiting top talent and building work teams.

## Organizational Design:

There are many approaches to the design of the Organizational Structure. The one that is most effective is the one that takes into account the purpose and the work of the company. Typical examples of organizational structures include:

### Functional structure

In the Functional Structure of organizational design, work is organized around typical functions within the organization. Such as, the payroll function, employee relations function, hiring function, etc. This leads to operational efficiencies within the group or the department. Coordination and specialization of tasks are centralized in a functional structure.

### Divisional structure

Divisional structure is sometimes known as product structure. Work is divided along product lines. Each division within a divisional structure contains all the necessary resources and functions within it. For example, a telephone company may divide its divisions into product specific topics such as cell phones, land lines, Internet access, etc. Other divisions may be divided based on geographic location such as Southeast United States, Northeast United States, or West Coast.

### Matrix structure

In a Matrix structure, employees serve two masters. They have a direct line reporting relationship to their immediate department head or supervisor, while also maintaining a dotted line reporting relationship to a project manager or team manager that they may have been temporarily assigned to. Matrix organizations frequently use teams of employees who are temporarily assigned to a project team to accomplish the work of the company. This type organizational structure is often confusing to employees who are trying to satisfy both of their reporting relationships.

## HR Policies and Procedures

HR's traditional duties include assisting in the development of the following:

- Formation and administrations of policies and procedures.
- Coordinating and updating policy manuals and employee handbooks.
- Overseeing and administering employee communications: written, oral, visual, electronic media, etc.

It should be pointed out, that the normal HR role isn't in the 'creation' of policies and procedures, that's top management's role, but in the 'interpretation' of those same policies and procedures.

## Integration and Coordination of HR Functions

### Staffing ratios

A 1:100 ratio is the commonly accepted standard in the industry for HR professionals per number of employees.

## Human Resource Inventory

A forecast of staffing needs begins with a study of current positions and employees' capabilities, past trends in an organization's workforce, and future business plans and market trends. An inventory that catalogs present employees' skills and abilities can help HR planners predict how closely internal candidates match the company's future HR needs.

Maintaining an inventory of current employees' skills makes it easier to find qualified internal candidates to fill openings. The same skills inventory also can be used in the staff planning process.

A skills inventory is easiest to maintain through an automated personnel recordkeeping system, although smaller employers can use a manual system. In either case, the process of tracking employees' skills involves several activities:

- Ask employees to keep the HR department informed of any new skills, interests, or qualifications they acquire, both on and off the job.
- Provide a standardized skills inventory form and remind employees of its purpose through occasional memos, newsletter articles, or other means of communication.
- When hiring a new employee, explain the promote-from-within policy and help the employee fill out a skills form. List the employee's skills that were discovered during the selection process and ask the employee to add any others to the form.

The same skills inventory can be used in the staff planning process. For companies with computerized personnel records, software programs can build an employee database that can be easily accessed through job specifications. For instance, a recruiter with a senior systems analyst position to fill could retrieve from the database all junior systems analysts with at least two years' experience and satisfactory or better performance ratings.

## HR Control Process

The HR department plays a vital role in enforcing company dictates and guidelines. The establishment of a company culture is predicated upon some group or body controlling and overseeing the HR process. Ways that HR helps to control this process is to:

- Maintain personnel and performance records.
- Monitor and control absenteeism, tardiness, and turnover.
- Develop and implement succession plans.
- Review proposals for classification changes.
- Develop job descriptions.
- Evaluate conformity of actual activities to job descriptions.

## Total Quality Management (TQM)

Reducing production costs and waste should be an ongoing companywide effort. Since minimizing controllable costs has a significant impact on bottom-line profitability, improving production processes plays an important role in total quality management (TQM) efforts. Through cost reductions, companies are able to provide more products or services with the same number of employees and thereby see an increase in profits.

To maximize benefits received from any cost-cutting plan, management should try to enlist the help of every employee to pinpoint areas of waste in company processes or their own daily practices. HR managers can guide waste management programs by making employees aware of the problem and involving them in the solution. Management should advise employees of recognized waste problems and enlist their help in identifying other problems.

Customer satisfaction is another product cost center important to any TQM program. The HR department can help create a culture where employees are committed to fulfilling customer expectations by revising such HR practices as interviewing and selection, orientation and training, job descriptions, standards of performance and performance appraisals, monetary and nonmonetary rewards, employee handbooks, and supervisory practices.

**TEST TAKING TIP**
If you run into a question that you don't know, mark it with the red exclamation marks (provided on the computerized test) and return later when time allows. Don't get hung up on a question you don't know and then can't finish the test because of a lack of time.

## Lean Manufacturing & Six Sigma

Lean manufacturing or lean production, which is often known simply as "Lean", is the optimal way of producing goods through the removal of waste and implementing flow, as opposed to batch and queue. Lean manufacturing is a generic process management philosophy derived mostly from the Toyota Production System (TPS). It is renowned for its focus on reduction of the original Toyota seven wastes in order to improve overall customer value, but there are varying perspectives on how this is best achieved.

Six Sigma is a business management strategy, originally developed by Motorola, which today enjoys wide-spread application in many sectors of industry. Six Sigma seeks to identify and remove the causes of defects and errors in manufacturing and business processes. It uses a set of quality management methods, including statistical methods, and creates a special infrastructure of people within the organization ("Black Belts" etc.) who are experts in these methods. Each Six Sigma project carried out within an organization follows a defined sequence of steps and has quantified financial targets (cost reduction or profit increase).[

Both Lean and Six Sigma can be seen as a loosely connected set of potentially competing principles whose goal is cost reduction by the elimination of waste by removing defects and errors.

## Performance Planning:  Identify Goals/Desired Behavior

Before setting performance goals, one should think through the job systematically and review the job requisition and the job itself to identify relevant factors such as:

- necessary skills and abilities— work experience, education, technical skills, communication skills, analytical skills, and specialized training;

- behavioral factors— motivation, interests, goals, drive and energy, reliability, and stress tolerance; and

- corporate culture— team orientation, independence, social effectiveness, and interpersonal style.

The first step in improving performance is to compare internal measures of performance to similar measures in other organizations (benchmarking).

Once areas for improvement are identified, the next task is to develop specific objectives for enhancing performance. Listed below are several effective goal-setting steps designed to boost performance:

### Specify the objective or tasks to be done

What must be accomplished? Are costs to be reduced? Is customer service to be improved? Beginning with the job description, an employee should know what is expected, what results the employee is responsible for, what deadlines must be met, what other jobs this job should be coordinated with, and what equipment should be used.

### Specify how the performance in question is to be measured

Work outcomes are usually measured by one of three standards:

- Physical units. This standard measures the quantity of production, market share, number of errors, and number of rejects.

- Time. Time standards examine the process of meeting deadlines, servicing customers, completing a project, and coming to work each day.

- Money. These standards look at the impact of profits, sales, costs, budgets, debts, income.

### Specify the standard or target to be reached

The method of setting a specific target can vary depending upon the context and purpose for which the targets are to be used. Examples of specifying a target might involve setting a production goal of 50 units per hour or completing a project by a certain date. Techniques often used for setting targets include the following:

#### *Time-and-motion studies*

In scientific terms, this method is the most precise way to set goals for routine, repetitive jobs. Motion studies analyze the job to eliminate unnecessary or wasted motion. Time studies examine the work cycle to determine the average time necessary to complete a cycle by one or more competent employees properly trained to perform the motions. Time is then prorated across the working day with allowances made for fatigue, set-up time, and interruptions. The resulting calculation is used to determine the expected production in a day.

#### *Participative goal setting*

Management develops targets with input from employees who have knowledge about a task.

#### *Cascading objectives*

This method of management by objectives sets goals first for the company, then for top executives. Next, senior managers meet with front-line supervisors to set objectives for helping management meet its goals. Finally, supervisors conduct similar goal setting meetings with employees.

#### *Average performance*

This method of setting goals is more readily understood and accepted by employees and management. Average performance rates are easy to determine from company records; however, if previous working conditions do not match present conditions, performance rates must be adjusted to account for new circumstances.

---

**Example**

A forest products company used average performance to set goals for its workers. First, the company developed mathematical equations to determine how much timber could be cut based on the number and type of equipment, the size of the tree, and the space between trees. The company then used statistical tables compiled from previous experience to determine an expected level of production for new locations.

---

### Specify the time span involved

Set a deadline for reaching a goal (e.g., answering a customer inquiry within 90 minutes). Setting daily goals is common for repetitive, manual work. When the level of responsibility increases, the time span across which goals are projected should increase.

Set a priority for goals. When the complexity of a job increases, the number of goals usually increases as well. When more than one goal is set, rank the goals in order of importance. This step directs action and effort in proportion to the rank of each goal.

### Rate goals by difficulty and importance (optional)

To achieve a high degree of measurement when setting multiple goals, rate each goal according to difficulty and importance. An overall performance goal can be calculated by combining its difficulty and importance rating with its goal fulfillment rating.

### Determine coordination requirements

Before deciding on a final set of goals, determine whether the achievement of these goals depends on the cooperation and contribution of others. If so, coordinate the goals of various employees and make sure that the goals of different people do not conflict.

## Setting and Communicating Performance Standards

The most formal opportunity to set and communicate performance standards is at the annual performance review.

Unfortunately, many supervisors and employees think of performance evaluation as a stressful exercise that happens once a year and they view it as more of a chore to be quickly finished than a valuable step in the planning and review process. However, if expectations are clarified and feedback is given throughout the year, the annual performance evaluations should become less stressful. The following steps will help you to more effectively implement the company's performance appraisal and disciplinary policies within your department.

### Decide on clear, objective expectations for the job

Setting expectations for a job affects every decision you make about an employee's career, from work assignments and recommendations for training opportunities to raises, promotions, transfers, and terminations of employment. It also shows the employee what behaviors or outcomes the company values, thus affecting employees' decisions on where to expend their greatest efforts.

The place to start when setting out objectives is the person's job description, which will give you and your employees a general idea of what the company expects from people in any given position. (Contact HR if you think the job description doesn't accurately portray the job.) Once you've examined the job description, you can start to break down the principal duties and accountabilities it lists into more concrete objectives and performance standards.

To make sure that everyone concerned can tell whether expectations have been met, performance standards should:

- be precise yet brief,
- be in writing,
- be realistic,
- help meet company objectives,

- be mutually agreed on, and
- be re-evaluated regularly.

---

**EXAMPLE**

If claims processing is a principal duty, you need to figure out a range of what is an acceptable number of claims processed in a given time period. Incorporate any measures of quality, such as the number of errors reported.

---

### Communicate expectations to the employees involved

Making expectations clear to employees is part of helping them do their jobs. Employees who know how their performance will be measured are much more likely to succeed in their jobs or to accept criticism if they fail. Making sure that everyone knows the expectations for their jobs is one way to show everyone that you are treating all employees equally and not making up reasons to discipline employees you don't like.

### Give constant feedback on whether employees are meeting the expectations

Nothing you say in an employee's annual review should be a surprise to the employee. Feedback —both positive and negative — should be ongoing throughout the year. This approach helps employees focus their efforts on tasks and behaviors that you find to be worthwhile for the company and improve in other areas.

### Stick to a fair procedure for implementing discipline

Our company uses a system called "progressive discipline." This means that for most rule infractions, you should go through the following steps: verbal warning, written warning, disciplinary suspension, and termination. We adhere to this system because it lets employees know where they stand and helps us make sure that people in different departments are treated equally. Your role as a supervisor involves making sure this disciplinary system is implemented in your part of the company.

**TEST TAKING TIP**

Some certification candidates plan to take the test twice. The first time is to sample the prep process and to gauge the difficulty of the exam process. The second exam is for all the marbles.

Disciplinary suspensions and terminations should be undertaken only after the HR department is consulted.

### Implement discipline consistently

Because personalities and "chemistries" between people differ, your interactions with each of your employees are bound to be different.

But if you, as a supervisor, do not implement discipline consistently, you leave yourself open to charges that you treated someone differently because of race, sex, age, disability, or other protected status. Getting into the habit of going through the progressive discipline steps and providing constant feedback will help improve your consistency.

If you encounter situations that haven't occurred in your department before, please call the HR department to see how the situations are normally dealt with. Also call to head off problems over something that could look like preferential treatment or discrimination. (For instance, is it OK to allow one employee who has child care obligations to be late while another employee gets disciplined for tardiness? Is it OK to start enforcing a rule that I didn't previously enforce because it never mattered until someone recently made a mistake after not following the rule?)

---

**Document employees' performance throughout the year, especially disciplinary measures**
Many a lawsuit has been lost because the only written records of an employee's performance show that the employee was performing wonderfully. But your need for documentation begins long before any lawsuit is filed. Disciplinary actions and even annual performance reviews are especially hard to undertake if you have no records on an employee's performance.

Spoken compliments or suggestions for improvements may come naturally to you and many times is the most appropriate way to work with an individual. But when it comes time to put an assessment of that employee's performance on paper, do you have any record of the ratio of compliments to criticism? Or of how many times you have pointed out a particular type of shortfall? Creating some written documentation along the way helps make sure that your appraisal of the employee's performance is based on incidents that happened throughout the year and not just on the most recent or memorable events of the year.

Written documentation can also decrease the chances that your communications will be misunderstood. It is hard for an employee to claim that you never told him or her that certain behaviors mattered if there is a memo in the file explaining why the behavior is important.

> **TEST TAKING TIP**
> You can't beat a formalized study program (class, lecture, study group) for helping most candidates prepare. Many of us aren't disciplined enough or have too many life distractions to prepare on our own without a structured program.

## Measuring Results and Providing Feedback

Feedback is essential in managing and measuring performance. People will not, however, give relevant feedback if they do not believe their feedback makes a difference or if they do not have easy access to those making the decisions.

Employees will need to know how they are doing in comparison with preset targets, as a way of measuring employee performance and assuring compliance. Encourage supervisors and managers to use these methods to tell employees how well they're doing:

- Give daily feedback to each person. Use a simple rating scale and be specific.
- Post individual and group indicators of progress towards productivity and performance goals.
- Conduct periodic performance appraisals based on measurable, observable targets.

Each organization will develop its own performance indicators based upon its business, products, services, or customers.

### 360-degree feedback method
An increasing number of companies now use performance appraisal systems that incorporate all or some of the concepts of "360-degree feedback" — a method of receiving evaluation feedback from representatives of virtually all persons who interact with the employee being evaluated. These persons typically include subordinates, superiors, outside consumers, inside consumers, and the employee. In short, the evaluation method is designed to provide a complete evaluation of the employee from every vantage point.

*Unique objectives*

A fundamental objective and by-product of 360-degree feedback is increased focus on customer service; productivity no longer is the exclusive concern. This increased concern with customer service is consistent with the incorporation of "total quality management" (TQM) concepts in business planning and evaluation. Both TQM and 360-degree feedback strive for broad-based review, including analysis of the quality of products and service. If the employee interacts with the public or with prospective consumers of the organization's services or products, input from those sources is valuable in providing a more complete picture of the employee's performance. It also is helpful to the organization in making general organizational decisions. The feedback might indicate broader problems — ones that are not limited to that employee or that employee's department. The organization can better evaluate its effectiveness in dealing with consumer complaints, questions, or suggestions and determine areas where it is ineffective. Similarly, the comments may reflect other problems with the general product or service provided by the organization.

## Implementing Performance Improvement Strategies

Experts recommend a three-step process for implementing a TQM process:

- Step 1. Management determines need, organizes a quality council, reviews and prioritizes project nominations, and identifies and trains teams.

- Step 2. Quality improvement teams review the organization's charter and mission statement, analyze symptoms, develop theories, test theories, identify causes, and develop remedies and controls.

- Step 3. Individual departments implement remedies and controls.

Taking these steps alone will not ensure success, however. For any TQM effort to produce results, these factors are important elements:

- Upper managers become personally involved as leaders of the quality revolution.

- Everyone in the organizational hierarchy receives training to manage for quality.

- Quality goals are added to strategic business plans.

- Quality efforts include "stretch goals" for improvement and are developed from benchmarking other companies.

- Quality improvement pushes forward at a rapid pace.

- Employee involvement and empowerment are extended.

- Upper managers personally review performance against quality goals.

- The organization makes greater use of recognition programs and revises the reward system to take into account the increased role of quality.

## Evaluating Results

### Difficulty of measurement

HR may have difficulty quantifying some aspects of TQM systems, such as customer satisfaction, employee morale, and the like. The most obvious measures of cost savings often ignore expensive hidden costs. In addition, if measurement methods among business units differ, the result is inconsistent results. The Baldrige Award's measurement criteria provide the lead in measuring quality initiatives.

## Purpose of the Baldrige Award

As U.S. Secretary of Commerce, Malcolm Baldrige urged U.S. companies to resist short-term thinking and focus instead on long-term goals of quality management and customer satisfaction. Congress passed the Malcolm Baldrige National Quality Improvement Act shortly after his death in 1987 to acknowledge and reward the quality achievements of U.S. companies and to publicize successful business strategies. The award represents the highest level of national recognition for quality that a U.S. company can receive.

Since its inception, only a few companies have received the Malcolm Baldrige National Quality Award, yet thousands more have applied. Baldrige Award winners may publicize and advertise their awards provided they agree to share with other U.S. organizations their successful quality strategies.

While the award itself confers prestige upon the winning organizations, it is the Baldrige measurement tool that provides HR and other divisions within the organization the means to achieve a competitive, customer-focused organization. The procedures that a company undergoes during award examination are designed not only to serve as a basis for bestowing the award, but also to diagnose quality management practices. The award provides organizations with a framework and with tools for measuring quality practices. In fact, many companies publicize their application for the award, since just the process of applying for the award requires a serious commitment by the applicant company.

**TEST TAKING TIP**
The test questions are written by certified HR professionals. Their goal is for the questions to be tough and broadly representative of the entire field of HR. They don't want any light-weights getting certified. Thus, the questions are challenging.

The importance attached to HR management in the Malcolm Baldrige Quality Award criteria is apparent by the total number of points assigned to this segment. The part of the Baldrige application that deals with HR issues looks at key elements summarized below.

## HR planning and evaluation

Questions on the application are designed to clarify how the company's HR planning and evaluation are aligned with its strategic and business plans, and how well HR addresses the development and well-being of the entire workforce. Areas to address include how the company translates overall requirements from strategic and business planning to specific HR plans. HR plans in the following areas are spotlighted:

- changes in work design to improve flexibility, innovation, and rapid response;
- employee development, education, and training;
- changes in compensation, recognition, and benefits; and
- recruitment, including expected or planned changes in demographics of the workforce.

In all these areas, companies are asked to distinguish between short- and long-term goals. The application also looks at how the company evaluates and improves its HR planning and practices and the alignment of those plans and practices with the company's strategic and business directions.

Applicants are asked to describe how employee-related data and company performance data are analyzed and used to:

- evaluate the development and well-being of all categories and types of employees;
- assess how HR practices are linked to key business results; and

- ensure that reliable and complete HR information is available for company strategic and business planning.

# Techniques to Sustain Creativity and Innovation

## Motivation Theories

### Behavioral science theories

HR management can draw on a wealth of behavioral science research to understand what makes individual employees tick. Experts agree that employee motivation depends heavily on a positive work environment, sympathetic management, employee participation, and some employee control over the individual job. In short, quality of work life issues is important in employee motivation. Insight into the motivation needs of employees enables an employer to influence the working relationship and make everyone feel valued as individuals working toward common goals.

### Reinforcement theories (operant conditioning)

Another theory of motivation is behavior modification, which is based upon psychologist B.F. Skinner's work. Instead of examining inner causes of behavior, Skinner's theory deals with modifying external factors. An employee's behavior, such as the performance of a specific task, can be modified by positive or negative reinforcement.

Positive reinforcement is more effective than negative reinforcement in achieving lasting change, so long as the reinforcement closely follows the behavior to be modified. Giving feedback, praise, encouragement, and recognition to employees who do a good job will motivate them to repeat the behavior. The most important thing about using behavior modification to train and develop employees is to make certain that rewards or sanctions occur soon after the performance of the task or behavior. Sometimes positive reinforcement can be generated by the employee, when the feeling of satisfaction from a task well done encourages the employee to perform in a similar manner.

> **TEST TAKING TIP**
> Some of the questions on the test are so simple you'll be fooled into over-thinking and over-analyzing the question. These are straight-forward questions.

While money may seem like an incentive to do a good job, it does not appear to be connected with day-to-day accomplishments. Money is therefore not viewed by Skinner as an effective reinforcer.

### Reward strategies

A primary objective of a compensation program is to motivate the employee behaviors needed to achieve business goals. Motivation begins with a pay program that employees perceive as fair and equitable. A good compensation program clearly links efforts to outcomes and behaviors to rewards. Some reward theories are discussed below.

### *Expectancy theory*

Expectancy theory holds that employees' expectations determine effort and performance. Expectancy theory indicates that compensation policies and practices can influence the extent to which employees believe that performance will be rewarded. A performance appraisal system ensures that employees receive the feedback they need to perform well; a well-designed pay system ensures that their performance is rewarded appropriately. Over time, effective performance appraisals and rewards can influence employees' expectations and behaviors.

### *Reward theory or reinforcement theory*

Reward theory is based on the idea that employees will repeat behaviors that are rewarded and will avoid behaviors that are not rewarded. According to reward theory, paying for time worked fails to motivate high performance because it automatically rewards average or standard levels of performance. Reward theory supports the idea that pay that is contingent on high performance can directly influence behavior.

### *Goal-setting theory (AKA: 'Management by Objectives (MBO))*

According to goal-setting theory, only those rewards that employees value can motivate behaviors. The key is to set mutual goals for an organization and its employees — goals that will reward both the company and its workers. Goal- setting theory holds that pay can motivate employees if:

- employees participate in setting the goals for which they will be rewarded and accept these goals as their own,

- the goals are specific and set at a sufficiently challenging level, and

- specific monetary rewards are designated for each goal achieved.

## Maslow's Hierarchy of Needs

Abraham Maslow has the view that human nature is an ascending hierarchy of five basic needs. When one need is fulfilled, a person strives to fulfill the need from the next level. Not everyone is striving to fulfill each need at the same time, which can explain the different reactions people have in similar situations.

Maslow's later writings point out that self- actualization is difficult to attain and not many people have the capacity for self-knowledge to realize their potential completely. An important point of Maslow's needs hierarchy in relation to employee motivation is that once a need is satisfied, it is no longer a motivator. If employees already have their first two needs satisfied (in that the company provides them with adequate wages, a secure position, a safe environment, and health insurance protection), the real or potential motivators will be the need for acceptance, esteem, and self- actualization. Listed in sequence, Maslow's hierarchy of needs as they relate to the workplace is as follows:

| | |
|---|---|
| **Basic needs** | sufficient salary and wages |
| **Safety or security need** | safe, nonthreatening environment, job stability |
| **Social needs** | a sense of belonging, interpersonal relationships that establish personal affection and acceptance |
| **Esteem needs** | a feeling of self-worth, a sense of achievement, recognition and appreciation from others |
| **Self-actualization needs** | fulfillment of one's full potential, becoming what one is capable of becoming |

# Work Teams

Many companies find that self-directed work teams boost productivity 30 to 50 percent over the long term. Team success stories have achieved more publicity than the failures, but employee work teams are not a quick fix for a company's economic woes. Leading experts believe that employers using SDTs may not see any increase in productivity for the first 12 to 18 months after they are implemented.

Work teams can reflect the uniqueness of each company, yet they are based on a common principle: Given resources, time, and encouragement, employees can pool their ideas and experience to achieve a common goal. Teamwork can best be achieved not by just focusing on human relations, but by addressing the structures and systems of the company to prevent defects and errors.

Team-building has been defined as a process that a group of people with interrelated jobs uses for purposes of:

- diagnosing how effectively they function as a team;
- identifying barriers in work procedures, interpersonal relationships, and leadership functions;
- improving team effectiveness in achieving business results or goals by reducing or eliminating barriers.

### Self-directed work teams

Self-directed work teams, a recent innovation, may be particularly well- suited to the HR function. Team structures have the following characteristics:

- a high level of self-determination,
- collective control of daily activities,
- group responsibility for solving problems and making decisions,
- shared leadership,
- job sharing, and
- pay for skill attainment.

> **TEST TAKING TIP**
> Most test centers will provide you with sheets of blank paper or an erasable tablet for you to take notes on. You'll have to turn them in when finished.

In contrast to most functionally organized HR departments, an HR function that uses self-directed work teams encourages cross-functional integration of otherwise separate HR disciplines. Clients or customers can deal with one team or one individual on a wide variety of issues, which produces more efficient service.

### Virtual Teams

A Virtual Team — also known as a Geographically Dispersed Team (GDT) — is a group of individuals who work across time, space, and organizational boundaries with links strengthened by webs of communication technology. In today's globally dispersed organization, it is imperative that cross-functional teams come from locations across the globe. This wide dispersal is an impediment to physically grouping employees in one location. Therefore, members of virtual teams communicate electronically, so they may never meet face to face.

They have complementary skills and are committed to a common purpose, have interdependent performance goals, and share an approach to work for which they hold themselves mutually accountable. Geographically dispersed teams allow organizations to hire and retain the best people regardless of location. However, most teams will meet at some point in time.

A **virtual team** does not always mean teleworker. Teleworkers are defined as individuals who work from home. Many virtual teams in today's organizations consist of employees both working at home and small groups in the office but in different geographic locations.

## Job Design and Redesign

Job design involves structuring job elements, duties, and tasks to achieve effective job performance and optimal employee satisfaction. Management approaches to job design in the past were based on the concepts of employer control and operational efficiency. Today's management approaches balance two needs: (1) the need to foster employee involvement, and (2) ownership and the need to increase productivity and improve quality.

## Assessing the need

To determine if job design is necessary in an organization, answer the following questions:

- Is the organization composed of motivated people?
- Does the organization have the flexible structure, jobs, and management that will keep employees motivated?
- Do employees have decision-making power in their jobs?
- Do employees have ready access to channels to help increase their productivity and efficiency and to improve the organization and their work?

If certain areas of the organization need job design, seek a long-term commitment from line management to change the way things are presently done and, in some instances, to give up responsibilities they currently hold. Shifting control cannot be done overnight. The mindset of both management and employees needs to be gradually transformed into a new way of thinking about work processes and management of work. The HR department should be the first to encourage a more open, less structured culture.

In assessing a company's readiness for job design, consider the following issues before going forward: wage and salary increases, implementation costs, facility and equipment additions and changes, and training costs. Look for answers to these questions:

- What organizational or structural adjustments are needed to respond to these design suggestions?
- How should the job classification plan be altered to respond to these structural changes?

## Common approaches

Some of the most common approaches to job design are listed below:

- **Work simplification.** Work simplification gives employees direct control over the management of their work areas.
- **Job enlargement.** Job enlargement increases the variety of an employee's job duties.
- **Job enrichment.** Job enrichment adds tasks to a job to increase the job's complexity, challenge, and responsibility.
- **Group tasking.** Group tasking creates work teams to handle certain tasks and decision- making for an area of responsibility.
- **Job sharing**. Job sharing splits a time position so that two or more part-time employees work cooperatively to fulfill the same job responsibilities.

# Employee Ownership/ESOPs

## Employee stock ownership plans

Some organizations provide for an Employee Stock Ownership Plan either as a substitute for, or supplement to, a conventional retirement plan. An ESOP is an employee benefit plan that is qualified for tax-favored treatment under the Internal Revenue Code. It is a type of deferred compensation plan that invests primarily in the employer's stock.

More specifically, an ESOP is a defined contribution retirement plan. Each participating employee's account is credited with an appropriate number of shares of an employer's stock over the period of employment. ESOP assets (cash and employer stock) are allocated each year to the accounts of employee participants by a formula usually based on the proportion of the employee's salary to total covered payroll. Upon retirement, death, disability, or other termination of service, the employee's account is distributed to the employee (or the employee's beneficiary) in shares of stock or in cash. This type of arrangement is a win-win for both the employee and employer. The employee derives the benefit of an asset-building investment while the employer gets its stock in 'friendly-hands' who have a vested interest in seeing the company successful and thriving.

## Employee Suggestion System

A well organized and properly administered suggestion system yields benefits for employees and employers alike. Effective programs provide a unique channel of communication and the potential to increase productivity, reduce safety and health hazards, improve products and services, and enhance employee dedication. Companies with suggestion systems can tangibly profit from employees' cost-cutting or process-improving ideas.

Suggestion systems are fundamental to developing and sustaining employees' interest in solving company problems. Just knowing that a suggestion program is there and that management takes it seriously can heighten employee morale. A carefully planned and effectively run suggestion program strengthens two-way communication and reminds employees that they are important to the company's success.

**TEST TAKING TIP**
Putting off your studying until the last minute is tantamount to giving up on passing. You must study over the long-haul. Cramming doesn't usually work for this type test.

## Alternative Work Schedules

As more and more workers strive to reconcile the competing demands of work and family, employers have begun considering alternatives to the traditional workday and workweek. Alternative work schedules and leave policies are options that allow employees to schedule their work hours and leave time to meet family obligations without neglecting job demands. Studies have shown that employees who have more flexibility to deal with family concerns may have less stress on the job, better productivity, and a more positive attitude toward work than employees with inflexible work schedules and policies.

Alternative work arrangements and leave policies can benefit parents of young children and employees who care for elderly persons as well as students, older workers, persons with disabilities, couples who want to share work and home responsibilities, and persons who wish to improve their skills or change careers by returning to school. Alternative schedules can also help employers to serve their customers outside the traditional workday or workweek; to use their capital more intensively; to attract better workers; to improve employee morale and productivity; and to reduce absenteeism.

Some employees feel hesitant to use flexible arrangements. They believe they will be seen as lazy or disinterested if they take advantage of the chance to work fewer hours or to work partly at home. Under these circumstances, the focus must be on changing attitudes and on recognizing the fact that flexibility is a business issue, important to all employees and to business competitiveness, not just to women.

Examples of alternate work schedules include:

- **Part-time schedules.** Employees work less than a full-time workweek, usually anywhere from 10 to 35 hours per week.

- **Temporary employees.** Employees are hired for short periods of time and are employed only for the time they are needed.

- **Flextime.** Employees vary their arrival and departure times, as well as the length of the workday or workweek. (Example: An employee can arrive anytime between 7:30 and 9:30 a.m.; eight hours later, the employee leaves. A sign-in sheet, time clock, or the honor system can be used to keep track of the individual times.)

- **Compressed work schedules.** Full-time employees work the equivalent of a full workweek in fewer than five days. (Four 10-hour days would be a compressed work schedule.)

- **Job sharing.** Two, or sometimes more, part-time workers do the work that traditionally would be given to one person. (If, for example, a company cannot recruit a full-time doctor, but two retired doctors are willing to work four hours a day each, job sharing would fill the job.)

- **Telecommuting.** Workers do their jobs away from the employer's premises, usually at a remote location, on the road, or at home. (A new mother able to work four or five hours a day might free-lance from her home; but if her employer installed a computer and internet connection in her home, the employee could bear her child, then remain a part-time employee telecommuting from her house.)

## Role of HR in Employee Involvement Programs

Organizations that can get every employee involved in ensuring quality products and services can better meet customer needs, develop new markets, and become world-class competitors. HR has the crucial function of making the connection between business and quality objectives, and employee contributions to those objectives, as clear as possible.

Employee empowerment means to give employees the authority and resources they need to effectively do their jobs. Employee involvement is not possible without giving employees the power to do what they need to do. The theory behind employee empowerment is that the person doing the job is best suited to make decisions regarding that job. For many employers, and especially middle managers, the idea of relinquishing control to employees has been uncomfortable. However, once put into place, managers generally find that they have more power because more is accomplished by pushing tasks down the line. Managers can concentrate on planning rather than "putting out fires."

When a company decides to empower employees, training for employees and managers is typically required. Overcoming managerial resistance is often a large obstacle and one that generally takes about two years to overcome.

Planning HR Policies and Goals:

- Assess the business from the employee's perspective.
- Develop policies and goals for employee involvement.
- Develop policies and goals for employee education.
- Develop policies and goals for a supportive work environment.
- Develop policies for recognition and reward.

# The Legislative Process:

HR Practitioners are impacted daily by the laws and regulations passed by the elected lawmakers. It is imperative for the HR Professional to understand this process with the possibility of exerting influence on the Legislative proceedings to affect a positive outcome for their organizations. This section examines the legislative process at the federal level.

As part of its Legislative process, the United States Congress considers thousands of bills each session. Some of which may have a profound effect on the Human Resources practitioner. However, only a small percentage of these proposals will ever reach the top of the president's desk for final approval or veto.

Along their way to the White House, bills traverse a maze of committees, debates, and amendments in both chambers of Congress, the House and the Senate. The following is a simple explanation of the process required for a bill to become a law and at which points individuals or advocacy groups will have an opportunity to influence the outcome of the proposal:

1.  Introduction: Only a member of Congress (House or Senate) can introduce the bill for consideration. The Representative or Senator who introduces the bill becomes its "sponsor." Other legislators who support the bill or work on its preparation can ask to be listed as "co-sponsors." Important bills usually have several co-sponsors.

2.  A bill or resolution has officially been introduced when it has been assigned a number (H.R. # for House Bills or S. # for Senate Bills), and printed in the Congressional Record by the Government Printing Office.

3.  Committee Consideration: All bills and resolutions are "referred" to one or more House or Senate committees according the specific rules of the House or Senate.

4.  Committee Action: The committee considers the bill in detail. For example, the powerful House Ways and Means Committee and Senate Appropriations Committee will consider a bill's potential impact on the Federal Budget.

5.  If the committee approves the bill, it moves on in the legislative process. Committees reject bills by simply not acting on them. Bills that fail to get committee action are said to have "died in committee," as many do.

6.  Subcommittee Review: The committee sends some bills to a subcommittee for further study and public hearings. Just about anyone can present testimony at these hearings. Government officials, industry experts, the public, anyone with an interest in the bill can give testimony either in person or in writing. Notice of these hearings, as well as instructions for presenting testimony is officially published in the Federal Register.

7.  Mark Up: If the subcommittee decides to recommend a bill back to the full committee for approval, they may first make changes and amendments to it. This process is called "Mark Up." If the subcommittee votes not to recommend or report a bill to the full committee, the bill dies there.

8.  Committee Action -- Reporting a Bill: The full committee now reviews the deliberations and recommendations of the subcommittee. The committee may now conduct further review, hold more public hearings, or simply vote on the report from the subcommittee. If the bill is to go forward, the full committee prepares and votes on its final recommendations to the House or

Senate. Once a bill has successfully passed this stage it is said to have been "ordered reported" or simply "reported."

9.  Publication of Committee Report: Once a bill has been reported, the bill is written and published. The report will include the purpose of the bill, its impact on existing laws, budgetary considerations, and any new taxes or tax increases that will be required by the bill. The report also typically contains transcripts from public hearings on the bill, as well as the opinions of the committee for and against the proposed bill.

10. Floor Action -- Legislative Calendar: The bill will now be placed on the legislative calendar of the House or Senate and scheduled for "floor action" or debate before the full membership. The Speaker of the House and House Majority Leader decide the order in which reported bills will be debated. The Senate, having only 100 members and considering fewer bills, has only one legislative calendar.

11. Debate: Debate for and against the bill proceeds before the full House and Senate according to strict rules of consideration and debate.

12. Voting: Once debate has ended and any amendments to the bill have been approved, the full membership will vote for or against the bill. Methods of voting allow for a voice vote or a roll-call vote.

13. Bill Referred to Other Chamber: Bills approved by one chamber of Congress (House or Senate) are now sent to the other chamber where they will follow pretty much the same track of committee to debate to vote. The other chamber may approve, reject, ignore, or amend the bill.

14. Conference Committee: If the second chamber to consider a bill changes it significantly, a "conference committee" made up of members of both chambers will be formed. The conference committee works to reconcile differences between the Senate and House versions of the bill. If the committee cannot agree, the bill simply dies. If the committee does agree on a compromise version of the bill, they prepare a report detailing the changes they have proposed. Both the House and Senate must approve the report of the conference committee or the bill will be sent back to them for further work.

15. Final Action – Enrollment: Once both the House and Senate have approved the bill in identical form, it becomes "Enrolled" and sent to the President of the United States. The President may sign the bill into law. The President can also take no action on the bill for ten days while Congress is in session and the bill will automatically become law. If the President is opposed to the bill, he can "veto" it. If he takes no action on the bill for ten days after Congress has adjourned their second session, the bill dies. This action is called a "pocket veto."

16. Overriding the Veto: Congress can attempt to "override" a presidential veto of a bill and force it into law, but doing so requires a 2/3 vote by a quorum of members in both the House and Senate.

# International Human Resource Management (SPHR-only section)

## International HR Management

Transportation and communication advances have created a global economy. Speedy telecommunications and cost-competitive air transportation allow international sales and far-flung operations that once proved too cumbersome to manage. The availability of low-cost natural resources and/or skilled labor drives business decisions and global competition, with government regulations posing the only restriction.

These changes have tremendous implications for U.S. companies and their HR managers. The consumer market has expanded from 230 million Americans to 4.5 billion potential purchasers worldwide. However, competition has increased along with expanding markets: International competitors exceed domestic ones by a wide margin.

> **TEST TAKING TIP**
> Do not leave any questions blank. There is no penalty for blind guessing on this exam. If you don't know the answer, guess at it but mark down something.

To help their companies succeed in the global free-for-all, HR managers must prepare to manage an increasingly international workforce. In addition, they must retain and train domestic employees who have the skills to produce and sell products and services that appeal to overseas customers. As a result of this global focus, training in foreign languages and customs will become part of employee development efforts.

Types of employees an HR manager may be responsible for include:

- **Expatriates.** A U.S. citizen or permanent resident who is assigned to work at a foreign location.
- **Third-country nationals.** A third-country national is a nonresident alien who is paid by a U.S.-based company, but works in a foreign country other than his or her home country. Nonresident aliens hired by U.S. employers to work in a third country generally are not subject to federal income and employment taxes on their earnings in the host country, but are subject to U.S. taxes with respect to any U.S.-source income.
- **Resident aliens.** Individuals are resident aliens if they pass either the "green card" test or the "substantial presence test" or if they elect to be treated as a resident alien during their first year working in the United States.
- **Host Country national.** Residents of the country that they are working in. These people are normally paid by the US based company but have a legal right to work in their country of residence.

## Expatriation and Repatriation

### Expatriation

In developing candidates for foreign assignments, a few companies are beginning to go beyond quickie cultural awareness and language courses. Realizing that grooming of candidates should start long before employees are picked for overseas assignments, some companies are implementing plans to ensure ongoing development of candidates. Whatever the exact methods used, companies can help develop international employees by projecting a global mind-set and showing that value is placed on international exposure. The sections that follow outline some of the ways to develop a pool of potential expatriates.

### Companywide education programs

Informational or orientation programs may help employees develop an image of themselves as an integral part of a global organization. Employees gain knowledge and exposure just by learning about the company's activities and the cultures in other parts of the world. Some companies are including global awareness training as part of new hire orientation and management development courses, while others are including it more broadly, in companywide programs.

### Internal referral networks

One of the best ways a company can help ease transitions for employees and their families is by letting them talk to someone who has been through a similar experience. The concept resembles assigning the whole family to mentors for guidance on personal as well as professional issues.

Employees who are living abroad or who have come home from foreign assignments are usually willing to share the knowledge they have gained. The family of an employee about to embark on an overseas assignment will be less jittery if they have someone to ask simple questions like, "What should we bring?" "What should we leave behind?" "How do the schools compare?" and "What would you do differently?" HR can facilitate sharing of information by setting up an internal referral network.

Expatriates willing to serve as mentor to the company's future expatriates can be encouraged to fill out a form volunteering their services as a mentor. It lists the overseas locations to which expatriates have been assigned, their job titles, and ways they can be contacted. If a company is very active in some areas of the world, HR may have a constant flow of returning expatriates who could help candidates' families learn about what they could be signing up for. In some cases, HR may be able to match family compositions; a family with teenagers will obviously have different experiences than those of a family with infants or no children. Where activity levels are lower, however, the best match may be someone who has been to a similar area or someone who could talk generally about what it is like to be away from one's home country for extended periods.

Referring a candidate to someone in the employee's own job function can help familiarize the employee with concerns unique to that function. For instance, people in sales and marketing may be very curious about cultural differences in buying habits and decision-making, while someone assigned to transfer technology in a manufacturing plant may be more interested in locals' work habits and job expectations.

### Counseling and employee assistance programs

Like anyone undergoing stress, employees and their families need ways to deal constructively with the stresses they will encounter. Preventive programs and counseling on substance abuse and depression may be especially needed.

### Support networks within the expatriate community

As the numbers of expatriates grow, employers are forming support networks in various industries and regions so that expatriates can help each other adjust. For example, firms involved in overseas construction and engineering have formed the International Occupational Program Association, a group that deals with alcohol, emotional, and other problems of overseas assignees.

### Repatriation

Many employees experience problems reentering the workforce and lifestyle of their home country when their 'off-shore' assignment is over. Common issues include:

### Increased communications with home

The culture shock of returning to an unfamiliar place can be decreased if expatriates are encouraged to keep up with events at home. Offer to buy them a subscription to a local newspaper for a few months before the end of the assignment, so that they can read up on the latest trends and the prices of goods. Encourage them to write to old friends and exchange photos with family members. A relative's new beard, receding hairline, or cane may be less surprising if first absorbed in small doses through photographs.

### Reentry counseling and workshops

Providing reentry workshops can help participants examine their overseas experience; identify important changes that have taken place in themselves, their company, and their country; explore the reentry shock process; and develop strategies to minimize stress during the transition period. Practical advice offered during such workshops can run from discussions of changes in the local real estate market to introductions to the latest technology. Remember that even the use of debit cards at supermarkets and gas stations is probably a new experience for someone returning from several years overseas.

### Spouse career assistance programs

These programs are designed to support the spouse who seeks employment or career-enhancing activities while abroad and at reentry. In some cases, companies offer financial reimbursement for career-related activities. At reentry, career counseling, job-search tips, resume-writing assistance, and other placement support are offered to the spouse.

### Monetary rewards and assistance

Rather than reward the employee "up front" for taking an overseas assignment, many companies save all or part of the expatriate's bonus for the return trip. This extra money not only serves the practical purpose of helping the employee cope with the expense of reestablishing a household, but there is a psychological boost provided in the sense of reward for a job well done. Similarly, providing temporary housing and transportation where needed can help the employee financially, as well as making him or her feel welcomed and supported during reentry.

> **TEST TAKING TIP**
> Just before entering into the test center, review your difficult concepts (laws, formulas, etc.) and write them down on the tablet the center will supply you when you first sit down at the computer table. Then, refer to your notes when you hit a question later in the test period.

### Time off

Understand that, above all, the re-entry process takes time for the expatriate and the expatriate's family. Children will need time to adjust or readjust to schools and neighborhoods, and spouses may need extra consideration while re-establishing careers. The expatriate may have postponed visits to the doctor or dentist until the "hometown" doctor could be consulted. Just the process of unpacking household goods can take weeks to complete. A supervisor's and HR specialist's awareness that all these personal pressures are compounding new work pressures can go far towards easing the strains of readjustment for the expatriate. Let the employee know that reasonable requests for time off are expected, and that the company will do what it can to allow "flex time" during the readjustment process.

## Reasons for failed assignments

Looking at the reasons expatriates come home early or embittered can help HR managers increase their success rate. The good news is that the problems are in areas where effective selection, training, and HR planning can make a difference.

Surveys taken of expatriates returning from assignment early consistently say that family discontent is high on the list of reasons for failed assignments. Employers and employees alike often underestimate the isolation and cultural adjustment involved in foreign assignments. One study of 123 U.S. corporations boiled down the most common reasons for failure to:

- the spouse's inability to adjust (69 percent),
- the employee's inability to adjust (51 percent),
- other family-related problems (30 percent),
- the employee's lack of skill to conduct business in the host country (30 percent),
- the employee's inability to merge talents with international scope (26 percent),
- personality or emotional immaturity (25 percent), and
- inability to adapt to changing business priorities or organizational alignment (20 percent).

Among the worst aspects of foreign assignments, according to a survey of expatriate managers: family consequences, personal consequences, separation from company headquarters, lifestyle/location, negative career consequences, and financial/material consequences. Note that family and personal consequences are considered worse than any job-related aspects in the list.

## Issues of Multinational Corporations

Multinational operations begin when a company expands into additional countries and begins to manufacture, distribute, and/or sell products from overseas. At this stage, HR staffers need to learn how to manage local workers at overseas subsidiaries and how to coordinate headquarters' policy and procedures with local requirements in all areas: accounting, staffing, policy development, strategic planning, product development, and marketing. Training still embodies the authoritarian, top-down, and forceful presence of a national, headquarters-dominated organization.

As businesses and governments expand their activity around the world, they need meetings to discuss mergers, sales, laws, and other matters. As a result, meetings will assume a more international flavor, and planners will have to consider the different languages, customs, and cultural values of participants. Again, technological tools such as electronic copyboards and keypad-based group decision support systems will be useful. Also, the growing number of diverse racial and ethnic groups in the labor pool will require staff meetings and training sessions to accommodate employees' cultural differences.

Also, HR should develop a country cluster or profile that takes into account the foreign subsidiary's environment. This profile should review the factors that may affect the expatriate's performance, i.e., languages, culture, politics, economy, government interference, labor and labor relations, financing, market research, advertising, money, transportation, communication, control, contracts, and trade barriers. These factors should be used to group the multinational firm's subsidiaries into country clusters based on similarity of environmental factors.

## The Three R's

Fons Trompenaars and Charles Hampden-Turner have developed their theory of the Three R's that help explain the challenge and process of successfully integrating multi-cultural operations into a cohesive unit. Before employees are sent on international assignment, they must be taught to utilize the three R's.

### Recognition
The first step for leaders is to help all players recognize the cultural differences between the team members. The leader must recognize the importance of these differences and how they have an impact on the team's function.

### Respect

Different cultural orientation and views about "where I am coming from" are neither right or wrong—they are just different. It is all too easy to be judgmental and distrust those who give different meaning to their world from the one you give to yours. Thus, the next step is to respect these differences and to accept other's right to interpret the world from their cultural perspective.

### Reconciliation

Once managers in multi-cultural environments are aware of their own mental models and cultural predispositions, and once they can respect and understand that those of another culture are legitimately different, then it becomes possible to reconcile differences yielding positive business benefits. This is the most difficult stage to put into actual practice.

> Their core finding is that great leaders reconcile seemingly opposing values—that's what they do, that's what makes them effective, and that's what makes them great.

In summary, senior leaders seem to know how to integrate objectives to deliver results. Successful leaders rarely give orders; rather, they create a culture of reconciled values. This transcultural competence encompasses these three R's.

## The Role of HR in International Business

In the largest sense, HR's main obligation regarding foreign assignments is to ensure the success of the assignment. "Success" can mean that the business mission gets accomplished, the employee returns at the scheduled time to a career that is every bit as promising (or more promising) as before the employee took the assignment, the family stays intact, and the expatriate feels good about working for the employer.

**TEST TAKING TIP**
Be sure to read over the glossary of terms in the back of this study guide. It has lots of information not covered elsewhere in this manual. Hang in there, you're nearly ready.

However, at an estimated cost of between $100,000 and $300,000 for each early return, this is clearly an area in which improved management of human resources can affect the bottom line. This cost must be added to the expenses already involved in overseas assignments: around $1 million for a three- to five-year assignment in Paris, for example. These estimates do not include the indirect costs of damage to relationships with the host-country's government and possible business partners, or loss of market share.

In addition to the early returns, many expatriates contemplate leaving their employer upon return home. A loss of valued employees because of a lack of support while on a foreign assignment obviously reflects poorly on HR and costs the company money.

In addition to the above, there are shortages of qualified American workers in some job categories, such as nursing, so employers recruit aliens to increase the workforce. Joint ventures with foreign companies create the need to quickly obtain permission for managers and other key employees of the foreign company to work in the United States, and increased globalization creates a need for foreign workers skilled in international business and foreign languages.

## DHR's Fast 20

1. **Repatriation:** The process of being reintegrated back into domestic operations after being on an international assignment outside of the United States.

2. **Expatriate:** An employer who is on assignment in a country other than their own home country.

3. **Human Resource Information System (HRIS):** The methods used by an organization to collect, store, analyze, report, and evaluate information and data on people, jobs, and costs.

4. **Strategic planning:** The process of determining what an organization's mission is and how it plans to achieve the goals that are associated with the mission.

5. **Quality circles:** A work group that usually meets once a week to solve work-related quality problems, usually self-directed.

6. **Turnover:** The net result of the exit of some employees and entrance of others in the workforce. One way of calculating turnover is finding the *quit rate.*
    a. Quit rate = (total quits ÷ average work force × 100).

7. **Scientific approach:** Used in evaluating research and consists of four stages: (1) observation (2) formulation of explanation (3) generation of predictions (4) verification of predictions using scientific methods.

8. **Benchmarking:** The first step in improving productivity is to compare internal measures of productivity performance to similar measures in other organizations.

9. **Attrition:** Reducing the workforce of an organization by simply not replacing those employees who retire or quit.

10. **Matrix structure:** A matrix structure couples a functional organization with a project or product organization. Responsibilities and reporting relationships remain organized by function, but the staff assigned to a particular function may temporarily work on various projects under the direction of a project manager.

11. **Qualitative analysis:** examines the types of programs and services an HR function is providing, how well it delivers those programs and services, and which HR areas or customers could benefit from new programs or improved processes.

12. **Quantitative analysis:** Calculates averages, ratios, or cost-benefit values for different HR activities. These measures can be tracked over time and compared to internal or external norms.

13. **Total Quality Management (TQM):** A customer-driven, quality improvement approach that recognizes the only way to eliminate waste is to improve work processes.

14. **McGregor's Model – Theory X and Theory Y:** Theory X managers view people by and large as lazy, not very bright, and irresponsible. Theory Y managers view people as basically bright, responsible, motivated, and wanting control over their work and lives.

15. **Hersey-Blanchard Model:** Also known as the **Situational Leadership Model**, plots leadership style against three dimensions: task behavior, relationship behavior, and task maturity. This theory asserts that in situations where task maturity is low, an effective leadership style is one that provides a fairly high degree of task structure for team members and at very high levels of task maturity, neither much direction (task behavior) nor contact (relationship behavior) is required because a team and team members function effectively autonomously.

16. **Hawthorne Effect:** Skews research since employees know they are being studied and therefore work differently (i.e., any changes in environment will have an effect on performance).

17. **Organizational Development (OD):** The most quoted definition is "an effort (a) planned, (b) organization wide, (c) managed from the top, to (d) increase organizational effectiveness, and health through (e) planned intervention in the organization's processes' using behavioral science knowledge.

18. **Consultative Manager:** Asks direct reports for their opinions during the decision-making process, but reserves the right to solely make the final decision.

19. **Third Country National (TCN):** A non-resident alien who is paid by a U.S. company but is not working in his/her home country.

20. **Lean manufacturing** or **lean production:** Often known simply as "**Lean**", is the optimal way of producing goods through the removal of waste and implementing flow, as opposed to batch and queue.

# Practice Quiz

1. Shared values and norms held by an organization's members that provide important cues as to what is acceptable behavior is called:
    A. Organizational mission
    B. Organizational vision
    C. Organizational culture
    D. Organizational development

2. A tool that balances the importance of financial measures by providing additional measures that try to evaluate future rather than past performance is called:
    A. Balanced scorecard
    B. Cost-benefit analysis
    C. Break-even analysis
    D. Return on investment

3. In the near future, outsourcing of HR functions will MOST likely:
    A. Decline in popularity
    B. Continue to rise due to cost reduction initiatives
    C. Become decentralized to the local plant level
    D. Decrease as electronic technologies progress to allow HR practitioners to assume additional duties

4. A method of budgeting that involves developing the entire budget from scratch is called:
    A. Incremental budgeting
    B. Formula budgeting
    C. Activity-based budgeting
    D. Zero-based budgeting

5. The Global HR Manager is pressured to predict the average level of employee performance and productivity for a new greenfield project the company is contemplating. With little raw data upon which to draw, and with the timeline nearly complete, the manager will MOST likely employ which technique to complete this task?
    A. Delphi method
    B. Regression analysis
    C. Judgmental forecasting
    D. Environmental scanning

6. An organization, in which almost all decisions of any importance are made by the CEO, would be MOST likely to have which organizational structure?
    A. Formalized
    B. Decentralized
    C. Centralized
    D. Specialized

7. The BEST term for situations when an individual has other competing financial, professional or personal obligations or interests that interfere with his or her ability to adequately perform required duties in a fair and objective manner.
    A. Ethics code
    B. Conflict of interest
    C. Operational values
    D. Nepotism standards

8. The BEST term for a description of what an organization wants to become or hopes to accomplish in the future (typically in the next 10 years).
    A. Mission statement
    B. Set of core values
    C. Vision statement
    D. Strategic business plan

9. In financial accounting, this is a statement of financial position and a summary of an organization's balances. Assets, liabilities and ownership equity are listed as of a specific date, such as the end of its financial year. This is often described as a snapshot of a company's financial condition.
    A. Profit & loss statement
    B. Trial balance
    C. Income statement
    D. Balance sheet

10. Which of Blake and Mouton's Managerial Grid theory of leadership styles is considered by the authors to be the pinnacle of leadership styles?
    A. Country club leadership
    B. Impoverished leadership
    C. Middle-of-the-road leadership
    D. Team leadership

11. This leadership style believes no single optimal profile of a leader exists. According to the theory, "what an individual actually does when acting as a leader is in large part dependent upon characteristics of the current state of affairs."
    A. Situational leadership
    B. Lewin's leadership styles
    C. Theory X & Y
    D. Trait theory

## Answers and Explanations to Practice Quiz:

1.  C

"Organizational culture" comprises the attitudes, experiences, beliefs and values of an organization. It has been defined as "the specific collection of values and norms that are shared by people and groups in an organization and that control the way they interact with each other and with stakeholders outside the organization. Organizational values are beliefs and ideas about what kinds of goals members of an organization should pursue and ideas about the appropriate kinds or standards of behavior organizational members should use to achieve these goals. This is the best answer from among the options.

2.  A

The Balanced Scorecard helps provide a more comprehensive view of a business, which in turn helps organizations act in their best long-term interests. This strategic management system helps managers focus on performance metrics while balancing financial objectives with customer, process and employee perspectives. Measures are often indicators of future performance.

3.  B

Combined with the pressure for cost containment measures, the organizational model continues to shift towards globalization, the use of specialists in their respective fields, and the downsizing of the HR department, it is commonly accepted theory that the typical HR department will continue to outsource many of its traditional duties.

4.  D

"Incremental budgeting" is the process of taking last budget period's budget and adding a percentage increase for cost-of-living increases, "formula budgeting" uses a method for calculating a budget based on a statistical system, and "activity budgeting" assigns values to each activity and when all activities are added together, you have a budget. The correct answer is ZBB.

5.  C

Under pressure to produce an immediate prediction, the HR Manager will use judgmental forecasting where she will simply use an educated guess as to future events. While the "Delphi method" and "environmental scanning" are commonly accepted forecasting models, they both take time to complete. "Regression analysis" is a statistical application for predicting future events but requires access to facts, numbers, and data.

6.  C

Centralization is the process by which the activities of an organization, particularly those regarding decision-making, become concentrated within a particular location, group, or person (in this case the CEO). Decentralization is the opposite case where decision making is dispersed to the lower levels in an organization.

7.  B

"Ethics code" refers to the operating philosophy guiding company conduct. "Operational values" refer to the issues in the conduct of the business upon which measures of integrity rely, and "nepotism" is the showing of favoritism toward relatives and friends. "Conflict of interest" is the correct answer since it concerns a person in a position of trust who has competing personal interests that may impair organizational judgment.

## 8.  C

A "mission statement" tells you what the company is now. It concentrates on present; it defines the customer(s), critical processes and it informs you about the desired level of performance. A "vision statement" outlines what a company wants to be. It concentrates on the future; it is a source of inspiration; it provides clear decision-making criteria. Many people mistake vision statement for mission statement. Don't you, and especially remember these tips on the PHR or SPHR exam.

## 9.  D

A company's balance sheet has three parts: assets, liabilities and ownership equity. It is a snapshot of the organization's finances.

## 10. D

According to the Blake Mouton model, Team Leadership is the pinnacle of managerial style. These leaders stress production needs and the needs of the people equally highly. The premise here is that employees are involved in understanding organizational purpose and determining production needs. When employees are committed to, and have a stake in the organization's success, their needs and production needs coincide. This creates a team environment based on trust and respect, which leads to high satisfaction and motivation and, as a result, high production

## 11. A

Situation leadership theory assumes that different situations call for different characteristics and responses. According to this group of theories, no single optimal psychographic profile of a leader exists. According to the theory, "what an individual actually does when acting as a leader is in large part dependent upon characteristics of the situation in which he functions.

# Appendix A - HR Acronyms

1. **AAP** — Affirmative Action Plan
2. **AD&D** — Accidental Death and Dismemberment
3. **ADA** — Americans with Disabilities Act
4. **ADDIE** — Analysis, Design, Develop, Implement, & Evaluate
5. **ADEA** — Age Discrimination in Employment Act
6. **ADR** — Alternative Dispute Resolution
7. **AMA** — American Management Association
8. **APA** — American Payroll Association
9. **ASTD** — American Society of Training & Development
10. **BARS** — Behavioral Anchored Rating Scales
11. **BFOQ** — Bona Fide Occupational Qualification
12. **CBT** — Computer Based Training
13. **CCP** — Certified Compensation Professional
14. **CDHP** — Consumer Driven Health Plan
15. **CEAP** — Certified Employee Assistance Professional
16. **CEBS** — Certified Employee Benefits Specialist
17. **CHRO** — Chief HR Officer
18. **COBRA** — Consolidated Omnibus Budget Reconciliation Act
19. **COLA** — Cost Of Living Allowance
20. **CSRA** — Civil Service Reform Act
21. **DBP** — Defined Benefits plan
22. **DCP** — Defined Contribution Plan
23. **DHS** — Department of Homeland Security
24. **DOB** — Date of Birth
25. **DOL** — Department of Labor
26. **DOT** — Dictionary of Occupational Titles
27. **EAP** — Employee Assistance Program
28. **EBSA** — Employee Benefits Security Administration
29. **EE** — Eligible Employee
30. **EEO** — Equal Employment Opportunity
31. **EEOC** — Equal Employment Opportunity Commission
32. **EEVS** — Electronic Employment Verification System
33. **EGTRRA** — The Economic Growth and Tax Relief Reconciliation Act of 2001
34. **EO 11246** — Executive Order 11246
35. **EPA** — Equal Pay Act
36. **EPO** — Employment Process Outsourcing
37. **EPPA** — Employee Polygraph Protection Act
38. **EQ** — Emotional Quotient
39. **ERISA** — Employee Retirement Income Security Act
40. **ERP** — Enterprise Resource Planning
41. **ESOP** — Employee Stock Ownership Plan
42. **FACTA** — Fair and Accurate Credit Transactions Act
43. **FCRA** — Fair Credit Reporting Act

| | | |
|---|---|---|
| 44. | **FICA** | Federal Insurance Contributions Act |
| 45. | **FLSA** | Fair Labor Standards Act |
| 46. | **FMLA** | Family and Medical Leave Act |
| 47. | **FSA** | Flexible Savings Account |
| 48. | **FTE** | Full-Time Equivalent |
| 49. | **FUTA** | Federal Unemployment Tax Act |
| 50. | **GPHR** | Global Professional in Human Resources |
| 51. | **HCE** | Highly Compensated Employees |
| 52. | **HCS** | Hazard Communication Standard |
| 53. | **HDHP** | High Deductible Health Plan |
| 54. | **HIPAA** | Health Insurance Portability and Accountability Act |
| 55. | **HMO** | Health Maintenance Organization |
| 56. | **HRA** | Health Reimbursement Account or (HCRA - "C" = Care) |
| 57. | **HRCI** | Human Resources Certification Institute |
| 58. | **HRD** | Human Resources Development |
| 59. | **HRIS** | Human Resources Information System |
| 60. | **HRM** | Human Resources Management |
| 61. | **HRMS** | Human Resources Management System |
| 62. | **HSA** | Health Savings Account |
| 63. | **I-9** | I-9 Form |
| 64. | **IBB** | Interest Based Bargaining |
| 65. | **ICE** | Immigration and Customs Enforcement |
| 66. | **IHRM** | International Association of HR Management |
| 67. | **IRA** | Individual Retirement Account |
| 68. | **IRCA** | Immigration Reform and Control Act |
| 69. | **JSA** | Job Safety Analysis |
| 70. | **KSA** | Knowledge, Skills and Abilities (or sometimes "Attitudes") |
| 71. | **LMRA** | Labor Management Relations Act (Taft Hartley) |
| 72. | **LMRDA** | Labor Management Reporting & Disclosure Act (Landrum Griffith) |
| 73. | **LOA** | Leave of Absence |
| 74. | **LOTO** | Lock-Out, Tag-Out |
| 75. | **LTD** | Long Term Disability |
| 76. | **LWOP** | Leave Without Pay |
| 77. | **MBO** | Management By Objectives |
| 78. | **MSDS** | Material Safety Data Sheet |
| 79. | **MSHA** | Mining Safety & Health Administration |
| 80. | **NLRA** | National Labor Relations Act |
| 81. | **NLRB** | National Labor Relations Board |
| 82. | **OD** | Organizational Development |
| 83. | **OFCCP** | Office of Federal Contract Compliance Programs |
| 84. | **OJT** | On The Job Training |
| 85. | **OPM** | Office of Personnel Management |
| 86. | **OSHA** | Occupational Safety & Health Administration |
| 87. | **OWBPA** | Older Workers Benefit Protection Act of 1990 |
| 88. | **PBGC** | Pension Benefit Guarantee Corporation |
| 89. | **PERT** | Project Evaluation & Review Technique |

| 90. | **PHI** | Protected Health Information |
| 91. | **PHR** | Professional in Human Resources |
| 92. | **PIE** | Period of Initial Eligibility |
| 93. | **PIP** | Performance Improvement Plan |
| 94. | **POLC** | Planning, Organizing, Leading, Controlling |
| 95. | **PPO** | Preferred Provider Organization |
| 96. | **QDRO** | Qualified Domestic Relations Order |
| 97. | **RIF** | Reduction in Force |
| 98. | **RONA** | Return on Net Assets |
| 99. | **SARBOX** | Sarbanes-Oxley Act of 2002 |
| 100. | **SHRM** | Society for Human Resource Management |
| 101. | **SIMPLE** | Savings Investment Match Plans for Employees |
| 102. | **SLEP** | Sick Leave Exchange Program |
| 103. | **SMART** | Specific, Measureable, Attainable, Realistic, and Timely |
| 104. | **SME** | Subject Matter Expert |
| 105. | **SNE** | Salaried, Non-Exempt Employee |
| 106. | **SOX** | Sarbanes-Oxley Act of 2002 (alternate acronym) |
| 107. | **SPD** | Summary Plan Description |
| 108. | **SPHR** | Senior Professional in Human Resources |
| 109. | **SRA** | Salary Reduction Agreement |
| 110. | **SSA** | Social Security Administration |
| 111. | **STD** | Short Term Disability |
| 112. | **SUTA** | State Unemployment Tax Act |
| 113. | **SWOT** | Strengths, Weaknesses, Opportunities, Threats |
| 114. | **TDA** | Tax-Deferred Annuities |
| 115. | **TIPS** | Threaten, Interrogate, Promise, Spy |
| 116. | **TQM** | Total Quality Management |
| 117. | **TSA** | Tax-Sheltered Annuities |
| 118. | **UGESP** | Uniform Guidelines on Employee Selection Procedures |
| 119. | **UI** | Unemployment Insurance |
| 120. | **ULP** | Unfair Labor Practice |
| 121. | **USCIS** | United States Customs and Immigration Services |
| 122. | **USERRA** | Uniformed Services Employment Reemployment Rights Act |
| 123. | **WARN** | Workers Adjustment and Retraining Notification Act |
| 124. | **WBT** | Web Based Training |
| 125. | **ZBB** | Zero Based Budgeting |

# Appendix B - Glossary of Terms

- **Ability To Pay -** This term is found in labor negotiations and refers to the ability of an organization to afford a wage or benefit cost increase.
- **Accretions -** Employees added to the bargaining unit once a union is certified as a representative of the bargaining unit.
- **Accidental Death And Dismemberment (AD&D) -** This describes common group benefit plan coverage where insurance pays for loss of a covered individual's permanent disfigurement, permanent loss of, or loss of use of a member or function of the body, or death.
- **Accrual Of Benefits -** As found in pension (defined benefit) plans, is the accumulation and counting of pension credits for years of experience, age, and earnings. In profit sharing plans (defined contribution), it is the vesting of funds accumulated in personal accounts.
- **Action Learning -** This is a continuous process of learning and reflection with the intention of getting something done. Learning is centered around the need to find a solution to a real problem… closely approximates the "scientific method." The six steps are:
    1. Formulate Hypothesis (an idea or concept)
    2. Design Experiment (consider ways of testing truth or validity of idea or concept)
    3. Apply in Practice (put into effect, test of validity or truth)
    4. Observe Results (collect and process data on outcomes of test)
    5. Analyze Results (make sense of data)
    6. Compare Analysis (relate analysis to original hypothesis)
- **Accumulated Funding Deficiency -** In the United States, this is the amount by which the accumulated promises of a Pension Plan as compared to the funds available do not meet certain minimum funding standards.
- **Acquisition -** When one organization purchases another, with the surviving organization being the purchaser. (As opposed to a Merger, where both organizations might change forms.) Acquisitions may be of two types - purchase of assets or purchase of stock.
- **Across-The-Board Increase -** A wage or salary increase where either a flat rate (common number of cents/hour) or a common percentage of salary is used. Also called a General Increase.
- **Actuary -** In life insurance, this is a professional who calculates mortality rates, morbidity rates, lapse rates, premium rates, policy reserves and other values. In pension work, a professional who applies these and other principles to calculate retirement plan obligations.
- **ADA, Americans With Disabilities Act -** National law forbidding discrimination against employees on the basis of disability and requiring reasonable accommodations for qualified disabled employees. The ADA is enforced by the Equal Opportunities Employment Commission (EEOC) and by private lawsuit.
- **ADDIE -** Analysis, Design, Development, Implement, Evaluate
- **ADEA, Age Discrimination -** In the United States, the Age Discrimination in Employment Act of 1967 protects employment rights of individuals age 40 and over.
- **Administrative Law Judge (ALJ) -** A civil service appointee of the National Labor Relations Board who conducts unfair labor practice hearings in the region where such cases originate.
- **Administrative Services Only (ASO) -** Common to health welfare plans, where an organization employs an outside organization to provide administrative services for self-funded plans. The ASO Contract or provider provides claim and policy administration, but the purchasing organization retains financial responsibility. ASO providers are also called 3$^{rd}$ Party Administrators.

- **Adverse Impact** - This is where a not obviously discriminatory practice affects a protected group of employees.
- **Advisory Arbitration** - Form of arbitration often referred to as fact finding where the decision of the arbitrator is not binding.
- **Age Discrimination** - In the United States, an employer is prohibited from treating individuals over age 40 differently because of their age.
- **Agency Shop** - A contract provision under which employees who do not join the union are required to pay a collective bargaining service fee instead. This service fee is usually the same as monthly dues. In some states public workers choose to pay service fee based on a percentage of the Union's budget spent on representing the bargaining unit's time and money spent on organizing and political action, not considered to be directly representing members.
- **All-Salaried Work Force** - A pay policy whereby all employees are paid on a salaried basis and all pay is defined in the same terms, such as a monthly or annual salary. Note: employees not meeting the salary-exempt test, as defined by FLSA, must still be paid time-and-one-half for all hours worked over 40 in a workweek.
- **Alter Ego Employer** - An employer who changes the name and outward appearance of a business but is in fact the same employer. An employer cannot rid himself of his obligation to recognize the legitimate bargaining representative through an alter ego.
- **Analysis Phase** - First of the Instructional System Design phases (ADDIE). The purpose of this phase is to determine what the job holder must know or do on the job and to determine training needs. Also see front-end analysis.
- **Andragogy** - Describes the theory of adult learning.
- **Annual Benefits Statements Under The Employee Retirement Income Security Act Of 1974 (ERISA)** - Employers are required to provide participants in qualified plans specific information about the status of their projected pension income or account balances.
- **Annuity** - A form of investment plan usually provided as a retirement plan that provides for income for a specified period of time, such as a number of years or for life.
- **Applicant tracking system** Known simply as ATS, it's computer software designed to help companies recruit employees more efficiently.
- **Aptitude** - The ability of an individual to acquire a new skill or show the potential for acquiring a skill when given the opportunity and proper training.
- **Arbitration** - A method of settling a labor-management dispute by having an impartial third party decide the issue. The decision of the third party (arbitrator) is usually binding.
- **Area Standards Picketing** - A form of picketing with the purpose of encouraging an employer to observe the standards in that industry in that locality. This kind of picketing has formed legal restrictions than picketing to force an employer to recognize a union or to impress employees' non-economic benefits.
- **Areawide Bargaining** - Collective bargaining agreement which covers all the unionized employers and their employees in a specific geographical and industrial setting.
- **Area Wage Surveys** - These are standard survey formats used across geographic boundaries so that consistent reporting can illustrate the same jobs and their different pay in various geographic areas.
- **Arithmetic Mean** - Arithmetic Mean (as defined by the U.S. DOL) is the rate of wages to be determined, to the extent feasible, by adding the wages paid to workers similarly employed in the area of intended employment and dividing the total by the number of such workers. This will, by definition of the term arithmetic mean, usually require computing a weighted average.
- **Association Agreements** - A collective bargaining agreement which governs a group of employers who ban together for mutual aid when bargaining with labor organizations. All employers belonging

to the association are bound by the agreement that was negotiated by the association and the union (AKA – coalition bargaining).

- **Attrition** - Reduction in the labor force of a company through natural causes such as voluntary quits, retirement, or death as opposed to layoffs.

- **Authorization Card** - A union card filled out by pro-union workers during a representation campaign. The card usually specifies the union as a collective bargaining agent of the employees and must be dated and signed. The NLRB will accept 30% of the employees signatures on cards or petitions as the "showing of interest" required to conduct an election. Usually unions will not file for an election unless a majority of the bargaining unit members have signed authorization cards.

- **Automatic Wage Adjustment** - Automatically increasing or decreasing wages according to a specific plan formula.

- **Automatic Wage Progression** - Automatically increasing wages after specified periods of service, until the employee reaches the top of his or her salary range. Automatic wage progression often is achieved through an automatic step-rate pay system.

- **Back Pay** - The amount of lost earnings accruing between the time a plaintiff terminates employment and a subsequent measuring date. Like Front Pay, it is not subject to the Civil Rights Act of 1991 $300,000 liability cap. Each can be awarded over and above any compensatory or punitive damages."

- **Background check** - Provides companies with a thorough understanding of an applicant's past actions. The term often is used inaccurately to describe the process of only checking references or an applicant's employment history.

- **Balance Sheet** - A financial statement of a company or other entity, showing what it owns (assets), what it owes (liabilities), and the owner's investment (shareholders equity) in the entity at a point in time such as the end of the fiscal year.

- **Balance Sheet Approach** - An accounting term that describes a situation where debits and credits must match. Often used to set expatriate compensation. The goal is to protect or equalize an expatriate's purchasing power while on assignment abroad.

- **Bargaining Agent** - Union designated by a government agency, such as the National Labor Relations Board, or recognized voluntarily by the employer, as the exclusive representative of all employees in the bargaining unit for purposes of collective bargaining.

- **Bargaining Rights** - The rights outlined in Section 7 of the National Labor Relations Act. Rights of workers to negotiate the terms and conditions of employment through chose representatives. The bargaining agent is designated by a majority of the workers in a bargaining unit to represent the group in collective bargaining.

- **Bargaining Unit** - A group of workers who bargain collectively with the employer. The unit may include all the workers in a single location or in a number of locations, or it may include only the workers in a single craft or department. Final unit is determined by the NLRB, or agreed to jointly by the union and the employer.

- **Base Rate** - The straight time rate of pay, excluding premiums and incentive bonuses.

- **Basic Plan With Major Medical** - A medical insurance plan that provides for coverage of almost all hospital and surgical charges and some other medical expenses, up to a specified amount without a deductible.

- **Basic Services** - Under dental insurance, dental services, such as fillings, periodontics and oral surgery, which are often covered at 80 percent of their reasonable and customary charges.

- **Behavior Based Appraisal** - Any performance assessment system that concentrates on the behaviors of those being rated (such as behavioral expectation scales, behaviorally anchored rating scales, or behavioral observation scales).

- **Benchmark Job** - A job that is commonly found and defined, used to make pay comparisons, either within the organization or to comparable jobs outside the organization. Pay data for these jobs are readily available in published surveys.

- **Benchmarking** - The process by which an organization seeks to identify top performing organizations and analyzes their strategies, policies and practices for the purpose of learning some or all of them.

- **Beneficiary** - The person, other than the plan member, designated to receive the benefit resulting from the death of an employee, such as the proceeds of a life or accident insurance policy or benefits from a pension plan.

- **Benefit Plans - Health Care** - The two types of health care benefit programs are indemnity programs and health maintenance organizations.

- **Benefit Plans – Retirement** - A Retirement Plan is an agreement on the part of management to provide a vehicle for the retirement income needs of employees. Such plans may be qualified or non-qualified for tax purposes.

- **Benefit Statements** - Each year employees must be given an individual benefit statement that explains accrued benefits to date and vesting status.

- **Benefits Cafeteria Plan** - A benefit program that offers a choice between taxable benefits, including cash, and non-taxable health and welfare benefits. The employee decides how his or her benefits dollars are to be used within the total limit of benefit costs agreed to by the employer.

- **Benefits Packages** - The total value of all non-cash compensation elements, including but not limited to income protection, health coverage, retirement savings, vacation and income supplements for employees, provided in whole or in part by employer payments.

- **Bennett Amendment** - An amendment to the Civil Rights Act of 1964 that states that it shall not be unlawful practice to differentiate compensation on the basis of sex if such differentiation is authorized by the Equal Pay Act.

- **Bereavement Leave** - Bereavement Leave or funeral leave provides time off for workers following the death of a family member.

- **Best Earnings Plan** - A benefit plan that calculates a recipient's retirement benefit based on the period during which the employee earned his or her highest income.

- **Beta** - A mathematical measure of the volatility of a particular stock, mutual fund, and/or portfolio in comparison with the entire market. Specifically, it measures the stock, fund or portfolio performance during the last 5 years. A beta of 1.0 indicates that an asset closely followed the market; a beta greater than 1.0 indicates a greater volatility than the market - a beta of less than 1.0 indicates that the asset was less volatile than the market.

- **Bi-weekly** - A bi-weekly pay period is one that occurs every two weeks (26 pay periods a year). Its pay day is on the same day every other week (for example, every other Friday). A bi-weekly pay period usually includes two full workweeks.

- **Birthday Rule** - A provision that specifies the manner in which benefits for dependent children are to be coordinated between two insurance plans. According to the birthday rule, benefits for dependent children will be paid by the plan of the parent whose birthday falls earlier in the year.

- **Blocking** - An NLRB decision not to proceed with an election in a bargaining unit where there are unresolved unfair labor practice charges.

- **Blog** - Short for "Web log," a blog is a way for computer users to exchange thoughts by posting messages online. A freewheeling electronic journal.

- **Blue Cross Plan** - A hospital expense insurance plan offered by a regionally-operated health care provider affiliated with a large national nonprofit health care organization. This plan typically provides benefits on a 'service-type' basis.

- **Blue Shield Plan** - A physician expense insurance plan offered by a regionally operated health care provider affiliated with a large national nonprofit health care organization. This plan typically provides benefits on a 'service-type' basis.

- **Bonafide Occupational Qualification (BFOQ)** - Typically refers to a valid job requirement, i.e., a knowledge, skill or an ability level that is required for competent job performance. Origin of the term BFOQ is found in Title VII of the Civil Rights Act (1964).

- **Bonus (Pay Plans)** - Plans that award cash or other items of value, such as stock or stock options, based on accomplishments achieved. Incentive plans are 'forward' looking; bonus plans are 'backward' looking.

- **Book Unit Award Plan** - A type of long-term incentive plan, whereby an employee is awarded stock valued at the book value per share. In a book value appreciation plan an increase in the book value of the stock accrues to the benefit of the employee.

- **Boycott** - A concerted refusal to work for, purchase from, or handle the products of an employer. Where the action is directed against the employer directly involved in the labor dispute, it is termed a primary boycott. In a secondary boycott, the action is directed against a neutral employer in an attempt to get him/her to stop doing business with the company with which the union is having a dispute. Secondary boycotts are illegal under the Taft Hartley Act.

- **Break In Service** - The length of time between the date on which an employee leaves an organization and the date on which the employee resumes working for that firm.

- **Broadbanding** - A pay structure that consolidates a large number of pay grades and salary ranges into much fewer bands with relatively wide salary ranges. These ranges typically have 100 percent or more differences between minimum and maximum. (e.g. $25,000 to $50,000)

- **Broker** - A person or firm who, for a fee or commission, acts as an intermediary between a buyer and seller. Usually a license is required (see also floor broker, agency).

- **Bureau Of Labor Statistics (BLS)** - This is the United States Federal Government's major fact-finding agency in the field of labor economics and statistics. Its responsibilities include finding data on wage, national pay, and industry surveys, such as the National Compensation Survey (NCS) and the Occupational Employment Survey (OES).

- **Business Agent (B.A., Union Representative)** - A full-time representative of a local union whose job is to represent members in the local.

- **Business Continuation Insurance** - An insurance type for closely held businesses, it is designed to provide funds to enable the remaining partners in a business, or the remaining stockholders in a closely-held corporation, to purchase the business interest of a deceased or disabled partner or stockholder.

- **Cafeteria Plan** - Also known as a flexible benefit plan, offers each employee several choices as to the types and or amounts of organization benefits. An employee is given a set amount, and he or she can choose how it is spent.

- **Call Back Pay** - A guarantee of pay for a minimum number of hours when employees, who are not scheduled to work and who are not on call, are called back to their work. They receive pay for at least the minimum number of hours established, even if they do not end up working up to those many hours.

- **Call-in Pay** - Compensation to workers who report for work and, for a variety of reasons, the employer decides to send back home. Examples of call in pay include: "show up pay" when a worker is called into work by error for overtime work and is sent back home; or, wages paid when the worker is required to report and there is insufficient work for a full day.

- **Canvass** - A method of talking individually to every member of a bargaining unit to either convey information, gather information on a survey, or plan for united action.

- **Canvass Coordinator** - A term sometimes used for the person at the "top" of a member-to-member action network. Other terms include "network coordinator" or "campaign coordinator". This person is responsible for establishing the one-on-one network and for planning and scheduling activities of the network.
- **Capital Expenditures** - Monies spent to acquire or upgrade physical assets such as buildings and machinery.
- **Captive Audience Meeting** - A union term for meetings of workers called by management and held on company time and property. Usually the purpose of these meetings is to try to persuade workers to vote against union representation.
- **Card Check** - Procedure whereby signed authorization cards are checked against a list of employees in a prospective bargaining unit to determine if the union has majority status. The employer may recognize the union on the basis of this card check without the necessity of a formal election. Often conducted by an outside party, e.g., respected member of the community.
- **Career Average** - A method used to calculate payout to a retiree in a defined-benefit pension plan by determining average annual salary. Years where less than 1,000 hours were worked may not always be included in the calculation.
- **Career Ladder** - This represents a series of outlined levels within a job category, where the nature of the work is comparable (e.g., engineering). The different levels represent the organization's requirements for increased skill, responsibility, and knowledge as the employee advances.
- **Case Management** - A cost-containment program designed to identify alternate, less costly methods of treatment for seriously ill patients without sacrificing the quality of care a patient receives. Also called large claim management or medical case management.
- **Case study** - A real-life situation that is presented under the guidance of an instructor or computer in order to achieve an instructional objective.
- **Cash Balance Pension Plan** - An established benefit plan resembling a defined contribution plan. The characteristics are usually annual or monthly account additions made at a predetermined rate (e.g., a percentage of pay). These contributions grow at a stated rate. Upon retirement or withdrawal, the participant may receive the full account balance in one lump sum, so long as the benefits are fully vested. The account balance may be used to purchase an annuity.
- **Cease and Desist Order** - An order to stop an action, to not repeat the action, and to take action to undo the wrong. A cease and desist order issued by the NLRB is a final order in an unfair labor practice case. It requires the guilty party to stop any conduct found to be in violation of the law and to take positive action to remedy the situation.
- **Central Tendency** - In statistics, central tendency is a measure THAT indicates the middle (mean, median or mode) of a data distribution.
- **Certificate Of Insurance** - A document given to the insured by the organization insurance plan. This document outlines the type and extent of coverage to which the organization member is entitled and the beneficiary of that coverage. Very often, the certificate will also contain a rundown of the contract terms as they affect individual organization members. See also master contract.
- **Certification** - Official designation by a labor board of a labor organization entitled to bargain an exclusive representative of employees in a certain unit.
- **Certification Bar** - The NLRB and many public sector agencies will prohibit another election in a bargaining unit for one year after a union has been certified following an election.
- **Certified Union** - A union designated by federal or state labor relations boards as the exclusive bargaining agent of a group of workers.
- **Charge** - Written statement of alleged unfair practices. Filing a charge with the NLRB State Labor Board is the first step in an unfair labor practice proceeding.
- **Charging Party** - The party filing a grievance or an unfair labor practice charge.

- **Check-Off** - A contract clause authorizing the company to deduct union dues from paychecks of those members who so authorize deductions. The company then transfers the money to the union.

- **Child Support** - There are two instances where an employer may become involved with an employee's Child Support: 1) Where there is a court order requiring the employer to withhold the support payment from the wages of the employee. Under the Child Support Enforcement Amendments of 1984 these payments take precedence over all other garnishment orders. 2) Under the Qualified Medical Child Support Order [QMCS], the child must be covered under the employer's health care plan to the extent that the plan covers dependents.

- **Civil Rights Act** - A provision in Title VII of the Civil Rights Act of 1964 that seeks to prohibit discrimination in all areas of employment on the basis of race, color, religion, national origin or sex.

- **Claim** - This is notification given to an insurance company asking for payment under the term of the insurance policy. May also be referred to as insurance claim.

- **Claim Frequency Rate** - In terms of health insurance calculations, the claim frequency rate is the anticipated percentage of insured that will make claims against the company and the number of claims they will make during a certain period of time. The claim frequency rate is used to calculate the estimated average cost of claims, which, in turn are used to establish premium rates.

- **Classification Method Of Job Evaluation** - A methodical system of job evaluation, where the focus is on the actual job as opposed to the individual carrying out the job. This evaluation method, therefore, determines the skills required to perform the job and measures the degree of difficulty of a particular job in comparison with another job through job analysis.

- **C-learning** - Classroom learning or conventional learning as compared to e-learning (electronic).

- **Cliff Vesting** - When, after a specified number of years of service, all benefits accrued vests without any gradual vesting before the set time.

- **Closed Shop** - An agreement between an employer and a union that, as a condition of employment, all employees must belong to the union before being hired. The employer agrees to retain only those employees who belong to a union. The closed shop was declared illegal by the Taft-Hartley Act.

- **Coach** - A person who instructs, demonstrates, directs, and prompts learners. Generally concerned with methods rather than concepts. There are four coaching roles/styles:
  1. hands-on - acting as an instructor for inexperienced learners
  2. hands-off - developing high performance in experienced learners
  3. supporter - helping learners use a flexible learning package
  4. qualifier - helping a learner develop a specific requirement for a competence-based or professional qualification

- **Coinsurance** - Found in most health insurance policies, this is an express requirement that the insured pay a particular percentage in excess of the deductible and of all eligible medical expenses.

- **COLA** - A Cost-of-Living Adjustment in which wage rates are periodically adjusted, usually upward, based upon changes in the cost of living.

- **Collective Bargaining** - A process which workers, through their bargaining committee, deal as a group to determine wages, hours and other conditions of employment. Normally, the result of collective bargaining is a written contract which covers all workers in the bargaining unit.

- **Commissions** - A commission is a sum of money paid to an employee based on the sale of a certain amount of goods or services. Commissions may be paid in the form of compulsory (or mandatory) service charges expressed as a specific percentage of the customer's bill (for example, charges imposed when a hotel rents out banquet facilities to a group). A commission may be paid in addition to or instead of any other method of pay. Some commission agreements include a "draw" on commissions. A draw is a fixed sum of money paid in advance of the settlement date for the earned commission pay.

- **Common Law Employees** - A common law employment relationship is deemed to exist in a situation where the person/company for whom services are being rendered the right to direct/control the person rendering that service. The said control must go beyond the employer having the right to control what the employee does. It must include the right to instruct the employee how to do it.

- **Common Review Date** - Also known as focal point, this is the date on which an entire organization will receive increases in pay. A company may, therefore, affect increases for all employees on June 1s. (Those employees who were hired half way through a cycle will normally have their increases prorated.)

- **Common Situs Picketing** - A form of picketing in which employees of a struck employer who work at a common site with employees of at least one neutral employer may picket only at their entrance to the worksite. The employees of neutral employers must enter the workplace through other gates. Picketing is restricted to the entrance of the struck employer so as not to encourage a secondary boycott on the part of the employees of a neutral employer.

- **Company Cars** - Excluded from Income. In general, when an employer provides a vehicle to an employee for business purposes, the value of the vehicle may be excluded from the employee's income. However, if the employee uses the vehicle for personal as well as business reasons, only the portion of the car's value that can be attributed to business use may be excluded.

- **Comparable Worth** - This is a doctrine that states that men and women who perform jobs of the same inherent value should be similarly compensated. *Comparable worth* focuses special attention on pay practices that perpetuate discrimination in the treatment of those holding female-dominated jobs whose content is similar but not equal to that of male-dominated jobs. *Comparable worth* means that women should be paid the same as men, excepting allowable differences (i.e. seniority plans, merit plans, production-based pay plans, or different establishments or locations).

- **Compa-Ratio** - The ratio of an employee's actual salary (the numerator) to the midpoint of the applicable (the denominator) salary range. To calculate an individual's compa-ratio, divide the actual salary by the midpoint of the assigned salary range.

- **Company Union** - An employee organization, usually in one company, that is dominated by management. The NLRA declared that such employer domination is an unfair labor practice.

- **Compensable Factor Degree** - In quantitative job evaluation plans, this is a term used to describe yardsticks used to measure and identify particular levels of compensable factor. Typically, there are about seven degrees for each factor.

- **Compensable Factor Weight** - In a job evaluation plan, this is the percentage, weight or influence, each compensable factor in a job is assigned.

- **Compensation** - A methodical approach to assigning a monetary value to employees in return for work performed. Compensation may include any or all of the following: base pay, overtime pay, commissions, stock option plans, merit pay, profit sharing, bonuses, housing allowance, vacations and all benefits.

- **Compensatory And Punitive Damages** - The intent of an award of compensatory damages is to compensate the plaintiff for loss suffered. To re-instate the plaintiff to the position in which they were before they suffered the loss. The intent of an award of punitive damages is to both punish the defendant and to act as a deterrent to others from similar behavior. Employees wrongfully dismissed may seek compensatory and punitive damages.

- **Compensatory Time Off** - Compensatory time off (comp time) is paid time off the job that is earned and accrued by an employee instead of immediate cash payment for working overtime hours. The use of comp time instead of overtime is limited by Section 7(o) of the FLSA to a public agency that is a state, a political subdivision of a state, or an interstate governmental agency.

- **Competency** - In terms of jobs, competency is an underlying behavior, skill, or characteristic of an employee. It is a good indicator of success.

- **Competency-based instruction** - Instruction that is organized around a set of learning objectives based upon the knowledge, skills and attitudes required to perform a set of skills called competencies. Evaluation of student success is based on competent performance of the skills.
- **Competitive Pay Policy** - Usually, this is a game plan that a company has, whereby they use the results of labor market surveys as means of evaluating and determining how to set pay levels.
- **Complaint** - Formal papers issued by the NLRB to start an unfair labor practice hearing before an Administrative Law Judge. The complaint states the basis for the Board's jurisdiction and the alleged unfair labor practice.
- **Compound Salary Growth Rate (CSGR)** - This term is employed to describe the growth rate, expressed as a percentage of a salary over a period of time.
- **Comprehensive Major Medical Insurance** - Health insurance coverage with a combination of both a major medical policy and a hospital expense policy.
- **Compressed Work-Weeks** - A term used to describe any alternative workweek schedules (10 hour days or more complex rotation resulting in extended weekends).
- **Compression** - Wage compression occurs when a new hire is paid the same as or more than employees with more seniority. It also occurs when employees are paid more than their supervisors. Often this occurs when the external labor market conflicts with a company's internal wage structure.
- **Computer-assisted instruction (CAI)** - The use of computers to aid in the delivery of instruction in which the system allows for remediation based on answers but not for a change in the underlying program structure
- **Concerted Activity** - The rights, protected by the National Labor Relations Act, of two or more employees to act in concert to form, join, or assist labor organizations in order to affect their wages, hours or work or working conditions.
- **Consent Decree** - An order of a court or agency which is entered into by agreement of all parties. In 1989 the General Executive Board of the IBT signed a consent decree which provided for rank and file elections of International Teamsters officers. This consent decree also established an Independent Review Board with the power to investigate and penalize officials judged to be corrupt.
- **Consent Election** - An election for union representation agreed to by management, employees, and the unions. The NLRB oversees the election.
- **Consolidated Omnibus Budget Reconciliation Act Of 1985 (COBRA)** - In the United States, this is a statute that mandates that employers sponsoring organization health plans continue to offer coverage under the organization plan to employees, their spouses, and dependent children who lost coverage due to the occurrence of a qualifying event (e.g. reduction in work hours, many types of termination of employment, death, and divorce).
- **Construct Validity** - The extent to which a measurement reflects the specific underlying construct it purports to assess. Construct validity requires gradual accumulation of evidence from a variety of sources.
- **Constructive Discharge** - A form of discrimination that forces a worker to "quit."
- **Consumer Picketing** - Picketing of a retail establishment that is legal if directed toward getting consumers not to buy a particular product of a supplier or of a producer with whom a labor dispute exists. Such picketing is illegal if it is aimed at getting customers to stop shopping at the store or at other parties, such as store employees or delivery to prevent personnel from crossing the picket line.
- **Content Validity** - The extent to which a measurement reflects the specific intended domain of content. Stated as a question: Do the ... thoroughly cover all relevant aspects of the conceptual domain they are intended to measure?
- **Contingent Compensation** - Similar to a BONUS, this is a payment or benefit that depends on the behavior and or performance of an employee.

- **Contingent staff** - Also known as "temps," contingent staff supplements a company's workforce without adding to its permanent ranks. Also known as independent contractors, contingent staff may be hired through a staffing firm or by the company that needs the temp and puts him on its own payroll.

- **Continuing Education (CE)** - An annual education requirement for many professionals to continue to receive certification in their respective field of work. CE credits are usually governed by various State Boards.

- **Contract Bar Doctrine** - Once a contract is executed, the NLRB does not (usually) permit a representation election in the unit covered by the contract until the contract expires up to a 3 year limit. This rule applies to a petition by another union to represent the employees, a petition filed by the employees to decertify, or a petition filed by the employer.

- **Contribution Limit** - In a defined contribution pension plan, this is the maximum allowed by law to be added to the participant's account. The annual contribution is inclusive of employer's contributions.

- **Control Point** - Within a given salary range, this is the point that represents the desired pay for a completely qualified and satisfactory performer (in a position or organization of jobs at the midpoint of the salary range).

- **Coordinated Bargaining** - Joint or cooperative efforts by several unions in dealing with an employer that has employees represented by each of the several unions.

- **Coordination Of Benefits (COB) Clause** - This is a clause included in health insurance policies that states that benefits will not be paid for amounts that are already covered by other organizational health insurers. The object of a coordination of benefits clause is to ensure that benefits from all eligible sources do not exceed 100% of permissible medical expenses. This also prevents an individual from profiting from duplicative organization health care coverage.

- **Corporate Campaign** - The use of strategic pressure on an employer's weak areas to gain leverage during a contract campaign or organizing drive. These campaigns involve analyzing an employer's social, financial, and political networks and mobilizing union members and community members in a comprehensive approach which does not rely on the strike alone as the basis of the union's power.

- **Corporate Culture** - The shared beliefs, norms and assumptions of an organization, which enable it to adapt to its external environment and to integrate its employees and units internally.

- **Craft Union** - A union whose membership is restricted to workers possessing a particular skill. Most craft unions today, however, have broadened their jurisdictions to include many occupations and skills not closely related to the originally designated craft.

- **Credited Service (ERISA Standard)** - This is the amount of service hours recognized in a benefit formula for the purpose of determining a pension. Typically, plans will credit one year of service for every year during which a beneficiary works a minimum of 1,000 hours.

- **Critical Incident** - A method of performance documentation in which the rater keeps a written record of on-the-job incidents and or behaviors, which may be examples of effective or ineffective behavior. The record is subsequently used as a source document to rate the employee. The purpose being to avoid subjective judgments, which feature in most ranking and rating methods.

- **Cross-training** - Providing training in several different areas or functions. This provides backup workers when the primary worker is unavailable.

- **Danger Pay** - Usually paid in addition to a hardship premium, danger pay is often given to expatriates who are required to live and work in a foreign country where a civil war, revolution, or some kind of terrorism could threaten the physical well-being of the expatriate. The State Department sets the rate and establishes where and when it is needed. The rate never surpasses 25% of the base salary. However, companies are free to exceed this rate if they so wish.

- **DART Rate:** Accident statistics that include, "Days Away, Restricted, and Transferred" (DART).

- **Day Rate** - A day rate is a flat sum paid for a day's work without regard to the number of hours worked in that day.
- **Decertification** - Withdrawal by a government agency, such as the National Labor Relations Board, of a union's official recognition as exclusive bargaining representative. The NLRB will withdraw certification if a majority of employees vote against union representative in a decertification election.
- **Deferred Benefits** - Non-monetary compensation that an employee may be entitled to at a future date, providing that he/she has accumulated enough credited years of service (for vesting purposes). These usually include, pension plans, 401(k) plans and stock option plans.
- **Deferred Compensation Plan** - Established by an employer in order to provide benefits to employees at a future date (e.g. upon the employee's retirement). Employers can provide future benefits to key employees through these nonqualified deferred compensation arrangements without the compliance costs or nondiscrimination restrictions placed on tax-qualified plans. Payable at some point in the future, these may be any number of compensation payments. May include voluntary or mandatory deferral of earned incentives.
- **Defined Benefit Plans** - There are basically two kinds of retirement plans: the defined benefit plan and the defined contribution plan. The defined benefit plan is one in which an employer comes up with a system that outlines how much an employee who is retiring will receive on a monthly basis for the rest of his/her life. The following are all taken into consideration when calculating the retirees' monthly stipend: years of employment with the employer, age and salary.
- **Defined Contribution Plans** - There are basically two kinds of retirement plans: the defined benefit plan and the defined contribution plan. The defined contribution plan is one in which an employer deposits a specific amount into an individual account for each employee. Accounts such as these are not required to specify how much is to be deposited into the account on a yearly basis, but they must specify how it is to be done. These kinds of plans are also known as Individual Account Plans.
- **Demotion** - When an employee is assigned to a position lower (in the company's hierarchy) than the employee's current position. This may be as a result of poor performance, company re-organization, or even at an employee's request.
- **Dependent Care Reimbursement Account** - Many flexible benefit programs include flexible spending accounts, which give employees the opportunity to set aside pretax funds for the reimbursement of eligible tax-favored welfare benefits. FSAs can be funded through salary reduction, employer contributions, or a combination of both. Employees can purchase additional benefits, pay health insurance deductibles and copayments, or pay for child care benefits with the money in their FSAs.
- **Dependent Care Spending Account** - Many flexible benefit programs include flexible spending accounts, which give employees the opportunity to set aside pretax funds for the reimbursement of eligible tax-favored welfare benefits. FSAs can be funded through salary reduction, employer contributions, or a combination of both. Employees can purchase additional benefits, pay health insurance deductibles and copayments, or pay for child care benefits with the money in their FSAs.
- **Dependent Variable** - This is a term used to describe something that must be numerically measured during a test or investigation, in order to answer a problem.
- **Diary / Log** - A method for gathering detailed information about a job by requiring the job incumbent to keep track of his or her specific activities during a determined period of time.
- **Dictionary Of Occupational Titles (DOT)** - Based on over 75,000 job analyses, this dictionary was developed and produced by the Department of Labor. It defines over 20,000 jobs.
- **Differential** - In expatriate compensation, this is used to describe an amount of money used to compensate for the discrepancies in costs between the home and the assignment locations.
- **Direct Cash Wages** - Direct cash wages are wages paid at an hourly rate by an employer directly to a tipped employee. Tips are not part of an employee's direct cash wages.

- **Direct Observation** - In order to thoroughly understand a job content, this method of job analysis involves the direct observation of employee(s) while they perform their duties. This method is usually used when analyzing production type jobs, which are very repetitive in nature.
- **Direct Pay / Cash Compensation** - Payments made to employees in direct exchange for their contributions to an organization (does not include bonuses, stock options, life insurance, 401K or other benefits).
- **Disability Income Insurance** - A kind of health insurance designed to provide periodic payments (usually monthly) in order to compensate insured people for a percentage of their income lost as a result of the disability. Also known as loss of time insurance.
- **Disability Under ADA** - Under the Americans with Disabilities Act of 1990 a disability is defined as a physical or other impairment, which substantially affects a person's ability to carry out one or more major life activities. In order for it to be said that a disability exists, it has to in fact substantially limit a major life activity. It is not enough that it could or might limit such an activity if corrective measures are not taken. A person whose impairment is not corrected by medication (or by other measures), therefore does not have an impairment as defined by the ADA.
- **Discretionary (Informal) Bonus Plan** - A bonus plan that is completely at the discretion of management. Management decides on the total amount of bonus to be dispersed, and the percentage each employee is to receive after a performance period. These types of bonuses have no pre-established formulas nor are there any guarantees attached.
- **Discrimination** - Disparate or unequal treatment of employees unrelated to qualifications, skills, or performance (e.g., race, religion, gender etc.). (1) The Civil Rights Act of 1964, the Age Discrimination and Employment Act of 1967 (ADEA), and the Equal Employment Opportunity Act of 1972 all forbid this kind of disparate treatment of employees.
- **Discrimination Testing** - This is a method used to determine whether benefits within a plan are being provided fairly and equally to a wide range of employees.
- **Disparate Treatment** - The treatment of members of a protected class of people (under Title VII of the Civil Rights Act or the Equal Pay Act), which is inconsistent with the provisions of the Civil Rights Act or the Equal Pay Act. This would include any company policy or practice that is deemed to be inconsistent with either of the Acts.
- **Distance learning** - (1) The use of any media for self-study. (2) A telecommunications-based instructional system evolved from the open learning movement used to overcome geographical "place-based" learning. (3) In its most common historical form, this refers to a broadcast of a lecture to distant locations, usually through video presentations.
- **Diversity** - Workplace diversity refers to race, gender, ethnicity, age, religion, and sexual orientation – attributes that carry with them a mix of legal requirements. However, socioeconomic status, education, national origin, and cultural backgrounds also are considered when designing a workforce that reflects the community at large.
- **DOL** - U.S. Department of Labor.
- **Domestic Partners** - Some organizations recognize, as a family unit for benefit purposes, committed relationships between two unrelated people (whether of the same or opposite sex). These relationships are similar to, but which does not involve, an official marriage.
- **Double Indemnity** - A type of death benefit policy that, if an insured's death is accidental / unnatural, pays an additional benefit that is equal to the basic benefit. Also known as accidental death benefit (ADB).
- **Downgrading** - The lowering of status, such as the lowering of a job to a lesser job grade or pay to a lower pay level.
- **Downsizing** - The reduction of the number of employees in the work force. This is usually an effort made by a company to reduce or eliminate inefficiencies or duplication of efforts.

- **Double Breasted Operation** - A condition where an employer operates two closely related companies—one with a union contract and one without. Under such operation, the employer will normally assign most of the work to the non-union segment of his two companies.
- **Draw** - A cash advance against future performance. May be recoverable or non-recoverable.
- **Drug Abuse** - Employees, who have been convicted of a felony drug offence, must be disciplined by their employers, per the Drug-Free Workplace Act (e.g. of discipline would be the completion of a drug abuse rehabilitation program).
- **Drugfree Workplace Act of 1988** - The Drug-Free Workplace Act of 1988 requires most federal government contractors and federal grantees to take specific steps to ensure a drug-free workplace. The law requires contractors to: 1. Develop and publish a policy statement notifying employees that the unlawful manufacture, distribution, dispensation, possession, or use of a controlled substance is prohibited in the workplace. 2. Establish a drug awareness program that tells employees about available drug counseling, rehabilitation, and the Employee Assistance Program (EAP), if the employer offers one. 3. Impose sanctions on employees who are convicted of a criminal drug offense, or require them to participate satisfactorily in a drug abuse assistance or rehabilitation program.
- **Dual Unionism** - Union members' activities on behalf of, or membership in, a rival union.
- **Due Diligence Process** - The objective of due diligence is to establish the financial and operating stability of a company prior to its being acquired.
- **Duty of Fair Representation (DFR)** - A union's obligation to represent all people in the bargaining unit as fairly and equally as possible. This requirement applies both in the creation and interpretation of collective bargaining agreements. A union is said to have violated its Duty of Fair Representation when a union's conduct toward a member of a collective bargaining unit is arbitrary, discriminatory, or in bad faith. A union steward, for example, may not ignore a grievance which has merit, nor can that grievance be processed in a perfunctory manner. It should be noted, however, that the employee in the bargaining unit has no absolute right to have a grievance taken to arbitration. The union is obligated to give fair representation to all union members, and also to collective bargaining unit members who have not joined the union in "right-to-work" states or in public service units.
- **Earnings** - Earnings include base pay, premium, overtime and bonuses. They are the total wages and or cash earned within a specific period of time.
- **Economic Strike** - A work stoppage by employees seeking economic benefits such as wages, hours, or other working conditions. This differs from a strike which is called solely to protect unfair labor practices.
- **Educational Benefits** - Companies may include educational benefits in their benefit package in a number of forms. The most common is an educational reimbursement plan, in which employees are reimbursed for the costs of schooling or training that can be shown to be related to their job or to their career in the company.
- **Effective Date** - Several definitions: (1) The date on which a health insurance policy and/or retirement plan kicks into effect and the insured party's coverage actually begins. (2) The date on which an increase in salary or pay rate goes into effect.
- **E-learning** - The use of innovative technologies and learning models to transform the way individuals and organizations acquire new skills and access knowledge.
- **Elder Care Programs** - Programs designed to assist the elderly in day-to-day activities. Usually this refers to the care of an elderly relative (financially, emotionally or even mentally).
- **Election Period** - This represents the 60 days, after having been notified of one's COBRA eligibility, during which an ex-employee may opt to accept the continuation of health coverage or decline.
- **Elective Contributions Or Elective Deferrals** - Contributions made to an employee's 401(k) plan, made by an employer on the behalf of the employee. Contributions are made with before tax monies from a reduction in the employee's pay check.

- **Eligibility Date -** This is the date on which an employee and/or his or her dependents are eligible for benefits.
- **Employee Assistance Programs -** An Employee Assistance Program (EAP) is an employer-initiated program to assist employees in dealing with problems such as substance abuse, marital discord, and employment problems.
- **Employee Retirement Income Security Act Of 1974 (ERISA) -** A Federal statute that establishes the following: (1) Rights of beneficiaries to pension benefits. (2) Standards that must be followed when investing pension plan assets. (3) Requirements that must be met before the disclosure of pension provisions and or funding. This law requires that persons engaged in the administration and management of private pensions act with the care, skill, prudence, and diligence that a prudent person familiar with such matters would use. The law also sets up an insurance program under the Pension Benefit Guarantee Corporation (PBGC) which guarantees some pension benefits even if a plan becomes bankrupt.
- **Employee Stock Option Plan (ESOP) -** A contract between a company and an employee giving the employee the right to purchase a specific number of shares in the company for a fixed price, during a certain period of time. Employee Stock Option Plans should not be confused with the term Employee Stock Ownership Plans (also ESOPs), which are retirement plans.
- **Employee Stock Ownership Plan (ESOP) -** Typically, this is benefit plan that requires that an employee meet certain requirements in order to participate and that has a portion of its investments (if not all) on company stock. An Employee Stock Ownership Plan (ESOP) is a type of defined contribution retirement plan in which the account of the employee consists of company stock.
- **Employment branding -** A strategy designed to make an organization appealing as a good place to work, this targeted marketing effort – online and off – attempts to shape the perceptions of potential employees, current employees and, in many cases, the public at large.
- **Equal Employment Opportunity Commission (EEOC) -** The purpose of the Equal Employment Opportunity Commission (EEOC) is to administer the various discrimination laws of the federal government. EEOC has the authority to investigate and conciliate charges of discrimination because of race, color, religion, sex, or national origin by employers, unions, employment agencies, and joint apprenticeship or training committees.
- **Equal Pay Act Of 1963 -** Makes gender based differentials in pay (wage discrimination) illegal, for jobs that are similar in terms of qualification requirements and that are performed under similar working conditions
- **Equal Pay For Comparable Work -** This doctrine goes beyond the Equal Pay Act of 1963. It states that women must be paid the same in a female dominated job type as a man for a job that is substantially of the same value in a male dominated job type. This doctrine is in effect saying that job value / worth can be measured.
- **E-Recruiting -** Recruiting services provided over the Internet are called e-Recruiting and offer the ability for job seekers to log in and post their resumes. Similarly, organizations may post job openings with these online services, using email and chat boards to further communication. Typically, the Internet service provider chargers the organization a fee for posting the open position information.
- **Ergonomics -** A methodical application of known information about every aspect (physical, psychological and social attributes) of human beings to the establishment and use of everything that may affect a person's working condition. This includes working environment, layout, training, the organization of the work-load and the job itself.
- **ERISA -** The Employee Retirement Income Security Act of 1974 (ERISA) was passed to ensure that pensions offered by private-industry employers met certain standards and were received by employees. ERISA does not require employers to offer pension programs. But ERISA does require that those who offer pension programs follow certain rules if they want favorable tax treatment for

their contributions and employee's deferral of income. ERISA's four basic requirements cover participation, vesting, funding and fiduciary duties.

- **Error And Omissions (E&O) Insurance** - A type of insurance which is designed to cover claims resulting from negligent acts and or mistakes of an insurance agent, including but not limited to (1) his or negligent acts or omissions or (2) mistakes made by individuals for whom the agent is vicariously liable.

- **Escalator Clause** - Union contract provision for the raising and lowering of wages according to changes in the cost of living index or a similar standard; most commonly referred to as a Cost of Living Adjustment (COLA).

- **Escape Clause** - A provision in maintenance of membership union contracts giving union members an "escape period" during which they may resign from union membership. Members who do not exercise this option must remain members for the duration of the contract.

- **Evidence Of Insurability** - This is proof that an individual is an insurable risk.

- **Excelsior List** - Established in the case of "Excelsior Underwear", the list of names and addresses of employees eligible to vote in a union election. It is normally provided by the employer to the union within ten days after the election date has been set or agreed upon at the NLRB.

- **Exclusive Bargaining Rights** - The right of a union which has been certified by the NLRB or other government agency to be the only union representing a particular bargaining unit.

- **Excess Benefit Plans** - Excess Benefit Plans are one form of non-qualified deferred compensation arrangements to supplement other retirement benefits for highly compensated executives. These plans are initiated in order to attract retain and attract motivated executives. They may also be used for early retirement, takeovers, and firing of top executives.

- **Exempt** - An exempt employee is one who is not entitled to the minimum wage and/or overtime pay protections of the FLSA. These employees are typically paid on salary.

- **Executive Order 10988** - Issued by President John F. Kennedy in 1962, the order recognizes the rights of federal employees to bargain with management.

- **Exempt Employee** - An employee who is not covered by the Fair Labor Standards Act and is therefore not eligible for time-and-one-half monetary payments for overtime. Exempt employees are generally paid a salary rather than an hourly rate.

- **Expatriate** - Also known as an international assignee or international staff, this is an individual who has been assigned to a country other than his or her home base for a period of time.

- **Expectancy Theory** - This is a theory that states that individuals make choices according to what they anticipate will give them the most payoffs. When applied to salaries, it follows that employees must hold the belief that the greater the effort that they make, the better their performance will be (the greater their results) and therefore the higher the salary they will command.

- **Expedited Arbitration** - An effort to streamline the arbitration hearing by reducing both time and cost. Transcripts and post hearing briefs are usually eliminated. Often the arbitrator issues a decision upon the completion of the hearing or shortly thereafter.

- **Experience Rating** - This rating system makes use of a group's premium and their claim experience to establish premium rates. Depending on the previous year's claim experience the insured party's premium will go up or down. See blended rates and manual rates.

- **Experiential learning** - A learning activity having a behavioral based hierarchy that allows the student to experience and practice job related tasks and functions during a training session.

- **External Equity** - The measure of a company's pay scales (pay levels or the going market rate) compared to the rate of other similar companies. External equity indicates that a company's pay levels are comparable to the market rate.

- **Extrinsic Rewards** - Rewards related to work and which is received for performance that can be measured in monetary terms. Contrast with intrinsic rewards, which stem from personal satisfaction stemming from a job well done.
- **Facilitator** - A person who makes it easier for learners to learn by attempting to discover what a learner is interested in knowing, and then determines the best way to make that information available to the learner by providing the knowledge, systems, or materials which enable the learner to perform a task more effectively. This is done by listening, asking questions, providing ideas, suggesting alternatives, and identifying possible resources.
- **Factor Comparison Method** - A method of evaluating jobs whereby a series of job rankings are performed in order to establish which particular job incorporates the most or the least of the factors considered to be compensable.
- **Fair Credit Reporting Act (FCRA)** - A federal law meant to ensure that consumer-reporting agencies are fair in their reporting (especially where the consumer's right to privacy is concerned. See consumer-reporting agency.
- **Fair Labor Standards Act Of 1938 (FLSA)** - The 1938 federal Wage-Hour Law which establishes minimum wage, maximum weekly hours and overtime pay requirements in industries engaged in interstate commerce.
- **Fair Share** - Under a union security clause of a union contract, the amount a nonunion member must contribute to a union to support collective bargaining activities. This arrangement is justified on the grounds that the union is obliged to represent all employees faithfully.
- **Family and Medical Leave Act (FMLA)** - Federal law establishing a basic floor of 12 weeks of unpaid family and medical leave in any 12-month period to deal with birth or adoption of a child, to care for an immediate family member with a "serious health condition", or to receive care when the employee is unable to work because of his or her own "serious health condition."
- **Federal Mediation and Conciliation Service (FMCS)** - Independent agency created by the Taft-Hartley Act in 1947 to mediate labor disputes which substantially affect interstate commerce.
- **Federal Service Impasse Panel** - In federal employment, it provides assistance in resolving negotiating impasses. The various techniques it employs are to serve as a substitute for the right to strike.
- **Federal Unemployment Tax Act** - FUTA, as it is commonly known, imposes tax on employers in order to pay for the unemployment benefits system. The tax represents the wages paid to employees.
- **Fee Basis** - Under FLSA, administrative and professional employees may be paid on a fee basis within the meaning of these regulations if the employee is paid an agreed upon sum for a single job regardless of the time required for its completion. These payments resemble piecework payments.
- **Fee Schedule Basis** - Compensation plan found in HMOs and PPOs whereby physicians are paid a pre-established amount for specific services that they provide. See Capitation basis.
- **FICA** - The Federal Insurance Contributions Act established the payroll deduction of OASDI and Medicare taxes from employers and employees.
- **Fixed Benefit Retirement Plan** - A type of retirement plan providing benefits only on a fixed amount or at a fixed percentage # such as 1 percent of monthly salary times the number of years of credited employment or 25 percent of the employee's average pay over the last few years prior to retirement.
- **Flexible Benefit Plan** - A benefit program under Section 125 of the Internal Revenue Code that offers employees a choice between permissible taxable benefits, including cash, and nontaxable health and welfare benefits such as life and health insurance, vacation pay, retirement plans and child care.
- **Flexible Spending Accounts** - Many flexible benefit programs include flexible spending accounts, which give employees the opportunity to set aside pretax funds for the reimbursement of eligible tax-

favored welfare benefits. FSAs can be funded through salary reduction, employer contributions or a combination of both. Employees can purchase additional benefits, pay health insurance deductibles and copayments, or pay for child care benefits with the money in their FSAs.

- **Flextime -** A system of working according to which people work a set number of hours within a fixed period of time, but can vary the time they start or finish work.
- **FLSA -** The Fair Labor Standards Act is a U.S. federal law that governs, amongst other things, child labor law, minimum wage and record-keeping requirements.
- **Form 5500 -** In the United States, a detailed report of membership and financial information pertaining to the operation of a pension plan. This report must be filed annually with the Internal Revenue Service.
- **401(K) Plans -** United States Internal Revenue Code Section 401(k) refers to Cash Or Deferred Arrangements. These are retirement plans typically described as a defined contribution plan used within private for profit firms.
- **403(B) Plans -** U.S. Internal Revenue Code Section 403(b) refers to Tax Sheltered Annuity Plans for nonprofit and public firms.
- **Free Riders -** Used in an open shop to refer to non-union members who receive all the benefits derived from collective bargaining without paying union dues or equivalent fees.
- **Fringe Benefits -** Non-salary employee compensation.
- **Front Pay -** The amount of lost earnings accruing between the time a plaintiff wins a legal judgment and is reinstated to his/her job or takes another job. Like back pay, front pay essentially is the equivalence of lost earnings. Neither Back Pay or Front Pay is subject to the Civil Rights Act of 1991 $300,000 liability cap. Each can be awarded over and above any compensatory or punitive damages.
- **FUTA -** The Federal Unemployment Tax Act (FUTA) levies an excise tax on employers to pay for the unemployment benefits system. The tax is a percentage of the wages paid to employees. Contributions to state unemployment funds are generally a credit against the FUTA tax.
- **Gainsharing / Gain-Sharing -** This type of variable pay ties bonuses or salary increases to increased productivity (vs. profit increases). This is performance-based incentive pay.
- **Garnishment -** Deductions made by an employer from an employee's wages and rendered to a creditor of the employee.
- **Gatekeeper -** The primary care provider responsible for managing medical treatment rendered to an enrollee of a health plan. Alternatively, this term has been used to describe third party monitoring of care to avoid excessive costs by allowing only appropriate and necessary care to be rendered.
- **Gender Discrimination -** Gender is one of the protected groups under the Civil Rights Act. Thus gender, in and of itself, may not be used in a whole range of human resource decisions regarding employees. In addition, the Equal Pay Act prohibits paying men and women differently for the same or substantially similar jobs, and Title IX prohibits discrimination by gender in educational institutions.
- **General Duty Clause -** OSHA requires each employer to, "furnish to each employee a place of employment which are free from recognized hazards that are causing or likely to cause death or serious physical harm."
- **General Strike -** A strike by all or most organized workers in a community or nation.
- **Geographic Salary Differentials -** The percent difference between pay levels for an occupation in two or more geographic areas. Due to the demand for and supply of labor, an employee may be paid more or less depending on where she works.
- **Glass Ceiling Analysis -** Refers to the analysis of how well (or poorly) women and minorities are doing at moving upwards in organizations. A Glass Ceiling Commission was authorized by law to study artificial barriers to the advancement of women and minorities in the workforce and to recommend means of overcoming such barriers.

- **Golden Handcuffs** - Rewards and penalties designed to discourage key employees from leaving a company.
- **Golden Parachutes** - A clause in an executive's employment contract specifying that he/she will receive large benefits in the event that the company is acquired and the executive's employment is terminated. These benefits can take the form of severance pay, a bonus, stock options, or a combination thereof.
- **Good Faith Bargaining** - Negotiations in which two parties meet and confer at reasonable times with open minds and the intention of reaching agreement over a new contract.
- **Goodwill** - Reputation for a product or service standard. A company's value over and above the physical property and accounts receivables.
- **Graded Vesting** - A vesting schedule under which an employee is partially vested, after a certain number of years of service, with the vesting schedule increasing until full vesting is achieved.
- **Grandfather Clause** - A contract provision specifying that employees on the payroll before a specified time will retain certain rights and benefits even though newer employees are not entitled to these rights.
- **Green Circle Rate** - An individual rate that is below the minimum of the established pay range for a specific job or pay grade.
- **Grievance** - Any type of worker dissatisfaction including violations of the collective bargaining agreement, violations of law, violations of employer policies, violations of fair treatment, and violations of past practices. The definition of a grievance is usually part of the contract, and therefore may vary from one contract to another.
- **Grievance Procedure** - A procedure usually established by a collective bargaining agreement to resolve disputes, problems or misunderstandings associated with the interpretation or application of the collective bargaining agreement. It consists of several steps with the last step of the procedure, usually being arbitration.
- **Gross Income** - Total income produced by a property before any expenses are deducted.
- **Group Grievance** - A grievance signed by many people in a workplace in order to show management that members as one in their opposition to a management's action.
- **Group Term Life Insurance** - A plan qualifying under Code Section 79 to provide employees with employer-paid life insurance coverage at little or no tax cost.
- **Group Universal Life Plan** - A form of group life insurance that combines term protection for designated beneficiaries with an investment element for the policyholder, which can be used to create nontaxable permanent insurance or to accumulate tax-deferred capital. Participation is entirely voluntary and the employee pays all premiums.
- **Handbook** - A document prepared specifically to provide guidance information. Handbooks are used for the presentation of general information, key benefits, policies, and general information about the employer
- **Hardship Distributions** - A withdrawal of an employee's contributions to a 401(k) plan prior to retirement at age 55 or attainment of age 591/2. A hardship withdrawal may be made only in cases of financial emergency provided there are no other sources available to meet the need the withdrawal is taxable as an early distribution and subject to a 10% excise tax.
- **Hazardous Duty Pay** - Work, which exposes the employee to a considerably greater risk than normal, working conditions. Pay is above normal rate tables due to the risk associated with each position and risks.
- **Headquarters Country** - The country where the center of operations or administration of a particular employer.

- **Health Care Reimbursement Account** - Allows employees to set aside pretax funds for eligible health care benefits such as physical exams, vision care and dental care, including deductibles and co-payments. See also Flexible Spending Accounts (FSAs).
- **Health Insurance** - Protection that provides payment of benefits for covered sickness or injury. Included under this heading are various types of insurance, such as accident insurance, disability income insurance, medical expense insurance, and accidental death and dismemberment insurance.
- **Health Insurance Portability And Accountability Act Of 1996 (HIPAA)** - The Health Information Portability and Accountability of Act demands that all HIPAA covered businesses prevent unauthorized access to "Protected Health Information" or PHI. PHI includes patients' names, addresses, and all information pertaining to the patients' health and payment records.
- **Health Maintenance Organization (HMO)** - A prepaid medical group practice plan that provides a comprehensive predetermined medical care benefit package. The government, medical schools, hospitals, employers, labor unions, consumer groups, insurance companies, can sponsor the HMO and hospital-medical plans. HMOs are both insurers and providers of health care.
- **Hierarchy Of Needs** - Abraham Maslow's classification of human needs and motives, ascending in a pyramid from the basic level of physiological needs, such as hunger and thirst, to the highest level of self-actualization.
- **Highly Compensated Employees** - Either a 5% owner or a person who earned more than $80,000 during the current or preceding year. Repeals rule treating highest paid officer as an HCE, the top-100 rule, and family aggregation rules in both the HCE definition and the $150,000 compensation cap. Discrimination in favor of this group is prohibited.
- **Hiring Bonus** - An extra sum of money provided at time of hire to entice an applicant to accept a job offer or to make up for compensation forfeited at the previous company.
- **Hiring Rate** - Refers to the wage or salary to which an employee is assigned upon entering the job.
- **Hiring Hall** - The process of the union dispatching workers to employers as needed. A hiring hall may be operated by a union alone or by an employer and union jointly. Hiring halls are monitored by the government to help prevent favoritism.
- **Hold Harmless Release** - A statement indicating that the individual will reimburse the insurance company if the claim is ever challenged and deemed to be fraudulent.
- **Holidays** - Days established by law or custom for which workers receive pay while absent from work. Law establishes statutory holidays. When the customary day tolls on a weekend a moveable holiday may be substituted for it on another day.
- **Home Country** - The expatriate's normal country of employment.
- **Homesourcing**: A euphemism for telecommuting. "Homesourced" workers who perform work at home on behalf of the company, from materials furnished directly or indirectly by the employer (AKA – **Homework**).
- **Host Country** - A nation in which representatives or organizations of another state are present because of government invitation and/or international agreement.
- **Hour Of Service/Work** - For purposes of retirement plans, an hour for which an employee is directly or indirectly paid by the employer for the performance of duties. An hour of overtime is still counted as only an hour of service, even though the pay for overtime may be higher. Hours during a leave of absence or a vacation with pay are counted.
- **Hours Of Work** - Standard hours worked in a year is 2,080 (52 weeks x 40 hours per week).
- **Hours Worked** - In general, hours worked includes all time an employee must be on duty, or on the employer's premises or at any other prescribed place of work. Also included is any additional time the employee is suffered or permitted (i.e., allowed) to work.
- **Hot Cargo Clauses** - Clauses in union contracts permitting employees to refuse to handle or work on goods shipped from a struck plant or to perform services benefiting an employer listed on a union

unfair list. Most hot cargo clauses were made illegal by the Taft-Hartley Act, but there are some exceptions.

- **Housevisits, Homecalls, and Housecalls** - Terms used to describe visits by union staff, volunteers, or organizing committee to the homes of workers they are attempting to organize. Such visits give organizers an opportunity to discuss the union and answer questions of unorganized workers in a relaxed and secure atmosphere.
- **HR Outsourcing** - A company entrusts HR operations to a third party. The outside HR service provider may take on specific traditional functions such as payroll, benefits administration and training. Or, it may handle broader assignments such as recruiting, call center staffing and applicant database management.
- **Human capital** - refers to the stock of productive skills and technical knowledge embodied in labor. An Adam Smith term. Smith saw human capital as skills, dexterity (physical, intellectual, psychological, etc.) and judgment.
- **Human Resource Development (HRD)** - An organized learning experience, conducted in a definite time period, to increase the possibility of improving job performance and growth.
- **Illegal Strike** - A strike that is called in violation of the law, such as a strike that ignores "cooling off" restrictions, or a strike that disregards a "no strike" agreement signed by the Union or imposed by a court of law.
- **Impartial Umpire** - Term often applied to a permanent arbitrator, named for the life of a union contract, and usually selected by mutual agreement. The term indicates his function of presiding over the union contract to enforce observance of it by both parties.
- **Impasse** - In general usage, a term referring to a situation where two parties cannot h agree on a solution to a dispute. In legal usage, if impasse is reached, the employer is legally permitted to unilaterally impose its latest offer.
- **Improshare** - Cost-saving group incentive plan in which a standard cost of production is established and the employees share in the cash savings of production costs under that amount. Improshare stands for improved productivity through sharing.
- **Incentive** - Additional pay (above and beyond the base salary or wage) awarded to an employee.
- **Incentive Compensation** - Rewarding the performance of an individual in an institution with added compensation, typically in the form of bonuses or percentage increments above the base salary.
- **Independent Contractors** - As distinguished from an employee by the IRS, the worker, not the employer, largely determines a person who works for another whose labor and how it is performed. Independent contractors pay their own taxes the employer does not, for example, pay Social Security or unemployment taxes for the worker.
- **Independent Review Board (IRB)** - The three-person board established as part of the 1989 consent decree signed by the International Brotherhood of Teamsters and the US Department of Justice as a settlement of the U.S. Government's RICO lawsuit. The IRB has the power to investigate and penalize officers it considers to be corrupt. The IRB has the power to investigate and penalize Teamster officials it considers to be corrupt.
- **Independent Variable** - A variable in a functional relation whose value determines the value or values of other variables, as x in the relation $y = 3x2$.
- **Indirect Labor** - Workforce not directly engaged in the manufacture of a product line.
- **Individual Account Plan** - A defined contribution plan or profit-sharing plan that provides an individual account for each participant, allows participants to choose, from a broad range of investment options, how their accounts will be invested, and whose benefits are based solely on the amount contributed to the participant's account, including income, expenses, gains and losses. Defined contribution retirement plans such, as 401(k) plans are examples of individual account plans.

- **Individual Retirement Account (IRA)** - Individuals, whether they are covered by a pension or not, are now permitted to save money on a tax-deferred basis in a qualified IRA plan. Although money can be withdrawn, a 10% penalty has been placed on those assets withdrawn prior to the individual turning 59 1/2, in addition to the normal taxes, which must be paid upon withdrawal.
- **Industrial Union** - A union whose membership includes all workers in a particular industry, regardless of the particular skills the worker exercises.
- **Informational Picketing** - Picketing done with the express intent not to cause a work stoppage, but to publicize either the existence of a labor dispute or information concerning the dispute. Picketing done with the express intent not to cause a work stoppage but to publicize either the existence of a labor dispute or information concerning the dispute.
- **Injunction** - A court order which either imposes restraints upon action, or directs that a specific action be taken and which is, in either case, backed by the courts power to hold disobedient parties in contempt.
- **Inside Strategy** - The use of mass grievances, working to rule, rolling sick-outs, informational picketing, and other forms of resistance designed to pressure an employer to meet the union's demands without the union resorting to a strike.
- **Insider** - A stockholder who owns 10% or more of a company, a member of the board of directors or an elected officer of a corporation, or anyone else who possesses information that is not publicly known about the company, but which is important in valuing its stock. Securities and Exchange Commission (SEC) regulations place restrictions on stock purchases and sales by insiders. Section 16 of the SEC regulations identifies 'insiders' as those precluded from profiting, unfairly from the sale and or purchase of company stock.
- **Insourcing** - The opposite of offshoring, insourcing is the transfer of foreign jobs to the United States.
- **Integrated Pension Plan** - A pension plan that is integrated with Social Security retirement benefits.
- **Intermittent Leave** - Leave taken in separate periods of time due to a single illness or injury. This is permitted under the FMLA.
- **Internal Equity** - Refers to the pay relationships among jobs.
- **Intervenor** - A union which wants to be on the ballot when another union has already petitioned for an election.
- **Intrinsic Motivation** - An incentive that originates from the behavior itself rather than from an external reward or reinforcement. Thus, intrinsically motivated behavior.
- **ISO 14001** - An environmental management standard that sets environmental management requirements. Its purpose is to help all kinds of organizations protect the environment, to prevent pollution, and to improve their overall environmental performance.
- **Job Action** - A concerted activity by employees designed to put pressure on the employer without resorting to a strike. Examples include: wearing T-shirts, buttons, or hats with union slogans, holding parking lot meetings, collective refusal of voluntary overtime, reporting to work in a group, petition signing, jamming phone lines, etc.
- **Job Analysis** - Systematic study of a job to discover its specifications, its mental, physical, and skill requirements, its relation to other jobs in your organization usually for wage-setting or job simplification purposes.
- **Job Descriptions** - A written summary describing a particular job classification or position that includes duties, qualifications, and responsibilities associated with a job.
- **Job design** - A process that results in a set of purposes, task characteristics, and duties based on the unique qualities of your organization and your employees.
- **Job Enlargement** - An increase in the number of tasks that an employee performs. It is associated with the design of jobs to reduce employee dissatisfaction.

- **Job Enrichment** - Act of making fuller or more meaningful or rewarding.
- **Job Evaluation** - The process of assessing job content and ranking jobs according to a consistent set of job characteristics and worker traits, such as skill, responsibility, experience etc. Commonly used for setting relative rates of pay.
- **Job Rate** - A job rate is a flat sum paid for doing a particular job without regard to the number of hours worked at that job.
- **Job Sharing** - Two people, typically in career-oriented professional positions, performing the tasks of one full-time position in order to enjoy more flexibility in their personal schedules, typically for child or dependent care. Salary and benefits are prorated.
- **Job Specifications** - A detailed, exact statement of particulars, especially a statement prescribing materials, dimensions, and quality of work.
- **Joint Committee or Panel** - A committee of equal numbers of union and management representatives established by a contract to hear grievances arising under the contract. If a committee is deadlocked on a grievance, the matter may be referred to a higher committee, to an arbitrator, or the employer and the union may be permitted economic recourse, depending on the wording of the contract.
- **Jurisdiction** - The specific industry, craft and/or geographical area which a local union is chartered to organize or represent.
- **Jurisdictional Dispute** - A conflict involving a dispute between two unions over which shall represent a group of employees in collective bargaining or as to which union's members shall perform a certain type of work.
- **Just Cause** - A reason an employer must give for any disciplinary action it takes against an employee. An employer must show just cause only if a contract requires it. Most contracts have just cause requirements which place the burden of proof for just cause on the employer.
- **Keogh Act** - The Self-Employed Individuals Tax Retirement Act of 1962 (also called HR-10 or the Keogh Act), and its subsequent amendments, made it possible for owner-employees of unincorporated businesses and other self-employed persons to be covered under qualified retirement plans. A tax deferred pension account available to the self-employed.
- **Key Employee** - A salaried employee who is among the highest paid 10 percent of all the employees employed by the employer.
- **Knowledge Based Pay** - Pay-for-knowledge rewards employees for increasing the depth and breadth of knowledge and skill and the utilization of those skills. Pay-for-knowledge is often an extension of work redesign efforts.
- **Knowledge Management** - Knowledge management is the name of a concept in which an enterprise consciously and comprehensively gathers, organizes, shares, and analyzes its knowledge in terms of resources, documents, and people skills.
- **Knowledge, Skills And Abilities (KSA)** - New hires and merit promotions are made on the basis of how applicants measure up to a set of factors, often called 'Knowledge, Skills, and Abilities' (KSAs) or 'Knowledge, Skills, Abilities and Other Characteristics (KSAOs).'
- **Knowledge supply chain** - A catchphrase coined to describe the vital connections between people that ultimately deliver qualified workers to the workforce.
- **L-M Reports** - The annual financial statement of income and expenses, including the salaries of union officers and staff. Unions are required by law to file with the Labor Management (LM) Division of the U.S. Department of Labor.
- **Landrum-Griffin Act of 1955** - Also known as the Labor-Management Reporting and Disclosure Act (LMRDA), it provides safeguards for individual union members, requires periodic reports by unions, and regulates union trusteeships and elections.

- **Lead Lag Structure Policy** - The practice of setting salary structures at the beginning of the year, to what the competition would reach at the middle of the year. This is based on competitive information and market research.

- **Leased Employees** - A three-party relationship whereby the user business purchases services of a worker, on a more or less full-time basis, from a business that pays the worker's salary. Any interrelationship between these parties can lead to an affiliated service group relationship, which is treated separately.

- **Lifetime Maximum** - The maximum amount of eligible medical expenses that the medical policy will pay for. This is during the lifetime of the insured.

- **Litigate** - To carry on a legal contest by a judicial process. For example, the employer will often go to the courts (litigate) to appeal a decision by the NLRB.

- **Living Wage** - A wage sufficient for a worker and family to subsist comfortably.

- **Local Area Network (LAN)** - An acronym for Local Area Network, LAN refers to a local network that connects computers located on the same floor or in the same building or nearby buildings.

- **Local Education Coordinator (LEC)** - In the Teamsters Union, a member designated by the local union and trained by the International Union to plan and implement educational programs for the members of the local.

- **Local National** - Employees hired by a local subsidiary or branch in the country of operation. Usually nationals of that country but may be citizens of any country.

- **Localization** - To become local, especially to become fixed in one area or part.

- **Lockout:** A suspension of work initiated by the employer as the result of a labor dispute. A lockout is the employer counterpart of a strike. Used primarily to pressure employees to accept the employer's terms in a new contract.

- **Long-Term Care** - A product designed to provide coverage for necessary diagnostic, preventative, therapeutic, rehabilitative, maintenance, or personal care services provided in a setting other than an acute care unit of a hospital, such as a nursing home or even one's own home. Also known as LTC insurance.

- **Made Whole** - A catchall phrase used in grievance and other legal action where a remedy is sought from an employer. Often used in discharge and discipline cases where the union seeks to have a worker who had been wrongly discharged or disciplined returned to work and reimbursed all wages, benefits, or other conditions lost due to an employer's unjustified action.

- **Maintenance of Membership** - Form of union security used in contract language under which the employee is not required to join a union but agrees to remain a member of the union for the duration of the contract if he/she is already a union member or does join the union during the life of the contract.

- **Managed Care** - A method by which insurance carriers attempt to manage healthcare costs by utilizing a pre-selected panel of physicians.

- **Managed Health Care** - A healthcare approach that delivers medical services while controlling cost and quality.

- **Managed Services:** The hiring of a third party, like a staffing firm, to run one or more of a company's HR functions or operations. It shares some characteristics with outsourcing but differs in that retained providers typically work at the client-employer's site.

- **Management By Objectives (MBO)** - A process by which management and employees set specific goals with feedback on goal progress.

- **Management Rights or Prerogatives** - The claimed rights of employers to control operational aspects of the workplace.

- **Mandatory Subject of Bargaining** - Those items included under wages, hours, and other terms and conditions of employment over which an employer must bargain. An employer may not make a change in a mandatory bargaining subject without providing prior notice to the union and an opportunity to bargain.

- **Mass Picketing** - Patrolling by large numbers of people in close formation, often preventing access to company premises.
- **Master Contract** - A union contract covering several companies in one industry.
- **Maximum Reasonable Compensation** - In the IRS determination of reasonable compensation for owner-managers, one of the main considerations is that of comparable wages. Maximum reasonable compensation would be the highest amount of compensation, both wages and bonus, which would be allowable to be used as a business expense for services rendered in comparable circumstances.
- **McCarran Ferguson Act** - The McCarran Ferguson Act allows employers to not include certain time and activities of employees, prior to and/or after work, as "work time." These activities are ones that are not required in order to accomplish the job. The most common of these is the time taken to commute to work. Examples of types of activities other than commuting that are non-compensable are: waiting to check in at the beginning of a workday or waiting in line for a paycheck at the conclusion of a shift.
- **Mean** - A mean is the result of dividing the sum of two or more quantities by the number of quantities.
- **Median** - One type of norm measure found by arranging the values in order and then selecting the one in the middle. Therefore, half of the numbers are less than the median, and half are higher than the median.
- **Mediation** - (Conciliation) The efforts of a third party to help parties to reach agreement in a labor dispute. Mediators help clarify issues and suggest possible solutions.
- **Medicaid** - An insurance plan funded by the government that provides medical coverage to individuals under age 65 who are low wage earners, and/or meet other criteria. Aide for those under age 65.
- **Medical Savings (Spending) Account (MSA)** - A savings account that can be used to pay for medical expenses that are not covered by insurance. The employee contributions to the plan are tax-deductible.
- **Medicare** - A medical plan that is available to those over age 65 and those with specific disabilities via the U.S. government through the Social Security Administration. There are two plans available through Medicare. Part A, provides for inpatient hospital services and post-hospital care. Part B, pays for medically necessary doctors' services, outpatient hospital services and a number of other medical services and supplies not covered under Medicare Part A. Care for those over age 65.
- **Member in Good Standing** - A union member in good standing is one who has fulfilled requirements for the organization and who has not voluntarily withdrawn from membership, been expelled, or suspended.
- **Member-to-Member Network** - A communications system designed to allow the leaders of a local union to communicate rapidly and personally with the members. A coordinator at the top of a pyramid communicates with approximately 10 leaders, each of whom communicates with approximately 10 members, each of whom may communicate with 10 other members, etc.
- **Mental Health Parity Act Of 1996** - Insurance plans that provide mental health benefits are not allowed to impose lifetime or annual dollar limits for mental health benefits that are less than those imposed on medical or surgical benefits. Substance abuse treatment is not included in these guidelines.
- **Merit Increase** - Increase in wages given to one employee by the employer to reward good performance. Unions often oppose merit increases because of a general lack of objective criteria for awarding increases, and thus allowing favoritism to enter into the decision to award the increase.

- **Metropolitan Statistical Areas (MSA)** - A geographic area consisting of a large population nucleus together with adjacent communities having a high degree of economic and social integration with the nucleus.
- **Midpoint** - The salary that is in the middle of a range of salaries.
- **Military Service Payments** - A salary payment agreement between an employee and employer when the employee is involved in such temporary duties as the National Guard or Reserve.
- **Minimum Wage** - The lowest allowable hourly-wage that an employer can pay an employee.
- **Minor** - Laws regarding work hours, work conditions and occupations for certain ages under 18 years of age.
- **Mode** - In a set of observations the worth that is most prevalent.
- **Money Purchase Plan** - A kind of defined contribution plan that utilizes a formula to determine the employer's contribution to the employees account. The formula and contribution are not related to profitability.
- **Moving And Relocation Expenses** - These expenses are paid for up front or reimbursed to an employee by the employer when the company needs to have that employee's skills utilized in another location.
- **Multiple Employee Welfare (MEWA)** - An employee benefit plan that is maintained by two or more employer groups to provide health and welfare benefits to the employees.
- **National Labor Relations Act Of 1935 (Wagner Act)** - A federal law giving employees the right to self-organize unions, bargain collectively through representatives of their own choosing. Federal law guaranteeing workers the right to participate in unions without management reprisals. It was modified in 1947 with the passage of the Taft-Hartley Act, and modified again in 1959 by the passage of the Landrum-Griffin Act.
- **National Labor Relations Board (NLRB)** - Agency created by the National Labor Relations Act, 1935, and continued through subsequent amendment, whose functions are to define the appropriate bargaining units, to hold elections, to determine whether a majority of workers want to be represented by a specific union or no union, to certify unions to represent employees, to interpret and apply the Act's provisions prohibiting certain employer and union unfair practices, and otherwise to administer the provisions of the Act.
- **National Mediation Board (NMB)** - Established under the Railway Labor Act, the NMB conducts representation elections, regulates major disputes, and appoints arbitrators and boards to decide minor disputes in the railway and airline industry.
- **Nearshoring** - Rather than offshoring – which involves transferring work to a firm located overseas – a company moves those jobs to a neighboring country. For a U.S. company, that means Mexico or Canada instead of India. The impetus for nearshoring is the same as with offshoring: lower costs.
- **Needs analysis / assessment** - A diagnosis that presents problems and future challenges that can be met through training or development.
- **No Raiding Pact** - An agreement between unions not to attempt to organize workers already under represented by another union.
- **Non-Compete Agreements** - A condition of an employment contract that states a specific time period that the employee cannot compete with the employer if the employee is terminated.
- **Noncash Incentives** - Incentives that are not a direct cash payment, such as comp time, a membership to a club and a reserved parking space.
- **Noncontributory Benefit Plan** - A term used when discussing employee benefit plans under which the employer pays, or contributes, the entire cost of the premium for benefits for the employees.
- **Nondiscrimination Rules** - An Internal Revenue code that states employee benefit plans are not to provide significantly greater benefits to higher paid employees and owners than to lower paid employees.

- **Nonexempt Employees / Non-exempt Employee** - Employees who are subject to the minimum wage and overtime pay provisions of the Fair Labor Standards Act.
- **Nonqualified Deferred Compensation Plan** - Typically used for senior executives and highly compensated employees, this retirement income plan does not meet the guidelines for a qualified plan, therefore they do not meet the criteria to be eligible for the tax advantages of a qualified plan.
- **Nonqualified Pension Plan** - A pension plan that does not meet IRS requirements, or receive the positive tax benefits, due to the increased benefits compared to what is allowable of a qualified plan.
- **Occasional Tasks** - Under the Fair Labor Standards Act (FLSA) new regulations, occasional tasks are infrequently recurring tasks that cannot practicably be performed by nonexempt employees, but are the means for an exempt employee to properly carry out exempt functions and responsibilities, are considered exempt work.
- **Occupational Safety and Health Act (OSHA)** - The Law which authorizes the OSHA agency to set standards, obligates employers to provide a safe workplace, and provides for enforcement of the standards. The law encourages the states to develop their own safety laws which displace the federal law.
- **Office Of Federal Contract Compliance Programs (OFCCP)** - Under the Vocational Rehabilitation Act of 1973, the agency is to enforce affirmative action for government contractors.
- **Offshoring**: - Moving work to an overseas location to take advantage of lower-cost labor.
- **On-Call Pay** - A pre-determined amount of compensation that is provided to an employee that is willing to report to work on short notice.
- **On-the-Job-Training (OJT)** - Formal training for learning the skills and knowledge to perform a job that takes place in the actual work environment.
- **Open Ended Questionnaire** - A technique used when analyzing a job using a written set of questions that requires a narrative response.
- **Open Pay System** - A compensation program that makes public salary information, including individual wage levels.
- **Open Shop** - Where employees do not have to belong to the union or pay dues to secure or retain employment in a company, even though there may be a collective bargaining agreement. The Union is obligated by law to represent members and non-members equally regardless of whether it is an open shop or a union shop.
- **Organizational review/analysis** - An analysis detailing what your organization is capable of doing in view of its resource profile. The objective is to match your corporate/organizational objectives and strategies with the realities that surround your organization and its leaders/managers.
- **Organizing Committee** - The employees in a non-union shop who are designated to represent their co-workers during the representation campaign. organizing committee members, among other things, usually sign up their coworkers on authorization cards or petitions, hand out leaflets, attend meetings and visit workers at home to gain support for the union effort.
- **Organizing Model of Unions** - The concept that the primary function of a union's officers and staff is to organize members to exert collective power to solve problems. This is in contrast to the Service Model of Unions.
- **Out Of Plan Services** - Healthcare providers that are not participating in a health plans network, therefore the insurer would require higher co pays or deductibles.
- **Out Of Pocket Limit** - The dollar amount that an employee is responsible for paying for medical care during a certain period of time, usually a calendar year, then the insurer pays 100% once the out of pocket limit has been paid.
- **Outplacement Assistance** - Counseling to employees that have laid off that can include assistance in regaining self-confidence, teaching job search skills, resume preparation and ultimately finding a new position.

- **Overfunded Pension Plan** - A defined-benefit pension plan that the assets have surpassed the company's current and projected future liabilities.
- **Over Learning** - Practice beyond what is required for retention. Also called over training.
- **Overtime** - Each hour worked in a workweek in excess of the maximum hours applicable. This usually means hours worked in excess of 40 in a workweek. Under the Fair Labor Standards Act of 1938 (FLSA), there is no limit to the number of hours that an employee may work, either daily or weekly. It simply requires that overtime pay must be paid at a rate of not less than 1½ times the nonexempt employee's regular rate of pay for hours worked over the maximum in a workweek.
- **Overtime Pay** - Overtime pay is the extra pay employers are required by the FLSA to pay to covered, nonexempt employees for the hours they work in excess of 40 in a workweek. Overtime pay must be computed at one and one-half times the employee's regular rate of pay. Extra pay for overtime hours worked may also be called an "overtime premium" payment.
- **Paid Sabbatical** - An executive benefit that allows a paid leave of absence for a predetermined period of time, usually to let the executive to follow another endeavor.
- **Paired Comparison** - An arranging technique that compares the occupations being evaluated to all other jobs to determine which of the positions has a higher value.
- **Parachute** - An employment contract that states if there is a change in control of the corporation, there will be an increase or accelerated payments or vesting or some other rights to the employee once the change is final as stated in the contract.
- **Passive Candidate** - A currently employed person who is not job hunting and who may or may not be happy in his current position.
- **Past Practice** - A customary way of doing things not written into the collective bargaining agreement. Past practices can sometimes be enforced through the grievance procedure if the practice has been longstanding, consistent, and accepted by the parties.
- **Pattern Bargaining** - Collective bargaining in which the union tries to apply identical terms, conditions, or demands to a number of employers in an industry although the employers act individually rather than as a group.
- **Pay At Risk** - A changeable pay policy that is funded by a reduction of base pay that is typically offset by the chance that a larger variable pay policy will payout when base pay is not at risk.
- **Pay Compression** - A term used to describe differentials in pay that is too little to be considered equitable. May be applied to the differences between (1) a supervisors pay and that of a subordinate. (2) The pay of an experienced employee versus that of a newly hired employee.
- **Pay equity** - Focus of pay equity is to eliminate the historical gap between the incomes of men and women, and to ensure that the salary ranges in your organization correspond to the value of work performed.
- **Pay for Performance** - Paying employees based upon their performance level. Employees are evaluated via performance appraisals and given raises based upon their performance ratings. Poorly performing employees have their wages frozen; they are not given wage cuts.
- **Pay For Time Not Worked** - An employee is paid for the time that was not actually worked, such as holidays, jury duty, and personal days.
- **Pay Period** - The pay period is the period of time in which compensation was earned for hours worked.
- **Pay Range** - Usually used to determine individual employee pay, this term refers to range of rates, from the minimum to the maximum for a particular class or grade of employees.
- **Pay Steps** - Specific levels in a pay range. An employee may move up grades depending upon their performance, time at the same grade, new job skills or performance.
- **Pedagogy** - Literally means the art and science of educating children.

- **Pension Benefit Guaranty Corporation (PBGC)** - A federal corporation that insures the benefits of defined benefit pension plans. The PBGC is supposed to ensure that all plan participants received their vested benefits, even in the event that the pension plan goes bankrupt.
- **Performance Appraisal** - The process by which you can evaluate employee job performance. A method used to determine how well an employee has performed during a specific time period. Usually utilized in determining salary increases.
- **Performance Based Restricted Stock** - Restricted shares of stock that are awarded to an executive and are contingent upon the attainment of internal or external performance goals or an increase in the price of the company stock.
- **Performance Management** - A process utilized by managers that is made up of planning a managing performance via observation and providing feedback. The process also includes bettering performance through development, assessing and rewarding performance.
- **Permanent Replacements** - Under current labor law, when employees engage in an economic strike, the employer has the right to hire permanent replacements. After the strike has ended, if there is no back to work agreement reached between the union and the employer, employees replaced during the strike are put on a preferential hiring list and must wait for openings to occur.
- **Permatemp** - Also known as a long-term temp. This is a temporary employee who continues to be retained for months or even years as a "temporary" employee.
- **Perquisite** - Special benefits, perks, for high level executives and other managerial employees. This income is taxable to the employee. Some of these perks may include club memberships, legal counseling, and special parking.
- **Person-Based Pay** - Compensation based on a skill or knowledge instead of a specifically defined job.
- **Personalized System of Instruction (Keller plan)** - A teaching technique that involves dividing course material into segments, evaluating learner performance on each segment for subject mastery, and allowing learners to move from segment to segment at their own pace.
- **Phantom Stock Options** - Options on units equal to stock shares; however they are not true shares, or rights to the increase in value of the shares not including related option rights.
- **Phone Banking** - The organized telephoning of large numbers of members to inform them of a union policy or action or to gather information. This is often done by volunteers who come into the union hall and telephone members during a certain time period.
- **Phone Tree** - A network of volunteer members in which one member calls a list of members, each of whom calls another list of members, etc.
- **Piece Rate** - A performance payment to an employee based upon production. Payment is given based upon each piece or quantity of work that is produced by an individual employee.
- **Piece Work** - Pay by the number of units completed. The theory is that the faster you work, the more you will get paid. Many workers have learned that if they exceed a certain quota, the piece rate will be lowered. A piece rate is a fixed amount paid per each item (dozen, gross, etc.) produced (manufactured, sold, etc.).
- **Plan Administrator** - The administrator of the plan is the plan sponsor, however someone else can be named as the sponsor in the plan document. The responsibilities include- 1) managing the plan assets to reduce risk of loss, 2) act on the interests of the beneficiaries, 3) act accordingly under the terms governing the plan.
- **Plan Document** - A document that states the terms of a pension plan for an employer. The document states the eligibility requirements and the specific benefits of the plan.
- **Point Factor** - A quantitative occupation evaluation technique that utilizes defined factors and degree levels in each factor.

- **Point Of Service Plans (POS)** - Health Plans that are a combination of an HMO and fee for service plan. The individual can choose at the point of service whether he wants to see a network provider or a non-network provider. The co pays and will be vary and deductibles may apply.
- **Policy** - A document that provides a written statement that reflects the employer's standards and objectives relating to various employee activities and employment-related matters.
- **PPO** - Preferred Provider Organization. A network of healthcare providers that will discount services to individuals or groups that participate in the particular plan.
- **Pre-Existing Condition** - Several definitions: 1) In individual medical plans, the condition is an injury that occurred or an illness that was diagnosed prior to the policy issue date, and in addition was not stated on the insurance application, 2) In group medical insurance the condition is one in which the employee received medical attention during a certain period of time (typically 3 months), just before the effective date.
- **Premium Pay** - An extra amount over straight time rates, sometimes a flat sum, sometimes a percentage of the wage rates, paid to workers to compensate them for inconvenient hours, overtime, hazardous, or unpleasant conditions, or other undesirable circumstances.
- **Prevailing Wage** - Generally the wage prevailing in a locality for a certain type of work. It is a wage determinant for many federal construction projects. (Prevailing wage does not necessarily refer to union wages.)
- **Primary Duty** - The principal, main, major, or most important duty that the employee performs. Determination of an employee's primary duty must be based on all the facts in a particular case, with the major emphasis on the character of the employee's job as a whole.
- **Profit Sharing Plan** - An agreement between an employer and the employees in which the profits of the company are shared with the employees.
- **Professional Employer Organization**: - A PEO acts as a full-service, outsourced HR department for a small- to medium-sized business. A PEO may administer payroll and benefits, recruit job candidates, train and develop employees, manage employee liability issues and ensure compliance with government regulations.
- **Programmed Learning** - A procedure that provides information to the learner in small steps, guarantees immediate feedback concerning whether or not the material was learned properly and allows the learner the pace with which she can go through the material.
- **Progressive discipline** - Type of discipline whereby there are stronger penalties for repeated offences.
- **Prudent Man Rules** - Common law standard that is supposed to be followed by the trustees of funds. The trustee is expected to act faithfully, with discretion, prudence and intelligence keeping in consideration the probable income and the security of the capital.
- **Qualified Domestic Relations Order (QDROS)** - Court orders from a state domestic court that are deemed qualified by the plan administrator. QDROs allow the employer to split the retirement benefits of an employee in the event of divorce without breaching ERISA or tax code.
- **Qualified Medical Child Support Order (QMCSO)** - A judgment, decree or order that is issued by a court that requires a group health plan to offer benefits to children of a plan participant.
- **Qualified Plan** - A pension or profit sharing plan that the Internal Revenue Service approves as meeting their requirements. These plans may have tax advantages.
- **Qualifying Event** - An event that qualifies a participant and dependents to be eligible for COBRA. This event may be a termination of employment (or a reduction in hours), divorce or legal separation, death of a covered employee, a dependent child's loss of dependent status, a covered employee's eligibility for Medicare or loss of coverage due to the employer's filing of a bankruptcy proceeding.
- **Quantitative Job Evaluation** - A technique that displays a hierarchy of job worth by examining occupations in terms of certain numerical indexes and factors.

- **Rabbi Trust** - This nonqualified arrangement, allows the employer to set money aside expressly to pay for excess pensions or deferred pay. Employers do not take a tax deduction, and the beneficiaries do not pay tax on contributions to the trusts until such time that they start receiving their money. Although funds are subject to employer's creditors, they are not accessible to current and future management.

- **Racketeering Influenced and Corrupt organizations Act (RICO)** - Federal law allowing the federal government to place in trusteeship organizations which are convicted of being dominated by racketeers or organized crime. The U.S. Department of Justice filed suit against the IBT under the RICO Act, and this lawsuit was settled by the 1989 Consent Decree.

- **Raiding** - A union's attempt to enroll workers belonging to or represented by another union.

- **Railway Labor Act of 1926 (RLA)** - This law regulates labor relations in the railway and airlines industries, guaranteeing workers in these industries the right to form a union and bargain collectively. The RLA severely controls the timing and right to strike. Also, bargaining units under the RLA are usually nation-wide, making it more difficult for workers to form a union.

- **Random Sampling** - A method under which sections of a population are drawn utilizing a procedure by which every member of the population has an equal opportunity to be chosen.

- **Range** - Several definitions: 1) The difference between the maximum value and minimum value, 2) In reference to a pay grade, the amount that the maximum pay exceeds the minimum pay.

- **Rank and File** - The members of a union.

- **Ranking Method Of Job Evaluation** - A job comparison that results in the ranking of jobs into a hierarchy beginning at the highest and ending at the lowest.

- **Ratification** - Formal approval of a newly negotiated agreement by vote of the union members affected.

- **Reasonable Compensation** - Reasonable compensation is a term used by the IRS to define the compensation amount that is a deductible business expense. The issue comes up because stockholder-employees can alter their wages and income distributions to avoid taxes. Under IRC 162 (a), wages are a deductible business expense to the extent wages are reasonable. In an S Corporation, under-payment of wages occurs in order to maximize pass-through income and avoid payment of FICA and Medicare contributions. In a C corporation, wages are maximized and dividends eliminated or minimized to avoid the double taxation of dividends.

- **Recognition** - Employer acceptance of a union as the exclusive bargaining representative for all employees in the bargaining unit.

- **Recognition Picketing** - Picketing to pressure or coerce an employer to recognize a union as a bargaining agent for the employees. Recognition picketing is subject to certain restrictions under the amendments to the NLRA.

- **Recognition Program** - A process in which employees efforts and successes are recognized.

- **Recruitment** - Process of finding and attracting capable applicants to apply for employment.

- **Recruitment Bonuses** - Reward payments that are given to new employees to entice them to accept the job offer. The rewards may be paid at the time the employee begins the employment, or over a pre-agreed upon period of time.

- **Red Circle Rate** - An employee pay that is higher than the already determined maximum that was assigned to the job. Increases in pay are not usually given unless the range maximum exceeds the employee pay rate.

- **Re-Enlistment Bonus** - A monetary incentive paid to an expatriate to stay on the current assignment longer than initially expected.

- **Referral Bonus** - Payments that are given to existing employees who recruit new employees as long as the new employee remains employed for a specific period of time, or for a new client that produces new revenue for the organization.

- **Regular Rate** - Generally, the regular rate includes all payments made by the employer to or on behalf of the employee. The regular rate is determined by adding together the employee's pay for the workweek and all other earnings and dividing the total by the number of hours the employee worked in that week.
- **Reinforcement Theory** - A behavior theory that hypothesizes that employees will act in ways that provide rewards as opposed to punishment.
- **Reliability** - The ability of a device or human to be free of error when taking measurements.
- **Religious Discrimination** - The failure of an employer to make a reasonable accommodation to allow the employee or employees to observe a religious holiday or practice, except in the event that the employees absence would create hardship on the employers business.
- **Remuneration** - Remuneration includes all pay for employment and certain payments made in the form of goods or facilities customarily furnished by the employer.
- **Reopener Clause** - Clause in a collective bargaining agreement providing for reopening negotiations on wage rates, etc., during the term of the agreement.
- **Replacement** - Workers hired to replace employees on strike. In the case of economic strikers, the strikers retain their employee status while on strike; however, the company may hire permanent replacements, and may legally refuse to reinstate strikers who have been permanently replaced. In this situation, if there are permanent replacements, economic strikers are generally entitled to reinstatement when the replacements leave. In the case of unfair labor practice strikes, the strikers must be reinstated with few exceptions.
- **Representation Election** - Election conducted to determine by a majority vote of workers whether they want a union.
- **Retroactive Pay** - Retroactive pay is pay that is related to a prior time period (for example, a pay increase resulting from a collectively bargained or other agreement, that was paid at a later time than the effective date of the pay increase).
- **Restructuring** - Describes any number of methods of reorganizing a company resulting in dramatic change within the company. Benefits are usually short term but may be long term and the main objective is typically to discourage take-over bids.
- **Return On Assets (ROA)** - This term describes the ratio of net income to total assets of an organization. This is a major financial measure, which is sometimes used as a determining factor in the establishment of incentive plans.
- **Return On Equity (ROE)** - Frequently used as an incentive plan measure, this is a term employed to describe returns due to shareholder by aligning profits to the equity of stockholders.
- **Return On Investments (ROI)** - This is a term employed to ascertain the earning power of assets. The ratio serves to measure the profitability of a company and therefore, is a good indicator of the effectiveness of management.
- **Return On Net Assets (RONA)** - This is a way of measuring the overall earning power and or profitability of a company. It is the ratio of the total assets (minus liabilities) to the net income. May be used as a measure for executive incentive plans.
- **Return On Sales (ROS)** - Sometimes used to establish executive incentive plans, this is an important financial measure, which represents the ratio of net income and sales.
- **Rewards System** - As more companies look for better ways to attract, retain and motivate good employees, in a competitive labor market, the pressure is growing to get rid of the old methods of compensation (which focuses on money and nothing else) and for new methods to be developed (which would be varied and which would encompass more). As much as money is important, it has been shown that both job seekers and employees value advancement possibilities, emotional rewards and learning and rank those highly on lists of today's best companies attribute list. The reward system is a compensation method/package, which includes all of those attributes.

- **"Right-to-Work" States** - States which have passed laws prohibiting unions from negotiating union shop clauses in their contracts with employers covered by the NLRA. There are more than 20 "right-to-work" states. Unions often refer to these as "right to work for less" states.

- **Rightsizing** - This is the term used to describe the elimination of non-essential / redundant positions in order to reduce the size of the work force to the smallest possible size that it can be without negatively affect operations. The employees who are not laid off at the end of this process are known as residual employees.

- **Rollover** - This is the process of re-investing distribution from one qualified plan of a prior employer to another or investing it in an individual retirement account (IRA). Roll-overs are tax -free transfers of account balances.

- **Rucker Plan - Share Of Production Plan - Gainsharing** - A program whereby certain cost savings resulting from an employee's effort will be shared with all employees.

- **Safe Harbor** - Safe harbors are regulations that describe certain acts or behaviors, which are not illegal under a specific law, even though they might otherwise be illegal.

- **Salary** - A salary is a predetermined amount of pay and is generally expressed as an amount paid weekly, bi-weekly, semi-monthly, monthly or yearly. A salary may be intended to cover straight-time pay for a predetermined number of hours worked during the period, or it may be intended to cover straight-time pay for all hours worked during the period.

- **Salary Continuation Plan** - A sick leave and or disability plan providing for employees to receive up to 100 percent of their salary for a certain amount of time, should they become sick or disabled.

- **Salary for Fluctuating Hours** - A salary for fluctuating hours is a predetermined amount of pay which, based on an understanding between employer and employee, is intended to cover straight-time pay for whatever hours the employee is called upon to work in a workweek, whether few or many.

- **Salary Surveys** - Salary surveys are used by organizations to determine what the 'market rate' is for jobs or skills used in their organization. Paying a competitive wage is important for attracting and maintaining an adequate workforce.

- **Sales Compensation Plans** - Sales compensation plans differ from the other types of compensation plans. Due to the fact that results are measurable in sales related jobs, compensation for those kinds of jobs are typically incentive (or commission) based. Compensation plans for sales type jobs may be fall into any of the following categories, Commission only, salary only plans, Commission-plus-draw plans, Salary-plus-commission plans, and or Salary-plus-bonus plans.

- **Sample** - In terms of statistics, this unit, which is representative of a class drawn from and studied in order to estimate the characteristics of an entire population. A random sample is where each member of the population has the same chance of being chosen. Convenience sample, on the other hand, is when units are selected, not at random but on the basis of what is easily available or accessible

- **Savings (Thrift) Plan** - Set up by employers, this is plan established for the purpose of systematically providing for capital accumulation by employees, whereby the employees make a contribution and the employer matches the contribution according to a pre-established rate and limit. See 401(k).

- **Scanlon Plan** - This is a profit sharing program whereby employees share in pre-established cost savings, which are due to employee effort. Formal employee participation is necessary with the Scanlon Plan, as well as periodic progress reporting and an incentive formula, all of which are pre-established.

- **Scattergram** - Also known as a scatter plot, this is a mathematical technique that displays a picture of the existing relationship between any two variable. It does this by plotting two (x,y) points.

- **Secondary Activities** - Strikes, picketing, boycotts, or other activities directed by a union against an employer with whom it has no dispute, in order to pressure that employer to stop doing business with, or to bring pressure against another employer with whom the union does have a dispute.

- **Section 401(K) Plan** - In the United States, a deferred profit sharing and or stock-bonus plan permitting participants to decide the extent to which their compensation is deferred. Contributions of participant are not taxable until that time when the funds are withdrawn. Contributions of sponsor and investment earnings are both also tax-deferred. Also known as Cash or Deferred Arrangement (CODA).

- **Section 403(B) Plan** - This is a type of retirement plan, typically established by certain tax-exempt organizations (i.e., charities, churches and hospitals). Section 403(b) plans are a creation of congress to serve as incentive to tax-exempt organizations, which ordinarily would not benefit from the tax advantages of qualified pension plans. The section 403(b) plan enables such organizations to offer their employees retirement compensation, albeit in a slightly different form. Educational organizations may also set up section 403(b) plans. May also be referred to as a tax-deferred annuity (TDA) plan or a tax-sheltered annuity (TSA) plan.

- **Securities And Exchange Commission (SEC)** - The SEC is the principal federal regulatory agency, which regulates the securities industry. The main function of the SEC is to promote full disclosure and it exists to protect investors, in the securities market, against practices that are fraudulent and or manipulative. SEC enforces several acts, including but not limited to the Securities Act of 1933, the Securities Exchange Act of 1934, the Trust Indenture Act of 1939, the Investment Company Act of 1940 and the Investment Advisers Act.

- **Self-Insured Organization Insurance** - A type of insurance whereby the organization sponsor and not an insurance company, has the responsibility for the payment of claims made by the insured parties. A company may be completely or partially self-insured. See also administrative services only (ASO) contract.

- **Self-paced learning** - Learning initiated and directed by the learner. The term is used by some organizations now to include computer-based, web-based and multimedia training.

- **Semi-monthly** - A semi-monthly pay period is a one that occurs twice a month (24 pay periods a year). For example, Pay Period 1 may begin on the first of the month and end on the 15th and Pay Period 2 begins on the 16th and ends on the 30th or 31st. A semi-monthly pay period will include full and partial workweeks.

- **Seniority** - Determined by the number of years that an employee has worked for a particular employer. Seniority is frequently the basis for benefits and privileges. The term is sometimes used to express the amount of time spent working for a division or in a specific occupation.

- **Service Model of Unions** - The concept that the primary function of a union, its staff, and its officers is to service the members or solve the members' problems for them. This is in contrast to the organizing Model of Unions.

- **Severance Pay** - In most countries, though not the U.S., severance pay is mandatory any time an employee is terminated. The purpose of severance pay is to soften the blow of unemployment, upon the termination of an employee. Typically, severance pay is equal to one week's pay for each year worked for the severing company (may be more and it may be less). Severance payments are taxable to employees and usually are subject to federal income tax withholding and FICA.

- **Sex Discrimination / Sexual Discrimination** - Gender is one of the protected groups under the Civil Rights Act. Thus gender, in and of itself, may not be used in a whole range of human resource decisions regarding employees. In addition, the Equal Pay Act prohibits paying men and women differently for the same or substantially similar jobs, and Title IX prohibits discrimination by gender in educational institutions.

- **Sexual Harassment** - In the United States, Title VII prohibits two kinds of sexual harassment: quid pro quo and hostile work environment. When a quid pro quo case is proven, employers automatically are liable. Employers are liable only under certain circumstances when hostile work environment is proven. Quid pro quo cases require that the unwelcome sexual demand on the employee be made by someone with the ability to grant or deny an employee some benefit. Also, there must be a link between the demand for sex and the granting or denial of the benefit. Hostile work environment cases must involve pervasive, unwelcome sexually charged behavior that is directed toward an employee by someone in the workplace.

- **Sherman Anti-Trust Act (1890)** - This Federal law was enacted in order to protect the general public from corporate monopolies. This law has, since 1908 applied to Unions, who have used the statute to ensure that competitive wages are paid.

- **Shift Differential** - A shift differential is an additional amount of pay received for working designated shifts. A shift differential is usually paid as an additional amount per hour. For example, an employee may receive an additional $0.75 per hour for each hour worked on the midnight shift.

- **Short-Term Disability Plan** - A benefit plan, whose goal is to provide income to employees who are absent from work either through illness or an accident but only when the employee is expected to return to his or her regular duties within a particular amount of time (typically 6 months).

- **Showing of Interest** - A requirement by the NLRB that must be met by a union when a union wishes to represent a group of employees. There are several showing of interest requirements used by the NLRB. A) A petitional union needs 30% of the eligible members in the union. B) Where a union has petitioned and another union wishes to intervene, the second union must have 30% of the unit it seeks. C) Where a union petitions and another union wishes to intervene in the same unit to the extent of blocking a consent election agreement, it must have 10%. D) Usually, a showing of one or two cards is enough for a second union to intervene only to have their name on the ballot or to participate in a hearing. E) A current or recently expired contract is also a criterion for showing of interest.

- **SIC** - The U.S. Standard Industrial Classification (SIC) system is a U.S. federally designed system that identifies companies by industry with a standard numbering system. It provides other information and is used by securities analysts, market researchers, and others. The SIC is being replaced by the North American Industry Classification System (NAICS).

- **Sick Leave** - Sick leave means providing pay for employees when not working due to illness or injury. It may start on the first day of illness or after two or three days. In developing a sick leave policy the following points need to be considered: (1) When are employees eligible? (2) Will proof of sickness be required? (3) What pay schedule will be used and will the employee receive full pay? (4) How much sick leave can be accumulated and what is done about unused sick leave? (5) May sick leave be used for taking care of family members?

- **Simple Plan** - First allowed in 1997, this is a kind of qualified retirement plan (IRA or 401(k)) for companies with over 100 employees.

- **Simplified Employee Pension (SEP)** - This is a pension plan that an employer may make contributions retirement income to, using individual retirement annuities or accounts. Under the SEP employers may directly contribute directly to Individual Retirement Accounts, amounts, which have been deferred by employees. Typically the SEP is cheaper to operate and therefore most commonly used by employers who are unable to afford more complex pension plans.

- **Single-Rate System** - This is a policy of compensation whereby employees are all paid at the same rate as opposed to being paid within a pay range. This is typical in a situation where the job being performed is so similar that there really isn't room for a wide range of skill level.

- **Sitdown Strike** - A work action which is currently illegal in which strikers refuse to leave the employer's premises.

- **Sixty Day Notice** - The notice that, under the Taft-Hartley Act, must be given by either party to a collective bargaining agreement when desiring to reopen or terminate it. No strike or lockout may begin during these 60 days.

- **Skewed Distribution** - This is a series of data that is plotted and non-symmetric in nature, which has a tail of extreme values going in a single direction.

- **Skill-Based Pay** - This is a compensation system, which is based on the set of skills an employee has and is capable of using should the need arise (even though the employee may not currently be using the skill).
- **Skills Inventory** - Typically used by employment agencies, personnel departments and contract programming companies who wish to set up and maintain a file for candidates and their associated qualifications. Once all the data is in place and information about a potential candidate is entered along with particular job requirements, then a search can be done for the candidate or candidates who meet the requirements.
- **Slotting** - The process of placing a position / a job into a hierarchy of jobs using other methods of evaluating jobs. This process entails the comparison of one job to others, already exist in the hierarchy of jobs.
- **Social Security** - Social Security is a federal government program that is part way between a tax plan and social insurance. Employers and employees pay payroll taxes to fund its two programs - Old Age Survivors' and Disability Insurance
- **Social Security Act** - The Social Security Act is the Act passed in 1935 establishing the social security system in the United States.
- **Social Security Tax** - Generally known as FICA taxes, after the Federal Insurance Contribution Act, these taxes are imposed on wages paid to employees to fund Social Security benefits for employees. Both the employer and the employee must pay FICA tax on an employee's annual wages from the employer up to the Social Security taxable wage base. This tax is divided into 2 components: Medicare and the Old Age Survivors and Disability Insurance (OASDI) component.
- **Sole Proprietor** - A sole proprietor is the 100% owner of a business, which is not incorporated.
- **Speed Up** - Any system designed to increase worker productivity without a compensating increase in wages.
- **Split Dollar Life Insurance** - The employer and employee share in the expenses, equity and death benefits of the policy.
- **Split Shift** - Any form of shift work where there are semi-regular work hours. In some cases, workers may work three different shifts in a work week. In all the various types of shifts, there is usually a break of several hours between the reporting times of the workers.
- **Stakeholder** - Any party that has an interest ('stake') in a firm.
- **Standard Deviation** - The square root of the variance. A measure of dispersion of a set of data from its mean.
- **Standard Industrial Classification System (SIC)** - This federally designed system identifies companies by industry with a standard numbering system. It provides other information and is used by securities analysts, market researchers, and others.
- **State Unemployment Tax Act (SUTA)** - The State Unemployment Tax Act (SUTA) provides that employers pay a payroll tax that supplies funds at the state level that are used to provide benefits for unemployed workers. The amount paid by the employer depends upon the experience of claims by former employees on the fund.
- **Step Rates** - A method of calculating benefits by assigning a different value to income below and above a certain breakpoint, such as the Social Security level.
- **Stewards Council** - An organization of the stewards within a local, stewards councils take some of the workload from the paid staff of the local and give the stewards an opportunity to compare their experiences and be more involved in the affairs of the union. Stewards' councils are governed either by their own bylaws or by a clause in the local union's bylaws.
- **Stock Option** - The right, but not the obligation, to buy company stock at a certain price within a particular period of time.

- **Stock Purchase Plan (Nonqualified)** - A plan that allows senior management or other key personnel to purchase employer stock. Certain restrictions apply: (1) the stockholder must be employed for a particular length of time, (2) the employer has the right to buy back the stock and (3) stockholders cannot sell the stock for a specific time period. (Qualified) A program under which employees buy shares in the employer's stock. The employer contributes a certain amount for each unit of employee contribution. Also, stock may be offered at a fixed price (usually below market) and paid for in full by the employees.
- **Stop-Loss Provision** - An insurance provision stating that the insurance company will pay all expenses after a set amount of out-of-pocket expenses has been paid.
- **Straight-Time Pay** - Straight-time pay is the employee's earnings before the overtime premium payment is calculated.
- **Strategic human resources** - The talent, technology and tactics that growing firms need in order to anticipate and adapt to changes in the workplace. The blending of these elements enables an HR professional to focus more fully on developing his company's business strategy.
- **Strategic Planning** - Determination of the steps required to reach an objective of achieving the optimum fit between the organization and the marketplace.
- **Strength Rating** - The overall physical strength required to perform a job is expressed as a strength rating.
- **Strikes** - To refuse to continue working because of an argument with an employer about working conditions, pay levels or job losses.
- **Struck Work** - A term to define a product which is produced by an employer during the period of a labor dispute with his employees. An employee who refuses to handle struck work is engaged in a sympathy work action. Workers who refuse to do the work of workers engaged in a strike may be replaced; however, they generally cannot be discharged. A struck work clauses in some collective bargaining agreements protect the rights of workers not to handle goods of a struck employer. There are limitations on such clauses in Section 8(e) of the NLRA.
- **Subchapter S Corporation** - This is a type of corporation, which does not have its gains taxed at the corporate level but rather the tax is passed down to the shareholders who then are required to report the gains on their individual tax returns.
- **Subcontracting** - (Contracting Out) An employer's practice of having work performed by an outside contractor and not by regular employees in the unit.
- **Subject Matter Expert (SME)** - A person who can perform a job or a selected group of tasks to standards. Her experience and knowledge of the job designates her as a technical expert.
- **Succession planning** - The process of making long-range management developmental plans to fill your future human resource needs.
- **Successor Employer** - An employer which has acquired an already existing operation and which continues those operations in approximately the same manner as the previous employer, including the use of the previous employer's employees.
- **Suggestions Awards** - Allows employees a monetary or incentive reward for company savings ideas or a unique idea.
- **Summary Plan Description (SPD)** - A requirement of ERISA for a written statement of a plan in an easy-to-read form, including a statement of eligibility, coverage, employee rights and appeal procedure. It is provided to participants, beneficiaries and, upon request, the Department of Labor.
- **Supervisor** - Those employees who have management rights such as the rights to hire, fire, or recommend such action. The employees who are defined as supervisors under the NLRA are not permitted to become members of the bargaining unit at the work location. In organizing campaigns, most employers will try to enlarge the ranks of their supervisory personnel. The employer will try to keep a certain group of supervisors as his anti-union workforce for future labor disputes.

- **Suffer or Permit to Work -** Time spent doing work not requested by the employer, but still allowed, is generally hours worked, since the employer knows or has reason to believe that the employees are continuing to work and the employer is benefiting from the work being done. This time is commonly referred to as "working off the clock."
- **Surface Bargaining -** Often referred to as a perfunctory tactic whereby an employer meets with the union, but only goes through the motions of bargaining. Such conduct on the part of the employer is considered as violation of the employer's duty to bargain, Section 8(a)(5) of the NLRA.
- **Sweetheart Contract -** Term of derision for an agreement negotiated by an employer and a union with terms favorable to the employer. The usual purpose being to keep another union out or to promote the individual welfare of the union officers rather than that of the employees represented.
- **Tactical Planning -** Deals primarily with the implementation phase of the planning process.
- **Taft-Hartley Act or Labor Management Act (LMRA) of 1947 -** An amendment of the NLRA which added provisions allowing unions to be prosecuted, enjoined, and sued for a variety of activities, including mass picketing and secondary boycotts.
- **Take Home Pay -** Pay actually received by an employee after adding on bonuses, but deducting taxes.
- **Talent Acquisition -** More than simply hiring people as openings occur, it's an ongoing, proactive, and strategic approach to developing a pool of high-potential candidates for current and future openings.
- **Talent Management System -** A specialized computer program that automates tasks related to the recruitment, selection, training, promotion and internal movement of employees.
- **Task Rate -** A task rate is a flat sum paid for doing a particular task without regard to the number of hours worked at that task.
- **Target Compensation -** Expected pay for a job or position. This would include all avenues of compensation. (Base pay, incentives, bonuses, etc.)
- **Tax Equalization -** A tax reimbursement system intended to ensure the expatriate neither gains nor loses, with regard to income tax, from undertaking an expatriate assignment. A hypothetical tax amount is deducted and the company then meets any additional host country tax liability on the entire package.
- **Telecommuting -** Working at home by using a computer terminal electronically linked to one's place of employment.
- **Temp-to-Perm -** The try-before-you-buy approach. Short for "temporary-to-permanent work arrangement. Workers that are hired as temporary employees for a set amount of time, knowing they may eventually be hired for the same jobs as full-time employees.
- **Third Country National (TCN) -** Citizens of one country who are employed by a company headquartered in a second country to work in a third country.
- **Third Party Administrator -** The party to an employee benefit plan that may collect premiums, pay claims and/or provides administrative services. Usually an out-of-house professional firm providing administrative services for employee benefit plans.
- **Thrift Plans -** A defined contribution plan to which employees make contributions on an after tax basis, usually as a percentage of salary. The employer also makes incentive matching or partially matching contributions on behalf of the participating employees.
- **Tiered Pay Plan -** A compensation system that distinguishes the salary based on time of hire, and work performance.
- **Time Off With Pay -** Compensation that is paid to the employee, based on pay for holidays, vacation, sick leave, lunch periods, and other approved time off.
- **Tipped Employee -** Tipped employees are those who work in occupations in which they customarily and regularly receive more than $30 a month in tips. An employer may count tips actually received by

tipped employees as wages when calculating wages for purpose of FLSA minimum wage and overtime pay requirements. This is known as a "tip credit."

- **Tip Pooling** - Tip pooling is an arrangement among employees who customarily and regularly receive tips to "pool" or share a customary and reasonable percentage of their tips received with others in the pool.

- **Top Hat Plans** - An unfunded deferred compensation plan or welfare plan that is maintained to provide deferred compensation for a select group of management or highly compensated employees.

- **Top Heavy Plans** - A qualified plan in which the share of benefits allocable to key employees is more than 60%. The plan may be subject to special accelerated vesting provisions and minimum contribution rates.

- **Tort** - A civil wrongdoing that creates a claim that's to be tried in court before a jury.

- **Total Compensation** - The sum of all payments made to an employee for a specific time period (usually annual) including base salary, incentives, and bonuses (and/or other variable pay such as commissions).

- **Transfer of Training** - The ability of persons to effectively apply to the job the knowledge and skills they gain in dissimilar learning situation.

- **U.S. Adopted Child Health Care Mandate** - Under COBRA, group health plans must treat adopted children like biological children covered by the plan, and plans are precluded from applying pre-existing condition exclusions to an adopted child where no such exclusion applies to a newborn biological child.

- **U.S. Minimum Wage** - The lowest wage, determined by law or contract, that an employer may pay an employee for a specified job.

- **U.S. Permanent Resident Alien Status** - A green card holder who is considered a permanent resident alien. They are entitled to all the rights, privileges and obligations of an American citizen except the right to vote.

- **Underwater Options** - An outstanding option where the option price is above the stock's current market price.

- **Unemployment Compensation** - Payments made under state-administered programs to workers who are unemployed and meet the requirements of the law involved to qualify for such payments. The requirements usually are (1) that the worker not be unemployed voluntarily. (2) That the worker has worked in employment that is 'covered' by the law. (3) That the worker be willing and able to take employment offered him or her. (4) That an initial period (the waiting period) of unemployment elapse before compensation is due. Programs are entirely employer financed except in four states that require small employee contributions.

- **Unfair Labor Practices** - Those employer or union activities classified as "unfair" by federal or state labor relations acts. Under the NLRA, employer unfair labor practices include employer threats against protected collective activity, employer domination of unions, discrimination against employees for collective activity, and employer failure to bargain in good faith with union representatives. Union unfair labor practices include failure to represent all members of the bargaining unit and failure to bargain in good faith, secondary boycotts. The RLA and many state public sector labor laws contain definitions of unfair labor practices which are similar to the NLRA definitions.

- **Union Security Clause** - A provision in a collective bargaining agreement designed to protect the institutional life of the union, such as union ship and union dues check-off clauses.

- **Union Shop** - Form of union security provided in the collective bargaining agreement which requires employees to belong to or pay dues to the union as a condition of retaining employment. It is illegal to have a closed shop which requires workers to be union members before they are hired. The union shop is legal, except in so-called right-to-work states, because it requires workers to join the union or pay dues within a certain time period after they are hired.

- **Union Welfare Fund** - A union organized fund, and one or more employers to which contributions are made by the employer(s) so that organization benefits can be made available to the union's members.
- **Universal Life Insurance** - A whole life insurance product whose investment component pays a competitive interest rate rather than the below-market crediting rate.
- **Validity** - The degree to which a test measures what it is intended to measure. Although there are several types of validity and different classification schemes for describing validity there are two major types of validity that test developers must be concerned with, they are content-related and criterion-related validity.
- **Variable Pay** - Rewards based on performance rather than rewards based on time spent on the job or the value of the job.
- **Vested Benefit** - Accrued benefits of a participant that have become non-forfeitable under the vesting schedule adopted by the plan.
- **Vestibule Training** - A variant of job rotation in which a separate work area is set up for a learner so that the actual work situation does not pressure the learner, (e.g. cockpit simulator).
- **Vesting** - The amount of time that an employee must work to guarantee that his/her accrued pension benefits will not be forfeited even if employment is terminated.
- **Video On Demand (VOD)** - A system by which viewers can watch video programs on their own television sets at the time they choose. The programs are supplied by cable or ISDN.
- **Virtual Classroom** - Where online learning takes place and where learners and instructors interact.
- **Visas** - A document that allows the resident of one country to enter another.  Two broad categories of visas in the US.  Nonimmigrant visas for temporary admission and Immigrant visas for permanent entry. Common nonimmigrant visas include: B-1 – Business Visa;  H-1B – Specialty Occupation;  L-1 – Intra-company transferee;  TN – Treaty Visa. These grant temporary rights to work.
- **Vision Care Benefits** - An insurance plan that provides participants with eye examinations, lenses, frames, and fitting of glasses.
- **Vocational Rehabilitation Act of 1973** - This act is intended to promote job access for qualified individuals with disabilities.
- **Voluntary Subject of Bargaining** - Subjects of bargaining other than those considered to be mandatory (see mandatory subject of bargaining). Either party may propose discussion of such a subject, and the other party may voluntarily bargain on it. Neither party may insist to the point of impasse on the inclusion of a voluntary subject in a contract. For example, the employer may not legally insist on bargaining over the method of selecting stewards or the method of taking a strike vote.
- **Volunteer organizing Committee (VOC)** - Term sometimes used to describe union members who volunteer for the union during organizing campaigns. Volunteers may donate their time and/or be compensated for lost wages while they assist the campaign by visiting workers at their homes, distributing leaflets, and attending meetings, etc.
- **W-2 Form** - Wage and Tax Statement.
- **W-4 Form** - The Employee's Withholding Allowance Certificate.
- **Wage** - The total of salary and also commissions, or bonuses, paid by an employer for services.
- **Wage And Price Controls** - Wages and prices are limited to some low percentage of growth through government regulation until they are deemed to be under control.
- **Wage Differential** - Of location of company, hours of work, working conditions, type of product manufactured, or a variety of other circumstances, there can be differences in wage rates.
- **Wage Level** - The average of all salaries paid to workers in an occupation, department, organization, or industry.

- **Wage Movement** - A decrease or increase in the wage levels for a particular position or occupation in a market.
- **Wage Rate** - The money rate paid to an employee per hour.
- **Wage Structure** - Usually established within an organization, this is the levels or hierarchy of job and pay ranges. The salary structure is also referred to as job grades, job-evaluation points and or policy lines.
- **Wage Survey** - A survey of the going rates for benchmark jobs, in a particular market.
- **Waiting Period** - Several definitions: 1) The duration of time between the beginning of an insured person's disability and the start of the policy's benefits. (2) The period between employment or enrollment in a program and the date when an insured person becomes eligible for benefits.
- **Waiver Of Coverage** - Relinquishing the right to a benefit, especially in regard to health benefits, flexible benefits or early retirement window plans.
- **Walsh-Healey Public Contracts Act Of 1936** - A federal law requiring that pay be at least be the federal minimum wage with certain employers holding federal contracts for the manufacture or provision of materials, supplies and equipment.
- **War Exclusion Provision** - A life insurance policy provision that if death were connected with war or military service, it would limit the insurer's liability to pay a death benefit.
- **Web-Based Training (WBT)** - Web-based training (sometimes called e-learning) is anywhere, any-time instruction delivered over the Internet or a corporate intranet to browser-equipped learners.
- **Weighted Average** - The average of the total population or number of incumbents reported. For each job, it is computed by multiplying each company's average salary by their number of incumbents, adding these values, and dividing by the total number of incumbents for each job.
- **Weighted Mean** - Reflects equally the number of incumbents in a survey. If companies participating are truly representative of the market, then the data should reflect the market value of the job. The weighted mean answers the question, 'On average, what are incumbents in a particular job paid?'
- **Weingarten Rights** - The rights of employees covered by the NLRA to request union representation during investigatory interviews if they reasonably believe that the interview could result in their being disciplined. Weingarten rights also guarantee the rights of union representatives to assist and counsel employees during interviews which could lead to discipline.
- **Welfare Benefit Plans** - ERISA defines welfare benefit plans to include medical, surgical, or hospital care, sickness, accident, disability, death, unemployment, vacation benefits, training programs, day-care centers, scholarship funds, prepaid legal services, or financial assistance for employee housing.
- **Wellness Programs** - Employer-sponsored programs and activities designed to promote and maintain the physical and psychological health of employees.
- **Whole Life Annuity** - A term for a series of periodic payments, each is made only if a designated payee is alive, with the payments continuing for that payee's entire life.
- **Whole Life Insurance** - Insurance payable to a beneficiary at the death of the insured, whenever that occurs. Premiums may be payable for a specified number of years (limited payment life) or for life (straight life). The premiums may remain level or decrease (by accumulating cash in the initial years of the policy).
- **Wildcat Strike** - A strike undertaken without official union authorization. Although not necessarily illegal, they are not necessarily protected by the NLRB.
- **Withholding** - Income tax withheld from employees' wages and paid directly to the government by the employer.
- **Witness Duty Leave** - Allowing employees to take time off from work to appear before a court of law or other judicial proceeding if they are subpoenaed or a party to the action.
- **Work-Design Variances** - Differences that exist in similar jobs within two or more organizations.

- **Workers' Compensation** - Government-mandated insurance that provides benefits to covered employees and their dependents if the employee suffers job-related injury, disease, or death.
- **Workforce Planning** - A systematic approach to getting the right people with the right talents, assigned to the right jobs at the right time. Also known as workforce optimization and workforce consulting.
- **Working Capital** - Assets available for use in the production of further assets.
- **Works Councils** - A council representing employer and employees of a plant or business to discuss working conditions etc. May also be a committee representing the workers elected to negotiate with management about grievances and wages etc.
- **Workstation** - A general-purpose computer designed to be used by one person at a time and which offers higher performance than normally found in a personal computer, especially with respect to graphics, processing power and the ability to carry out several tasks at the same time.
- **Workweek** - Generally a fixed period of 168 hours (7 consecutive 24-hour periods). The employer establishes the workweek. It may begin on any day of the week and at any hour of the day. Under FLSA, a workweek is 40 hours long with no daily hour limit.
- **Year Of Service** - As defined by ERISA, a 12-month period during which an employee completes at least 1,000 hours of service to the employer.
- **Zipper Clause** - A standard contract clause which precludes any renegotiation of conditions covered in the contract during the life of the contract. It is designed to prevent the employer from trying to change the contract before the next round of bargaining.

# Index

# Revised and improved for the new 2015 exams!

The PHR/SPHR Study Guide is written by a leading expert and former question writer for the PHR/SPHR Exams!  Content is based on the HRCI outline to design the PHR and SPHR exams. **David Siler**, SPHR, GPHR, HRBP, & HRMP is the creator and instructor for the Distinctive HR learning system that has helped thousands achieve the Professional in Human Resources (PHR), Senior Professional in Human Resources (SPHR), and Global Professional in Human Resources (GPHR) certification by the Human Resource Certification Institute (HRCI).

## Want to dramatically increase your exam score?

The PHR/SPHR Web-based Certification Study Course offered through CAI is taught by none other than the author himself.  In typical David Siler fashion, this interactive course/webinar will give you the confidence and test-taking secrets to ensure you are prepared!!

While the national pass rates in most PHR/SPHR test periods have been 60% OR LESS for the past 4 years, **David's PHR/SPHR students have an extremely impressive pass rate of more than 90%!!** Now, from the convenience of your own home or office, you can participate in this comprehensive PHR/SPHR certification prep program.

Choose from the following webinars:
- Friday afternoon sessions (1:00pm - 4:00pm EST)
- Tuesday evening sessions (6:00pm - 9:00pm EST)

****SPECIAL RATES AVAILABLE!!!  MENTION **"CAI PROMO"** WHEN CALLING.****

**For more information about the
PHR/SPHR Web-Based Study Course
call 1-919-878-9222.**